A Complete Treasury
of Stories
for Public Speakers

Compiled and edited by

MORRIS MANDEL, 1911-

 JONATHAN DAVID PUBLISHERS
MIDDLE VILLAGE, N.Y. 11379

A COMPLETE TREASURY
OF STORIES
FOR PUBLIC SPEAKERS
Copyright © 1974
by
Morris Mandel

JONATHAN DAVID PUBLISHERS
68-22 Eliot Avenue
Middle Village, N. Y. 11379

Library of Congress Cataloging in Publication data
Mandel, Morris, 1911-
    A complete treasure of stories for public speakers.

    1. Anecdotes.   II. Title.
PN4193.I5M3   808.88'2   73-8433
ISBN 0-8241-0160-2

PRINTED IN UNITED STATES OF AMERICA

To My Grandchildren:

SHAYNE FRIMMET

RACHEL

REBECCA

ISAAC

who kept me on my toes searching for new stories.

ACKNOWLEDGEMENTS

My thanks are due to a number of people who graciously helped in the preparation of this book. I especially wish to acknowledge my indebtedness to Mrs. Anita Blumenson who read the manuscript, and the proofs, and who made my task much easier.

M. M.

ABILITY

It's not so much what we *have*, as what we *do* with what we have, that makes the difference in this world. For example:

Longfellow could take a worthless sheet of paper, write a poem on it and make it worth $6,000. That's genius!

Rockefeller could put his name to a piece of paper and make it worth a million. That's capital!

Uncle Sam can take silver, stamp an emblem on it, and make it worth a dollar. That's money!

A mechanic can take metal that is worth only five dollars and make it worth fifty dollars. That's skill!

An artist can take a 50¢ piece of canvas, paint a picture on it and make it worth thousands. That's art!

There was a contest to raise money at the county fair:

A strong man had squeezed a lemon dry, and a prize was offered to anyone who could get another drop from it. Many men tried, but the lemon did not yield another drop. Finally, a little man said he could squeeze more juice from the lemon. Amid the laughter of the group, the little man was handed the dry lemon. He took it into his hand and squeezed a jet of juice.

"Extraordinary! Marvelous!" the onlookers shouted.

"Not at all," the little man replied. "You see, I work for the Internal Revenue Bureau."

ACCEPTANCE

It is related that a child born to King David became critically ill. All through the child's illness, David prayed and fasted and would not sleep in his own bed. Instead, he slept on the earth.

After a week, the baby died . . . but the servants were afraid to reveal the death to David. Finally, they were compelled to tell him the sad tidings. Thereupon, David arose, changed his clothes, entered the sanctuary, prayed, and then sat down and ate a meal.

1

His servants were astonished at this strange behavior and asked him to explain his actions.

"What are you doing?" they asked. "When the child was alive you fasted and wept. Now that the child is dead, you rise and eat bread?"

David's answer was an expression of acceptance. "While the child was yet alive I fasted and wept, for I thought: Who knows whether the Lord will not be gracious to me, that the child may live? But now he is dead, wherefore should I fast? Can I bring him back again?"

A minister was once asked to accept a difficult pulpit in a distant city, and refused the assignment. His wife was not too happy with his decision, but he advised her to be patient and to wait until the Christmas holidays would be over, and that then she would understand his reasons. In the meantime, he asked her to buy the most beautiful Christmas tree that she could find, and he helped her to decorate it very ornately. They put much effort into it, and the results were beautiful and striking.

It was customary for the minister to have open house for his parishioners daily, beginning with Christmas Eve right through New Year's day. People came and went in and out of his home, and there was not a soul who did not find the tree breath-taking; nor could they resist touching it. By the time the minister and his wife had said good-bye to the last of their guests, you can imagine the condition of that most beautiful Christmas tree after having been touched by so many hands. The bright green had faded and most of it had turned brown. The fresh smell was gone, and the needles were falling to the ground.

Pointing to the sad looking tree, the minister said to his wife: "Observe this tree and you will have my explanation for refusing the assignment. I could not fare better than this tree when subjected to public abuse."

There was once a beautiful pitcher so exquisitely lovely and graceful that all who saw it remarked on its extraordinary beauty. The pitcher itself was far from ignorant of its attributes, and became very vain indeed.

One day, the man who owned it poured vinegar into the pitcher. The pitcher was outraged that it should be filled with such a lowly commodity, and when the man had left the room it tipped itself, and spilled its contents. Of course, the owner was

2

astonished to find the vinegar all spilled out, and could not understand how this happened.

Shortly thereafter the owner filled the pitcher with wine. This time the pitcher became indignant because the wine was not of the right vintage to be poured into so elegant a pitcher. Once more, when its owner was out of sight, the pitcher tipped and spilled the contents.

When the man found the wine spilled he concluded that there was something wrong with the pitcher which he could not detect, and since it could not be put to any good use, he discarded it.

Life is pretty much the same. One must learn to accept the vinegar as well as the wine, for as we go through life we are sure to get varying doses of each.

ACCOMPLISHMENT

Max Nordau, the famed Zionist leader and author of the work, *The Lies of Modern Civilization,* has the following story in his book:

There was a convention of missionaries from all parts of the world. Each one reported how with his fiery speeches, his pioneer work, and his exemplary conduct, he had converted the natives to Christianity. Among those reporting was a missionary from the cannibal area of Africa. He, too, boasted of his progress with the natives.

After all the reports had been submitted, a question was directed to the missionary from the cannibal area. Had he stopped the cannibals from eating human flesh?

The missionary answered that he had not stopped cannibalism, but while formerly they were eating with their hands, he had achieved the great goal of having them eat with knives and forks.

During the period of the French Revolution, King Louis XVI reigned over France. When he entered the courtyard amidst the heralding blares of bugles and unfurled flags, all of his subjects and soldiers snapped to attention. When complete silence reigned, the loudspeakers pronounced the king's schedule for the day: *Le roi ne fera rien!* "Today the king will do nothing." And so we find that King Louis XVI is referred to in the histories of the French Revolution as the *Roi Fainéant,* "the magnificent do-nothing king."

3

Sarasate, the great Spanish violinist of the last century, was once called a genius by a famous critic. In reply to this, he shook his head and bellowed:

"Genius! For thirty-seven years I've practiced fifteen hours a day, and *now* they call me a genius."

ACTION

Perhaps you may have noticed, over the years a particular type of statue that is found in many of our cities.

There are many around. They all look very much alike. It is a statue of a horse. The sculptor always places the horse's weight on its hind legs, and the front legs are poised high—as if ready to leap, ready to take off; but it hasn't actually started to make the leap.

You can pass such a statue many times and you will always find the horse in the same position. Ready to take off—but never quite getting started.

There was once a wealthy man who prided himself upon being a good and pious Jew. Each day he would lead his family in prayer for all the sick and needy in the world. In particular, he prayed that God might help an aged couple who lived near his estate and who were ill as well as poor.

One morning his son asked him whether he ever stopped to visit the unfortunate couple. When he received a reply in the negative, the boy remarked, "Dad, I wish I had your money."

"Why?" the father asked.

"Because," the boy responded, "then I would answer your prayers."

It is related that a fire broke out in a house. Within, a man was sleeping. They tried to carry him out through the window, but could not. They tried through the door, but could not.

One wise man said, "Wake him up, he'll get out by himself!"

They were debating: "Which is more important—learning or action?"

Said one: "Action is more important; learning has no value unless put into practice."

4

Said the other: "Learning is more important because it teaches right from wrong."

They finally compromised: "Learning is more important when it leads to action."

~~~

Two men were walking by the seaside at low tide when they saw an oyster. They both stopped at the same time to pick it up. One pushed the other, and a dispute ensued. A third man came along, and they decided to ask him which of the two had the right to the oyster.

While each was telling his story, the arbitrator gravely took out his knife, opened the shell, and loosened the oyster. By the time the two disputants had presented their arguments and were waiting for the decision, the arbitrator had swallowed the oyster. Giving each a shell, he said, "The Court awards each of you a shell. The oyster will cover the costs."

~~~

"People can be compared to books," remarked the preacher to the well-dressed man sitting in his office, "because their thoughts and deeds are written in their lives. Though it is important for a book to have a good title, it is more important that the contents of the book be worthwhile. Likewise, it is important for a person to make a fine appearance, but it is more important to live a worthy life."

~~~

The head of a seminary entered the study hall and found his students involved in a heated debate. He was surprised to discover that the students were discussing ways to banish the bad habit of wasting time! They never realized that what they were doing was itself a waste of time!

~~~

ADAPTABILITY

A reporter once was assigned to interview a famous marksman who was reputedly the most unbelievably accurate sharpshooter the world ever beheld. At the country home of the sharpshooter, the newspaper man found targets hanging from fences, trees, shrubbery, and hedges. Each target had a bullet hole in the center of the bull's eye.

5

Overcome with amazement and admiration, the reporter asked: "How do you do it? What is the secret of your amazing skill?"

"There is really nothing to it," replied the marksman. "First I shoot the bullet, and then I draw the target around the bullet hole."

ADEQUACY

A laborer was once asked what he would do if he suddenly inherited a million dollars. "The first thing I would do," he answered, "would be to buy a longer handle for my pick!"

A successful manufacturer was asked why he did not sell out and retire to a life of ease, instead of enlarging his factory. "What would I do with myself?" he replied. "I must keep on working, planning, building, creating, growing or else I die. My satisfaction is making things that people need."

Like the laborer, all he needed to keep him happy was to have the right tools to continue to do his job adequately.

Sholem Aleichem tells of the forgetful man who never could remember in the morning where he had put his clothes the night before. To remedy this embarrassing situation, he hit upon the idea of writing down on a piece of paper before he went to sleep exactly where his things were.

While sitting in bed, he wrote: My shoes and socks are under the chair near the window. My shirt is draped over the kitchen chair. My suit is hanging in the closet, and I am in bed.

In the morning, with the paper guiding him, he went to the one chair to get his shoes and socks, then to the other chair for his shirt, then to the closet for his suit and finally to the bed to find himself. But, unfortunately as hard as he searched he could not find himself.

So it is with man, who knows the cost of everything and the value of nothing.

A little girl was getting ready for kindergarten one morning, and called down, "Mommy, will you please hurry up here and button my dress!"

"No, mother is too busy; you must do it yourself."

"My gosh," she exclaimed, loud enough to be heard, "whatever would I do without myself?"

ADJUSTMENT

Dr. Norman Vincent Peale tells of a trip he took on a sailboat in the Near East.

"The ocean is a tremendous force," the first mate said to him, "and a ship is only a very small force, but we know how to make our powerful engines adapt themselves to the timing of the sea. We don't drive them relentlessly through the waves; instead, we adjust our speed to the timing of the waves, so we are practically carried along by the sea."

Ella Wheeler Wilcox, an American poet, advised people to adjust to life's demands with these words:

This world will never adjust itself
To suit your whims to the letter;
Some things must go wrong your whole life long
And the sooner you know it the better.
It is folly to fight with the Infinite,
And go under at last in the wrestle,
The wiser man shapes into God's plan
As the water shapes into a vessel.

ADMIRATION

The first day of school was about to begin. The bell rang and the class was seated. The teacher, with her notebook in front of her, glanced at the names of the boys and girls who were to be in her class. After each student's name was a number, such as 135, 137, 139, 146. The teacher was both astonished and happy.

"Look at these I.Q.'s," she said to herself. "I've got myself an honor class."

With this in mind, she tried out new methods, brought in objective material, went on field trips. The students responded exceptionally well to her enthusiasm and her creative approach.

It was fortunate that it wasn't until much later in the term that the teacher learned that those numbers represented the locker numbers for the pupils in her class.

ADVANCEMENT

Life is not built on a level. It is built on an incline, so that when you stop climbing, you are liable to slip, and a slip may result in a slide. So keep on advancing.

7

ADVERSITY

Three hundred years ago, a prisoner condemned to the Tower of London carved on the wall of his cell this sentiment to keep his spirits high during his long imprisonment: "It is not adversity that kills, but the impatience with which we bear adversity."

⌘

Happy is the man who resolves that no matter how much life may confuse or wound him, it will, in the end, bless him.

⌘

ADVERTISING

Paderewski arrived in a small Connecticut town about noon one day and decided to take a walk in the afternoon. While strolling along, he heard a piano, and following the sound he came to a house bearing a sign which read: "Miss Jones—Piano Lessons 25¢ Per Hour."

Pausing to listen, he heard the young woman trying to play one of Chopin's nocturnes, but not succeeding very well.

Paderewski walked up to the house and knocked.

Miss Jones came to the door and recognized him at once. Delighted, she invited him in. He sat down and played the nocturne as only he could, and then spent an hour in correcting her mistakes. Miss Jones thanked him and he departed.

Some months later he returned to the town, and again he took the same walk.

He soon came to the home of Miss Jones and, looking at the sign, he read: "Miss Jones— (Pupil of Paderewski) —Piano Lessons $1.00 Per Hour."

⌘

A Scotsman joined a golf club and was told by his caddy that if his name were on his golf balls they would be returned to him when found. This pleased him greatly.

"Put my name on each ball," he said.

The caddy did so.

"Would you also put M. D. after it?" said the new member. "You see, I'm a doctor."

Again the caddy obeyed.

"While you are writing," continued the Scot, "could you squeeze in: 'Hours 2-4 and 6-8.'?"

⌘

Said a tiger to a lion as they drank beside a pool, "Tell me, why do you roar like a fool?"

"That's not foolish," replied the lion with a twinkle in his eyes. "They call me king of all the beasts because I advertise."

A rabbit heard them talking and ran home like a streak. He thought he would try the lion's plan, but his roar was a squeak. A fox came to investigate—and had his lunch in the woods.

The moral: when you advertise, be sure you've got the goods!

ADVICE

A religious person was once asked how it was possible for someone like himself, who lived in a spiritual realm, withdrawn from the affairs of this world, to offer advice to his followers on secular matters.

The holy man replied: "When one steps a little distance away from a problem, the perspective is better, one's insight becomes keener, and one can see things with a great deal more clarity. Justice is no longer justice when personal feelings enter the picture. Personal involvement obscures vision. A penny will hide the biggest star in the universe, if you hold it close enough to your eye. Perhaps it is because I am not personally involved in mundane matters that my view of things is all the more clear."

A fable is told of a centipede with arthritis who sought the advice of a wise old owl.

"Centipede," the owl said, "you have a hundred legs, all swollen up. Now if I were you, I'd change myself into a stork. With only two legs, you'll cut your pain by 98%, and if you use your wings you can stay off your legs altogether."

The centipede was elated, "I accept your suggestion without hesitation," he said, "Now just tell me, how do I go about making the change?"

"Oh," said the owl, "I would not know about the details. I only make general policy."

A college professor was admonishing his class: "Every man should know himself," he said.

"That may be true," countered a student, "but in doing so he wastes a great deal of time that he might have spent making more desirable acquaintances."

He had just completed his first book of poetry and was seeking poetic laurels.

Turning to the editor of a well-known magazine, he asked, "Do you think I ought to put more fire into my poetry?"

"Not at all," the editor replied calmly, "just put the poetry into the fire."

AFFAIRS

They belonged to the same group. One was the president and the other was a middle-aged lady who had been doing too much reading of stories about the permissive society and free love, the cheating that was going on in suburbia.

"Tell me," she asked of the president, "just how do you start an affair?"

The president didn't hesitate a second. "Always the same way," she said. "First with Hatikvah, then the Star Spangled Banner, and then the invocation!"

AGE

At a party, the guests were discussing which season of life was the most happy. The host, an octogenarian, asked if the guests had noticed a grove of trees before the house, and then said, "When the spring comes, and in the soft air the buds are breaking on the trees, and they are covered with blossoms, I think, 'HOW BEAU-TIFUL IS SPRING!' And when the summer comes, and covers the trees with its heavy foliage, and singing birds are all among the branches, I think, "HOW BEAUTIFUL IS SUMMER.' When autumn loads them with golden fruit, and their leaves bear the gorgeous tint of frost, I think, 'HOW BEAUTIFUL IS AU-TUMN.' And when it is winter, and there is neither foliage nor fruit, then I look up, and through the leafless branches, as I could never until now, I see the stars shine through."

James Barrie was once asked how he managed to grow old so gracefully. He smiled as he answered, "My dear lady, I give all my time to it."

Chauncey M. Depew said: "Give me five minutes talk with a man about politics, or weather, or neighbors, or finances, and

I will tell you whether he is going to reach 95 in good shape or not. If he says he has the finest neighbors in the world, and adds that times never have been better, or politics cleaner, or the weather finer, then you may be pretty sure he will be a winner at 95, or any other age. No matter how long you live, there isn't time to worry."

"How old did you say you were?" asked the doctor.

"I never mention my age," retorted the woman, "but, as a matter of fact, I've just reached twenty-one."

"Indeed!" said the doctor. "What detained you?"

A forty-year-old man married a girl of twenty. He was subjected to much criticism about the difference in their ages.

"It's not as bad as you think," he said, "When she looks at me, she feels ten years older, and when I look at her I feel ten years younger. That makes each of us thirty. So what's wrong?"

One of the witnesses in a lawsuit was trying to appear much younger than she actually was. She was hopelessly overdressed, her hair was dyed, and she was bedecked with jewels—all in a vain effort to conceal her real age.

When she appeared on the stand, she was asked how old she was. Calmly she replied: "Twenty-six."

"Twenty-six!" the judge exclaimed in astonishment. "When were you born?"

"1920," was her answer.

"Well, said the kindly judge, "let the record show that she was founded in 1920 and restored in 1966."

Turning to the jury the judge added, "If we would spend as much time growing up inside as we do trying to keep youthful on the outside, we would be better off."

The family was seated around the dinner table. The visitor pushed his chair back with obvious satisfaction. He turned to the youngster at the table and inquired, "How old are you, sonny?"

"That is difficult to say," was the answer. "According to my latest school tests I have a psychological age of eleven and a moral age of ten. Anatomically I am seven and mentally I am nine. But

11

I suppose you are referring to my chronological age. I am eight—but nobody pays much attention to that these days."

～～～

"You ask me what old age is?" repeated 85-year-old Bernard Baruch. "To me old age is always fifteen years older than I am."

～～～

By the time a man is wise enough to watch his step . . . he's too old to go anywhere.

～～～

"It's not how old you are, but how you are old that counts," counseled a woman in her eighties.

～～～

An 80-year-old grandmother walked six blocks from her home to the village library. When she arrived there, she requested the librarian to reserve a copy of the latest racy best-seller for her.

"Why," remarked the librarian, "I thought you only read history."

Without as much as a glance, the 80-year-old grandmother replied, "My dear young lady, at my age, *this is history.*"

～～～

The family was talking about their uncle who had reached his one hundredth birthday.

"A hundred years old!" repeated a distant cousin. "I suppose all you nieces and nephews are proud of him."

"I really don't know," remarked a thirty-year-old niece. "He hasn't done anything except grow old, and look how long it took him to do that."

～～～

There is a well-known sixteenth century engraving which represents an old man sitting in a child's wheelchair, with the inscription *ANCORA IMPARO* (I still learn). This phrase was constantly on the lips of Michelangelo, who in old age, carved at the marbles and refused to rest.

～～～

AGING

When Oliver Wendell Holmes was still on the Supreme Court bench, he and Justice Brandeis took walks every afternoon.

12

On one of these occasions Holmes, then 92, paused to gaze in frank admiration at a beautiful young girl who passed them. Turning to Brandeis, he sighed: "Oh! to be ten years younger again!"

⁓

Youth says: "The world belongs to me. My future is beautiful and my path is strewn with blossoms. I need never worry about the future when I have today and will surely enjoy tomorrow."

Age counsels: "Spend not all your energy at once. Divide your strength equally over the span of years and you will never feel tired or feeble. If you do not preserve your vigor, your little good fortune will soon melt away while you are still young."

⁓

A reporter asked Justice Hugo Black about his rumored retirement from the Supreme Court, and the 75-year-old Justice replied that he had not time to talk because he was on his way to play a set of doubles.

⁓

On the subject of aging, Beecher remarked, "In the morning, we carry the world like an atlas; at noon, we stoop and bend beneath it; and at night it crushes us to the ground."

⁓

A dear old Quaker lady, distinguished for her youthful appearance, was asked what she used to preserve her appearance. She replied sweetly:

> I use for the lips, truth;
> for the voice, prayer;
> for the eyes, pity;
> for the hand, charity;
> for the figure, uprightness;
> for the heart, love.

⁓

An elderly grandmother was receiving congratulations on her birthday. Her grandchild said to her, "Grandma, you are beautiful."

Without a moment's hesitation, she replied: "I ought to be. I'm 74. Such beauty is not decorative. It is structural."

⁓

13

I overheard someone say to a kindly old man: "Why, Samuel, you're already eighty, how much longer do you think you'll be here?"

Quickly, Samuel replied: "Well, it should be a long time. Statistics indicate that few people die after eighty."

⁓

W. Somerset Maugham once said that when he was young he was amazed at Plutarch's statement that the elder Cato began to learn Greek at the age of eighty. "I am amazed no longer," he added. "Old age is ready to undertake tasks that youth shirked because they would take too long."

⁓

Shakespeare, in his oft quoted passage in *As You Like It,* divides life into seven stages. Man begins as "the infant mewling and puking," and then, he is "the whining school-boy, with his satchel and shining morning face, creeping like a snail, unwilling to go to school." Later he is the lover "sighing like a furnace," then the soldier "seeking the bubble reputation even in the cannon's mouth." In his fifth stage, he is "the justice in fair round belly with good capon lined." In his sixth stage, we find him "with spectacles on nose and pouch on side." Shakespeare brings man to an inglorious conclusion by ending with "second childishness," when we find our hero "sans teeth, sans eyes, sans taste, sans everything."

⁓

A reader of her column once wrote to Ann Landers:

"Lord, Thou knowest that I am growing older. Keep me from becoming talkative and possessed with the idea that I must express myself on every subject. Release me from the craving to straighten out everyone's affairs. Keep my mind free from the recital of end-less detail. Give me wings to get to the point. Seal my lips when I am inclined to tell of my aches and pains. They are increasing with the years and my love to speak of them grows sweeter and sweeter as time goes by. Teach me the glorious lesson that occa-sionally I may be wrong. Make me thoughtful but not nosy— helpful but not bossy.

"With my vast store of wisdom and experience, it does seem a pity not to use it all. But Thou knowest, Lord, that I want a few friends at the end."

⁓

An ancient Greek fable tells of a mother who had a beloved child. She prayed to the gods on behalf of her child.

Moved by her prayers, the gods said: "Oh, mother, ask any gift that you will for your child and we shall grant it."

The mother replied: "Oh great and high gods, grant my child eternal life."

The wish was granted.

Decades later the mother died and went to her reward. After many, many years the mother one day returned to earth to see how her child had fared. The child still lived, but great age had caused the eyes to sink. The face was a mass of wrinkles. The cheeks had shrunk to hollow cavities.

The mother cried out in anguish: "See what has happened to my child, whom you promised to bless with eternal life."

The reply came back: "Oh, mother, you asked for eternal life, not eternal youth."

A 102-year-old man was asked on a radio program how he faced life. He answered with a recipe that might be followed by many: "Every morning when I get out of bed, I have two choices: to be happy or to be unhappy. I always choose to be happy."

When asked how he felt about aging, Henry Ford replied: "Anyone who stops learning is old, whether at twenty or eighty. Anyone who keeps learning stays young. The greatest thing in life is to keep your mind young."

Perhaps Oliver Wendell Holmes gave the best illustration about aging. When he became 90, Congress cut his pension. When he heard of it, the great jurist chuckled and remarked: "I have always been a prudent man, so this cut in pay will not hurt me, but I am distressed that I cannot continue to lay aside as much as usual for my old age!"

AIRPLANES

A story once appeared in the *New York Journal American,* written by correspondent Jack Smith, which sounds apocryphal, but could very well have been true. It ran somewhat like this:

A plane that had taken off from Los Angeles was getting ready

15

to land in London ahead of schedule because of strong tailwinds. The stewardess grew alarmed and ran into the cockpit and said to the pilot, "You can't land yet! The movie isn't over!"

"What's playing?" asked the pilot.

"*The Greatest Story Ever Told*," replied the stewardess. "It's a story about the Bible."

The pilot called the Tower and asked for permission to orbit the field at 20,000 feet. "We're in the middle of a movie," he said.

"What's playing?" asked the Tower.

"*The Greatest Story Ever Told*," was the answer.

"Permission granted. But make sure you stay at 20,000 feet and don't bump into flight 808. They're up there, somewhere, finishing *Cleopatra*."

About half an hour later, the pilot grew impatient and called in the stewardess.

"I can't stay up here any longer!"

"But we can't land now!" she complained. "The movie isn't over yet."

"Just cut it off, and tell them how it ends," said the pilot.

"But I don't know how it ends," she protested.

"Didn't you ever read the book?" asked the pilot.

"I read the Bible," she answered. "But you know the movies! They change everything! The movie is never like the book!"

AIRS

Mark Twain, checking in at a hotel in Canada, noticed that the arrival just ahead of him had written on the hotel register: "Baron von Blank and valet."

Mark Twain was not to be outdone by this show of elegance. He wrote: "Mark Twain and valise."

ALIVE

One mark of man's greatness is his ability to live on after death. A serious danger which confronts him is the possibility of dying while he is still alive.

Some time ago, a religious sect took as its motto these words: "Millions now living will never die." Whereupon, someone commented. "That may be so. But the tragedy is that millions now living are already dead and don't know it."

ALTRUISM

There was once a very kind-hearted man who always gave away whatever he possessed. A friend of his once asked him: "How come you give away everything you own when the sages explicitly stated that whoever gives alms should give no more than a fifth of his property?"

The generous man replied: "To transgress against the precepts established by our sages is indeed a great sin which merits Hell. But in the morning, after I have distributed a fifth of my income and a man comes to me and complains that he has no bread for his wife and children, I cannot refrain from committing this sin, and I give away the rest. Ah, were it only for sins such as these that men would go to Hades!"

AMBITION

All three were out for the company promotion. They were walking along the beach, each concerned about how to win the coveted promotion. Suddenly, they came upon several boys looking for crabs. As each crab was caught, it was placed into a wicker basket. One of the men warned: "You'd better cover the basket, otherwise the crabs will climb out and run away."

"Not so," replied one of the boys. "If one crab tries to climb up, the others will pull him down."

A little watch, dissatisfied with being in a pocket, envied Big Ben, the great tower clock. "I wish I could be up there," said the little watch. "I could serve the multitude."

And suddenly, the little watch had its wish. It was drawn up to the tower. But from below, it was invisible. Its elevation had become its annihilation.

A farmer sent his son to college. The lad came home at the end of the first year jubilant, announcing that he stood second in his class.

"Second!" said his father. "Why were you not first? What do you think I am sending you to school for anyway?"

Filled with determination, the boy plowed into his books and returned home from his sophomore year with top honors. His father looked at him silently for a few minutes, then shrugged his

17

shoulders and grumbled, "At the head of the class, eh? Well, it cannot be much of a college!"

Carl Sandburg once advised, "Before you go to sleep, say to yourself, 'I haven't reached my goal yet whatever it is, and I'm going to be uncomfortable and, in a degree, unhappy until I do.'"

A man who was able to quote the Bible by heart, had a questionable reputation in his community. During a conversation, he confided his secret ambition to his grandfather.

"More than anything else," he said, "I would like to go to the desert which our forefathers crossed, and then to Mount Sinai where the Ten Commandments were given. I would then like to climb the summit of the mountain and from there read the Ten Commandments aloud. That would be the crowning achievement of my life."

His grandfather looked at him intently for a while and then said, "Instead of going to Mount Sinai to read the Ten Commandments, why not stay at home and observe them!"

ANCESTORS

In creating the world, God created countless trees, animals, birds, and fish. But when He created man, he created only Adam, and then Eve. The wise men have offered many reasons for this:

By creating this one couple, nobody can say, "I came from better stock than you do."

It has also been pointed out that when one saves the life of another, it is like saving the entire world; when he kills another human being, it is as though he killed the entire world.

A boorish fellow took the liberty of questioning Alexander Dumas rather too closely about his genealogical tree.

"You are a quadroon, Mr. Dumas," he began.

"I am, sir," quietly replied Dumas.

"And your father?"

"Was a mulatto."

"And your grandfather?"

"A Negro," hastily answered the dramatist, whose patience was waning.

18

"And may I inquire what your great grandfather was?"

"An ape, sir!" thundered Dumas. "An ape, sir. My pedigree commences where yours terminates."

~~~

He had been boasting throughout the evening that his ancestors had come across on the Mayflower. It became just too much when he turned to one of the others and asked, "Were your ancestors Pilgrims?"

"No," was the terse comment, "my ancestors came over when the immigration laws were more stringent."

~~~

Oliver Wendell Holmes once said: "He is a wise child who chooses a good grandfather."

~~~

An old proverb declares: "The man who has not anything to boast about but his glorious ancestors can be compared to a potato: the best part of him is underground."

~~~

"One of my ancestors signed the Declaration of Independence," boasted a bigot.

"That's pretty recent," replied one of the men. "One of my ancestors signed the Ten Commandments."

~~~

When Ney, one of Napoleon's famous marshals, was asked who his ancestors were by a woman who had been discussing her wonderful ancestry, he replied, "Madam, I myself am an ancestor."

~~~

ANGELS

There is a legend which states that every man has two angels who always go with him. One is on his right shoulder and one on his left. When he does something good, the angel on the right shoulder writes it down and seals it, because what is done is done forever. When he does evil, the angel on the left shoulder writes it down. However, he waits until midnight. If before that time the man repents and asks for forgiveness, the angel erases it. If not, at midnight he seals it and the other angel weeps in sorrow.

~~~

ANGER

Charles Dickens, the English novelist, relates how a man handled himself when he realized that his ill temper was bringing misery to the others living with him:

He built a special room in his house which he named the GROWLERY. There he would retire whenever he was in a nasty mood. He would enter the room alone, shut the door, and growl to his heart's content. When he felt better, he returned to face family and friends.

A well-known humorist tells of a young man who attended a golden wedding celebration and could not help but wonder how two people could stay happily married for fifty years. He finally mustered enough courage to ask the elderly "bridegroom" if he had ever thought of divorce during the fifty marital years. The old man thought for a moment and answered, "Divorce—never; Murder—many times."

An illiterate tailor regularly attended the debates at the town hall. When he was asked whether he understood the language, he replied, "No, but I know who is wrong in any argument."

"How?" was the next question.

"By observing who gets angry first," was the wise reply.

Abraham Lincoln once read to a member of his cabinet a harsh letter he had written in answer to an attack upon his integrity. When he finished reading it, Lincoln tore the letter into shreds and tossed it into the wastebasket.

"Why did you do that?" the astonished official asked.

"I never mail such letters," the President answered. "I just write them to blow off steam."

"I have been badly insulted," said the young man to his preacher, "and I am going to the home of the man who insulted me and see that justice is done."

"Better go home," advised the preacher.

"What do you mean go home?" retorted the young man. "I've been insulted. He muddied my name and I'm going to clean it up."

20

"That's just my point," replied the preacher. "The whole world knows that mud brushes off a lot more easily when it is dry."

ANTI-SEMITISM

Bismarck once remarked to Disraeli, "The Germans have just bought a new country in Africa where Jews and pigs will not be tolerated."

Without a moment's hesitation, Disraeli answered, "Fortunately we are both here."

In the early days of the Hitler era when Jews were persecuted for no valid reason, Einstein once stated: "If my theory of relativity is proved successful, Germany will claim me as a German and France will claim me as a citizen of the world. Should my theory prove untrue, France will say that I am a German and Germany will say I am a Jew."

"You are a Jew, are you not?" said the bigoted and prejudiced Yankee to the small man he found seated next to him on the train.

"Yes," admitted the man, "I am a Jew."

"Well, I'm not," the Yankee said proudly, "and I am happy to say that in the little village I come from there is not a single Jew."

His neighbor replied quietly, "That is why it is still a village."

George M. Cohan once wrote to an expensive hotel for reservations. The answer he received was that the hotel catered to a restricted clientele. It was evident that they had mistaken him for a Jew. The famous Broadway producer wired back, "Apparently there has been a mistake on both sides: you thought I was Jewish and I thought you were gentlemen."

ANXIETY

A wise man once observed: "It is not the experience of today that drives men mad—it is remorse or bitterness for something

21

which happened yesterday, and the dread of what tomorrow may bring."

❦

APOLOGY

Two men collided on a busy street. One of them raised his hat and said, "My friend, I don't know which of us is to blame for this sudden meeting, and I don't feel it is important enough to investigate. If I ran into you, I beg your pardon; if you ran into me, don't mention it."

❦

"My briefcase is missing," said one man to another, "and I believe you have taken it." In a few minutes, the man discovered his briefcase in a corner of the room. "I must apologize for having accused you," he said.

"Never mind," said the second man. "You thought I was a thief and I thought you were a gentleman, and we were both mistaken."

❦

APPEARANCE

When Chaim Auerbach was rabbi of Lenschitz, he had many critics, most of whom were observant but not sincere in their practices.

One day Chaim was seen conversing with a woman in the marketplace, and his opponents seized upon this in an effort to discredit him: "The supposedly devout cleric—conversing with a strange woman—a veritable outrage!"

When word of this outcry reached the ears of the rabbi, he commented: "Far better to converse with a woman, and have in mind thoughts of God, than to converse with God and have thoughts of women."

❦

There was once a beautiful clock which had kept ticking away for many years. It had ticked for grandma and grandpa, for mother and father. It ticked accurately and dependably. There was but one thing wrong with this beautiful clock: it had no hands. One could hear the regular tick-tock, tick-tock, but the face of the clock revealed nothing.

❦

A college president was asked what he thought about the newest women's hair style. He answered, "I am not as concerned about the uniformity of women's heads on the outside, as I am by the uniformity of women's heads on the inside."

~~~~~

She came running downstairs one morning, lighthearted as only a child can be. She rushed into the kitchen and noticed that her mother wore a glum expression.

"Mommy," she said, "aren't you happy?"

"Why certainly I'm happy," the mother replied.

"Well," said the little girl, "you certainly haven't told your face yet."

~~~~~

About a year ago a group of archeologists excavated an ancient temple in Egypt. After being buried for centuries, the temple still retains its lovely splendor. It is studded with precious jewels and plastered with gold. But a hieroglyphic inscription on the altar reads: "Here human hearts are sacrificed to the gods."

What a gulf there exists between the exterior beauty and the inner inhumanity of that temple. Art so glorified, and hearts so mercilessly torn from the bodies of men!

~~~~~

APPRECIATION

As a simple, unpretentious admirer of fine art, Elbert Hubbard derived much pleasure from visiting the great art galleries. One day he was admiring a priceless painting in a New York gallery when a friend jokingly remarked, "Elbert, why do you allow yourself to become so enthused over things you can never afford to own?"

"Joe," replied the sage of East Aurora, "I would rather be able to appreciate things I cannot have, than have things I cannot appreciate."

~~~~~

Oliver Wendell Holmes once said, "If anyone should give me a dish of sand and tell me there were particles of iron in it, I might look for them with my eyes, and search for them with my clumsy fingers, and be unable to detect them; but let me take a magnet and sweep through it, and how it would draw to itself the almost invisible particles by mere power of attraction. The unthankful heart, like my finger in the sand, discovers no mercies; but let the thankful heart sweep through the day, and as the magnet finds the iron, so it will find in every hour some heavenly blessing. Only the iron in God's hand is as precious as gold."

"How can I ever show my appreciation?" said a woman to Clarence Darrow, after he had resolved her legal troubles.

"My dear woman," replied Darrow, "ever since the Phoenicians invented money, there has been only one answer to that question."

A woman bounced into an art gallery and made a superficial tour of the exhibits.

"Are these the masterpieces I have heard so much about?" she asked, with a scornful tone of voice. "I do not see anything in them."

Quietly, the curator said: "Madam, don't you wish you could?"

A gentleman gave a friend some first-rate wine, which he tasted and drank, but upon which he did not comment. The host, disgusted at his guest's lack of appreciation, then offered him some strong, but inferior wine. The guest had no sooner tasted it that he exclaimed that it was excellent wine.

"But you said nothing of the first," remarked the host.

"Oh," replied the other, "the first required no comment. It spoke for itself. I thought the second needed someone to speak up for it."

Thomas Carlyle's wife was a highly gifted person, one of the most clever women in England in her time. She loved her husband dearly and, to the extent that he was capable of loving any woman other than his mother, he loved her too. After her death, he read this entry in her diary: "Carlyle never praises me. If he says nothing, I have to be content that things are all right."

She had hungered for appreciation which this man of letters never brought himself to express.

A father and son were discussing the importance and significance of success. The son finally said, "It must be great to be famous and have people remember you. Now, there was Paul Revere. He was a great man."

The father responded, "Yes, Paul Revere was a real man, but do you know the name of his horse?" Of course the boy did not know the name of the horse, nor do we, for tradition or history does not record its name.

The father then said, "Did you ever stop to think that Paul Revere could not have taken the ride if it had not been for the horse?"

Like the boy, we do not often give much consideration to the horse, with the result that we do not completely understand success, or develop true appreciation for the unnamed persons who help us achieve it.

Mozart once said to a critic, "If you and I were both melted down together, we should not furnish materials for one Haydn."

Haydn said of Mozart: "If every friend of music, and great men in particular, appreciated Mozart's genius as I did, nations would vie with each other to possess such a jewel."

A non-Jewish scholar once asked a learned rabbi why the Jews hate non-Jews, and as a reason for his question he said to the rabbi: "Every morning you say a benediction: 'Thank you, God, for not having created me a heathen.'"

The rabbi replied: "In the very same benedictions, the Jew also thanks the Almighty for not being created a woman, and you will surely not say that we hate our wives."

A woman visiting a large city, saw a ragged, cold and hungry young girl gazing at some cake in a shop window. She took the child by the hand, led her into the store and bought her some of the cake. Later, she took her into a clothing store and bought her some clothes. The grateful young child looked at the lady and with sincere thanks asked, "Are you God's wife?"

A man came to the Louvre and began to inspect the art galleries. He turned to the guide and said: "I don't see why people are so excited about these paintings! I can't see anything extraordinary to rave about!"

"Monsieur!" the guide replied with deep resentment. "These

paintings are no longer on trial. The greatest critics have already expressed their great admiration and approval. It is you who are on trial, to determine if you are wise enough to appreciate what you see."

———

There is a story of a boy who was sitting on his father's shoulders and was enjoying the experience very much. As they were walking the boy saw something on the ground that he wanted. "Please get it for me," he asked of his father.

The father, devoted to his son's happiness, though carrying his son on his shoulders, bent down and picked up the article. A short time later, the son saw something else on the ground, and again he desired it, and the father smilingly picked it up. This happened several more times. Soon, the young man met another young man. The boy, sitting on his poor father's shoulders, shouted to the boy on the ground, "Have you seen my father?"

When the father heard this he became very angry. "Here I have been carrying you all this time, doing everything you ask, and now you ask where I am!" He immediately threw him from his shoulders, claiming that his son felt no appreciation.

———

A monk, who had tarried outside the monastery admiring a lovely sunset, was scolded by his confrères for being late for devotions.

"Oh," said the tardy one, "I was so enraptured by God's world that I forgot it was time to worship Him."

———

ARGUMENT

They were having a terrific argument. One of the men raised his voice and thundered, "My argument is absolutely sound."

"Yes," replied the other, "Your argument is sound, just sound."

———

ARITHMETIC

Three men pooled their cash to purchase seventeen horses. One man paid half of the cost, another a third, and the third man a ninth.

When the time came to divide the horses, they were at a loss, and so went to a judge. The judge brought them to his house and pulled his horse out alongside their seventeen horses. Looking at the three men, he said, "Now there are eighteen horses. You, who paid one half of the cost, take one-half of the horses—*nine of* them. You, who paid a third, take *six* horses. And you, who paid a ninth, take *two* horses."

Having distributed 17 horses, the judge walked his horse back into the barn.

～

ART

An old artist in Italy called one of his pupils aside and said, "I hoped this would be my masterpiece but I am old and feeble. Please complete it for me. Do thy best."

The young man breathed a fervent prayer for divine help, and then began to paint. After several weeks, the picture was finished. With ecstasy the old artist gazed upon it. "Thou hast done well, my son. I will paint no more."

And so Leonardo da Vinci began his climb to fame.

～

An art dealer was describing a friend who had become wealthy. "He has his Cadillac now, and his wife has a mink coat and a sable coat. He's buying a house, and he asked me if I thought I could get him a genuine Renoir. I told him of one I could bring in for about $7,000 and so help me, he asked, 'Does that include the frame?' "

～

Michelangelo was not only the world's foremost sculptor, he was also a superb psychologist. His own generation at first ignored him. However, Michelangelo had faith in his ability and decided to use applied psychology to convince his critics.

Knowing that they were fascinated by supposedly priceless works of art discovered in the excavation of old ruins, he tinted one of his masterpieces and then had it buried where it would surely be found. The critics were enraptured with their discovery. They pronounced it a rare antique. The Cardinal of San Giorgio paid a huge sum to add it to his collection. Then Michelangelo let the cat out of the bag, and the critics could do nothing less than proclaim the genius of Michelangelo.

～

ASPIRATION

An artist must see his finished oil painting in his mind's eye before he begins it, or he will seldom ever do a masterpiece. An architect must have his finished building down on his blue-print before the digging of the foundation takes place. So it is with life. Our goals and aspirations must be clearly in our minds and hearts if we are to be successful.

Four fellows decided to climb the mountain to see the view. One of them wore new, expensive shoes which did not fit, and he complained constantly of his feet. The second was a jealous individual who kept wishing for this house or that farm. The third kept looking at the skies, seeing storm clouds and worrying that they might get caught in the rain. The fourth really saw the marvelous view. He was not caught in the valley of his experiences but was climbing to higher things.

There is an old legend of a prince who had a crooked back. Being very proud, he suffered mentally. One day he said to his most skillful sculptor: "Make a statue of me, but with a *straight* back. I would see myself as I might have been."

When the perfect statue was finished, it was suggested that it be set up before the palace gate, but the prince said, "Place it in a secret nook in the palace garden where only I shall see it."

The affair was soon forgotten, but every day the prince would steal away and look long and earnestly at the statue, and each time something seemed to set his blood tingling and his heart throbbing. Months passed and people began to say: "The prince's back is not as crooked as it was," or, "The prince seems much more noble-looking than he used to."

Hearing this, the prince went back again into the garden and stood before the statue, and behold, his back had become as straight as the statue's and his brow as noble. He had become the man of the statue.

ASSIMILATION

Two significant events occurred in European Jewish history during the year 1848.

It was in that year that the Russian Czar, Nicholas I, instituted his infamous cantonist system, whereby young Jewish children were torn from their parents and brought up by priests, eventually being drafted into the army. It was in the same year that the Austrian Emperor, Franz Josef I, ennobled the first Jews in his empire.

The story was told that the two emperors met, and Nicholas angrily reproved Franz Josef for his actions.

"Here am I out to destroy the Jews, and you make them barons!"

To which Franz Josef is supposed to have replied, "I also wish to destroy the Jews, but you will see that my method is more effective than yours."

ASSISTANCE

A small boy was struggling to lift a heavy stone, but he could not budge it. His father, passing by, stopped to watch his efforts. Finally he said to his son: "Are you using all your strength?"

"Yes, I am," the boy cried, exasperated.

"No," the father said calmly, "you're not. You have not asked me to help you."

ASSOCIATION

There are localities in Switzerland where a canary is caged with a nightingale so that it may catch the sweetness of the latter's song and breathe into its notes that harmonious melody that delights all tourists in Europe. It is a demonstration of the power of association. The canary can be trained by a nightingale.

The farmer was having trouble with his corn, which was being destroyed by cranes that fed in his field. Finally, he set a trap to ensnare the birds.

When he visited the snare, he discovered a beautiful stork caught with the cranes. The stork pleaded that he was innocent, and in fact had not ever touched any of the farmer's crop.

"That may be true," answered the farmer, "but I find you among them and I judge you accordingly."

ASSURANCE

A nervous driver approached an extremely narrow pass in the Rocky Mountains. He was frightened at the thought of driving his car along this narrow road. A sign on the highway reassured him. It read: "Oh, yes, you can. Millions have!"

ATHEIST

An atheist came to a rabbi with a peculiar request. "Rabbi," he said, "I have made up my mind to violate every precept in the Torah. I have already broken every one I can think of, but I am afraid I missed one or two."

"*Nu*, what do you want of me?" asked the rabbi.

"This. I'll enumerate all the commandments I have transgressed, and if you find that I forgot any, tell me so I can break them too."

The rabbi listened stonily as the sinner recited a long list of the most shocking misdeeds he had perpetrated.

"There is just one more sin you will have to commit to make your record complete," said the rabbi when the libertine had finished.

"Fine! Tell me what it is and I'll do it!"

"You forgot the injunction against suicide," snapped the rabbi.

"God, strike me dead in five minutes, if You can," shouted an atheist.

When the five minutes had expired, he jeered to his audience. "What did I tell you?"

A man standing by asked, "Sir, have you any children?"

"Yes, why?"

"Well, if one of them handed you a gun and said, 'Dad, kill me,' would you do it?"

"Of course not, I love them."

"God loves you too and that's the reason he didn't strike you dead."

A religious leader was once challenged to a debate by an atheist. When the religious leader refused, the atheist asked, "What's the matter? Are you afraid?"

"Let me tell you a story," replied the leader, "and perhaps you will understand my reason." He then said, "A skunk once challenged a lion to single combat. The lion promptly declined the honor of such a meeting.

" 'Are you afraid?' demanded the skunk.

" 'Very much so,' said the lion, 'for you would only gain fame by having the honor of fighting a lion, while everyone who would meet me during the next month would know that I had been in the company of a skunk.' "

An insightful man once defined an atheist with these words: "An atheist is a man who has no invisible means of support."

ATOMIC AGE

According to some of our present day nuclear scientists, an entry was made in a scientific journal, some 90 years ago, which foresaw that within 100 years man would discover the secret of the atom. When that time comes, the journal suggests, "God, with His white beard, will come down to earth swinging a bunch of keys and will announce to humanity, as they do at 5 o'clock in the saloon: 'Closing time, gentlemen, closing time!' "

ATROPHY

Harold Nicholson reminds us of the story of the fish in Mammoth Cave, Kentucky. These fish have lived for generations in the dark and their optic nerves have become atrophied. The fish are quite blind.

Similarly, Darwin tells us that he lost his love of poetry and music, once very strong within him, simply because he ceased to develop them.

This is true of all our powers: memory, concentration, capacity for hard work. We must use them or lose them.

ATTENTION

It had snowed all through the night and the three young lads were playing. A man came up to them and said, "Would you like to try a race and win a prize?"

The boys agreed and the man informed them that this would

be a different type of race. "I will go to the other side of the field," he explained, "and when I give you the signal, you will start to run. The one whose footsteps are the straightest in the snow will be the winner."

The race began and the first boy kept looking at his feet to see if his steps were straight. The second lad kept looking at his friends to see what they were doing; but the third boy just ran on with his eyes fixed on the man on the other side of the field.

The third young fellow was the winner, for his footsteps were straight in the snow. He had kept his eyes on the goal ahead of him.

A rather frail woman was married to a lumberman. They had five sons, all engaged in the same business. When she was asked how she made her soft voice heard above the roars of her husband and sons, she replied: "It's very easy. I whisper."

A man who had been condemned to die in the electric chair was asked if he had a final statement to make. He looked at the many reporters, photographers, and officials who surrounded him and then said bitterly: "If I had been shown so much attention when I was a boy, I would not be here today."

A doctor was busy in his study when his small son came in and stood silently by. The doctor, preoccupied with his work, put his hand in his pocket, took out a coin and offered it to the boy.

"I don't want any money," the lad said.

After a few moments the doctor opened a drawer of his desk, took out a candy bar, and offered it to his son. Again he was refused.

A little impatient, the busy doctor asked, "Well, what *do* you want?"

"I don't want anything," replied the boy. "I only wanted to be with you."

ATTITUDE

Two young children, just coming out of their Sunday School class, were discussing what they had just learned. "Do you really believe there is a devil?" asked one.

"No," replied the other promptly, "of course not. It's just like Santa Claus—he's your father."

A man was driving in the country one day, and he saw an old man sitting on a fence watching the automobiles go by. Stopping to pass the time of day, the traveler said, "I never could stand living out here. You don't see anything, and I'm sure you don't travel like I do. I'm on the go all the time."

The old man on the fence looked down at the stranger, and drawled, "I can't see much difference in what I'm doing and what you're doing. I sit on the fence and watch the autos go by, and you sit in your auto and watch the fences go by. It's just the way you look at things."

He was an old man yet every Sunday he could be seen walking to church. Because he was deaf, he could not hear the sermon; nor could he hear the music of the choir, or the hymns sung by the congregation. A scoffer asked, "Why do you spend your Sundays in church when you can't hear a single word?"

He replied: "I want my neighbors to know which side I'm on."

There was a lively wedding taking place in the small village. Men and women were dancing to the strains of the village band. A totally deaf stranger came accidentally upon the scene. Since no strains of the music reached his ears, and he noted the strange behavior of the guests, capering about and grimacing, he decided that they were absolutely mad.

AUTHORITY

Parents' discipline should be based on four F's: FIRMNESS, FONDNESS, FRANKNESS, and FAIRNESS. Parents who cannot say "No" to a child often rear offspring who have contempt for authority.

AUTHORS

A young writer who had just completed his first work, once approached W. Somerset Maugham and asked: "Mr. Maugham,

33

I've just written a novel, but have been unable to come up with an intriguing title. Your books have such wonderful titles: *Cakes and Ale, The Razor's Edge.* . . . Could you help me with my title by reading the book?"

"There is no necessity for reading your book," replied Maugham. "Are there drums in it?"

"No, it's not that kind of a story. You see it deals with—"

"Are there any bugles in it?"

"No, certainly not," was the response.

"Well then," replied the famous author, "Call it, *No Drums, No Bugles.*"

AUTOMATION

Years ago, a man was just a cog in a wheel. Today, he is ten holes in an I.B.M. punch card.

There is a story told about Thomas Edison. He and a friend were watching a new earth-mover in operation.

The friend said sadly, "That machine will put a great number of men out of work."

Edison turned to him and said, "Many more men could be put to work if they would move that earth with teaspoons."

AWARENESS

It took an unknown author to point out that happiness is sometimes in our own back yard:

> He searched the wide world over
> To find a four-leafed clover
> Which all the while had grown beside his door.

The Chinese tell a story of the little fish who heard about water for the first time and swam frantically from pond to river to ocean in search of it. He had overheard a fisherman say that without water no living creature could survive. Then, a wise old fish convinced him that he had been living in water since he had been born. The little fish began the long swim home, saying: "I had water all the time, and I did not know it."

BALANCE

A story is told about a party of native bearers in Central Africa who suddenly set down their packs and refused to go forward. When asked the reason, one said, "Our bodies have gone too quickly for our souls, and we are waiting for our souls to catch up with us."

A man had a habit of presenting a pair of scales to his children as they grew up. The children wondered why their father had selected scales as a sign of maturity. The father explained: "A pair of scales is one of the most important things in life. If you tend to be too gay and carefree, see to it that you balance the scales with the more serious aspects of life."

A young man lived in a small town where he bore the distinction of being the only musician. Since he was a very talented young fellow and could play several instruments, he was invited to every social function in the vicinity. As his reputation for livening up parties spread, his work took him further and further away from home, and he attended more and more happy occasions.

The young man's father, who was a pious and good man, feared that living constantly in a festive atmosphere might give the boy a wrong perspective of life. The father did not want his son to lose all sense of proportion and come to believe that life was nothing more than a round of parties. After much thought the father spoke to his son.

"My son," said the wise old man, "promise me that you will make it a habit to visit either the aged, the sick, or the poor before you go off on a round of merry-making. This will help you bear in mind that in life the scales are always balanced; there is no good without some bad; there is no joy without some sadness; there is no affluence without some deprivation."

BEAUTY

An unknown poet once described what he believed were four beautiful things:

> These things are beautiful beyond belief:
> The pleasant weakness that comes after pain,
> The radiant greenness that comes after rain,

The deepened faith that follows after grief,
And the awakening to love again.

～～～

Rabbi Joshua, the son of Hananiah, is described in the Talmud as one of those men whose minds are far more beautiful than their bodies. His great learning, wit, and wisdom had earned for him not only the love and respect of the populace, but even the favor of Emperor Trajan.

Being often at court, one of the princesses remarked on his ugliness.

"How is it," she said, "that such glorious wisdom is enclosed in so ugly a vessel?"

The rabbi, not in the least offended, asked the princess in what sort of vessels her father kept his wines.

"Why, in earthen vessels," replied the princess.

"Oh," exclaimed the clever rabbi, "this is what ordinary people do; an Emperor's wine should be kept in more beautiful vessels."

The princess, thinking him in earnest, ordered the wine to be transferred from the earthen jugs into gold and silver vessels. But to her great surprise she found that in a very short time the wine became unfit to drink.

"Very fine advice, indeed, Joshua, hast thou given me!" said the princess. "Do you know that all our wine is sour and spoiled?"

"Now you should be convinced," said the rabbi, "that wine keeps best in plain vessels. And the same is true of wisdom."

"But," continued the princess, "I know many persons who are both wise and handsome."

"True," replied the sage, "but they would most probably be still wiser were they less handsome."

～～～

The French artist, Pierre Auguste Renoir, suffered a great deal from an old malady, rheumatism. It was extremely painful for him to continue painting, which he nevertheless did, seated in a chair.

A friend, who was visiting with him, noted Renoir's obvious pain. "You have done enough already, Renoir," he commented. "Why do you continue to torture yourself?"

The famous artist looked at him for a long moment and replied, "The pain passes, but the beauty remains."

～～～

Frank Lloyd Wright, a genius who lived a full, rich life and whose contributions in architecture will live on and on, once wrote:

"The longer I live the more beautiful life becomes. If you foolishly ignore beauty, you'll soon find yourself without it. Your life will be impoverished. But if you wisely invest in beauty, it will remain with you all the days of your life."

A young man sat in a train looking out of the window. Beside him sat an elderly workman. Suddenly, on the opposite track, an express train came thundering by, hiding the countryside view.

The young man snapped his fingers and, turning to the workman, exclaimed: "There it is. It's always there. That's my train."

"Is that so?" returned the older man with a smile. "You look all hot and bothered about your train."

"Well," said the boy, "a few moments ago I was enjoying the countryside through the window of the train. I was admiring the beautiful scenery—the trees, the farmhouses, the grass . . . and along came this train and blotted out the view."

The other nodded thoughtfully and said, "That often happens to us, but did you ever stop to think that there are windows on both sides of this train? Look over there now."

As the man looked across the aisle and out through the other window he saw the water of a lake, blue under the summer sky, small ships with sails, all quite lovely to behold.

"You will often find," the old workman murmured, "that a lot depends on which way we look."

BEGINNING

A student minister was about to be tested by his superiors in what they said was going to be an extemporaneous speech. They told him that they would not give him the text of the sermon until he was on the pulpit facing the audience.

At the appointed time, the young aspirant took his place behind the pulpit, and there he found a slip of paper. It was completely blank. He picked it up and turned it over. The back side was also blank. He looked straight into the eyes of his audience as he kept turning the paper over and over and then in a strong voice said: "Nothing on this side, and nothing on that side—out of nothing did God create the earth." This became his text.

"Life is full of ends," wrote Phillips Brooks, "but every end is a new beginning, and we are continually coming to the point where we close one chapter, but we always can turn and open a new and better and a diviner chapter."

~~~

BELIEF

A minister once delivered a sermon at a medical school on the meaning of having a soul. Following the service a medical student came up to the minister and said in a tone tinged with sarcasm, "I have just dissected a cadaver completely. I opened every organ of the human body, but no place did I find a soul. How can you stand up before people and claim that a soul exists?"

"That is very interesting," replied the clergyman. "But let me ask you, when you opened the brain, did you find a thought?"

"No," was the answer.

"When you opened the heart, did you find a feeling of generosity?" And the student was once again compelled to answer in the negative.

"And when you dissected the eye, did you discover vision?"

Once more, the young scientist had to answer, "No."

"Well, then," said the minister, "you found none of these but you know very well that thoughts, and feelings of generosity, and vision exist. You know this because you have experienced them yourself and you know this because without these attributes mankind would have perished." He stopped for a minute and then added: "You must understand, my young friend, that just because we cannot see or prove something conclusively, it does not necessarily follow that it does not exist."

~~~

One of the most stirring poems to come out of World War II was one found on the body of an unknown American soldier. He was obviously not an accomplished poet but his sincerity was eloquent.

> "Look God, I have never spoken to You.
> But now I want to say 'How do You do?'
> You see, they told me You didn't exist.
> And like a fool, I believed all this.
>
> Last night from a shell hole, I saw Your sky;
> I figured right then, they had told me a lie....

Funny I had to come to this hellish place
Before I had time to see Your face."

And a few stanzas later he concludes:

"Well, I have to go now, God, goodbye.
Strange, since I met you, I'm not afraid to die."

⁓

When the earth was created and the birds had acquired the art of singing their melodious songs, God placed wings upon their backs. When this took place, a storm of protest arose, and the birds decided to send a delegation to plead their cause. The delegates approached the throned Majesty and eloquently implored the Lord to remove their obnoxious wings.

"Is it not enough," they said, "that we are as feeble and must drag the weight of our bodies around, that you have also burdened us with the weight of wings?"

The Lord smiled and replied to his feathered delegation. "I see the justice of your complaint. However, let us wait one week, and if at that time you still desire to have your wings removed, I shall comply with your request."

Greatly pleased, the delegation left. But then a very strange thing happened. One day later they felt a certain force lifting them upward from the ground. When a second and a third day passed, the birds found themselves flying and enjoying heavenly sensations.

After one week had passed, the delegation again appeared before the Lord, but this time they were humble. "Merciful Father," they said, "how could we have doubted your infinite wisdom? These very wings which we ridiculed as unnecessary burdens we now cherish, for they enable us to soar aloft into the very heavens."

⁓

A very severe earthquake hit a tiny village. All the villagers were alarmed, with the exception of one elderly lady who seemed to be cool and calm. When asked why she was not afraid, she replied, "I am not afraid. In fact, I rejoice that I have a God who can shake the world."

⁓

Two men built houses that were exactly alike. They had the same walls, the same kind of roof, the same doors, and the same windows. Then a storm came, and when the storm was over, one was a heap of rubble, and the other stood just as it was before the storm. The difference was due to the fact that one was built on sand and the other on rock.

—

Clarence Darrow, the famous criminal lawyer, once said during a debate: "They tell me there is a God; but I have never seen him, nor have I ever touched him. I have no personal acquaintance with him."

Roy L. Smith replied: "It is credibly reported that Mr. Darrow has a mind; but I have never seen it, nor touched it. In fact, I have no proof of it at all."

—

BIBLE

Don't just own a Bible; read it.
Don't only read it; understand it.
Don't only understand it; believe it.
Don't only believe it; live it.

—

Asked what he'd learned at Sunday school, the ten-year-old began, "Well, our teacher told us about when God sent Moses behind the enemy lines to rescue the Israelites from the Egyptians. When they came to the Red Sea, Moses called for the engineers to build a pontoon bridge. After they had all crossed, they looked back and saw the Egyptian tanks coming. Quick as a flash, Moses radioed headquarters on his walkie-talkie to send bombers to blow up the bridge, and that is how he saved the Israelites."

"Bobby," exclaimed his startled mother, "is that really the way your teacher told that story?"

"Well, not exactly. But if I told it her way, you'd never believe it!"

—Dr. John F. Anderson, in *Dallas News*

—

Voltaire said that in 100 years the Bible would be a forgotten book, found only in the museums. When the 100 years were up, Voltaire's home was occupied by the Geneva Bible Society.

—

A young man preparing for a long trip remarked to his companion, "I am just about packed. I only have to put in a guidebook, a lamp, a mirror, a microscope, a telescope, a volume of fine poetry, a few biographies, a package of old letters, a book of songs, a sword, a hammer, and a set of books I have been studying."

"How can you pack all this?" his friend protested. "It is impossible to get all that in your suitcase."

"Oh, but it doesn't take much room," replied the young man, as he placed his Bible in the corner of the suitcase and closed the lid.

An old man once said, "For a long time, reading Scripture presented many difficulties to me. I finally came to the conclusion that reading the Bible was like eating fish. When I find a difficulty, I lay it aside, and call it a *bone*. Why should I choke over the bone when there is so much nutritious meat for me? Some day I may find that even the bone may afford me nourishment."

Atheist: "I am surprised you still read the Bible. I am convinced it is a fraud."

Minister: "And what makes you say that?"

Atheist: "Many things. Any sane person who thinks logically can see that the Bible contains impossible stuff. Take for example, the story of Balaam's ass. How could a dumb animal talk?"

Minister: "There is logic to that story. If hundreds of humans talk like asses, it is perfectly possible for at least one ass to talk like a human being."

A minister was once visiting in the home of a wealthy parishioner who was a collector of Bibles. He had the Bible in a great number of forms and in many languages; he had ancient scrolls and parchments, rare manuscripts of early times, and elaborate modern editions.

"Loving the Book as you seem to," said the pastor, "you must get a great deal of pleasure from reading it."

"Oh," was the reply, "I am so busy running around the country looking for these rare finds, I don't have the time to read it."

A skeptic once said to a minister, "How do you reconcile the teachings of the Bible with the latest scientific conclusions?"

41

The minister took no time in replying, "I haven't seen this morning's papers. What are the latest conclusions of modern science?"

⟲

A young boy noticed a Bible on the book shelf. It needed a dusting badly.

"Whose book is this?" he asked of his mother.

"It is God's book," she answered.

"Well, he replied, "Don't you think we ought to return it? Nobody seems to be reading it here!"

⟲

A skeptic, speaking of the Bible, said that it was quite impossible, these days, to believe in any book whose authorship was unknown. A student asked him if the compiler of the multiplication table was known.

"No," was the immediate answer.

"Then, of course, you do not believe in it?"

"Oh, yes, I believe it because it works so well."

"So does the Bible," was the rejoinder, and the skeptic had no answer.

⟲

BIRTH

There is a beautiful legend which tells us that while the child is in its mother's womb a candle burns by whose light the unborn infant is able to see from one end of the world to another, and from one generation to the other.

At the moment of birth, the candle is extinguished. An angel playfully flicks its finger under the baby's chin—hence the dimple —and then it forgets. But in its memory the experience lingers on.

⟲

BIRTH CONTROL

Clarence Darrow, the eminent criminal lawyer, was once asked whether or not he believed in birth control.

"Whenever that question is put to me," he answered, "I always remember that I was the fifth."

⟲

BLESSING

More than seven centuries ago, Francis of Assisi composed this beautiful prayer:

Where there is hatred, let me sow love;
Where there is injury, pardon;
Where there is doubt, faith;
Where there is despair, hope;
Where there is darkness, light;
Where there is sadness, joy.

O, Divine Master, grant that I not so much seek to be
    consoled as to console;
To be understood as to understand;
To be loved as to love;
For it is in giving that we receive;
It is in pardoning that we are pardoned;
It is in dying that we are born to eternal life.

A traveler wandering in the desert became faint with heat, hunger and thirst. Suddenly he spied a large, shady tree laden with luscious fruit. Nearby flowed a clear, sparkling stream. The weary man hungrily devoured the fruit, quenched his thirst with the fresh flowing water, and reclined in the shade of the tree.

When he prepared to set out again, he turned to the tree and said, "Benevolent tree, how can I thank you? Shall I bless you that your fruit be sweet? Your fruit is sweet. Shall I bless you that your shade be soothing? It is soothing. Shall I wish for water to flow through and nourish your roots? You already have a stream at your feet. There is just one blessing that I can give you. May the twigs which are cut from you and planted in other soil, flourish and blossom like you."

BLINDNESS

In a letter to John Greenleaf Whittier, Helen Keller wrote, complimenting him upon his poetry:

"It is very pleasant to live here in our beautiful world. I cannot see the lovely things with my eyes, but my mind can see them all, and so I am joyful all the day long."

Helen Keller offers sage advice in *The World I Live In*. She says: "I have walked with people whose eyes are full of light but who see nothing in woods, sea or sky, nothing in the city street, nothing in books. What a witless masquerade is this seeing.

"It were better far to sail forever in the night of blindness with sense and feeling and mind than to be thus content with the mere act of seeing.

"They have the sunset, the morning skies, the purpose of distant hills, yet their souls voyage through this enchanted world with nothing but a barren stare."

Helen Keller, famous American, once counseled a group by saying: "I who am blind, can give one hint to those who see: Use your eyes as if tomorrow you would be stricken blind."

BOASTING

He just kept on boasting about his ancestors. "Yes," he finally declared, "my family can trace its ancestry back to William the Conqueror."

"I suppose," sneered a listener, "you'll be telling us that your ancestors were in Noah's Ark."

"Certainly not," said the boaster, "my people owned a boat all of their own."

A Chicago matron was present at a dinner party. She was seated next to Mrs. Cabot, who insisted on talking about her native Boston. "In Boston," said Mrs. Cabot, "we place all our emphasis on breeding."

The Chicago woman listened quietly and then squelched her with, "In Chicago, we too think it's a lot of fun, but we manage to have a great many other outside interests."

Booth Tarkington was not to be topped. While in Naples, he was present at an eruption of Vesuvius.

"You haven't anything approaching that in America, have you?" asked an Italian with pride.

Tarkington smiled as he replied, "No, but we've got the Niagara Falls . . . and that would put the blooming thing out in five minutes!"

A rather pompous city dweller who had turned to farming showed a young lad his acreage. He bragged about all his accomplishments, finally concluding with the proud boast: "And I grew it all by myself, sonny. Started with absolutely nothing, and now look at it!"

"From nothing?" echoed the impressed lad. "Golly, sir, without even a seed?"

Bacon reprimanded one of his friends who loved to boast. "The less you speak of your greatness," he said, "the more I shall think of it. Mirrors are the accompaniments of dandies, not heroes. The men of history were not perpetually looking in the glass to make sure of their own size. They were absorbed in their work, and the world noticed what they accomplished."

There is an ancient fable about the ant and the elephant crossing a bridge. The bridge shook under the weight of the elephant. When the two reached the other side, the ant exclaimed: "Boy, we sure shook that bridge, didn't we?"

BOOKS

"A book is a garden," wrote Henry Ward Beecher. "A book is an orchard. A book is a storehouse. It is good company. It is a counselor. It is a multitude of counselors. The best things that the best men have ever thought in past times, and expressed in the best manner, lie in books; and he who knows how to use these may be said, almost, to have control of the world. I would give more for the ownership of books than for all the gold in California, if in ownership I sought happiness—various, self-respecting happiness, continuous amidst care and burdens and disappointments in youth, in middle age, and in old age. There is nothing like a book to one who knows how to pluck fruit from it, and how to prepare it for his palate."

Kingsley, who loved to read, once said, "Consider! Except for a living man, there is nothing more wonderful than a book—a message to us from the dead, from human souls whom we never saw, who lived, perhaps, thousands of miles away; and yet these, in those little sheets of paper, speak to us, amuse us, terrify us, teach us, comfort us, open their hearts to us as brothers."

Someone asked his friend: "If you were shipwrecked, alone, on a distant island, and could have one book, which one would you choose?"

The friend wisely replied, *"Johnson's Manual of Ship Building!"*

The French writer, Balzac, spent an evening with friends who talked about everything in general, but said nothing of significance. When he got home, he went to his study, took off his coat, rubbed his hands, and, regarding the books of the masters on the shelves, cried, "Now for some real people!"

BORROWING

Sir Walter Scott had difficulty in getting back the books friends had borrowed. One day, as he again was urged to lend a book, he cautioned the borrower to return it promptly. "I must do this," he said, "for though all my friends are poor mathematicians, I notice that most of them are good bookkeepers."

BRAGGARTS

A doctor, an engineer and a banker were arguing which profession was the oldest.

Doctor: Mine is; God's operation—making Eve out of Adam's rib.

Engineer: Mine is; Creation was made out of chaos.

Banker: But who created the chaos?

BRAVERY

At Gettysburg, there is a monument in memory of a color-bearer who became isolated from his regiment. The regiment had retreated after an unsuccessful charge, but the color-bearer remained.

The commanding officer sent a messenger to the boy, "Bring the colors back to the regiment."

The boy replied, "Bring the regiment back to the colors."

The Duke of Wellington was a heroic English general. It is reported that he once remarked: "The British are not braver than the French. They are only brave for five minutes *longer*."

BREVITY

A soldier who had just lost his three stripes for a slight infraction of regulations, emerged from his Commanding Officer's tent muttering: "That guy is a man of few words. He calls me in and says: 'Hello, sit down, Sergeant; get up, Corporal; goodbye, Private.' "

Mark Twain was attending a meeting where a missionary had been invited to speak. Twain was deeply impressed. Later he related, "The preacher's voice was beautiful. He told us about the sufferings of the natives, and he pleaded for help with such moving simplicity that I mentally doubled the 50 cents I had intended to put in the plate. He described the pitiful misery of those savages so vividly that the dollar I had in mind gradually rose to five. Then that preacher continued, and I felt that all the cash I carried on me would be insufficient, and I decided to write a large check."

"Then he went on," added Twain. "He went on and on and on about the dreadful state of those natives, and I abandoned the idea of the check. And he went on. And I got back to five dollars. And he went on, and I got back to four, two, one. And still he went on. And when the plate came around . . . I took 10 cents out of it."

"There are four requisites to a good short story," exclaimed the teacher of journalism to the aspirants. "They are brevity, a reference to religion, some association with society, and an illustration of modesty. Now, with these four points, write a short story in thirty minutes or less."

In five minutes Murray announced that he had finished.

47

"That is fine," said the teacher. "Read your story to the class."

Murray read: " 'My Gawd!' said the duchess. 'Take your hands off my knee!' "

The Wright brothers were both present at a meeting of inventors. Wilbur Wright was called upon to make a speech.

"There must be some mistake," he said. "Orville does all the talking."

So Orville was called upon. His speech was even shorter. "Wilbur has just made our speech," he said.

A reporter, travelling through the South, picked up what he believed to be a "big story." He telegraphed his editor asking whether the story should be sent in. The answer arrived promptly: "Send six hundred words."

The enthusiastic reporter was depressed and wired back, "Can't be told in less than twelve hundred words."

Then came the final reply: "Story of creation of world told in six hundred. Try it."

BROTHERHOOD

It is told of the great Russian novelist, Turgenev, that once he was walking in the streets and was stopped by a beggar. Turgenev dug his hands into his pockets and found that he had brought no money with him. He turned to the beggar and said, "I'm sorry, brother, but I have no money to give you."

The beggar smiled and said, "You don't have to give me any money. You have already given me a precious gift. You've called me *brother*."

Two men entered a forest from opposite directions. Each of them was fully armed and carried a lighted lantern. After a while, each imagined that he was being followed stealthily by some unknown enemy.

Greatly terrified, each anxiously attempted to avoid the other by following a narrow, crooked path instead of the much shorter, main path. How amazed they were when coming upon one another in the middle of the forest, they held their lanterns aloft and recognized each other. They were each other's brother!

A young boy was seen carrying a heavy baby in his arms. He looked tired and his thin arms seemed to sag under the load he was bearing.

"Isn't he too heavy for you?" asked a kind lady.

"No, he's not heavy," was the reply. "He's my brother."

Abou Ben Adhem—may his tribe increase—
Awoke one night from a deep dream of peace,
And saw within the moonlight of his room,
Making it rich and like a lily in bloom,
An angel writing in a book of gold.

Exceeding peace had made Ben Adhem bold,
And to the presence in the room he said:
"What writest thou?" The vision raised its head,
And with a look made all of sweet accord,
Answered: "The names of those who love the Lord."

"And is mine one?" asked Abou. "Nay, not so,"
Replied the angel. Abou spoke more low,
But cheerily still, and said: "I pray thee then,
Write me as one that loves his fellow-men."
The angel wrote and vanished. The next night
He came again with a great wakening light,
And showed the names whom love of God had blessed,
And lo! Ben Adhem's name led all the rest.

—Leigh Hunt

When the Nazis urged the King of Denmark to institute anti-Jewish legislation, he replied, "But you see, there isn't any Jewish problem here. We do not consider ourselves inferior to them."

Harold Hender wrote a valuable book entitled, *Rescue in Denmark*. It is a testimonial to a nation that defied Nazism while so many nations stood by silently. Here is one episode from his book:

The Nazis planned a lightning raid upon the Jews of Denmark on the first day of Rosh Hashanah, 1943. They chose that day because they knew that many Jews would be gathered in the synagogue. Chief Rabbi Marcus Melchior of the Copenhagen Synagogue had been informed of the Nazi plan, and warned his congregants. He urged them to leave the synagogue immediately, and to spread the word to every Jew. Not only did Jews warn fellow Jews, but, throughout that day, Christian policemen, mailmen, taxi drivers, shopkeepers, doctors, teachers and students went about, quietly passing the warning to their Jewish friends and acquaintances.

Jorgen Knudsen, a young, newly-married ambulance driver, was leaving his apartment to report for work when he noticed some of his friends rushing up and down the street, stopping people to talk to them. When they told him, in response to his question, that they were warning Jews of the impending disaster, he decided that he, too, must help.

He went to a corner telephone booth, took out the telephone directory, hid it under his coat, and went to the garage where his ambulance was parked. There, he went through the entire book and circled all the names that appeared to be Jewish. He did not report to the hospital with his ambulance that day. Instead, he drove through the streets of Copenhagen, calling on total strangers to give them warning. When some of the Jewish people became frantic, not knowing where to run, he put them into his ambulance and drove them to the hospital where they were welcomed, and hidden from the Germans.

A young child seeing two nestling birds pecking at each other, inquired of his elder brother what they were doing. "They are quarrelling," was the answer.

"No," replied the young child, "that cannot be. They are brothers."

"Brothers," said an old tea kettle that lay in the corner of a shed in which some worn-out locomotives had been stowed away, "I am sorry to see you in this place. I was not brought here till I had more than once lost my spout and had been patched and soldered, till very little of my original shape was left. I conclude, therefore, that like me, you have seen your best days, and are to be laid aside as useless."

The locomotives frowned at one another, but did not answer.

"Well, brothers," cried the kettle again. "Don't be down-hearted. We have played busy and useful parts in our day and have earned the right to be retired."

"What are you talking about, you broken-down tin-whistle? Why do you refer to us as brothers?" questioned the locomotives.

"So you do not want to own up to our relationship? Well, let me tell you! I am a mother and father to you as well; for who would ever have heard of a steam engine if it had not been for a tea kettle?"

In an engine room, it is impossible to look into the great boiler and see how much water it contains. But running up beside it is a tiny glass tube, which serves as a gauge. As the water stands in the little tube, so it stands in the great boiler. When the tube is half full, the boiler is half full; when the tube is empty, the boiler is empty. Your love for God can be measured the same way. The way you love your fellow human being is the measure of your love for God.

BUILDING

When an engineer builds a bridge, he figures on three loads that the bridge must bear: the dead load, the live load, and the wind load. The dead load is the weight of the bridge; the live load is the weight of the traffic on the bridge; and the wind load is the pressure of the wind on its superstructure.

This is a parable of life. Life's "dead load" is concerned with managing one's self; its "live load" is the pressure of daily wear and tear; its "wind load" is adversity and unalterable circumstances.

BURDEN

"What is life's heaviest burden?" asked a youth of a sad and lonely old man.

"To have nothing to carry," was his pensive answer.

On a hot day, an old man was walking and carrying a heavy load upon his back. A rich man, passing by in his convertible, took pity on him, and invited him to take a seat in the back.

51

Shortly after, turning around, the rich man saw that the old man still had the bundle on his back. "Why don't you put it down?" he asked.

"Is it not enough that you carry me?" replied the poor man, "must you also carry my burden?"

"Foolish man!" was the reply. "If I am willing to carry you, am I not equally willing to carry your burden?"

BUREAUCRACY

During World War II, a Japanese spy was sent to Washington to spot targets for a Japanese raid. Reporting to his superiors, the spy said, "It is useless to bomb Washington. The American government has been very forehanded. If you completely destroy one building and everyone in it, you accomplish nothing, for they already have two other buildings completely staffed with people doing exactly the same thing."

BUSINESS

The town sage was holding court. "I have a horse that is a problem to me," said one of the farmers. "Sometimes he appears to be normal, and at other times he is quite lame. What advice can you give me?"

"The next time your horse appears normal, sell him," was the immediate answer.

BUSY

A wise man once remarked that what he fears most is to stand at last before the great throne and hear a voice asking: "Well, what did you see in My world?" and having to answer, "I never saw it, I was busy working."

CAMOUFLAGE

Alexander the Great engaged an artist to paint his portrait. He set down only two conditions: It was to be an exact likeness, unfalsified, and it was to be handsome and attractive.

The artist had a difficult time, for over his right eye, Alexander had a prominent battle scar. The artist was confronted with a painful dilemma. To omit the scar would be a violation of the first condition. To include it would be a violation of the second.

Finally, the artist decided to paint Alexander in a pensive mood, his face supported by his right hand with his forefinger covering the scar.

CARES

One winter day, some boys made a snowball and rolled it along until it had grown too large and heavy for them to move.

"Here," said the father of one of the boys, "we have an example of human cares. They are often insignificant, but we magnify them by impatience and lack of faith until they become greater than we can bear."

CAUTION

A gentleman wishing to test the character of some men who had applied for the position of chauffeur, took them to a narrow road which bordered on a deep precipice.

"How near this dangerous cliff can you drive without fear?" he asked.

One said, "A few feet." Another replied, "A few inches." A third man answered, "I should drive as far from it as possible, the place is dangerous and I would avoid it altogether if it were possible."

The third man was engaged because he could be trusted. He was too wise to encounter needless peril.

CHALLENGE

A man endangered his own life to rescue a small boy from drowning.

The boy said, "Thank you, sir, for saving me."

The man replied, "That's all right, son. Just be sure you're worth saving."

A new engineer was being put through the usual routine at the General Electric Company. The same joke had been tried on every embryonic engineer since the electric light was an idea in the brain of Edison. He was assigned the impossible task of frosting electric light bulbs on the inside. Not being aware that it was a joke, he discovered a way not only to frost bulbs on the inside, but also to etch the glass with soft, rounded pits which gave the bulbs added strength. It was indeed fortunate that no "smart alec" had told him that he had been assigned the impossible, because he might otherwise not have accomplished it.

The difference between the pessimist and the optimist can be summarized this way: "The pessimist sees the difficulty in every opportunity; the optimist sees the opportunity in every difficulty."

A traveler in Africa saw one of the large butterflies of the tropics struggling to free itself from the cocoon. He pitied it and, with his knife, cut the cords at which it was straining.

It was released, but all the brilliant coloring was gone! The struggle was necessary to make the color appear.

The beautiful colors of the soul are won in the struggle with, and the victory over, trial and adversity.

CHANGE

When Galileo was summoned before the Inquisition to be tried for the "heresy" of affirming the revolution of the earth, he said to the judges: "I can convince you. Here is my telescope. Look through it and you shall see the moons of Jupiter."

They refused to look. They were convinced that the earth did not revolve around the sun and no evidence could convince them otherwise.

A peasant entered a nearby city for the first time in his life. Everyone stared at him because his garments were so odd and so shabby. Impressed with the clothes he saw others wearing, he went into a store and bought a new suit. When he returned home and put on his new suit, it did not fit. He complained about this to all his friends, until one pointed out, "Of course it does not fit! You put on the new suit right over your old clothes. You have to take off the old before you can put on the new."

George Bernard Shaw once remarked that the only intelligent man he knew was his tailor, who would take a new measure of him every time he ordered a new suit, and would not assume that he always remained the *same* George Bernard Shaw.

CHARACTER

An elderly Quaker woman with a beautiful complexion was asked what kind of cosmetic she used. In reply, she offered this prescription:

"I use for my lips, truth; for my voice, prayer; for my eyes, pity; for my hands, charity; for my figure, uprightness; for my heart, love. This prescription can be filled without expense, and the supply will increase with continued use."

> We are all blind until we see
> That in the human plan
> Nothing is worth the making, if
> It does not make the man.
> Why build these cities glorious
> If man unbuilded goes?
> In vain we build the work, unless
> The builder also grows.
>
> —Edwin Markham

There is a story told of Alexander the Great, the all powerful Greek ruler of the fourth century B.C.E., who was sitting in judgment over one of his subjects. The man had been found guilty and was condemned to death.

"Have you anything to say?" asked the king.

"Yes," replied the criminal.

"Well, what is it?" asked Alexander the Great.

"I want to appeal the verdict," replied the prisoner.

"Appeal! Appeal to whom?" cried Alexander. "I am the judge and I am the king!"

"I want to appeal," answered the subject, "from Alexander the Small to Alexander the Great."

Have you ever noticed how an icicle is formed? If you have, you have noticed how it froze one drop at a time until it was a.

foot or more long. If the water was clear, the icicle remained clear, and sparkled almost as brightly as diamonds in the sun; but if the water was slightly muddy, the icicle looked foul and its beauty was spoiled.

Just so our characters are forming—one little thought at a time, one action at a time.

The passenger trains in Europe are divided into three classes. One can purchase either an expensive first-class ticket and travel in luxury, or a second class ticket and travel in relative comfort, or a third-class ticket and ride with the poor.

There was a poor man who had to travel from Bialystok to Warsaw. He stood at the end of a long line to purchase a third-class ticket. By the time he reached the window, there were no more tickets left for third or second classes. As he had to be in Warsaw the next day on an urgent matter, he bought a ticket for the first.

The splendor of the car and the luxurious dress of the passengers dazzled his eyes. His shabby dress and his empty pockets made him self-conscious and ill-at-ease. Feeling out of place, he fidgeted and trembled in his seat. The conductor, noticing the peculiar behavior of this passenger, eyed him with suspicion. The official thought he had no ticket, so he approached the passenger and demanded, "Let me see your ticket." The frightened man fumbled in his pockets and finally produced it.

The conductor examined it carefully, and finding it in good order, said to him, "Mister, you have a first-class ticket; why don't you act like a first-class passenger?"

A young girl said to her mother, just after a white-haired visitor had left their home, "If I could be such a nice old lady as that—so beautiful and sweet—I wouldn't mind growing old."

The mother replied, "Well, Shayne, if you want to be that kind of old lady, you'd better begin now. She didn't become a lady like that in a hurry."

CHARITY

The speaker had finished making an emotional appeal for funds. He had claimed that by donating to this particular cause, they would obtain seats in heaven. The donations started coming

in. One man gave $10,000, another $7,000, and still another
$5,000. Men were donating by the hundreds and thousands. One
woman, sitting next to her husband, whispered, "Don't give more
than a dollar."

"Listen," he yelled back. "Jack Weber gave $10,000 for his
seat in heaven. Emanuel Farber gave $7,000 for his. Where do
you think I'm gonna sit for a dollar?"

A rich man, who was also a great philanthropist, once discussed his future with his father. "You know, Dad, that I give
a great deal of money to different charities. I would, therefore,
like to be assured of my share in the 'World to Come.'"

His father replied: "Why do you give to charity? Perhaps an
unfortunate poor man comes to you, tells you about his terrible
plight, and pours out his bitter heart. To salve your own conscience, you give him charity. Your giving affords you far greater
pleasure than the poor man can derive from receiving it; and for
having acquired pleasure do you want an eternal reward as well?"

A sainted scholar was aware of the fact that there were wealthy
people who never gave charity but were intent on amassing large
fortunes. "It is a pity," he once remarked, "that the rich are not
aware of the fact that there are no pockets in shrouds."

A scoffer once ridiculed a preacher. "You constantly solicit the
wealthy for help, but they never come to you for knowledge."

"This is a good observation," replied the preacher. "I realize
I need money so I go to those who possess it. However, the rich
don't realize that they need knowledge, so they don't come to me."

"When I look at the congregation," said the preacher, "I ask
myself, 'Where are the poor?'

"But then, when I hear your response, I say to myself, 'Where
are the rich?'"

A striking epitaph was written for Edward Earl of Devonshire
in 1419:

"What we gave, we have; what we spent, we had; what we kept,
we lost."

In the land of Israel there are two seas. One is the sea that has fish in it; and has vegetation surrounding its banks. During the hot summer months it serves as a beach area. The water coming into this sea is the water of the Jordan and flows on southward.

In the second sea of Israel there are no fish, and no vegetation grows on its banks. The water is unfit for human consumption. The river Jordan flows into both seas, yet the first is usable and the second is not. In fact, the second is called "The Dead Sea." What makes them so different?

The difference is not in the source of the waters, but what happens later. The Jordan flows into the first, the Sea of Galilee, and the Sea sends the water onward . . . it receives a drop, and it gives a drop. It is constantly receiving and giving, so it is constantly fresh.

The second sea, however, receives but does not give. All the water it receives it keeps. It releases nothing freely. The water is stagnant and bcause of this no life can be sustained in it. It is truly a "Dead Sea."

In Ireland and Wales there are a great many bee-keepers. Every third year, each owner is required to distribute some of his honey among his neighbors, because his bees have gathered their nectar from the flowers in the neighborhood.

We owe a great deal to our friends and neighbors. They have added materially to our happiness and prosperity. And because of this we are bound, by the law of brotherly-kindness, to distribute among them some of the honey of our own prosperity and comfort.

The wealthiest man in a certain town was an importer of wool. One day, he received word that a large shipment of wool had been lost. He immediately demanded that a list of all the poor people in town be drawn up and that a package of food and money be sent to each.

His wife turned to him and asked, "You have just sustained a heavy loss. Why do you pick this time to be so charitable?"

"I am surprised at you," he answered. "Did you not see how quickly part of my wealth was snatched from me? The loss was not an accident. It was the will of God. Before any more of my wealth is lost, I want to snatch a part of it for myself—to benefit my soul."

A lesson in concern for others was taught by a woman who was the object of much curiosity in her neighborhood because of a most unusual habit. Every time she shopped, ate in a restaurant, or went to see a motion picture, she would take a little book out of her purse and write in it.

"Do you keep a record of all your expenditures?" someone finally asked her.

"Not at all," she replied. "I only keep a list of what I spend for luxuries."

"What for?" asked the bewildered questioner.

"I feel," answered the woman, "that if I am able to enjoy the comforts of life in the midst of so much poverty in the world, I should donate part of what I spend for luxuries to the homeless and the sick."

A wise man had an original plan for alleviating human ills. He explained to his wife: "Some people have so much, that they are unhappy. They eat too much and get sick. They worry about their possessions and cannot sleep. Others have so little, that they are unhappy. They go hungry, their houses are shabby."

"Well, what is your plan?" the wife inquired.

"It is very simple. I have suggested that the rich unload some of their burden on the poor so that both might be happier. All we need is a little cooperation."

"How are you doing?" the wife asked.

"Oh, very well . . . in fact my job is half done. The poor have already promised to accept."

A man had a heart attack, and when he was brought to the doctor, the doctor proceeded to take his blood pressure. The man naively said, "Doctor, it's my heart that hurts, not my hand."

"Ah," cried the doctor, "When I examine your hand, I can tell if everything is right with your heart."

Between the acts at a benefit performance for a local charity, an appeal was made for charitable contributions, but unfortunately the response was poor. The speaker turned to the audience and said, "This appeal is for the benefit of the poor, but they all seem to be present here this evening."

59

There are some who ask why grace is not said over an act of charity, as it is done in the performance of other blessings.

An eminent man, versed in such knowledge, straightened this matter out in the following manner. The performance of every blessing requires certain preparations, such as washing the hands, saying a thanksgiving prayer, etc. Charity, however, is an exception to the rule, for the time spent in preparations may render the recipient of charity past help. The Bible therefore enjoins us: If a poor man knocks at your door, lose no time in saying prayers, but help him promptly.

An indigent scholar once visited a prominent author of many works, one of which was entitled *The Hand of Ephraim*, and asked him for a donation. The author gave him an insignificant pittance and took the opportunity of inquiring whether the poor man liked his books.

The poverty-stricken scholar, not a little annoyed by the small contribution he had received from the wealthy author, replied cryptically: "I like all of your books; but I do not like *The Hand of Ephraim*."

The message struck home immediately, and the author, realizing the slight of his earlier donation, presented the poor scholar with a sizeable sum.

A destitute man once asked a wealthy but very stingy person for a contribution. The rich man refused him and said, "I give to no one, and I shall not make an exception of you. So get out, and don't show your face here again."

"Very well," said the shamed and unhappy pauper, "but after I leave, I will send it to you."

Upon hearing these words, the rich man ran after the poor fellow and asked what it was that he was going to send him.

The poor man replied, "I am going to send you *poverty* to plead for itself."

The rich man became frightened, apologized to the poor man, and gave him a substantial donation.

A very wealthy man was asked for a contribution to a worthy cause. The miserly millionaire tried to get out of giving anything and made all kinds of excuses. His best excuse was that he gave a lot of charity, but that he did so secretly, and nobody knew about it.

"This is really a most peculiar phenomenon," replied the fundraiser. "We are quite well aware of the sins which you commit secretly, despite the fact that you take great care to conceal them; but of your good deeds and secretly-given charity, we have never heard a thing. Really, a most remarkable phenomenon."

There was once a saintly man who lived in dire poverty. All the money he earned, he distributed equally between himself and the poor.

His son, too, found it extremely difficult to make ends meet, for his father gave him just enough to keep body and soul together.

When the father was asked why he paid so very little attention to his son's personal needs while the bulk of his attention went to others, the saint replied, "If I were to meet all my son's requirements, I am afraid he would perhaps forget the necessity of relying upon Providence."

A keen-witted scholar was once asked the following riddle: "It is well known that the *manna* which fell from heaven was received by everyone in accordance with his needs. How then, could anyone at that time fulfill the commandment to be charitable?"

The scholar replied without a moment's hesitation: "It is well known that the *manna* contained all possible flavors. Charity, therefore, consisted in the rich telling the poor what flavor to choose since the poor man had no idea of what a good flavor was like."

A Quaker, once hearing a person tell of how deeply he felt for another who was in distress and in need of assistance, dryly asked: "Friend, has thee felt in thy pocket for him?"

A sinner died and came before the Heavenly Court. The Tribunal was about to condemn him to Hell when his counsel called the attention of the Judges to an unusual act of charity the man had once performed. During the rainy season, a poor peddler had the misfortune of having his horse and wagon bog down in the deep mud. His wares were ruined and the poor fellow was in misery. When this man saw the trouble the peddler was in, he helped him pull the horse and wagon out of the mire and extended him a loan to enable the poor fellow to buy a new stock of wares.

Upon hearing about this incident, the Court ordered that the horse, the wagon, and the wares be put on the scales of justice; but even these did not outweigh the sins of the accused man.

Then the counsel made a final plea, "Since the horse and wagon were entirely covered with mud, let the mud also be placed on the scales."

His request was granted. The mud tipped the scales, and the sinner was saved from Hell by his act of charity.

A famous philanthropist was once asked, "How are you able to give so much, and still have so much?"

It took him only a moment to reply, "As I shovel out, He shovels in; and the Lord has a bigger shovel than I have."

A rich man once bragged to a friend about the thousands of dollars that he contributed for charitable purposes. As was his habit, the rich man prefaced his boasting with: "I don't want to talk about it, but I gave. . . ."

"It certainly should be talked about," the friend interrupted. "Speak as much as your heart desires about your deeds, as long as you continue to give, give, and give even more."

A cartoon appeared in a magazine some time ago. It showed two old women in rags shivering over a meager fire.

One of the women asks, "What are you thinking about?"

The other responds, "About the nice warm clothes the rich ladies will be giving us next summer."

A beggar was standing in the street soliciting alms. A passerby stopped and said to him:

"You ought to be ashamed of yourself! A healthy man like you should not be begging in the street."

Whereupon the beggar shot back:

"Would you want me to become a cripple on account of your contemptible penny?"

A fast-talking businessman was approached by a young woman who was selling tickets for a charity concert. "I regret I will be unable to attend the concert," he said, "but I assure you that I will be there in spirit. After all it is a worthy cause."

"Fine," replied the persistent young woman. "Now where would you like your spirit to sit? The tickets range from $5.50 to $12.00 a pair."

"You'll pull through," said the doctor to his patient, "but you are a very sick man."

The patient was obviously frightened. "Please, doctor," he pleaded, "do everything you can for me. And if I get well, I'll donate $25,000 to the fund for your new hospital."

Several months later the doctor met the patient on the street. "How are you?" he asked.

"Just marvelous, doctor," replied the former patient.

"I have been meaning to speak to you," continued the doctor, "about that money for the new hospital."

"What are you talking about?"

"You said that if you got well," the doctor reminded him, "you would donate $25,000 to the fund for the new hospital."

"If I said that," the former patient exclaimed, "then I really must have been sick."

The young boy was on his way to Sunday school. His mother had given him two dimes: one for ice-cream, and the other for a donation. As he walked along, one dime fell into the sewer. "God," he exclaimed, "there goes your dime!"

CHILDREN

A census-taker rang the bell and was admitted by a woman with several children hanging on to her skirts.

"How many children do you have?" he asked.

She replied, "Let me see now, there is Elsie and Mendy, and Jonathan. . . ."

At this point, the visitor interrupted her, rather irritated. He said, "I am not interested in their names but only in their number."

The woman looked him squarely in the eye and answered with

63

indignation, "Sir, my children have no numbers, they have names!"

—————

A youngster, being scolded for a poor report card, asked: "Dad, what do you think is the trouble with me—heredity or environment?"

—————

In Hollywood, the movie stars and their families live a glamorous life. Some time ago, a well-known star approached his 8-year-old son and said, "I'm sorry, son, but tomorrow morning I have to use the chauffeur and limousine for business."

"But Dad," objected the youngster, "how will I get to school?"

"Go to school like every other kid in America," answered the actor angrily. "Take a cab!"

—————

A bachelor, entering his friend's home and seeing all his children eating their lunch meal, said, "Children make a rich man poor."

Immediately, he received this answer: "No, sir, children make a poor man rich for there is not a person who would part with one of them for all the wealth you could offer."

—————

"I thank God for my sons," said an elderly man. "My first-born is a doctor, the second is a lawyer, the third a chemist, the fourth an artist, and the fifth a writer."

"And what do you do?" he was asked.

"I," said the man, "have a dry goods store, not a big one, but I manage to support them all."

—————

A poor man had five children and his wife presented him with twins.

The priest met him on the street and said, "I see that the Lord has smiled on you again."

"Smiled!" said the poor man. "He laughed right out loud."

—————

A humorist once remarked, "When I was young, my parents told me what to do; now that I am old, my children tell me what to do. I wonder, when will I be able to do what I want to do?"

—————

Years ago, at the White House Conference on Child Health and Protection, the members, coming from every state in the Union, drew up "The Children's Charter." These are some of the highlights that this important document sought as goals:

1. For every child a home, and the love and security that a home provides.
2. For every child a dwelling place, safe, sanitary, and wholesome, with reasonable provision for privacy, freedom from conditions which tend to thwart his development; and a home environment harmonious and enriching.
3. For every child the right to grow up in a family with an adequate standard of living and the security of a stable income as the surest safeguard against social handicaps.
4. For every child understanding and the guarding of his personality as his most precious right.
5. For every child such teaching and training as will prepare him for successful parenthood, homemaking, and the rights of citizenship; and for parents supplementary training to fit them wisely with the problems of parenthood.

It is related that a woman once asked Freud, "How early can I begin the education of my child?"

"When will your child be born?" Freud asked.

"Born?" she exclaimed, "Why, he is already five years old!"

"My goodness, woman," the famous psychoanalyst cried, "don't stand there talking to me—hurry home! You have already wasted the five best years!"

A wise man once observed that a great many children are like wheelbarrows: not good unless pushed. Some are like canoes: they need to be paddled. Some are like kites: if you don't keep a string on them they fly away. A few are like a good watch: open face, pure gold, quietly busy and full of good works.

A family was seated in a restaurant. The waitress took the order of the adults and then turned to their young son.

"What will you have, sonny?" she asked.

"I want a hot dog," the boy began timidly.

Before the waitress could write down the order, the mother interrupted.

"No hot dog," she said. "Give him potatoes, beef, and some carrots."

But the waitress ignored her completely. "Do you want some ketchup or mustard on your hot dog?" she asked of the boy.

"Ketchup," he replied with a happy smile on his face.

"Coming up," the waitress said, starting for the kitchen.

There was stunned silence upon her departure. Finally, the boy turned to his parents. "Know what?" he said, "she thinks I'm real."

———

A father was wearily completing his work at home. His nine-year-old son was eager for companionship and kept annoying his father with questions. Finally, in desperation, the father scattered on the floor the pieces of a jigsaw puzzle of a map of the world. Certain that he had won at least an hour's respite, he advised his son that as soon as the jigsaw was put together, he would spend time with him.

In less than ten minutes, the boy cried happily, "Look, Daddy, it is finished."

The father was amazed when he examined the work. It was put together accurately. "How did you do it so quickly?" he asked.

"It was easy," replied the boy. "On the other side of the map, there was a picture of a child. When I put the child together the world came out all right."

———

The young girl had finished reciting her prayers, yet she kept staring as though she were still deep in prayer. Finally, the mother, thinking that it was just a trick to remain up for a while longer, asked her what she was waiting for. And the answer came quickly: "I am waiting to see if God has anything to say to me!"

———

A little boy was given a globe of the world as a gift. Cherishing the gift he placed it in a secure spot in his room.

One night, his parents found themselves debating a point of geography and needed the globe for reference. The father quietly tiptoed into his child's darkened room to reach out for the globe, when suddenly he heard the child's voice unexpectedly directed to him, "Daddy, what are you doing with my world?"

———

A young boy kept firing questions at his father.

"Why is the grass green?"

"I don't know," was his father's answer.

"What keeps the stars hanging in the skies?"

Again the father responded, "I don't know."

This went on and on and the boy was getting nowhere. He made one last attempt and began to ask a question. In the middle of the sentence he stopped himself and shouted, "Oh, never mind."

At this point the father retorted, "Go ahead, son, ask your question. How else are you going to learn?"

One of the finest sermons ever preached was delivered by a young child who was asked by her teacher to repeat the twenty-third Psalm from memory. She didn't recite the Psalm as most of us know it, but what she said makes sense for our day and age. *"The Lord is my shepherd,"* she began, *"that's all I want."*

There is a story of old Rome which tells of a fashionable lady who, visiting the noble Cornelia, did nothing but boast of her fine robes and jewels. "You must have jewels, too," she remarked; "pray, show me your most precious possessions."

Cornelia rose and went out, returning with her two little sons. Holding each by the hand, she said, "These are my jewels."

Dr. Beecher, years ago, counseled parents about how children should be raised.

"Many children," he said, "grow up like plants under bell-glasses. They are surrounded only by artificial and prepared influences. They are house-bred, room-bred, nurse-bred, mother-bred—everything but self-bred. The object of training is to teach the child to take care of himself, but many parents use their children only as a kind of spool on which to reel off their own experience, and they are bound and corded until they perish by inanity, or break all bonds and cords, and rush to ruin by reaction."

Preacher: "Can you tell me who made you, Joey?"

"Well, sir, God made part of me."

67

"Part of you? What do you mean?"

"I mean He made me little—I *growed* the rest myself."

～

A woman arrived home in the United States after a long stay in Europe. She had with her a young nine month old son. When she came to customs, her heart sank as the official looked at the large pile of baggage.

"What articles of value have you acquired abroad in the last twelve months?" he demanded.

"Well, there's the baby . . ." began the woman.

He looked at the sleeping infant, and then with a wave of his hand said, "Lady, original works of art are exempt from duty."

～

There was an oriental philosopher who once said that parents who are afraid to "put their foot down" usually have children who step on toes.

～

When General Robert E. Lee was once asked for advice as to the method of guiding a child, he answered, "Teach him to deny himself."

～

The difference between theory and practice is well illustrated by the story of a young man who thought that he knew a great deal about child education. As a student of child behavior, he frequently delivered a lecture called the "Ten Commandments for Parents."

He married and became a father. The title of the lecture was altered to "Ten Hints for Parents."

Another child arrived. The lecture became, "Some Suggestions for Parents."

A third child was born. At this point, the lecturer gave up lecturing.

～

"If we paid no more attention to our plants than we have to our children," Luther Burbank said, "we would now be living in a jungle of weeds."

～

Henry Ward Beecher compared the influence on children with the making of good china. He wrote: "Once china or porcelain has been inscribed, and put into a furnace, and baked and glazed, you cannot rub the inscription off. It is too late then. If you want to rub it off, you must do it while the ware is in the 'biscuit.' When children come into our hands they are in the biscuit, and we can inscribe on them what we please."

It is unfortunate that some fathers place the accumulation of wealth before the training of their children.

Socrates once said: "Could I climb to the highest place in Athens, I would lift my voice and proclaim: 'Fellow citizens, why do you turn and scrape every stone to gather wealth, and take so little care of your children to whom one day you must relinquish it all?'"

"My children just don't appreciate anything that is done for them," complained a father.

"Maybe," a friend suggested, "you have tried to give them too much to live with and not enough to live for."

Small boy at piano to his mother: "Gee, Mommy, I wish you hadn't been deprived of so many things as a child."

CHOICE

A young child and his mother entered a candy store. The child wandered from case to case, studying the contents with a very grave expression. His mother, tired of waiting, called to him, "Hurry up son, spend your money. We must be going on."

The boy stopped for a moment, looked at his mother, and replied: "But mama, I've only got one nickel to spend and I've got to spend it wisely."

A man was marooned on an island for years. One day he saw a ship in the distance, to which he signalled. A little boat was sent out to him. As the boat approached the shore of the island, a sailor threw him a pack of newspapers and called out to him,

"Read them! Tomorrow I will return and see if you still want to return to civilization."

A young skeptic, wishing to test the wisdom of a seer, held his closed fist before the venerated man.

"What have I in my hand?" the youth asked.

"A bird," was the answer.

"Is it alive or dead?" queried the youth.

The old man knew that the youth was sporting with him. If he replied dead, the youth would open his hand and let the bird fly away. If he replied alive, the youth would close his fist and crush the bird.

Very wisely the seer said: "As you will it, my son, as you will it."

In *The Merchant of Venice*, Portia's portrait was placed in one of three caskets. The suitor who chose the casket containing the portrait was to win her hand.

Each of the caskets carried a legend, sufficient to guide one to the wisest choice. On the casket of gold was written, "Who chooseth me shall gain what many men desire." On the casket of silver was written, "Who chooseth me shall get as much as he deserves." On the casket of lead, dark and uninviting, were the words, "Who chooseth me must give and hazard all he hath."

Interesting are the words on each: "Who chooseth me shall GAIN," "Who chooseth me shall GET," "Who chooseth me must GIVE."

It was in the casket of lead that Bassanio found his heart's ideal. Shakespeare surely wanted to point out that the best things in life are discovered not by getting, but by giving.

The honeybee makes her honey from exactly the same nectar with which the hermit spider distills one of the deadliest poisons known. The real question is how you treat your opportunities. Do you distill them into success or into failure?

CHURCH

The minister was trying to get the millionaire to attend church services. However, the millionaire was most patronizing. "I never go to church," he said. "Perhaps you have noticed that?"

70

"Yes, I have noticed your absence," said the minister seriously.

"Well, my reason is that I don't want to go to church because there are so many hypocrites there."

"Don't let that keep you away," said the minister, smiling. "There is always room for one more, you know."

One day, the telephone in the office of the Rector of President Roosevelt's Washington church rang, and an eager voice said, "Tell me, do you expect the President to be in church this Sunday?"

"That," explained the Rector, "I cannot promise. But we expect God to be there, and we feel that will be incentive enough for a reasonably large attendance."

A devout member of the congregation never missed a prayer service. Suddenly he stopped coming. The preacher inquired around if the man was ill. No, he was feeling fine. He had just decided he did not need religion or the company of others any longer.

One day the preacher paid him a visit. He found the man sitting in his library near a roaring fire blazing in the fireplace. The preacher sat down next to his parishioner, and without saying a word, picked up the tongs and moved one hot coal a distance away from the others. The fire continued to blaze but the single coal that had been moved aside grew paler and paler, and soon died out. Not a word had passed between the two men. Then the preacher got up to leave.

"Will I see you next week?" asked the preacher as he put on his overcoat.

"I'll be there," replied the parishioner, lamely.

CIVILIZATION

When Albert Schweitzer revisited Europe after his long stay in Africa, one of his admirers asked him, "Well, what do you think of civilization?"

"It's a good idea," replied the famous man. "Somebody ought to start it."

Rev. Peter Marshall was, at one time, chaplain of the U.S. Senate. In one of his prayers, he said: "Give us clear vision, that

71

we may know where to stand and what to stand for—because unless we stand for something, we shall fall for anything."

~~~

COMPARISON

A teacher had assigned some problems to his class. One of the students was having a great deal of trouble answering them. Finally, the teacher, in exasperation, told the student, "You ought to be ashamed of yourself. At your age George Washington was a surveyor!"

The boy looked straight into the eyes of the teacher and replied, "Yes, and at your age he was already President of the United States."

~~~

COMPASSION

E. V. Lucus tells of a school in England where compassion is taught. In the course of the term every child has one blind day, one lame day, one deaf day, one day when he cannot speak. The night before the blind day, his eyes are bandaged. He awakens, blind, and needs help and other children lead him about.

Through this method he gets a grasp of what it is really like to be blind. And those who help, having been "blind" themselves, are able to guide and direct the blind with understanding. This method accomplishes what all of us need—daily training in how we can establish a sense of real fellowship with others.

~~~

After the tragic sinking of the *Titanic,* an American newspaper carried two pictures. One showed the ship's side torn open and about to sink—and underneath the picture were these words: "The weakness of man; the supremacy of nature."

The other illustration showed the passengers stepping back to give the last place in the lifeboat to a woman with her baby in her arms. Under this picture were the words: "The weakness of nature; the supremacy of man."

~~~

Moses was tested by God through sheep. The Midrash tells us that while Moses was attending Jethro's flock in the wilderness, a lamb strayed from the herd. Moses endeavored to overtake it, but it ran much faster than he could run. Then the lamb came upon a spring, and suddenly it stopped and took a drink of water.

"You dear little innocent creature," said Moses, "I see now why you ran away. Had I known your need, on my shoulders would I have carried you to the spring to quench your thirst. But come little innocent one, I will make up for my ignorance. You are no doubt fatigued after so long a journey; you shall walk no further." He immediately took the little creature into his arms, and carried it back to the flock.

God approved of the deed, and a heavenly voice was heard to exclaim: "Moses, benevolent Moses! If a dumb animal thus excited your compassion, how much more will the children of men! What will you not do for your own brethren? Come, from now on you shall be the shepherd of my chosen flock, and you will teach them by your example that the Lord is good to all, and that His mercies are over all His works."

***

A resident was making an impassioned plea to a politician, seeking aid for a friend who badly needed assistance. The politician replied, "I've become so busy I can no longer concern myself with individual cases."

"Fortunately," replied the resident, "God hasn't reached that stage yet."

***

COMPETITION

A pile of books on a book shelf were arguing, each claiming to be the most important to man.

The History Book claimed: "I am the most useful book in the world. Who could give a knowledge of the past were it not for me? What else contains a detailed account of the great deeds, discoveries and inventions that have transpired over the ages?"

"Stop boasting," exclaimed the Geography Text. "I am greater than you! Who would know even that there was a world were it not for MY pages? I describe countries, tell what peoples inhabit them. Were it not for me, would it even be known that the earth is round?"

"Enough, enough!" exclaimed the Philosophy Text. "You are important but were it not for me, who would understand why the apple falls to the ground instead of rising to the sky? Who could comprehend gravitation or the other laws which govern the earth?

Who could tell how steam was made man's servant, or how news can be flashed around the world on telegraph wires?"

Up jumped the under-sized Spelling Book. "Stop all this squabbling!" it exclaimed. "I am the greatest among you! Were it not for these twenty-six letters, not one of you would ever have had an existence. To me you owe all your greatness; without me, you are nothing."

———

Benjamin Franklin had tenacity of purpose to a wonderful degree. When he started in the printing business in Philadelphia, he carried his materials through the streets on a wheelbarrow. He hired one room for his office, workroom, and sleeping room. He found a formidable rival in the city and invited him to his room. Pointing to a piece of bread from which he had just eaten his dinner, he said: "Unless you can live cheaper than I can, you cannot starve me out."

———

COMPLACENCY

A well known columnist refused to attend a reunion of his college class. "I refuse to eat with dead men," he explained. "When they were young students, each a bundle of potentialities, they were strong in their will to strive, to seek, to find, and not to yield to the thinking of the organization man. They were full of life . . . yet they died quietly. And in their place has come earthbound complacency."

———

COMPLAINT

A preacher once had a dream. In it he heard a proclamation that every mortal should bring his griefs and calamities and throw them together in a heap. The whole army of mankind, coming from every part of the globe, marched, led by a somewhat nebulous figure called *"Imagination."*

What a procession it was! The long never-ending parade of those who bear burdens stretched far into the distance where sky and earth met. There were people with visible physical burdens —the burden of failing strength, or chronic illness, or other "thorns in the flesh." There were burdens of lost happiness, of lost ambition, of disappointment; burdens of anxiety and care; burdens of temptation, and even burdens of guilt. Each person laid down his burden of real and imagined woe. Slowly, the heap of discarded burdens grew until it reached the heavens.

Then, a second proclamation was issued: each person was now at liberty to exchange his affliction and return to his home with any other burden he might select. *"Imagination"* now took the lead. As each person stood at the heap, unable to decide which package to pick, *"Imagination"* made a recommendation.

The deluded mortals eagerly selected their new burdens. But, instead of joy, the whole plain was filled with lamentation and murmuring, for the people discovered very quickly that their new condition was much worse than their former state.

Taking pity on them, an angel ordered them to lay down their burdens a second time so that each might resume his own. With that, the phantom *"Imagination"* was ordered to disappear, and a new figure, called *"Patience,"* stationed itself near the mountain of misery. Very soon, the mountain shrank in size as each man took back his original burden.

When the preacher awoke, he knew the lesson he was to preach: "Men have their own burdens, and their own burdens are the ones best suited to them."

Levy met Lapidus and complained, "Lapidus, I know you for many years and I always remember to inquire about your family. In all this time you never once asked me how things were with me?"

"Perhaps you are right," replied Lapidus, "how are things with you?"

"Don't ask!" was the immediate answer.

COMPROMISE

The strangeness of a man's way with a maid has been attested to, but the way of a maid being courted has always been a mystery to the male.

A girl dismissed her sweetheart with the statement that she could not think of marrying him until he saved a few thousand dollars.

Several months later she met him on the street and asked him how much he had saved.

"Thirty-five dollars," he said.

"Well," she remarked, blushing, "I guess that is near enough."

CONCEIT

The servant of a great scholar was very conceited. He was proud because he was privileged to serve the great and renowned scholar, and also because he was the nephew of the richest man in town.

When the servant's arrogant behavior was brought to the attention of his employer, the learned man said to him, "Now do me a favor and listen to reason. If you had as much knowledge as I have, and as much money as your uncle has, there would be some semblance of an excuse for your conceit. But since you possess as little money as I do, and as little learning as your uncle, what reason have you to be conceited?"

The Talmud tells us that Rabbi Yanai was once walking along feeling very pleased with himself when he met a man and stopped to exchange a few words with him. The person happened to be very ugly, and Rabbi Yanai forgot himself and said: "Oh, how ugly you are."

The man was, of course, very hurt. "You are right," he replied. "I am ugly. Why don't you go to my Maker and tell Him what an ugly person He has created?"

The Bible warns humanity to beware of that terrible characteristic—CONCEIT. It is difficult to conceive that such a trait exists among mankind whose life is a continuous chain of mishap, caprice, and suffering, interspersed with a bit of happiness here and there to weld the chain together.

Man is not master of his own life even for a moment. The only certainty in the life of a mortal being is his mortality. Being faced with the threat of death at every moment, how dare he be conceited?

A young woodpecker, who felt exceedingly vigorous one morning, looked around the forest and decided to start the day by pecking at a huge oak. He had just gotten off to a good start when a bolt of lightning split the tree from top to bottom. The bird hustled out from under the debris, looked up at what was left of the tree, and murmured with a shudder, "My! I did not even know my own strength."

A Congressman once said to Horace Greeley: "I am a self-made man."

"That, sir," said Greeley, "relieves the Almighty of a great responsibility."

A novelist suddenly became famous. One of his books had been purchased for the movies and television, and he was much sought after as a lecturer.

One evening he came home and found his wife weeping bitterly. "The eternal triangle is wrecking our marriage," she said.

"Nonsense, my dear!" exclaimed the novelist. "I'm world famous, but I have never as much as glanced at another woman. How can you say there is a triangle?"

"But there is a triangle," sobbed the wife. "And a vicious triangle too. Both you and I are in love with you."

There is a story of the mighty Roman general, Titus, who conquered Palestine after waging a long and fierce campaign against the Jewish people. The Jews displayed tremendous courage, and sacrificed greatly in their defense of their homeland. Titus boasted that he was stronger than the God of Israel.

"If it were otherwise," said he, "I would never have been victorious over the people of Israel."

Then a voice was heard to say: "Titus, you fool! You are a slave to vanity! Do you really believe that you are mightier than God? Why, you will be destroyed by the smallest creature created by God."

Soon afterwards, an insect of microscopic size entered his nostril. It could not be removed. Infection followed simple irritation, and eventually it destroyed him.

CONCERN

A poet was sitting in his study complaining bitterly, "The world is selfish. . . . Every man thinks only of himself. . . . No one is concerned with the next person."

He kept on writing when suddenly his peace was shattered by the sound of a child crying. Pen in hand, he rushed out of his room to the street. Then a feeling of relief came over him. He realized that it was only a strange child crying—not his child, only a strange child.

CONCLUSIONS

Jumping at conclusions can be fatal, as was illustrated by the story of a motorcycle driver who, on a wintry night, reversed his jacket so that the bitter winds would not come through the openings between the buttons. The jacket was somewhat uncomfortable back-to-front, but it served the purpose. As he sped along the road, the motorcycle skidded on an icy spot and crashed into a tree. When the ambulance arrived, the first-aid men pushed through the crowd and asked a man who was standing over the victim what happened. He replied that the driver had seemed to be in pretty good shape after the crash, but by the time they got his head straightened out he was dead.

CONDUCT

A nobleman once tendered an official banquet for some of his friends. While the guests were at the table, two masked individuals, no larger than children, entered the hall. One seemed to be impersonating a lord, the other a lady. They were both dressed in splendor and danced beautifully. Everybody admired the skill of the two polite children.

Suddenly, one of the guests tossed an apple between the two. The lord and lady rushed after the apple as though frantic. In the struggle, they tore off each other's mask, and, behold, they were not children but a couple of monkeys.

The guests laughed at the joke played on them, but someone made this wise remark: "Fools and monkeys may dress themselves in fashion, but the day soon comes when they reveal their true identity."

CONFESSION

A sinner once came to a minister to beg repentance. Since the man was ashamed to admit that he was the sinner, he told the minister that a friend of his committed the sins but was too embarrassed to appear personally, and so had asked him to go. He then gave the minister a list of sins his friend had supposedly committed.

"What a fool the other man is," the minister knowingly smiled. "He could have come himself and said that his friend sent him."

CONFIDENCE

Cardinal Manning, the English churchman, authored a book called, *Confidence in God!* One day, wanting a copy of the book for his own use, he called the local book shop for it.

The clerk called downstairs to the keeper of the storeroom. "One copy of Manning's *Confidence in God!*" In a few moments, the answer came up the stairs: "Manning's *Confidence in God!* all gone."

John Singer Sargent, the famous American painter, once painted a still-life consisting of a panel of roses. The painting won great praise and admiration. Sargent refused to sell the picture, though he was offered a high price for it. Whenever he was discouraged, Sargent would take a look at the panel of roses and recall, "I painted this picture." Somehow, confidence and skill would return to him.

When Rear Admiral DuPont explained to his superior officer, Farragut, the reason why he had failed to take his ships into Charleston Harbor, Farragut heard him through to the end and then said, "Admiral, there is one explanation which you have not given."

"What is that?" asked DuPont.

"It's this: You did not believe that you could do it."

Two boys were conversing about Elijah's ascent to heaven in the chariot of fire.

Said one: "Wouldn't you be afraid to ride in such a chariot?"

"No," was the immediate reply, "not if God drove."

CONGREGATION

The late Woodrow Wilson was the son of a minister. His father, who was tall and very thin, would often take young Woodrow with him on his parish calls, which he made with a horse and buggy.

One day, on one of these calls, a parishioner asked: "Reverend, how is it that you're so thin and gaunt, while your horse is so fat and sleek?"

Before the father could reply, young Woodrow said, "Probably because my father feeds the horse and the congregation feeds my father."

CONGRESS

A man planning to make a business trip to Washington decided to further his young son's education by taking him along. After the father's business was concluded, he took his son to visit the Corcoran Art Gallery, the Congressional Library, the National Museum, and ended up in the gallery of the Senate. Nothing escaped the keen observation of the wide-eyed boy.

In the Senate, a man, dressed in black, walked to the podium and began to speak.

"Who is that man, Daddy?" asked the boy.

The father whispered: "That man is the chaplain of the Senate."

"Does he pray for the Senate?" persisted the boy.

"No," replied the father with evident feeling, "he comes in, looks at the senators, and then prays for the country."

CONSCIENCE

When Samuel Johnson was a boy, his father sold books at a stall on market days in various towns. One day he was taken ill and wanted young Samuel to take his place in the market at Uttoxeter, but the boy was proud and refused to go. His poor father, ill as he was, had to go himself. That night his father returned very tired and worn out but never uttered a word of reproach to his son.

Fifty years later, when Samuel Johnson had become famous throughout England, he traveled to Uttoxeter one market day, and stood there for hours, bareheaded, close by the spot where his father's bookstall had been. People stared at the big burly man standing there without his hat in the wind and in the rain, and some of them wondered if he had not gone mad. But Johnson was remembering his old unkindness to his father, and by that strange act was trying to do penance, hoping to win forgiveness.

There was a king who owned a magic ring. On his finger, it looked like any other ring, yet it had mystic qualities. Whenever an evil thought entered his mind, or when he was tempted to do something evil, or actually perpetrated a wrong, the ring would press painfully upon his finger. The name of his ring was conscience.

⬿

A dying man once confided to a friend that he was bothered by an incident that had occurred during his childhood. "When I was a boy," he said, "I once twisted a sign post so that it pointed the wrong way. Just now, for some reason, I've been worried about the number of travelers I've sent along the wrong road."

⬿

An anonymous New York taxpayer sent a letter to the State Income Tax Department in Albany, saying that he had cheated on his income tax return ten years ago, and had not been able to get a good night's sleep since.

He enclosed $25, and added, "If I still can't sleep, I'll send the balance."

⬿

A poor and sick man once approached a wealthy man for money to purchase a chicken from which he could make some broth, which had been prescribed by the doctor for his ailment. The rich man, however, gave him only enough money with which to purchase a piece of beef.

Shortly, thereafter, the poor man died, and when he heard the news the wealthy man said: "Weep for me, for I have killed him!"

⬿

Abraham Lincoln addressed these words to a committee from Missouri:

> I desire so to conduct the affairs of this administration that if at the end, when I have come to lay down the reins of power, I have lost every other friend on earth, I shall at least have one friend left, and that friend shall be down inside me.

⬿

A man decided to steal corn from his neighbor's field. He took his young son along with him to be the look-out, to give warning in case anyone should come along. Before the father commenced, he looked all around, first one way and then the other. Not seeing any person around, he was just about to fill his bag, when his son cried out, "Father, there is one way you haven't looked yet!" The father, alarmed that someone was coming, asked his son which way he meant. Then the son answered, "Father, you forgot to look up!" The father, conscience-stricken, took his boy by the hand and hurried home without the stolen corn.

There was a prophet who appeared in the square of a city every day, preaching love and brotherhood. His words fell on deaf ears. In fact he was jeered and ridiculed, but, undaunted, he continued to plead for peace.

His friends tried to dissuade him, saying, "There's no use preaching to them when they won't even listen to you."

The prophet replied, "Even if I can't save the world, at least I can save my own soul."

CONSIDERATION

Abraham Lincoln once received a letter requesting a "sentiment" and his autograph. Lincoln replied:

Dear Madam:

When you ask from a stranger that which is of interest only to yourself, always enclose a stamp. There's your sentiment, and here's my autograph.

A. Lincoln

A man placing a bouquet of flowers on a grave noticed an old Chinese gentleman placing a bowl of rice on a nearby grave, and asked: "What time do you expect your friend to come up and eat the rice?"

The old Chinese gentleman replied with a smile: "At about the same time your friend comes up to smell the flowers."

CONTENTMENT

A man decided to sell his home and consulted a real estate broker. After visiting the house, the agent wrote an elaborate description of it and gave it to his client for approval. "Is that my house?" asked the seller. "If it is, I've changed my mind about

82

selling. It's just the house I've always wanted, and I never realized that I had it all the time."

<hr>

A young farmer once came to his minister and complained about his poor financial situation. Weeping bitterly, he said: "We are twelve members in our family and barely have place to move around. We are so overcrowded that it makes life unbearable. Please help me."

"Have you a goat?" asked the minister.

"Yes," was the immediate reply.

"Good," said the minister. "Take the goat into your house."

The ignorant farmer was a bit astonished by this advice, but did as he was told. In a few days, he returned, saying: "Reverend, things are even worse than before. I don't have a place to rest my weary bones."

"Have you any chickens?" again queried the minister.

"Yes, we have chickens," said the farmer.

"I want you to take all your chickens into the house," was the advice this time.

Once again the farmer did as he was told. He would not dare disobey his minister whom he respected greatly. But in a day or so he was back again bemoaning his fate.

"Reverend," he said, "I can't stand it another day. You must help me get some room in my house."

"Are the chickens and the goat still in your home?" asked the minister.

"Yes, sir, they are still there as you ordered."

The minister thought for a moment and then said: "Drive them all out of your home!"

Some days later, the farmer again returned to the minister. "You have helped me far more than I can say. You have saved my family. I drove out the chickens and the goat and now we have plenty of room."

<hr>

He was 70 years of age and complained a great deal. Nothing could ever please him. Suddenly, he changed. He was gentle and a glint of optimism was always in his eyes. "What caused you to change so suddenly?" he was asked.

"Well," he replied, "I've been striving all my life for a contented mind. It's done no good, so I've decided to be contented without it."

<hr>

A king said to a sage, "Make thou such a request of me, that thou wouldst have sufficient for thy needs throughout thy life."

The sage replied, "Why should I make such a request of thee, seeing that I am richer than thou art?"

The sage answered, "Because I am more content with the little I possess than thou art with thy great wealth."

A poor widow, not having sufficient blankets to shelter her young son from the snow which used to blow in through the cracks of her hut, would cover him with boards. One night the boy asked: "Ma, what do poor folks do on such cold nights, who have no boards to put on their children?"

A philosopher, who was passing through a market place filled with articles of luxury, made himself feel much better with this simple yet sage reflection, "How many things there are here that I do not want."

A traveler, on a rather wet morning, asked a shepherd what weather it would be. "It will be," replied the shepherd, "what weather pleases me."

"What do you mean by your statement?" asked the traveler.

"Sir, it shall be what weather pleases God," he answered, "and what weather pleases God pleases me."

Two ears to hear all I should know.
Oh, God, forgive me when I whine:
I'm blessed indeed, the world is mine.

If we could see our own blessings and privileges as others see them, would it not add to our contentment with our lot?

At a particularly dull academic meeting a fellow guest remarked sympathetically to Albert Einstein, "I am afraid you are terribly bored, Professor Einstein."

"Oh, no," replied Einstein, pleasantly. "On occasions like this I retire to the back of my mind, and there I am happy."

Somewhere this fable is told: The dove complained to its Maker that it had not been dealt with fairly. "Why do I not have plumage as gorgeous as that of the peacock?"

God replied: "I will grant your desire on one condition."

"Name your proposition," said the dove eagerly.

"You must part with your gentleness and your lovable qualities which for so long have been the admiration of the world."

The dove debated the matter, then declined.

"No," he said, "I would not part with my gentle graces for all the colorful plumage of the peacock."

~~~~~

A hard-working mailman once met a millionaire who was working continuously, and becoming wealthier every year. The civil service employee made just enough to support his family, and take them on a short vacation once a year.

One day, delivering mail to the millionaire, he remarked, "I am richer than you are."

The rich man looked puzzled. "How can that be?" he asked.

The mailman smiled. "Why," he said, "I have as much money as I want and you haven't."

~~~~~

If I had been made a firefly, it would not become me to say, "If God had only made me a star, to shine always, then I would shine." It is my duty, if I am a firefly, to fly and sparkle, and fly and sparkle; not to shut my wings down over my phosphorescent self because God did not make me a sun or a star.

~~~~~

A king went into his garden and found wilted and dying trees, shrubs, and flowers. The oak said it was dying because it could not be tall like the pine. Turning to the pine, he found it drooping because it was unable to bear grapes like the vine. And the vine was dying because it could not blossom like the rose. He found heartsease blooming and as fresh as ever. Upon inquiry, he received this reply:

"I took it for granted that when you planted me you wanted heartsease. If you had desired an oak, a vine or a rose, you would have planted them. So I thought, since you had put me here, I should do the best I can to be what you want. I can be nothing but what I am, and I am trying to be that to the best of my ability."

~~~~~

There was once a young stonecutter who was very happy and contented with the work he was doing. Once he delivered a piece of stone to a merchant. There he saw a beautiful bed and he wished aloud, "Oh, I wish I were a merchant and had such a bed."

In the twinkling of an eye, his wish was granted. And he was happy . . . until one day he saw a parade passing him by. Slaves were carrying a prince. "I wish I were a prince," he said. Immediately he became a prince. However, while being carried about by the slaves of his household, he felt extremely hot because of the bright sun.

To be a prince is nothing," he said. "I wish I were the sun, for it is greater than any man." He became the sun and now he was happy. Happy, that is, until a cloud came between him and the earth and cut his rays so that he couldn't reach the earth. His heart became heavy. "I wish I were the cloud!" he exclaimed. Again his wish was granted.

So he rained down on the earth to his heart's content, until there were floods everywhere. He came to the mountain and poured rain on it, but it made no difference. The mountain stood firm.

Now the cloud was unhappy. "That mountain is greater than I; I wish I were the mountain!" Instantly, he became the mountain. And he thought, "Now indeed I am the greatest of all."

But on the following day a little man climbed up the mountain and with a hammer and chisel started tapping at the slab in his side. The mountain could not stop him. "Why, that little man is greater than I," said the mountain. "I wish I were a man!"

And so once again his wish was granted and he became a stone-cutter. He lived a long useful life and everyone marveled at how happy he was.

~~~~~

One of the world's wealthiest men was once interviewed on television.

He was asked, "How much money does a man need to be satisfied?"

The wealthy man was also wise. He thought for a moment before he replied, "A man always needs just a little more."

~~~~~

CONTRADICTIONS

William Saroyan, in a moment of self-examination and introspection, put it this way when he wrote of himself in his autobiography, *Here Comes, There Goes, You Know Who*: "I am enormously wise and abysmally ignorant. I am also downright stupid."

An Irishman visiting America remarked about the strange American customs. "You take a glass of ginger-ale," he said, "and add whiskey to make it strong and then water to make it weak; lemon to make it sour and sugar to make it sweet. You raise the glass and say, 'here's to you,' and then you drink it down yourself."

CONTRAST

When Lincoln Steffens was a boy, he observed an artist at work painting an oil of a muddy river. Steffens looked at the finished product and then criticized the picture because there was so much "mud" in the picture.

The artist, also looking at the finished product, replied: "You see the mud in the picture young fellow. No doubt, there is mud and lots of it. But I see the beautiful colors and contrasts, the beautiful harmonies of light and dark, of water and mud."

CONTRIBUTION

There was once a village that wanted to have a great celebration. So it was decided that each household would contribute a pitcher of wine which would be placed in a great barrel and then, at the feast, each could come and draw wine for the celebration. But each thought: what will my little pitcher mean in that enormous barrel? So, instead of wine, each brought a pitcher of water. On the day of the feast the barrel was tapped and only water came out. . . . There was no celebration.

A little fellow was sitting in the bus when an enormously fat woman entered. She stood for a minute glaring at the seated passengers and then demanded, "Isn't some gentleman going to offer me a seat?"

The tiny fellow got up and said timidly, "Well, I'll make a small contribution."

CONVERSATION

The best recipe for the art of conversation comes from the Arabic. The pupil asked the sage how he could be a good conversationalist.

"Listen, my son," replied the sage, holding up an admonishing finger.

"I am listening, father," said the pupil after a silence. "Continue your instruction."

"There is no more to tell," replied the sage.

A tourist, who was spending the night in a small town in Vermont, decided to join a group of men sitting on the porch of the general store. They were a quiet lot. After several attempts to start a conversation, he became annoyed and finally asked, "Is there a law against talking in this town?"

One of the natives spoke up, "There is no law against talking, but we have an understanding that no one is to speak unless he is sure he can improve on the silence."

COOPERATION

During the night a house caught fire. The fire spread rapidly to other houses. Each family ran frantically about, attempting to save its individual possessions. A wise bystander, noticing this, remarked: "You are silly selfish people. Instead of each one trying to save his own possessions, why don't you all get together and put out the fire, so that it will not spread any further."

A great king made a feast and sent messengers to all the cities and towns of his kingdom, asking the people to come, and promising not only food but wealth.

In one town there was a strong, robust man, who, unfortunately, was blind; and he loudly bemoaned the fact that his affliction would prevent him from accepting the king's invitation. But then he heard that in the same town there was a lame man who was also disturbed because he too would be unable to attend the feast.

The blind man and the lame man thereupon made an agreement: the blind man would carry the lame man on his shoulders.

So it happened that the man who had sight, but could not walk, guided the man who could walk, but could not see; and the two went together to the king's feast.

~

All the fruits had gathered to determine why no other fruit but the grape contained the juice from which the finest wines are made.

"Her drink is famous throughout the world. Why is she more worthy than we, to be blessed with this gift of God?"

A cluster of grapes hanging within earshot decided to answer. "All of you grow individually," she said, "but we grapes grow together in bunches and are faithful to each other. For that reason our substance is tasty and fragrant."

~

A certain gentleman was being taken on a tour of the other world. On reaching the nether regions, he was greatly surprised to find the people all seated at a banquet table laden with appetizing food. On the wall was a sign listing the one law of the place, which was strictly enforced. Everyone must use the knives, spoons, and forks provided by the management. But the utensils had such long handles that no one could get a morsel of food near his mouth. They were all starving to death! And that was Hell!

In the heavenly city, where the man visited next, he also found the people seated at banquet tables laden with the same delicious food and holding the same long-handled forks. But they were having a delightful time, for each person was feeding his neighbor across the table. This was Heaven!

~

The great industrialist, Charles Schwab, was noted especially for inspiring an amazing degree of cooperation from people who worked for him, as well as from those with whom he had business dealings. When he was asked what he considered the prime ingredient in his character that had helped make him such a towering success, he answered, "I consider my ability to arouse enthusiasm among people the greatest asset I possess."

~

A blind woman stood on a busy corner in New York waiting for someone to help her across the intersection. A man stepped up and asked: "May I go across with you?"

"I'd be very happy if you would," she replied.

When safely across the street, the man thanked her and said, "You know, when someone has been blind as many years as I have it's a mighty big favor to have someone help him across the street."

It has been said that the gates of heaven are too narrow for one man to walk through alone. Two men walking side by side, one of whom has helped the other, will find it easy to enter. And when ten men come, men who have served one another in love, they find the gate wide and welcome.

A young child went off to play in a nearby field. A short time later, his mother discovered his absence and began to search for him with little success. She called her husband to help, but neither could find the boy. The neighbors were soon called in to help. No luck!

Men and women from nearby towns went looking in the field, but they, too, had no success. Finally, one suggested: "Everybody's going off in all directions. Let's join hands, make one huge circle, spread out, and then close in. We can't miss finding him that way!"

Asked to give an example of true cooperation, the speaker thought for a minute, and then said, "When you see a Methodist bishop umpiring a Sunday baseball game between the Knights of Columbus and the Ku Klux Klan for the benefit of Jewish charities, that would be true cooperation."

COSMETICS

A certain perfume manufacturer ran out of superlatives to describe the perfection of his product. He hit upon a statement that described, in a novel and compelling way, the last word that could be said concerning it: "As we couldn't improve our product, we improved the box."

90

COURAGE

A medical student who was seriously crippled was obliged to walk with crutches. Of course, his walk was hesitating and painfully slow. Though he suffered greatly, he was friendly, optimistic, intelligent, and quite cheerful.

During his years at medical school, he won many scholastic honors. During all this time his friends, out of consideration and respect, refrained from questioning him as to the cause of his deformity. They did not want to bring up a subject that might be painful to him. But one day a close friend of his asked the fateful question.

"Infantile paralysis," was the quick matter-of-fact answer.

"Then tell me," said the admiring friend, "with such a misfortune, how can you face the world so confidently and without bitterness?"

A warm smile appeared on the young man's face as he replied, "You see, the paralysis never touched my heart."

Charles Steinmetz, who rose to be one of the world's most outstanding men in the field of electrical research and engineering, was born with a spinal weakness that had plagued his father and grandfather before him. He knew that his deformed body could never be strengthened. Yet, this poor, crippled boy, who arrived in New York in 1889 from Europe, lived to fashion a distinguished career for himself because he had the will to do it.

As the ship began to sink in mid-ocean at the height of the storm, the captain called together the dismayed crew and said to them: "You have been a most faithful and courageous crew. Our ship is now sinking, but I don't want you to be disheartened. I have measured the depths of the sea and discovered that even after the ship will have sunk its flag will continue to flutter above the raging waters."

In the Louvre, there is a beautiful painting of Goethe's Faust. It depicts Mephistopheles and Faust, with a chessboard between them on the table. Mephistopheles points with a leer; and Faust sits there dejected. Mephistopheles says, "Checkmate."

One day, a great chess player looked and admired the painting. Suddenly he lunged forward and exclaimed, "Satan, one minute! Faust has one more move!"

In facing a crisis, we too should keep on saying to ourselves "I HAVE ONE MORE MOVE."

Back in 1812, when three-year-old Louis Braille was boring holes into a heavy piece of leather, an accident caused his blindness. Seventeen years lated, the totally blind youth invented the Braille system, a system now used all over the world, and which has brought incalculable blessing to thousands of blind persons. Not only did the invention bring "sight" to young Braille, but his tragedy served as a means of helping many generations of sightless people to lead a fairly normal life.

"Can you fight?" Dr. Charles W. Eliot, president of Harvard University, once asked a young professor who had come to him with a disconcerting problem.

"Why, yes," the man replied. "That is, I think I can."

"Can you fight when you are in the minority?"

"I have done so occasionally."

"Can you fight when everybody is against you, when not one person is ready to lend you support?"

"I am ready to try it if necessary."

"Then you need have no fear. But if you have convictions, it will sometimes be necessary to do no less."

Robert Louis Stevenson wrote a friend in 1893 that he hadn't had one day of good health in fourteen years. "I have wakened sick and gone to bed weary, and yet I have done my work unflinchingly. I have written my books in bed and out of bed, written them when my head swam for weakness. I have now done this for so long that it seems to me I have won my wager. . . .

"But the battle still goes on—ill or well is a trifle so long as it goes."

In 1966, a story was run by the Associated Press which concerned itself with pretty Roberta Scott, a youthful, talented water-skier and artist who, in 1961, was runner-up for the Miss Oklahoma beauty-queen title, and three years later had to have a leg amputated as a result of cancer. For years, she continued being a water-skier and artist. Then she began to help elementary school students who were slow or retarded.

She said, "I'd rather lose my leg than my life. I get too much enjoyment out of life to sit and gripe about it."

Her philosophy is centered around six magic words: "I'm so glad to be alive."

Greatness is a measure of one's ability to rise above defeat. Glance at the handicaps of others and take courage. Beethoven was deaf; Homer was blind; Milton was deaf; Rembrandt, troubled; Alexander Pope, a hunchback; Edgar Allen Poe, a psychoneurotic; Charles Darwin, an invalid; Julius Caesar, an epileptic; Franklin D. Roosevelt, a polio victim—just a few of the great who made it despite serious handicaps.

Reinhold Niebuhr, the famous theologian, wrote the following little prayer in 1934:

Oh God, give us—
Serenity to accept what cannot be changed
Courage to change what should be changed
And the wisdom to distinguish the one from the other.

A writer once catalogued Abraham Lincoln's adverses, and they were many. He ran for the Legislature in Illinois and was badly swamped. He engaged in business, failed, and spent 17 years of his life paying off the debts of a worthless partner. He fell in love with a beautiful lady to whom he became engaged, but she later died. He married a woman who was a burden to him. Upon entering politics again, he was badly defeated in a Congressional race. He failed to get an appointment to the U.S. Land Office. He failed dismally in his bid for the U.S. Senate. In 1856, he became a candidate for the vice-presidency and was defeated. In 1858, he was defeated again by Douglas.

COURTESY

It has been estimated that the people of the United States pay $10,000,000 a year in telegraph tolls to add just one word to their messages. The word is "please." The price seems high, but when you consider that the returns from an investment in courtesy are respect, friendship, and good will in business, you see that it is money well spent.

A consultant was once called upon to help rescue a failing business. After making a survey he recommended: "I suggest you start advertising, and use three media: radio, direct mail, and courtesy. The first two will cost money. The third is free, but it's the most important one of all."

Nicholas I of Russia had asked Liszt, the great pianist, to play at court. Right in the middle of the opening number the great musician looked at the Czar and saw him talking to an aide. He continued playing, but was very much irritated. As the Czar continued, Liszt finally stopped playing. The Czar sent a messenger to ask why he was not playing and Liszt said, "When the Czar speaks, everyone should be silent." Thereafter there was no interruption during the concert.

Recently, a young girl walked boldly up to a concert pianist as he was leaving the concert hall where he had given a brilliant performance and had received a standing ovation.

"May I have your autograph?" she asked somewhat timidly.

"No, dear," he answered rather curtly, "my hands are extremely tired from playing."

"And my hands are tired too," she beamed, "they're tired from applauding."

She got his autograph with a smile.

COURTSHIP

They met on the street. He was married, the other was a good-looking bachelor. Said the married man: "How in the world have you managed to remain single so long?"

Replied the bachelor: "It's not difficult. Every time I watch television and see the commercials, I learn that women are anemic, have stringy hair, large pores, rough hands, underarm odor, and are overweight."

The marriage broker had brought him an ugly girl, but wealthy. The boy's father was urging the match because he felt that he could improve his financial lot. "But father," protested the son, "she's so ugly she'll make me miserable if I marry her."

"Use your head," replied the broker. "I admit, she's ugly. So what? All day long you will be at your office and will not look at her. At night you will be eating supper and you won't look at her. Later you will be watching television and you won't look at her. When you go to bed at night, you won't look at her. When you are asleep you won't look at her. Finally, in your leisure time —will you want to look at her? No! So, I ask you—what's all the excitement about? When will you look at her?"

A matchmaker was asked by a young artist to find him a suitable mate.

"I know just the girl for a creative man like you!" cried the marriage broker.

The next day the matchmaker brought the girl to the artist's house. The young man was shocked with her appearance and at the first opportunity he drew the broker aside.

"What kind of a monster do you call that?" he hissed. "One eye slanted up, the other down; the left ear way up here, the right ear way down there; the forehead sloped back like a. . . ."

"Look, you're an artist," interrupted the matchmaker. "You should know better than anyone else—you either like Picasso or you don't!"

CREATION

Kirschner, the famous astronomer, had a scientist friend visiting him. The friend professed disbelief in God. One day, this friend was admiring a working model of the solar system that stood upon a table. By turning a handle, the planets could be made to revolve in their respective orbits around the sun.

"Very ingenious indeed," he remarked. "Who made it?"

"Oh! Nobody in particular," replied Kirschner.

"No, really tell me, I want to know who made it."

"Nobody made it, it just made itself."

The friend began to see the point and was annoyed.

"I see you are trying to be funny."

"Is it not rather you that are funny? You cannot believe that this little model made itself, and yet you can believe that the

95

real sun and moon and stars, the vast universe in fact, came into existence somehow without any maker!"

⁓

A serious dispute was taking place between three men about which profession was first established on earth.

Said the surgeon: "The Bible says that Eve was made from one of Adam's ribs. I guess that makes mine the oldest profession."

Claimed the engineer, "Not at all. An engineering job came before that. In six days the earth was created out of chaos—and that was an engineer's job."

Said the politician, "Yes, but who created the chaos?"

⁓

A man walking beneath the shade of some trees exclaimed, "How beautiful are these trees! But how odd," he continued, "that so large a tree should bear a fruit as small as the acorn!" He then cast his eyes upon a gourdvine, with its tender stem, and wondered how it could yield a fruit weighing one hundred pounds. "If I had been God," he said, "I would have arranged creation differently. I would have put the small fruit on the small plant and the large fruit on the large tree."

It was a hot day and the man decided to take a nap under the spreading branches of the oak tree. An acorn landed on his face. Awakened by the falling of the tiny fruit, a thought flashed through his mind. "Had that been the gourd of one hundred pounds, I should probably have been a corpse at this time!"

"There *is* a wise God," he said, "who planned what is best for man."

⁓

A teacher was once asked, "Why didn't God create Eve before Adam?"

"That's very simple to understand," replied the teacher. "Because it's dangerous to start with a woman."

⁓

CREATIVITY

There is a difference between a thermometer and a thermostat. When a room is cold, the mercury in the tube of a thermometer drops. When the room is warm, it rises. The thin red line adjusts itself automatically to the temperature of the room.

The thermostat works quite differently. No sooner does a room become cold than it sends a message to the furnace saying, "Send up more heat." When the room is too warm, it calls down, "Enough, stop for a while."

People can be thermometers or thermostats. The thermometer people merely follow. As the saying goes, they follow the idea that "when in Rome do as the Romans do." The thermostat type of person is not molded by society. He protects against evil. He does something about his convictions.

CRISIS

The ship was slowly sinking and all was being done to save the passengers and the crew. One particular old lady was much distraught. To cheer her up, the captain said, "Just trust in Providence."

Looking even more worried she replied, "Is it as bad as that?"

CRITICISM

Abraham Lincoln once said, "If I tried to read, much less answer, all the criticisms made of me, and all the attacks leveled against me, this office would have to be closed for all other business. I do the best I know how, the very best I can. And I mean to keep on doing this, down to the very end. If the end brings me out all wrong, ten angels swearing I had been right would make no difference. If the end brings me out right, then what is said against me now will not amount to anything."

It was the youthful custom of a celebrated Persian writer, to rise from his sleep, to wash, to pray, and to read the Koran. One night as he was thus engaged, his father, a man of practical virtue, awoke.

"Behold," said the youth to him, "thy children are lost in irreligious slumbers, while I alone am awake and praise God."

"Son of my soul," said the father, "it is better to sleep than to be awake and to remark upon the faults of thy brethren."

There are always some who scoff at the ideas of others. Even the Baal Shem Tov, the founder of Hassidism, did not escape the lash of tongues that did not understand, but criticized his teachings. His reply to them was the following little story:

Once, at a wedding celebration, while the musicians played merry dance tunes in one corner of the room, the guests danced and laughed and were gay. A deaf man happened to pass by, and as he looked through the window, he saw the dancers leap into the air and fling their arms about. "Just observe their antics," he cried. "The house is full of madmen."

***

A lady complained to a friend who was visiting her that her next door neighbor was a poor housekeeper, her children were dirty, and her house was filthy. She felt disgraced even living near her.

"Just look," she said, "at those clothes she has out on the line. See the black streaks up and down those sheets and pillowcases."

"It appears to me, my dear," said the visitor, "that the clothes are perfectly clean; the streaks that you see are on your own window."

***

Mullah Naser-Ed Din, an ancient Persian poet, was walking with his son along a country road behind their donkey, who was contentedly nibbling grass along the way. A man, seeing Mullah and his son walking and sweating profusely, remarked, "Look how foolish they are, walking instead of riding."

Hearing this remark, Mullah and his son climbed on the donkey and rode through the next village where they heard an old man exclaim, "They ought to be ashamed, making the poor donkey carry two riders."

Mullah dismounted and walked while the son rode the donkey to the next village. There, Mullah heard this comment: "Poor old man. That boy ought to be ashamed, making his father walk."

Then Mullah got on the donkey, while his son dismounted and walked for some distance.

Finally, another villager observed, "Look at that old man, riding, while his son has to walk. How cruel!"

Mullah rubbed his beard, shook his head, and said to himself, "You cannot please all of the people any of the time."

***

"Your sermon was truly wonderful," said the lady shaking hands with the preacher. "Wonderful sermon," she repeated. "Everything you said applies to someone I know."

There is an old story of a woman who made artificial fruits of such perfection that people could not tell them from the real fruit. Yet she had some critics who would find fault with the shape of the fruit, the color, and other things. One day as the critics stood before a table on which the woman had placed several pieces of fruit, they criticized one apple in particular. When they had finished, the woman picked up the apple, cut it in half, and began to eat it, for it was a real apple.

One day a housewife was particularly sharp in rebuking her maid publicly. "The house has not been cleaned and dusted properly," complained the mistress. The maid flushed with embarrassment and amazement, for everything looked immaculately clean. Finally, a visitor turned to the housewife and said, "Madam, I think the dust you see is on your own glasses." The woman removed her glasses and, sure enough, the lenses were covered with dust.

An ancient emperor had a minister who never failed to speak freely of the king's faults. This happened so frequently that the emperor became displeased, and determined to rid himself of so candid a counsellor. The queen mother, upon being informed of it, instantly presented herself to the king and wished him joy.

"Joy!" said the emperor. "Of what?"

"Why, my son," she answered, "of a circumstance that has seldom ever happened to a monarch before. You have a subject who has the courage to admonish you, and who, because of that very honest quality, is the very finest courtier, since he thus insinuates that you have the greatness to hear it."

An editor, wishing to please fault-finders, inserted this item in his newspaper: "If you find an error, please understand it was there for a purpose. We try to publish something for everyone, and some people are always looking for something to criticize."

The dinner was over and the musicale was about to begin. The hostess began playing on the piano. As she continued a second selection, one of the guests leaned over to a charming young woman seated next to him, and asked, "What do you think of her execution?"

The girl turned and replied coolly, "I am in favor of it."

CULTURE

In the *Ethics of the Fathers,* we read: "There are seven marks of an uncultured man, and seven of a wise man. The wise man does not speak before him who is greater than he in wisdom, and does not break in upon the speech of his fellow; he is not hasty to answer; he questions according to the subject matter, and answers to the point; he addresses himself to first things first and to last things last; regarding that which he had not understood he says: 'I do not understand it,' and acknowledges the truth."

CURE

A man who devoted a good deal of time to charitable deeds once visited a miser. The rich man sat with his family around a well-laden table and asked this good man: "Can you tell me the purpose of your unexpected visit?"

"I came to pay you a sick call," answered the charitable man.

"I am, praise be to God, quite well. Perhaps you have made a mistake?"

"Not at all," replied the visitor. "I am not in the least mistaken. You are a very sick man suffering from what is known as 'propertyitis.' You and your property are welded together; you have no ability to separate yourself from even a little of your possessions to help the needy. This, my friend, is a very grave illness."

Not daring to contradict his guest, the rich miser asked politely, "Well, then, what is it that you want of me?"

And the visitor said: "It is stated that a visit to a sick person removes a sixtieth part of his ailment. With my visit here, I should like to remove one sixtieth of your 'disease,' for the sake of the needy."

CURIOSITY

An advertising executive had a client who wanted to read his literature to every married woman in a specific town. The executive thought for a minute and then hit upon what he believed to be a surefire success. "The solution to your problem is simple," he said, "just address letters to every married man in town, and mark the envelope, PERSONAL."

The local sexton was a bit depressed because his wife had gone out of town on a visit which she would not shorten in spite of his appeals to her to come home. He finally hit upon a plan to induce her to return. He sent her a copy of each of the local papers with just one item clipped out. When she wrote asking what had been clipped out, he refused to tell her. In less than one week she was home to find out what had been going on that her husband did not want her to know!

A woman visiting the Bronx Zoo looked intently at a hippopotamus, turned to the keeper, and asked, "Is this one a male or a female?"

"Madam," replied the keeper sternly, "that is a question that should be of interest only to another hippopotamus."

CYNIC

The cynic loves the world with a terrible hate.
The saint hates the world with a terrible love.

DAY-DREAMS

There is an old legend about a fisherman who lived on the banks of a river. Walking home with his eyes half-closed one evening after a hard day's toil, he was dreaming of what he would do if he became rich. Suddenly his feet struck against a leather pouch filled with what seemed to be small stones. Absentmindedly, he picked up the pouch and began throwing the pebbles into the water. "When I am rich," he said to himself, "I'll have a large house." And he threw a stone. He threw another and thought, "I'll have servants and wine and rich food."

101

This went on until only one stone was left. As the fisherman held it in his hand, a ray of light caught it and made it sparkle. He realized then that it was a valuable gem, that he had been throwing away real riches in his hand while he dreamed idly of unreal riches in the future.

***

DEATH

A shepherd was mourning over the death of his favorite child. He sobbed and bemoaned the fact that what he had loved most dearly had been taken from him.

Suddenly, a stranger appeared and beckoned him forth into the field. Said the stranger: "When you select one of these lambs from the flock, you choose the best and most beautiful among them. Why should you murmur because I, the Master Shepherd of all the sheep, have selected from those which you have nourished for me, the one that was most fitted for my eternal fold?"

The shepherd, hearing these words, was comforted.

***

When, during the war, Sir Harry Lauder, the famous Scot comedian, heard that his son had been killed in France, he said: "In a time like this there are three courses open to a man. He may give up in despair, sour upon the world, and become a grouch. He may endeavor to drown his sorrow in drink or by a life of waywardness and wickedness. Or he may turn to God."

***

A famous Scottish explorer, in his old age, was holding some young people enthralled by telling of some of the most exciting moments in his life: how he shot a tiger springing at him, how he saved himself after being shipwrecked and afloat on a raft for two days, how he saw a marvelous sunrise from a peak in the Himalayas, and so on.

"But I am expecting to have another thrill soon, bigger than any of these."

His audience listened with wonder, for they assumed that his exploring days were over.

"Are you planning another journey, then, sir?"

"No," he replied, "I was thinking of the first five minutes after death."

***

Some time ago, the Metropolitan Museum of Art held a display of contemporary art at which $52,000 was awarded to American sculptors, painters, and artists. The award for the best painting went to an Illinois artist. His canvas was described as "macabre, detailed work showing a closed door bearing a funeral wreath." Equally striking was the work's title: "That Which I Should Have Done, I Did Not Do."

An English nobleman gave a jester a wand, saying: "Keep this until you find a greater fool than yourself."

The jester laughingly accepted the wand and flourished it on festive occasions.

One day, the nobleman lay dying. Calling the jester to his bedside, he said: "I am going on a long journey."

"Where to?" asked the jester.

"I don't know," came the reply.

"How long will you be gone?" asked the jester.

"I shall be gone forever," said the dying man.

"What provisions have you made for the trip?" the jester asked.

The nobleman shrugged his shoulders. "None at all."

"Then," said the jester, "take this." And placing the wand in the nobleman's hands, he added: "It belongs to you."

A miser died suddenly, and while the body remained in the house, his son shed no tears. But as soon as the professional criers went about the town with their boxes, crying "Charity delivereth from death," the son began to weep bitterly. When he was asked why he was in tears now, when he seemed so calm before, he replied: "When people go about asking for charity and my father doesn't run away, it is certain proof that he is really dead."

To most humans, death is life's major catastrophe, and they either refuse to think of it or attempt to rationalize away its grim finality, as Whittier revealed in his *Snowbound,* when he says—

> Alas for him who never sees
> The stars shine through his cypress trees!
> Who, hopeless, lays his dead away,
> Nor looks to see the breaking day
> Across the mournful marbles play.

Who hath not learned, in hours of faith,
The truth, to flesh and sense unknown,
That life is ever lord of death
And love can never lose its own.

⟜

There was a little girl who was asked to tell the story of Enoch. She rose from her seat and said, "Enoch used to go on long walks with God. One day they walked farther than usual, and God said: 'Enoch, you are tired. Come into my house and stay and rest.' "

What a beautiful way to speak of death!

⟜

Love of life is a strong human instinct, but the fear of death comes from ignorance. One prepares for life by learning to walk and to talk; by acquiring an education and seeking a vocation. One must prepare for inevitable death with equal diligence, learning to share and to give, to be compassionate and to love. A good, clean life crowds out the fear of death. A pious and wise man once said: "I am not afraid of death. I am certain that death means going out through one dor and immediately entering through another door; going out of one room and entering another."

A man who had lived a full life was at the point of death. Knowing that his minutes were numbered, he turned to a friend seated at his bedside. "Don't mourn for me," said the dying man. "I have lived a rich life. Rather, mourn for the living dead." Speaking earnestly he continued:

"Go tell the others that I am dead
But they need shed no tears,
For though I'm dead, I'm no more dead
Than they have been for years."

⟜

A tailor left instructions that at his death his coffin was to be made out of his worktable. Why? So that the very wood might testify on his behalf when God asked him the first question: Have you done your work faithfully?

⟜

Upon the death of a devoted, though poor man, the preacher said:

"When he came there was no light;
When he died there was no darkness."

⟜

DEBATE

Shortly after Winston Churchill left the Conservative bench of the House of Commons, he was asked to escort a certain young woman into dinner. While she clung to his arm, she looked coyly at him and remarked, with the frankness and audacity of youth, "Mr. Churchill, there are two things about you I dislike very much."

"And what are they?"

"Your new politics and your mustache."

He looked deeply into her eyes for a moment and then replied with a lofty air, "My dear, pray do not disturb yourself. You are not likely to come into contact with either."

DEBTS

The Dubner Maggid, one Yom Kippur, came to the synagogue, and noticed that the synagogue was more crowded than usual. He saw men and women whom he had not seen before. Later in the afternoon, he ascended the pulpit and, addressing the congregation, related the following parable:

There was a merchant who after many years built up a wonderful business. He had toiled and labored before becoming a success. However, because of a series of poor investments he lost everything, and in fact, was in debt to one creditor for $8,000.

The poor man was miserable. He did not know where to turn. His friends advised him to go to his creditor and plead his cause. This he did. When the creditor heard the entire story he said, "Stop crying. You owe me nothing. I'm ripping up all your promissory notes. You now have a clean slate. Begin all over again and you can count on me for help."

When the story of this man's generosity reached the ears of another citizen, he decided that he would try to liquidate his debt with the same creditor. He felt that he would succeed since he owed but $5,000. That very evening he approached the creditor and sobbed in feigned tragedy. "Stop your crying," said the creditor. "It will do you no good. You will have to pay me every cent of the $5,000 you owe me."

"But why did you forgive the other person?" he demanded.

"How can you compare yourself to him?" explained the creditor. "I have been doing business with him for years. He has made deposits of honesty and sincerity, but you—you, I hardly see. You come only when I have bargains."

105

"Need I be more explicit?" asked the Dubner as he left the pulpit.

～～～

Dag Hammarskjold, in his book *Markings*, which presents his innermost feelings about life, pinpointed a basic attitude which all people must achieve:

> It is *now*, in this very moment, that I can and must pay for all that I have received. The past and its load of debt are balanced against the present. . . . Is not beauty created at every encounter between a man and life, in which he repays his debt?

～～～

DECEIT

The story is told of an old lady who rented a furnished villa for the summer, and along with the villa went a large dog. In the sitting room of the villa there was a very comfortable armchair. The old lady liked this chair better than any others in the house. She always headed right for it.

However, much to her regret, she nearly always found the chair occupied by the large dog. Being afraid of the dog, she never dared bid it harshly to get out of the chair. Instead, she would go to the window and call, "CATS!" Then the dog would rush to the window and bark, and the old lady would slip into the vacant chair quietly.

One day, the dog entered the room and found the old lady in possession of the chair. He strolled over to the window and, looking out, appeared very much excited and set up a tremendous barking. The old lady rose and hastened to the window to see what was the matter, and the dog quietly climbed into the chair.

～～～

A rich miser who had never given a penny for charity, once fell ill and the attending physicians gave up hope for his life. In his dying hours his wife and children stormed heaven with their prayers and recited the Psalms. The dying man himself vowed that if he would only recover he would donate large sums of money to charity. When, with God's help, the miser rose from his death bed he regretted that he had promised to donate so much for charity and said, "Now I first realize how terribly sick and how feverish I was. One must really have a high temperature to promise such a large amount."

DECISION

Two neighbors appeared before the famous judge. They were disputing the ownership of a piece of ground. Neither would yield to the other.

"The land is mine," said the first.

"It is mine," replied the second.

"Let the earth render the decision," replied the judge. With these words, he bent down to the ground as if to listen to the voice of the earth.

In a few moments, he rose and said: "My dear friends, this is the decision of the earth 'I belong to *neither* of you, but you both belong to me. Both of you will some day sleep in my bosom, so when you walk upon me, walk in peace!' "

DEDICATION

On Arturo Toscanini's eightieth birthday, someone asked his son, Walter, what his father ranked as his most important achievement. The son replied, "For him there can be no such thing. Whatever he happens to be doing at the moment is the biggest thing in his life, whether it is conducting a symphony or peeling an orange."

DEEDS

Emperor Hadrian, passing near Tiberias in Galilee, noticed an old man digging a large trench in order to plant some fig trees. "If you had properly used the morning of your life," remarked Hadrian, "you would not now have to work so hard in the evening of your days."

"I have not wasted my early days, nor will I neglect the evening of my life. Let God do what He thinks best," was the reply of the old man.

"How old are you?" asked the Emperor.

"One hundred years old."

"What!" exclaimed Hadrian. "A hundred years old and you still plant trees! Do you hope, then, to ever enjoy the fruits of your labor?"

"Mighty Emperor," rejoined the hoary-headed man, "yes, I do hope. If God wills it, I may even eat the fruit of these very trees; if not, my children will. Have not my forefathers planted trees for me, and shall I not do the same for my children?"

Hadrian, pleased with the man's reply, said, "Well, old man, if you ever live to see the fruit of these trees, let me know."

The old man did live long enough to see the fruits of his industry. The trees bore excellent fruit. As soon as they were ripe, he gathered the choicest figs, put them in a basket, and marched off toward the Emperor's palace. Hadrian happened to be looking out of one of the windows. Seeing a man bent with age, with a basket on his shoulders, standing near the gate, he ordered him to be admitted to his presence.

"May it please your Majesty," replied the man, "to recollect seeing once a very old man planting some trees, and you desired him, if ever he should gather the fruit, to let you know. I am that old man and this is the fruit of those very trees. May it please you graciously to accept them as a tribute of gratitude."

Hadrian ordered that the basket be emptied of the fruit and filled with gold which he presented to the old man.

A sage said: "There are three ways in which a man can go about performing a good deed. If he says, 'I shall do it soon,' the method is poor. If he says, 'I am ready to do it now,' the method is of average quality. If he says, 'I am doing it," the method is praiseworthy."

DEFECTS

John Ruskin, the famous nineteenth century English author, once called on a literary collaborator and found her in mental distress because she had ruined a costly handkerchief by a blot of ink.

"Nothing can be done with it," she cried. "It's absolutely worthless."

"Are you sure?" said Ruskin. "Let me have it awhile."

Sometime later, Ruskin sent the handkerchief back and the blot could not be recognized. He used the blot as the basis for a design of surpassing beauty. It was now many times more valuable than its original loveliness.

The story is told that when the first steam engine was ready for its trial run in the early nineteenth century, a large crowd of skeptical onlookers had assembled. It got up steam and began to hiss. They shouted, "It will not start!" The whistle blew and, puffing and snorting, the locomotive began to move. They were amazed, but still not convinced. "It will not keep going!" they yelled. Strangely enough it kept right on going. Still stubborn in their disbelief, they challenged, "But will it stop?"

DELINQUENTS

An old railroader once said, "A switch has put many a delinquent on the right track."

A hermit was conducted by an angel into a wood where he saw an old man cutting down boughs to make up a load. When it was large he tied it up, and attempted to lift it to his shoulder and carry it away. However, finding it very heavy, he laid it down again, then cut more wood and heaped it on. Again he tried to carry it off. This he repeated several times, always adding something to the load after having failed to raise it from the ground.

The hermit, astonished at the old man's folly, asked the angel to explain what this meant. The angel replied, "You observe in the foolish old man an exact representation of those who, being aware of the burden of their sins, resolve to repent, but tire of the attempt. Instead of lessening their burden, they increase it every day. Each time they try to repent they find the task harder than before, and so postpone it a little longer, in the vain hope that later they will be more able to succeed. Thus they go on adding to their burden until it grows too heavy to be borne. Then, in despair, and with their sins unrepented, they lie down and die."

DELIVERY

A distinguished minister questioned an equally distinguished actor concerning the difference in their appeal to people:

"Why is it," asked the minister, "that you appear night after night before great crowds, and I am getting no crowd at all? Your words are sheer fiction, and mine are essential and unchangeable truth."

The actor's answer was, "It is all quite simple. I present my fiction as though it were truth. You present your truth as though it were fiction."

DELUSION

A minister was cautioned by one of his members, who said, "Don't talk as plainly as you do about sin. Our children hear you talking so much about sin, they will more easily become sinners. Call it a mistake, if you will, or some other milder term."

The minister went to the medicine shelf and brought back a small bottle of strychnine marked 'Poison.' "I see what you want me to do," he said. "Suppose I take this label and replace it with some mild label like 'Essence of Peppermint.' What do you think would happen?"

DEMOCRACY

When Gladstone was premier, he insisted that Queen Victoria sign a bill just passed by the House of Commons. Victoria refused his request and, resenting his insistence, exclaimed, "Mr. Gladstone, you forget who I am . . . I am the Queen of England."

To which Gladstone replied, "Your Majesty, you forget who I am. . . . I am the people of England."

Nikita Khrushchev, Harry Truman and Chaim Weizmann were discussing the complexities of their respective positions.

"There are two million Communist Party members in Russia," remarked Khrushchev. "That should give you an idea of my difficulties."

Said Truman: "Two million? What's two million? In the United States there are 180 million people, and I am responsible to every one of them!"

"Your job is easy compared to mine," commented Weizmann. "How would you like to be president of two-and-a-half million presidents?"

DEPENDENCE

A legend tells us about a horse who was too weak to contend with a stag. He asked a man to help him get rid of the other animal. The man got on the horse's back and quickly put the stag to flight. Unfortunately, the horse could never get the man off his back, nor the bit out of his mouth.

DESCENDANTS

"Well, yes," said Mrs. Garner proudly, "we can trace our ancestors back to . . . to. . . . Well, I don't know exactly who, but we've been descending for centuries."

DESIRE

According to an ancient legend, Alexander the Great, after he had made himself master of the world, was shown a pair of scales. In one cup he placed all of the gold and silver he had amassed, but it was outweighed by the other, which contained a single human skull with the socket of an eye, the symbol of man's limitless desires.

"There are two tragedies in life," wrote George Bernard Shaw. "One is not to get your heart's desire. The other is to get it."

DETERMINATION

A crow, half dead with thirst, came upon a pitcher which had once been full of water; but when the crow put its beak into the mouth of the pitcher, he found that only very little water was left in it, and that he could not reach far enough down to get it. He tried and he tried, but at last had to give up in despair. Then a thought came to him, and he took a pebble and dropped it into the pitcher. Then he took another pebble and dropped it into the pitcher. Pebble after pebble, he dropped into that pitcher. Finally, the water was near him and he was able to quench his thirst and save his life.

Rabbi Akiba began his studies at the late age of forty and wondered if he could succeed at study at such a late age. One day, as he walked along the road, he said to himself, "I am almost forty years old and now it may be too late for me to study the Torah. Who knows if I will ever achieve my goal?"

Suddenly he came upon several shepherds sitting near a spring. At the mouth of the spring lay a stone which had many grooves.

"What caused these grooves?" he asked the shepherds.

"They were made by drops of water that steadily trickled upon the stone."

Hearing this, Akiba rejoiced. He said to himself, "If a stone may be softened, how much easier will it be to soften my mind!"

Beethoven knew early in his career that deafness was closing in on him, but it didn't depress him. He wrote: "I will seize fate by the throat; most assuredly it shall not get me wholly down." His most beautiful music is testimony to the fact that he succeeded.

A small boy had a new pair of skates that he had wanted for a long time. He was trying his best to balance himself, but was not doing too well. Again and again, he fell to the ground. A passerby, noticing the boy's difficulties, advised, "Sonny, if I were you I would give up. Otherwise you might get hurt."

With tears in his eyes the boy looked up from the sidewalk where he had fallen and replied, "I didn't get these skates to give up on, I got them to learn on."

A father was seeing his son off on the steamship. The young man was going to a new land with the intention of seeking his fortune.

"Now, my son," said the father, as they parted, "remember the three bones, and you will be successful."

A stranger who had overheard the remark asked about the three bones.

"I'll tell you," explained the father. "They are the wishbone, the jawbone, and the backbone. It's the wishbone that keeps you going after things; it's the jawbone that helps you find out how to go after them if you are not too proud to ask a question; and it's the backbone that keeps you at it till you get there!"

A saint once heard about the evil city of Sodom. Being a saint, he went to the city with love and concern for its people. When he saw wickedness all about him, he began to preach and plead

112

and protest daily. After many years of this, a friend asked, "Why all the bother? You have not changed them a bit!"

The saint replied, "In this city of madness and sin, I must go out to shout, to preach and plead and protest—not that they should become like me, but that I should not become like them."

It is said that one day Michelangelo, the great sculptor, visited a contractor who sold rough pieces of marble. He came upon an ugly, misshapen piece that was obviously worth little or nothing. No doubt it had fallen or been broken in handling. The great sculptor stood pensively and looked long at the stone. Then he said quietly, "I will take it. There is an angel within that stone and I must release it."

DEVOTION

A bird once set out to cross a windy sea with its three fledglings. The sea was so wide and the wind so strong that the father bird was forced to carry his young, one by one, in his claws.

When he was half-way across with the first fledgling the wind turned to a gale, and he said: "My child, look how I am struggling and risking my life in your behalf. When you are grown up, will you do as much for me and provide for my old age?"

The fledgling replied: "Only bring me to safety, and when you are old I shall do everything you ask of me." Whereupon the father bird dropped his child into the sea, and it drowned, and he said: "So shall it be done to such a liar as you."

Then the father bird returned to the shore and set forth with his second fledgling. Midway across the sea he asked the same question, and receiving the same answer, drowned the second child with the cry, "You, too, are a liar!"

Finally he set out with the third fledgling, and when he asked the same question, the third and last fledgling replied: "My dear father, it is true you are struggling mightily and risking your life in my behalf, and I shall be wrong not to repay you when you are old, but I cannot bind myself. This though I can promise: when I am grown up and have children of my own, I shall do as much for them as you have done for me." Whereupon the father bird said: "Well spoken, my child, and wisely; your life I spare and I will carry you to shore in safety."

—*Autobiography of Gluckel of Hamlen*

A young artist, who was studying under a great master, came one day to the studio and pleaded for permission to use his master's brush. The request was granted, and with a happy heart the young man left to take care of his own painting. He felt that, with the master's brush, his work would be much better.

A day or two later he returned with the brush, confessing that he could do no better with it than he could with his own.

An assistant in the studio, having overheard the young man's complaint, said to him, "My young friend, it is not the master's brush you need, but the master's devotion and spirit."

DIETING

George Bernard Shaw was a noted vegetarian. At a dinner with Sir James Barrie, Shaw was once served a vegetarian concoction. Barrie looked at Shaw's plate and remarked, "Tell me, my good friend, have you eaten that or are you going to?"

It is related that George Bernard Shaw and Alfred Hitchcock once met in London. As is well known, Hitchcock eats full meals . . . and his tummy shows just that.

When they met, Hitchcock said, "To look at you, Mr. Shaw, one would think there already was a famine in England."

Shaw immediately answered with, "And to look at you, one would think you had caused it."

DIGRESSION

The farmer had just returned from a drive in his carriage. His dog, who had been running alongside threw himself on the grass, his sides heaving with his heavy panting.

"It is not the road that tires him," explained the farmer, "but his zigzagging. We have ridden for about 5 miles, but the dog has covered 25 miles. There wasn't a cat he didn't chase, not a dog he didn't bark at, not a driveway he did not investigate. Straight traveling didn't tire him, only the zigzagging did."

DIPLOMACY

The three animals were having a debate about which one of them had made the greatest contribution to the war. The horse claimed first honors, because he made it possible for men to ride off to war. The cow claimed that were it not for her staying home, the civilian population would starve. But the donkey was not to be outdone. "None of you contributed as much as I," he said, "for had I not been in diplomacy at the head of the governments, there would never have been a war."

A wise old man who was a judge was asked to settle a dispute between two brothers about the fair division of a large estate left them by their father.

"Let one brother divide the estate," said the judge, "and let the other brother have first choice."

An American visiting the Holy Land entered a book store and selected a Bible which he wished to purchase. However, the proprietor looked very grieved and pointedly remarked, "We do not sell the Bible. It is too sacred."

Finally, the American hit upon an idea. Pricing the Bible at ten piastres, he took forth the sum of money and said to the proprietor, "May I offer you a gift of ten piastres?" The latter received the money and, wrapping the Bible, handed it to the American while remarking gravely, "And now may I present you with a copy of the Bible?"

The height of diplomacy was reached by a young man who entered an elevator and neglected to take his hat off. The only other passenger in the elevator was a fussy, middle-aged school teacher who asked: "Don't you take off your hat to ladies?"

"Only to old ones, madam," he replied with a smile and a bow.

After the American Revolutionary War, Benjamin Franklin, the English ambassador, and the French minister, were dining together. They agreed that each should offer a toast.

The English ambassador began: "To George the Third, who, like the sun at noonday, spreads his light and illuminates the world."

The French minister followed with: "To His Majesty, Louis the Sixteenth, who, like the moon, fills the earth with a soft, benevolent glow."

Franklin said the following: "To George Washington, General

115

of the Armies of the United States, who, like Joshua of old, commanded both the sun and the moon to stand still, and both obeyed."

DIRECTION

Oliver Wendell Holmes once boarded a train in Massachusetts, then promptly lost his ticket. The conductor recognized him and said, "Never mind, when you find your ticket I am certain you will mail it in."

"Mr. Conductor," replied Holmes, "the question is not, 'Where is my ticket?' but, 'Where am I going?' "

One ship drives east and another drives west
With selfsame winds that blow;
It's the set of the sails and not the gales
That tells them where to go.

Like the winds of the sea are the winds of fate,
As we voyage along through life;
It's the set of the soul that decides its goal,
And not the calm or the strife.

DISCONTENT

Grant a man the necessities in life, and he wants the conveniences; give him the conveniences, and he prays for the luxuries; grant him the luxuries, and he yearns for the elegances; let him have the elegances, and he asks for the follies; grant him everything that he wishes and he will complain that the price was too high and the quantity too small.

A canary and a goldfish lived in the same room. One hot, sweltering day the master of the house heard the fish complain, envying the sweet song of his companion overhead. "Oh, I wish I could be up there singing as sweetly as my friend!" he sighed.

At almost the same time, the canary was eyeing the inhabitant of the cool-looking watery globe. "How comfortable he looks," remarked the discontented bird. "How I wish I could change places with him!"

116

"I'll grant both your wishes," said the master of the house. With these words, he placed the fish in the air and the bird in the water. It did not take long for both to realize their folly and to plead for a return to their natural habitats.

⚬⚬⚬

> As a rule a man's a fool;
> When it's hot he wants it cool;
> When it's cool he wants it hot.
> Always wanting what is not.

⚬⚬⚬

DISCRIMINATION

A Negro boy stood watching the balloon man at the country fair. Suddenly, a red balloon broke loose and soared upward until it could scarcely be seen. So many people watched that balloon go upward that the vendor thought it would be good business to let another go. This time a yellow one went up, followed by a white one. The young boy watched. Finally he said, "Mister, if you sent the black one up, would it go as high as the others?"

The balloon vendor understood. With a smile, he released the black one and said, "Sonny, it isn't the color—it's the stuff inside that makes it rise."

⚬⚬⚬

A certain man made it his custom to invite some of his poorest neighbors, who were usually spurned by everyone else, to share the joys of the holidays with him and his family. When friends asked why he went out of his way to be particularly nice to such people, he replied: "You see, in the 'World to Come' all the virtuous and scholarly men will be invited into the most hallowed parts of heaven. I will surely want to be a guest there, too, but the angel will probably stop me at the door and ask me sternly: 'How does a man of mediocre station like yourself dare to assume that he may be a guest at such a distinguished gathering?' I shall then be able to reply to him: 'Please forgive me, but in my home I also invited neighbors who were not my equals.'"

⚬⚬⚬

DISHONESTY

A wealthy merchant was taken to task by a citizens' committee for his dishonest dealings with his customers. The merchant was angered by this accusation and said rather sharply: "Gentlemen, why don't you isolate yourselves in a secluded place and meditate, like the monks in the days of Robin Hood?"

The committee was not disturbed by this question and the spokesman replied: "In the days of Robin Hood, the robbers lived in the forest, and the monks lived nearby to pray for the neighbors. Today, however, shrewd "operators" live in big cities, and good people who see through their schemes must live there as well so that they can protect the poor, unsuspecting public from heartless profiteers."

Two large turtles and one small one started out on a journey. After travelling a few weeks, they came to a tavern and bought some beer. Then they remembered that they had forgotten something at home. They drew lots to see who would return to get it. The lot fell on the little one. "I'll go," he said, "provided you won't drink my beer." They agreed.

A week, a month, a year; two years passed and finally the two turtles decided they had better not let the beer go to waste. Just as they were about to begin sipping, the little turtle looked in—"I saw you. . . . I won't go if you drink it."

DISPOSITION

An old man surprised all who knew him with his constant cheerful attitude, despite an unusual amount of trouble. When asked about the secret of his cheery disposition, he replied "Well, I learned it from the Bible. Where it often says, 'And it came to pass,' never does it say, 'It came to stay.' "

DISSATISFACTION

There is a strange plant in South America which finds a moist place and rests there for a while, sending its roots down and becoming green. When this bit of earth dries up, the plant draws itself together and is blown along by the wind until it finds another moist spot, where it repeats its performance. On and on it rolls, stopping wherever it finds a little water and staying until the water is exhausted. But after all the journeying, it is nothing but a bundle of dead roots and leaves. The life of this plant tells the story of those who drink only at the world's springs of sensual pleasures.

They go from spring to spring, but at the end of the longest life, they are nothing but bundles of unsatisfied desires and burning thirsts.

DIVORCE

A young woman walked into her bank and demanded to see the manager. "I'd like to make a loan," she told him. "You see I need the money to get a divorce."

The manager looked surprised at this odd request. "We don't give money for this reason," he answered. "We make loans for businesses, automobiles, and home improvements."

"That's what I mean," shouted the lady. "This is a home improvement."

If the rising divorce rate is making America the land of the free, then the tremendous marriage rate is making America the land of the brave.

An unhappy, henpecked husband came to his preacher asking for a divorce.

"What! How can you, a religious man, think of such a thing! Don't you realize that our good book tells us that when a man divorces his wife not only do the angels cry but the very stones weep?"

"Listen," replied the husband, "if the angels and stones want to cry, let them. I want to rejoice!"

DOCTORS

A specialist who devoted much time to charity work in clinics was surprised to see a bearded old gentleman ushered into his elaborate consulting room.

"Remember me, Doctor?" asked the man. "You treated me over at the clinic. Well, I've been left a little money and I guess I can afford my doctor now."

"But what made you come to *me?*" the physician wanted to know. "I wasn't the only doctor who treated you at the clinic."

"I know," the old man said quietly. "But you were the only one who helped me with my coat."

The doctor had decided to tell the sick man the entire truth. "I feel I should tell you," he began very seriously, "that you are a very sick man. I am certain that you would want to know the facts. Now—is there anyone you would like to see?"

Bending down towards his patient, the doctor heard a feeble "Yes."

"Who is it?"

In a slightly stronger tone the sick man replied, "Another doctor."

DONATIONS

A wealthy man attended a meeting where the building of a new church was being discussed. The wealthy man was of the opinion that the old building would do for a while but said he would give five dollars if they did decide to build. As he took his seat, a piece of plaster fell from the ceiling and struck his head. The man stood up immediately and said that the need for a new church was more pressing than he had thought and that he would raise his pledge to fifty dollars. A pious congregant who had observed the good effect of the providential accident fervently prayed, "Lord, hit him again!"

A gentle landlord was approached by the town rabbi for a donation for the poor.

"Why should I give to a Jew?" argued the landlord. "If my religion does not suit you, then neither should my money."

"Sir," the rabbi answered gently, "the people who farm your lands are all Jews; it is they who provide you with your wealth. As to your religion, let me answer it this way: We may not eat pork, but there is nothing in the Scriptures that forbids us to wear pigskin shoes."

DRINKING

Once upon a time, a Mohammedan came to one of his religious leaders called a Kadi, and asked: "If I eat dates is that against the commands of religion?"

"No," said the Kadi.

"And may I add some water?"

"Certainly."

"And is it wrong to take a little yeast?"

"Oh, no."

"Well," went on the questioner, "date wine consists only of these three ingredients. Why, then, is it forbidden by the laws of our religion?"

The Kadi thought a moment and then he said, "If I throw a handful of dust on your head, will that cause pain?"

"Not in the least."

"And if I add some water—will it hurt you then?"

"I think not."

"Now, if I mix dust and water together and burn it into a brick and hit you on the head with it, what then?"

—*Dry Legion*

DURABILITY

A soldier who was stationed in England, sauntered into the West London Synagogue for the New Year Holy Days services, and asked: "What kind of a show do you have here? Is it good?"

"It should be," replied the rabbi who had overheard the question. "It has been running for nearly six thousand years."

DUTY

How does one best serve God? Hundreds of years ago a pious scholar, Eliezer ben Isaac, spelled out the answer in a letter to his son:

"My son, give God all the honor and gratitude which is His due. Thou hast need of Him, but He needs thee not. Fear the Lord, the God of thy fathers. See that thou guardest thy soul's holiness, and when thou prayest, think well before Whom it is, thou standest. Visit the sick and suffering man, and let thy countenance be cheerful when he sees it, but not so that thou oppress the helpless one with gaiety. Respect the poor man by gifts whose hand he knows not of. Rather feed thyself with the vilest weed than make thyself dependent on other human beings. Seek not greedily after power and pre-eminence in the world. Spend not thy time among people who speak ill of their fellowman. Be not as the fly that is always seeking sick and wounded places. Dare not rejoice when thine enemy falls to the ground; give him food when he hungers. Purge thy soul from angry passion, that in-

121

heritage of fools. Love the society of wise men, and strive to know more and more of the ways and the works of thy Creator."

~~~

"What did God ever make such a world for anyway?" a young lady complained, adding, "I could make a better world than this myself."

"That's just the reason," suggested her friend, "that God put you into this world—to make it better. Now go ahead and do your part."

~~~

How true of life! She had gone to bed and when she arose, she remarked, "I slept and dreamed that life was beauty. I awoke— and found that life was duty."

~~~

ECONOMY

Edison's summer home was full of labor saving devices—with one exception. One had to pass through a stiff turnstile which required considerable force to push.

Finally, one guest gathered the courage to ask the inventor, "Mr. Edison, why is everything so perfect here except that awful turnstile?"

"Shh!" replied Edison. "Everybody who pushes the turnstile pumps eight gallons of water into the tank on my roof."

~~~

EDUCATION

A five-year-old was asked by her mother what she and her classmates had learned at nursery school. She replied, "Oh, the kids who hit were taught not to hit, and the kids who don't hit were taught to hit back."

~~~

The famous Greek philosopher, Aristotle, said, "They who educate children well, are more to be honored than they who produce them: for these only gave them life, those the art of living."

~~~

A prominent businessman was enrolling his son in a well known university. He shook his head dubiously when he began to examine the institution's catalogue of studies. "Does my son have to take all these courses?" he asked the dean. "Can't you make it shorter? He wants to get through quickly."

"Certainly he can take a shorter course," replied the dean, "but it depends on what he wants to make of himself. When God wants to make an oak, he takes twenty years. He only takes two months to make a squash."

Charles W. Eliot, famous president of Harvard University, was being honored one night by a group of well-known educators.

"Permit me to congratulate you on the miracles you have performed at the university," said one educator. "Since you became president, Harvard has become a storehouse of knowledge."

"That is true," laughed Eliot. "But I scarcely deserve credit for that. It is simply that the freshmen bring so much and the seniors take away so little."

A well known educator, making a high school commencement address, presented a strong case for higher education. After the ceremony, one of the graduates asked, "How can you really prove to me what it is like to be college-bred? I want definite proof."

The speaker asked for a banana, peeled it, and ate it as everyone watched. On finishing, he asked the young graduate, "Do you know what the banana tasted like?"

"Certainly not," came the reply. "Only the one who ate it can tell that."

"So it is with a college education," concluded the educator. "You must taste it yourself."

When Woodrow Wilson was president of Princeton University, an anxious mother was questioning him closely about what Princeton could do for her son. Wilson replied: "Madam, we guarantee satisfaction or you will get your son back."

A successful businessman returned to his alma mater for a visit with his former economics professor.

Just for the fun of it, he wanted to see how well he could make out on a current exam and asked to see the questions. He was amazed to find the questions to be the same as in his own student days. The professor noticed that his visitor was bewildered, and explained: "Certainly the questions are the same, but in economics we always change the answers."

⁓

Thoreau and Emerson, both Harvard men, were once discussing higher education. What particularly pleased Emerson was the fact that Harvard now included all branches of learning in its curriculum.

Thoreau's quiet but meaningful answer was: "Yes, all branches but none of the roots."

⁓

A teacher who wanted to discourage his students from staying up too late explained to them: "Keeping very late hours is a ruse of the evil spirits. They come to plague you and nag you into ill-spent wakeful hours so that when the sun rises, and it is indeed time for you to commence your activities, you will be too tired to perform properly at work and studies."

⁓

At a conference, a speaker began a tirade against education in general and expressed thankfulness that he himself had never been corrupted by contact with a college. After a while, someone interrupted with the question, "Do I understand, sir, that you are thankful for your ignorance?"

"Well, yes, you can put it that way if you wish."

"Well, then, all I have to say," the other replied sweetly, "is that you have much to be thankful for."

⁓

The young man had just received his degree from college. He was elated and rushed out and exclaimed, "Here I am, world; I have my A. B.!"

And the world replied, "Sit down, son, and I'll teach you the rest of the alphabet."

⁓

Many years, ago, when a wise and well-loved professor was lecturing at a small college, a group of young students sought to unhitch the horses from his wagon and pull it themselves.

The professor, smiling, protested: "All my life I have worked to make people out of horses, and now you want me to make horses out of people."

⁓

A young mother was looking at a toy for her small child. "Isn't this toy awfully complicated for him?" she asked the salesman.

"That, madam," replied the salesman, "is an educational toy, designed to prepare the child for life in today's world. Any way he puts it together is wrong."

⁓

EFFECT

Several men were adrift in a boat. One of the men suddenly grasped an awl and began to bore a hole through the hull under his seat. His fellows remonstrated with him, warning of the disaster that would befall all the occupants. The man continued with his boring, stopping for a moment to reply, "Mind your own business; I am boring the hole under my own seat."

⁓

Charles M. Schwab believed in hard work. When he obtained a large contract, he remarked, "Some people call it luck but they are mistaken. Success comes from hard work. I remember a businessman who crossed the ocean with me one winter. The country was in a depression. "And you, Mr. Schwab," he asked, "are you like the rest of us praying for better things?"

"No, not only praying. I have rolled up my sleeves and am working for it as well."

⁓

"How can I get life to give me maximum happiness?" asked the student of his teacher.

"Your question reminds me of the farmer who owned a cow," was the reply. "Someone once asked him, 'How much milk does your cow give?' To which the farmer replied, 'She doesn't give any, you have to take it away from her.'"

⁓

Two frogs fell into a bucket of cream. They tried to get out by climbing up the side of the bucket. But each time they would slip back into the cream.

Finally one frog said: "We'll never get any place doing this. I give up!" So down he went and drowned.

125

The other frog, seeing the consequences of giving up, decided to keep trying. Even if he didn't succeed, it would be better to go down fighting. So time and again he tried to climb with his front legs while he kicked with his back legs. Suddenly he hit something solid. He turned to see what it was. Lo and behold, he found that all his kicking had churned up a lump of butter! So hopping on top of it, he leaped out of the pail to safety.

EFFICIENCY

An efficiency expert died and was being carried to his grave by six pallbearers. As they approached their destination the lid of the coffin popped open and the efficiency expert sat up and shouted, "If you'd put this thing on wheels you could lay off four men!"

A harassed-looking man was wandering around a large retail store during a special sale day. It was obvious that he was worried about something. Finally, the store manager approached him and asked, "Can I help you, sir?"

"I've lost my wife," the man began.

"Yes, sir," replied the much too efficient manager, "mourning clothes on the fifth floor."

EFFORT

A king once placed a heavy burden in the middle of the road. It proved a great inconvenience to those who walked down the road as well as to the horsecarts that were driven. Many people stumbled over the rock and hurt themselves. A cart turned over and was badly damaged. But no one stooped down to remove the boulder. Finally, one man came along, saw the obstruction, picked it up and dropped it in the field. Then he returned with some earth to fill the crater that was formed. As he began to fill the hole, he noticed a purse lying there. He opened it and found the gold-filled purse that the king had placed there for the man who was thoughtful enough to remove the obstacle from the road. "Lucky man!" everyone said. But he was not lucky. His reward was the result of effort expended.

126

Leonardo Da Vinci, one of the three greatest painters the world has known, and a remarkable success in five other fields of activity, once said, "Oh, God, thou givest everything for the price of an effort."

⁓

"If I had the wings of an angel," said a young boy, turning the pages of a travel magazine, "I'd fly to the top of his mountain pictured here. It is beautiful." Then, after brief meditation, he observed, "I haven't any wings. But I have feet and legs with which to reach the top."

⁓

At Chamonix, on a stone which marks the grave of a guide who perished ascending the Alps, are written these three suggestive words: "He died climbing."

To be victorious over the world does not mean that we shall never stumble nor fall; that is impossible. It means that after every fall we shall rise undaunted, undefeated, undismayed, and climb, and keep on climbing, and "die climbing."

⁓

A college instructor in an agricultural school figured out that man does only 5% of the work on an ear of corn, and that God does 95%.

⁓

"It is only a little further," a father would say to his tired, leg-weary son on the long Sunday afternoon walks they took together. The child would brace up and struggle on a little longer, looking for the first familiar landmarks that would indicate they were back in their own neighborhood. One day the boy asked the father how far a little further was.

"It is further than you can see, but not as far as you can go," he replied.

⁓

An apple was hanging from the ceiling. One man saw it, reached up, but couldn't quite reach it. Disappointed at his failure he walked away. Another man also saw the apple. Said he to himself, "It may be readily obtained by placing a chair near it and standing on it so that my hand is within reach of the fruit." This he did and was rewarded.

⁓

127

A rough diamond lay in the sand among many common stones. A boy, walking by, picked up a handful of stones and took them home, the jewel among them. The boy's father observed his son playing and noticed the rough jewel. "Please hand me that stone," he said to his son. The boy smilingly obliged, thinking, "What is my father going to do with that stone?"

The father took the stone and polished it skillfully into smooth planes and angles and, behold, a diamond glittered brilliantly. "See," his father exclaimed, "this is the same stone you gave me."

The boy wondered at the splendor and brilliance of the diamond and remarked in astonishment, "Dad, how did you accomplish this?"

"I knew the hidden virtue of the stone. I knew its value," replied the father. "Therefore, I freed it from its coating of dross. Now it sparkles with natural radiance."

A poor woman was abandoned by her husband and was left with no visible means of support. Her case came up in court and the judge asked her, "Madam, have you any means of support whatever?"

"Well, your honor," she answered, "I have three, to tell the truth."

"Three!"

"Yes, sir."

"What are they?" asked the astonished judge.

"My God, my health, and my hands," was the reply.

I'M GONNA TRY

I'm gonna try to play the game, and play it hard, and play it fair. I may not win, but just the same I'm gonna try to do my share. I may not always meet the rest as well as some more clever "guy," but while my heart beats in my chest, I'm gonna try.

I'm gonna try to stand the gaff, yet keep my nerve; I'm gonna seek to love and work and play and laugh, and never show no yellow streak. I'm gonna struggle to be kind, and not grow hard of face and eye. I'll flop at times, but never mind, I'm gonna try.

I'm gonna try to be a friend that folks can trust, and who they know will be the same way to the end, whether the luck runs high or low. I'll hitch my wagon to a star, and set my goal up in the sky; and though I may not get that far, I'm gonna try!

—Anonymous

Hanan of Sepphoris once illustrated how a difficult task could be made simpler with these words: "The study of the law may be compared to a huge heap of dust that is to be cleared away. The foolish man says, 'It is impossible for me to remove this immense heap; I will not attempt it.' The wise man says, 'I will remove a little today, some tomorrow, and more the day after, and thus, in time, shall have removed it all.' "

A man went to the town sage and said that he was going to close his bakery and move elsewhere.

"Why are you closing up shop?"

"You see," replied the depressed storekeeper, "my competitor gets a good deal of the business; most of the customers seem to go into his bakery."

"How do you know that most of the townspeople go to his store?" inquired the sage.

"It's quite simple. When I stand at my door, I see many people entering and leaving his bakeshop."

"That's just the trouble," counseled the wise sage. "If you were not so intent on watching his store, but would spend your time building up your own business, success might be yours."

James Ulman, a famous mountain climber, in his book, *The White Tower*, describes his experience when he introduced his two sons, Jim, eight years old, and Bill, six years old, to mountain climbing. They started on a modest mountain in the Hudson River Highlands. Almost from the beginning, the two boys reacted differently to the climb. Jim was eager, curious, excited. Bill wanted none of it.

With each turn of the trail, Bill's pace grew slower and his expression more grimly tense. First he fell on his face and then he sat down with a grunt. He tore his jacket and scraped his knees. For a while he withheld comment, but presently the time came when he could keep his question back no longer. "Dad," he asked, raising a puzzled face, "are we doing this for fun?"

EGO

A small and a large chicken were playing on a farm. The small chicken dug a hole where the big chicken was standing so that

129

the big chicken would become a little shorter and he would appear of equal stature.

The little chicken could have achieved the same effect if he had stood on something to raise him up. The point is, however, that there are many who belittle others so that they themselves may appear to better advantage.

The five-year-old, who has just succeeded in putting a simple toy together, declares with great joy, "Daddy, I know how to do everything."

"Just ask me anything," confidently advises the twenty-year-old.

"If it's in my line, I can tell you because I know my business like an open book," says the man of forty.

"The field of human knowledge is so vast that even a specialist can hardly know all of it," admits a man of fifty.

"I have lived a good many years," confesses the man of seventy, "and I've realized that what I know is little; what I am ignorant of is immense."

One day, a sixth grade teacher asked her class, "What is here in the world today that was not here fifteen years ago?" She rightly expected the class to tell her of some of the new inventions and discoveries. One young boy raised his hand.

"All right," she asked, "what is here that was not here fifteen years ago?"

He startled her with his reply: "Me!" he said.

When two egotists meet, it results in a tie:
A vocal dead heat,
With an I for an I.

A father and son were sitting at the dinner table when the son turned and asked, "Dad, what do pro and con mean?"

"Well," replied the father. "It's like this. Pro is your convincing, unalterable argument, and con is the other fellow's contemptible drivel."

EGOTISM

"I am afraid I sin each morning," said the young lady to her minister.

"And what makes you think you are?" asked the minister.

"Because every morning when I gaze into the mirror, I think how beautiful I am."

The father confessor didn't think for more than a moment before he said, "Never fear. That isn't a sin; it's only a mistake."

⁓

A certain popular singer, the proud possessor of a very fine bass voice, confided one day to a friend that he had had a remarkable dream. "I was in a mighty choir: 5,000 sopranos, 5,000 altos, 5,000 tenors—all singing at once. Suddenly, the conductor stopped the choir and, turning to me, said, 'Not quite so loud in the bass, Mr. Jones.'"

⁓

A wise man pasted this in his hat to serve as a reminder along the way of life:

"Any man can spoil himself for himself. He can allow himself to grow so sensitive that he lives in constant pain. He can nurse his grudges until they are an intolerable burden. He can think himself insulted until he is apt to be. He can believe the world's against him until it is. He can imagine troubles until they are real. He can hold so many under suspicion that no one believes in him. He can insult his friends until they are no longer friends. He can think himself so important that no one else does. He can have such a good opinion of himself that no one else enjoys his friendship. He can become so wrapped up in himself that he becomes very small."

⁓

A snob walked into a doctor's office and said, "Doctor, I feel terrible. I want you to give me a thorough examination and tell me what is wrong with me."

"Fine," said the doctor. "But first let me ask you a few questions. Do you drink much liquor?"

"I have never touched the vile stuff," the man replied indignantly.

"Do you smoke?" the doctor continued his inquiry.

"I have never touched the filthy weed."

"Do you run around much at night?"

"Of course not! I am in bed every night by ten o'clock for a good night's rest."

"Tell me," the doctor continued, "do you have sharp pains in the head?"

"That's just it!" the snob replied. "I have sharp pains in the head."

"That's the trouble, my dear man," the doctor advised. "Your halo is on too tight!"

EMPATHY

A woman once visited her analyst about some domestic problems. She said, "I wouldn't come to bother you, but all this has given me a splitting headache. I couldn't stand it anymore."

The analyst listened to her problems. After twenty minutes of steady talking she smiled and said, "Doctor, it's wonderful. My headache has disappeared!"

The analyst sighed and answered, "No, my dear, your headache didn't disappear. Now I have it."

In his book, *The Bond Between Us*, Dr. Loomis relates a significant personal experience. Shortly after he settled in California, his wife died of pneumonia. Within the next few days, three doctors came, individually, to console him. Each of them gave him a signed blank check, and told him to fill in any amount he needed and to return the sum whenever he became affluent enough to do so. In recalling the incident, Dr. Loomis writes: "This act in a way prompted every decent thing I have done in all the years since."

A minister visited the home of one of his wealthier members. It was cold outside so he came dressed in his warm fur-lined overcoat. The minister was welcomed into the parlor, and was asked to remove his coat. He was then served a cup of hot tea. They talked a while and then the minister prepared to leave. He put on his warm overcoat and beckoned to his host to escort him into the outer hall, as he wanted to say something to him in the greatest privacy. The host, thinking that this would only take a minute, did not bother to put on his own overcoat although he was going out into the unheated hall. The minister proceeded to engage in small talk, much to the discomfort of the host. He became so cold,

132

his teeth started to shake. But the minister continued with his small talk. Several times the host asked the minister to come back into the parlor, but each time the minister replied that it would only take another minute.

Finally, the rich man said: "If you do not tell me what you want I'll freeze to death. I'm so cold my blood has almost stopped flowing in my veins."

"I'll tell you what I came for," replied the minister. "I need $50 to buy coal for some poor people."

"Here is the money, but couldn't you tell me this inside? Why did you have to take me out into the cold hall?"

"Inside, perhaps you would not have realized what it means to be cold. Now, you too have a taste of it," replied the wise minister.

A soft-hearted man who invariably suffered along with those who were troubled as if their problems were his own, was asked by a curious friend where he drew the strength to participate so intimately in another's sorrows.

The good man replied: "I see something of myself in everyone. Therefore, I do not merely share the troubles of another; his sorrows become my own, and have you ever seen a man who is not made strong in the face of personal sorrows?"

A child had to walk past a haunted house every evening. Filled with fear, each trip was an agonizing experience. His elders sought to give him courage. One gave him a good-luck charm to ward off the ghosts. Another asked the city council to erect a street light on the corner. Another said earnestly, "It is sinful to be afraid. Trust God and be brave." Each one gave the child advice, but held himself aloof. But one with genuine understanding said, "I know what it is to be afraid. I will walk with you past the house." This person did a great deal to remove the fear by lifting it from the child's shoulders and placing part of it on his own.

The rabbi was late for the Day of Atonement service. The congregation could not understand how he could be tardy on this most important day. The time came to recite the prayers and still he was not there, so they began without him.

What had happened to the rabbi? He had started for the synagogue and on the way had overtaken another worshipper. But the latter was lame and could not walk fast. The rabbi knew he should hurry; the congregation was waiting for him. Nonetheless he walked beside the lame man, matching paces with him. The rabbi knew that if he were to hurry forward in great strides he would have left the lame man behind, overwhelmed by a feeling of inferiority, weighed down by a feeling of overpowering loneliness. So the lame man and the rabbi arrived late—but together.

When a painter asked Albert Einstein to sit for a portrait, the famous mathematician replied, "No, no, no, I do not have time."

"But I desperately need the money I'll get for the picture," the painter confessed.

"Well, that's another story," Einstein replied. "Of course I'll sit."

William Phelps Lyons related how he became aware of how many people walk with crutches. After an automobile accident, he spent several days hobbling about on crutches. For the first time in his life he took notice of how many others were similarly afflicted.

ENEMIES

President Lincoln was once taken to task for his attitude toward his enemies. "Why do you try to make friends of them?" asked an associate. "You know they will only be traitors. You should try to destroy them."

"Am I not destroying my enemies," Lincoln gently replied, "when I make them my friends? And a friend is never a traitor."

ENVIRONMENT

A maker of violins searched all his life for wood that would be best suited for making instruments which produced a certain beautiful, haunting resonance. He found what he was looking for in the wood gathered from the timberline of a great mountain range, the last stand of trees growing 12,000 feet above sea level. Up there, where the winds blew so fiercely and steadily that the

134

bark had no chance to form, where the branches all pointed one way, and where a tree in order to live, had to remain bowed down all through its life, grew the world's most resonant wood. The trees survived because they had learned to overcome the difficulties and dangers of their environment.

A forest ranger was walking along a city street with his metropolitan brother. "Did you hear that bird?" he suddenly asked.

"In this city traffic, how could you hear anything?" was the immediate reply.

They continued to walk, when suddenly the city brother stopped. "Why did you stop?" asked the ranger.

"I thought I heard the sound of a coin dropping to the ground," was the reply.

"In this busy noisy traffic?" marvelled the ranger.

It is true that each one heard what his ears had been trained to hear.

When Leonardo Da Vinci was painting his famous picture of the "Last Supper," he took as a model an angelic-faced young man who sang in the choir of the Milan Cathedral. Years later, the painter was seeking a model who could pose for a sinner. One day he came across a man in the streets of Rome whose features seemed to portray greed and vice. He asked him to pose. When they both got to the studio the man looked familiar and da Vinci asked him for his name.

"Oh, you know me," was the answer. "I posed for your picture of the 'Last Supper.'"

ENVY

An incident is related in Greek history of a youth who so distinguished himself in the Olympic games that his fellow citizens raised a statue to perpetuate his victory. This statue excited such intense envy in the heart of another youth whom he had defeated, that he decided one night to destroy it. After prolonged effort, he succeeded in removing it from its pedestal, but then it fell and crushed him to death.

A man once died leaving his possessions to be divided equally between his two sons. During the old man's lifetime the sons had worked happily together, but as soon as it came to dividing their father's estate each was afraid that the other would get more than his fair share, and they wrangled and bickered from morning till night. At last they sought the advice of an old friend of their father. "How would you advise us? How can we be sure that each will get an equal share?" they asked.

"You must pull down the house, and count the bricks, one by one," he replied. "You must saw the furniture in half, chop the cows and the horses in two, break the plates in half, cut up the sheets and blankets. . . ."

As the old man spoke the brothers were ashamed. They saw that their suspicious natures were leading them to destruction.

There is no doubt that envy in one's heart bars joy from entering. A man was out walking in the park on a beautiful warm summer day. As he was walking, he met a friend who remarked, "It's a glorious day, isn't it!"

"It sure is," was the immediate answer.

"Then why do you look so glum?"

"Because my enemies are enjoying it too."

The person who envies others is not to be envied. The trouble is that envy is a progressive disease, and if it is not stamped out in its early stages, it will surely grow to incurable proportions.

There was once a woman who, one may say, "envied" herself to death. She always wished to have at least a little of what others had. She even envied her own children. Soon this poison took hold of her completely; it became the master of her every waking hour and brought unrest to her in her dreams. She really did not know what she was envying because she could only imagine what others possessed.

One day, at a friend's home, she was introduced to the friend's niece, a young lady with large, beautiful eyes. The woman, who was already on in years, had to depend on glasses to help her vision. "How I detest wearing eye-glasses," she confided to the young girl. "I wish I had eyes like yours."

"How I wish I could wear eyeglasses," replied the girl. "You see," she continued, "my eyes are completely sightless."

An onion once decided that it was not an onion at all, but a tulip bulb. And so it boasted loudly to the other onions that it was better than they. It would grow into a gorgeous tulip.

Eventually it was planted, it grew, and it proved to be a very nice little onion. After this it became the laughing-stock of the garden, and was so humiliated that it drooped and died at an early age. Thus it lost its chance to be a superior sort of onion, forgetting in its fruitless ambition that there is a need in the world for both onions and tulips.

There is a story of a frustrated sea captain and his envious chief engineer. The engineer and the captain had been arguing right along as to which of them was more important to the ship. Being unable to agree, they resorted to the altogether impractical plan of swapping places.

The chief ascended to the bridge, and the skipper dived into the engine room. After a couple of hours, the captain suddenly appeared on the deck covered with oil and soot. One eye was swollen shut, and he was very much the worse for wear. "Chief," he called, wildly beckoning with a monkey wrench, "you'll have to come down at once. I can't make her go!"

"Of course you can't," replied the chief, calmly removing his pipe from his mouth; "She's ashore!"

There is a tale of a fisherman who was in his small boat on the Mediterranean. Gazing at the shore, he is overawed by the splendor of a prince's magnificent palace. Just then, the prince appears and comes out on his balcony. From afar, the fisherman envies him, saying, "Oh, how fortunate is the prince! He has such a beautiful palace, the most delicious foods to eat, and all kinds of servants to wait on him. How I wish that I were a prince and not a fisherman!"

At that selfsame moment, the prince on the balcony espying the fisherman far down below on the water, observes, "Oh, how I envy that fisherman! He has no problems or responsibilities at all. How I wish I could go out in a small boat and just relax with a fishing pole in my hand!"

"How can a man achieve happiness?" a philosopher was once asked. "I'll explain with a parable," he answered. And then he related this story:

A group of blind men were conversing quietly with one another when someone approached them and said, "Here is a gold ring. Divide it among yourselves."

Each of the blind men thought that the one standing next to him had received the ring. Soon a fight started.

"How foolish they are," said the spokesman. "They are blind and do not know that they are fighting for nothing because I did not give the ring to any of them."

"We, the living," continued the philosopher, "are like that group of blind men. Each of us thinks that our neighbor possesses the golden ring called happiness. Only contentment is true happiness."

Envy is the daughter of pride, the author of murder and revenge, the beginner of secret sedition, the perpetual tormenter of virtue. Envy is the filthy slime of the soul; a venom, a poison, a quicksand which consumes the flesh and dries up the marrow of the bones.

The benevolent have the advantage of the envious. The envious is tormented not only by all the ill that befalls himself, but by all the good that happens to another. The benevolent man is the better prepared to bear his own calamities unruffled because of the complacency and serenity he has secured from contemplating the prosperity of those around him.

EPITAPH

After recovering from a severe illness, a man bought two grave plots for himself and his wife. He then ordered a double tombstone, at the same time instructing the engraver to inscribe the following on his wife's side of the stone: "She died of an insatiable desire for things."

"And what shall I inscribe on your side?" asked the engraver.

His answer was: "On my side of the stone you will inscribe, "He died trying to provide them.'"

The following was found on a tombstone:

Remember man as you pass by
As you are now, so once was I;
As I am now, so you shall be;
Remember this and follow me.

Underneath someone wrote:

> To allow you I'll not consent
> Until I know which way you went.

~~~

EQUALITY

Diogenes was looking attentively at a large collection of human bones piled one upon another. Alexander the Great took note of what was going on and asked the philosopher what he was looking for.

"I am searching for the bones of your father," said Diogenes, "but I cannot distinguish them from those of his slaves."

~~~

EVIL

A Japanese peasant went to heaven, and the first thing he saw was a long shelf with something very strange looking upon it.

"What is that?" he asked. "Is it something to make soup of?" (The Japanese are very fond of soup).

"No," was the reply, "those are ears. They belong to people who, when they lived on earth, heard what they ought to do in order to be good, but they did not pay any attention to it, so when they died their ears came to heaven, but the rest of their bodies could not."

After a while, the peasant saw another shelf with very odd looking things on it.

"What is that?" he asked again. "Is that something to make soup of?"

"No," he was told, "these are tongues. They once belonged to people in the world who told people how to live and how to do good, but they themselves never did as they told others to do. So, when they died, their tongues came to heaven, but the rest of their bodies could not."

~~~

Two clergymen were walking along a river bank when they came upon a tree which had been blown down in a recent gale. It was a mighty tree, tall, substantial, with large outspreading roots and abundant foliage. It must have been the growth of a greater part of a century; and anyone who had seen it would have said there was no cause why it should not have remained standing a century longer. Upon examining the tree, the clergymen found it had been snapped off just above the roots; that there was only an outer shell of good wood, and the heart was rotten. Apparently, the decay had been going on for years.

"A tree never breaks off in this way, unless there has been previous decay," said one.

"A very suggestive lesson for us and our people," remarked the second. "Men seldom fall all at once. They begin to fall through the years."

~~~~~

When David Shlome, Rabbi of Sorocco, served there as spiritual leader he often criticized the members of that community for their lack of religious zeal, their laxity in matters of charity, and considered Sorocco the worst city of all.

Eventually he left to settle in Israel. Every man, woman, and child escorted him to the outskirts of the city as he departed, and not a living soul was left in the city.

The rabbi then turned around to face the city of Sorocco:

"What a beautiful city!" he exclaimed enthusiastically.

"What?" exclaimed some of the elders, "You always claimed it was the worst."

"True," replied the rabbi, "but now that all of you have left the city, it is, indeed, a most beautiful city."

~~~~~

EXAGGERATION

A Scotch giant once journeyed to Ireland, to destroy a certain Irish giant who loved to brag.

The Irish giant looked out of his window, saw the Scotch giant moving in his direction, and was frightened by his size and tough appearance.

With rare presence of mind, the Irishman climbed into his baby's carriage, his feet hanging out.

The Scotch giant approached the house, saw the big pair of feet hanging out of the baby's carriage, and said to himself, "If the Irish giant has a baby that size, the old man must be a whale. Maybe there is something to those stories I have been hearing." And with that he turned away and went back to Scotland.

~~~~~

EXAMPLE

"I never want to catch you lying again," cried the mother, who had just caught her son in an obvious untruth. As she lectured to him about the evil of lying, her phone rang.

"Please answer it," she told her son, "and if it's Mrs. Murphy, tell her I am not at home."

＊

When Theodore Roosevelt was a boy, his father said to him, "Theodore, do you know what a thoroughbred is? Well, I'll show you. See those two dogs? Well, this one"—and he picked up an ugly looking low-bred pup and gave him a gentle shaking, causing yelps and barks and howls to pierce the air—"this is not a thoroughbred." Then he picked up a fine looking, handsome dog and shook him hard, but not a sound came forth. "There," said the father, "that is your thoroughbred."

"Be a thoroughbred, my boy, and whatever happens, don't squeal."

＊

One winter day, a man found it necessary to visit a neighbor who lived beyond a steep and rugged mountain. He had climbed the dangerous trial for several minutes, through the drifted snow and along the edge of a precipice, when he heard a voice call: "Be careful, daddy. I'm walking in your steps."

＊

A little boy, with his parents, moved into a house overlooking a deep ravine. One day, because of a reprimand, the little boy became very angry with his mother. In order to give vent to his feelings, he ran to the edge of the ravine and shouted as loud as he could: "I hate you!" Almost immediately there came rumbling back at him an angry, hollow voice: "I hate you, I hate you!"

The little boy was terrified and, running back to his mother, sobbed that there was a wicked man in the ravine who hated him and wanted to harm him. The wise mother took the little boy by the hand and led him back to the ravine. Then in a tender, pleasant voice she called: "I love you, I love you." A kind, happy voice echoed back the same sweet words which she had just spoken.

＊

A crab said to her son: "Why do you walk so one-sided, my child? It is far better to walk straight ahead."

141

The young crab replied: "Quite true, mother. If you will show me how to walk properly, I will certainly try to follow."

Example is better than lecture.

—————

EXAMINATIONS

An English teacher used the Honor System when he gave examinations. At the end of an examination, he would require that each student write and sign an "honesty pledge." With tongue in cheek, one student wrote: "I didn't get no help on this here exam, and the good Lord knows I couldn't give none."

—————

EXCUSE

On hearing the excuses given by the Russians for not favoring certain Balkan measures in the United Nations, Warren Austin was reminded of the story about the Vermont farmer whose neighbor wanted to borrow an axe.

"Sorry, Jim," said the farmer, "I've got to shave tonight."

Later, his wife took him to task, saying, "Why did you give Jim such a silly excuse?"

"If you don't want to do a thing," the farmer replied, "one excuse is as good as another."

—————

In a small town in Europe, there lived a rather wealthy man. An old maid also lived in this same town. Unfortunately she was somewhat less than pretty, with pockmarked face, flattened nose, and twisted mouth. The rich man was a skinflint and had never been known to give donations for any purpose whatsoever. When asked for a contribution, his standard reply was that he would only contribute to a dowry for some poor maiden.

Naturally, the citizens of the town were more than a little piqued at this miser and decided to "fix" him. They searched the entire town for eligible bachelors, found an elderly tailor, and promised him a big dowry if he would consent to marry the homely spinster. Upon his consent they thought they had the old miser. He would finally have to make good his promise to contribute towards the dowry.

A committee hastened to the wealthy man's home and reminded him of his promise about the dowry. He listened to them, questioned them closely, and finally informed them that he would not give them a penny.

"Why?" the delegation asked in rage.

"Because I don't like the match," the miser promptly retorted.

⁓

EXPERIENCE

Turner, the famous artist, once invited Charles Kingsley into his studio to see a picture of a storm at sea. Kingsley was full of admiration for the reality of the painting. "How did you do it, Turner?" he asked.

The artist's answer taught a lesson: "I wished to paint a storm at sea, so I went to the coast of Holland, and engaged a fisherman to take me out in his boat in the next storm. The storm was brewing, and I went down to his boat and asked him to bind me to its mast. Then he drove the boat out into the teeth of the storm. The storm was so furious that I longed to lie down in the bottom of the boat and allow it to blow over me. But I could not: I was bound to the mast. Not only did I see that storm and feel it, but it blew itself into me, till I became part of the storm. And then I came back and painted that picture."

⁓

A firm was interested in filling an executive position. The firm bypassed the man next in line and selected an outsider to fill the post. The man who had seniority was so upset that he went to talk to the president. In very strained tones he said, "But I have had fifteen years of experience with this firm."

The president replied, "That is not so. You have had one year of experience fifteen times."

⁓

As a king and his officers passed the customs house, he asked them to stop and pay the usual tariff.

"Your Majesty," they cried in astonishment, "all that is collected belongs to you; why then give what they will soon return to your treasury?"

"Because," answered the king, "I wish travelers to learn from what I do, and I want them to see how I detest dishonesty."

⁓

Mrs. A. sought her neighbor's aid in solving a very vexing problem. "How do you get your children to go to church on Sunday?" she asked.

143

"I don't," replied the neighbor.

"What do you mean?" asked Mrs. A.

Whereupon the neighbor exclaimed: "I don't get them to go. I take them!"

~~~~~

A man had caught his young daughter telling a lie. "I'm surprised at you," he said. "When I was your age, I never thought of telling a lie."

She looked at him inquiringly. "How old were you when you started to think of it, Dad?" she asked.

~~~~~

A young rabbi about to be ordained stated that at one period in his life he was nearly an unbeliever. "But," said he, "there was one argument in favor of Judaism, which I could never refute— the consistent conduct of my father."

~~~~~

EVOLUTION

A rather talkative young man had much to say to a clergyman at a dinner they were both attending. He droned on and on about Darwin's *Origin of the Species*. At one point he said, "I can't see what difference it would make if my grandfather was an ape."

"I can't see that it would make any difference to you either," said the clergyman, "but it must have made a great difference to your grandmother."

~~~~~

FAITH

An old preacher once told some of his Sunday School students the Bible lesson he would be using on the following Sunday morning.

The boys decided to have some fun. During the week, they located the preacher's pulpit Bible. They found the chapter and glued the connecting pages together.

When Sunday morning came, and the preacher started quoting Scripture, he began reading on the bottom of one page:

When Noah was 120 years old, he took unto himself a wife, who was . . .—then turning the stuck-together pages he continued—140 cubits long, 40 cubits wide, built of gopher wood, and covered with pitch inside and out.

144

The preacher was naturally puzzled at this. It didn't sound familiar, and so he read it again and verified it. Then he turned to the congregation and said:

"My friends: This is the first time I ever met this in the Bible, but I accept it as evidence of the assertion that we are fearfully and wonderfully made."

In Ben-Gurion's book, *Ben-Gurion Looks at the Bible,* he discusses the ancient port city of Eilat.

In 1934, when Ben-Gurion visited it for the first time, it was not called Eilat, but *Umm Rashrash.* As he contemplated the area, he became convinced that it was extremely important for the Jewish people to acquire this port area. He foresaw its great significance for the future of a Jewish state.

Louis Brandeis was visiting Palestine that year—in 1934— and Ben-Gurion went to see him. Brandeis was not only a distinguished member of the U.S. Supreme Court, but a very wealthy man as well. Ben-Gurion describes how he went to Brandeis and presented him with a carefully worded memorandum in which he wrote that in the near future Eilat will play an economic role greater than the one which it played during the biblical period.

"It is important that we establish a pioneering Jewish settlement here. It will not bring a profit, and it might cost $100,000," Ben-Gurion explained.

Brandeis had no sooner finished reading the memorandum, when he took his pen, and wrote a check, and said: "Here is $100,000."

Ben-Gurion was flabbergasted, and quickly protested, "Mr. Justice, I didn't come to ask you for money. I came to get moral support for this matter."

"I want to be the first," said Brandeis, "to help stake a claim on this important spot."

The Brandeis gesture was an act of faith that brought to Ben Gurion's life a new momentum that was beyond measure.

Perhaps the most beautiful reply to "What is faith?" was given by a young child who answered, "Faith is doing God's will, and asking no questions."

An infidel on his deathbed felt himself adrift, terribly troubled by surges of doubt and uncertainty. Some of his friends urged him to hold on to the end. He replied, "I have no objection to holding on, but will you tell me what am I to hold on to?"

~~~

A father and his young son were making their way through a dense forest. Their only light was a lantern which was held by the boy.

"Father," said the young boy, "let us turn back. The light shines but for a short distance."

"No," replied the father. "Let us proceed as far as we can see, and the light will continue to shine in advance of us."

~~~

A young boy was standing along the edge of the river. A man approached him and inquired, "What are you waiting for?"

Without hesitation the youth replied, "I am waiting for that steamboat to pick me up."

"Foolish boy," said the man, "boats don't stop everywhere. You must wait at the pier." The boy did not reply, and to the amazement of the stranger, the boat turned to pick up the youngster.

"You see!" exclaimed the boy as he boarded the boat. "My father is the captain."

~~~

A young child once taught the significance of faith to her mother. Both mother and daughter were preparing to retire for the night, and both were a bit frightened of the darkness. After the lights were extinguished the child caught a glimpse of the moon outside the window.

"Mother," she whispered, "is the moon God's light?"

"Yes," replied the mother, "God's lights are always shining."

The young child was silent for a moment and then asked, "Will God blow out His lights and go to sleep?"

"No, my child," replied the mother, "God never goes to sleep."

"Well, so long as God is awake, I am not afraid," said the child.

~~~

A little boy stood in the sun, on the edge of an open trap-door to a cellar. From above, nothing was visible in the cellar, only blackness.

Up from the cellar came the voice of the boy's father: "Jump down son, I'll catch you!"

"But I cannot see you, father."

"Never mind, I can see you! Jump!"

Summoning his courage, the boy jumped, and in a moment felt himself held safely, with his father's arms around him.

When the fall of the Confederacy was at hand, General Grant invited Lincoln to come down to visit him at his headquarters at City Point on the James River. As they sat that night around the campfire, Lincoln related some of his characteristic anecdotes, and then sat in silence, looking into the fire. Grant looked up and said, "Mr. President, did you at any time doubt the final success of the cause?"

Straightening himself up in his camp chair, and leaning forward and lifting his hand by way of emphasis, Lincoln replied with great solemnity, "Never, for a moment!"

The Human Comedy, by William Saroyan, describes, in a very touching and dramatic scene, little Ulysses standing at the railroad tracks waving to the passengers of a moving train. He goes unnoticed by the passengers and his gesture receives no recognition. His spirits fall and his arm becomes heavy as it falls to his side. But just when his spirits are at their lowest ebb, a Negro hobo, perched on the platform of the last car, sees him and waves back to him smilingly. He even sings out a message to him, telling him that he is going back home.

Throughout his life Ulysses thinks back upon that moment when despondency was turned once again into hope through the smile and song of the Negro hobo who restored his faith in human beings.

A young soldier of Protestant faith was in emergency need of a chaplain. Since the Protestant chaplain was on leave, the Catholic chaplain went to see the boy. The soldier was somewhat anxious and apprehensive and said, "Father, I appreciate your coming to see me, but I want you to understand that I am a Protestant. I hope you won't try to change my faith."

With a gentle smile, the Catholic chaplain replied, "My son, I don't want to change your faith. I want your faith to change you."

During a particularly hot summer, a group of farmers met in their church to pray for rain. After the services, a little girl asked her father if the people truly expected that it would rain. "Of course," replied her father. "Otherwise, we wouldn't be here."

"But Daddy," she protested, "how come no one came to church with an umbrella?"

A wife once taught her despondent husband a lesson in faith. When he came home, he found her dressed completely in mourning black.

"What's wrong?" he asked.

"Don't you know? God in heaven is dead."

"What nonsense!" he exclaimed. "How can God die? He is immortal and will live through all eternity."

"If that is so," she answered quietly, "don't go about so helpless and discouraged."

A man was being conducted by a guide over a dangerous Alpine trail. At length they came to a place where a great rock jutted out over the precipice, leaving only the fragment of the pathway. The guide laid hold of the rock with one hand, put his other hand down on what was left to the trail, his arm extending over the abyss. He told the other man to step on his hand and forearm and thus pass around the rock in safety. The man hesitated and was afraid, but the guide said, "Do not fear to stand on my hand. That hand has never yet lost a man!"

A young child's doll was broken. As she cried over the tiny pieces, she said to her brother, "I'm going to pray to God to put the pieces together."

"Do you expect God to answer your prayer?" he asked.

"You will see that God will answer," she predicted.

A few hours later, when the brother returned he demanded of the little girl, "Well, has God answered?"

"Yes," she replied, pointing to the pieces. "He said, 'No.' "

Some years back, a statesman who had responsibility for world affairs could not sleep at night. His servant found him pacing the floor. When the disturbed servant asked what he could do, the statesman shook his head, and continued with his pacing. "It is

148

the terrific problems of the world that keep me awake. You can do nothing about them," he finally said.

"Sir," asked the servant, "who watched over the world before you came into it?"

"Why, God, of course."

"And, sir, will God watch over the world after you have gone out of it?"

"Certainly," the statesman replied.

"Then, sir, why don't you let Him watch over it just long enough for you to get a good night's sleep?"

The statesman had a good sleep that night.

A young man undertook a difficult trip each week to visit his priest. "What benefit can you possibly derive from these audiences with your priest?" a scornful and doubting friend asked.

"When I come from my priest, I know that there is a God in the world," the young man replied.

"Nonsense," the friend rejoined. "Ask a person of any faith, and he will tell you the same thing: that he believes in God."

"Anyone can tell me that he believes in God, but when I come from my priest, I *know* there is a God," said the young man with deep feeling.

A frail old lady continued to work as a seamstress although she was well on in years. Her friends marveled at her patient endurance.

One asked, "How do you manage to work so steadily?"

"Often," she replied, "I get up in the morning feeling exhausted. It seems impossible to get through the day's work. But I'm like a street-car before it is connected with the power wire. Upon rising I connect with power from on high. I pray and put my hand in God's hand. I feel His power surging through me. Then I go about my daily business."

The woman was showing a beautiful, massive piece of family silver. As she took it from the cupboard where it had been kept, she apologized, saying, "Dreadfully tarnished! I can't keep it bright unless I use it." How true this is of faith. It cannot be tucked away for some emergency. It cannot be kept bright unless it is constantly used.

149

There was once a man whose faith in the goodness of man remained unshaken in spite of his awareness of the unwholesome state of the world.

"Give me any young man who is immersed in the sins and corruption of this world of ours, and I assure you I will make sin and idleness so obnoxious to him that even the mere thought of a sinful act would sicken him. It requires but time and patience to find the proper approach, and you will eventually strike a sympathetic chord—even in an apparently bad person.

In a country known for its intolerance, an edict was issued to round up and arrest all who observed religions other than the one approved and observed by the sovereign of the state. Arrest for religious reasons meant certain death.

One of the men who was arrested was very old and wise, and strictly faithful to his beliefs. When one of the arresting officers asked him, "Does it pay to lose such a beautiful world because of your orthodox beliefs?" the sage looked at him and replied: "I am quite undisturbed by this. Whereas you believe in one world and many gods, I believe in one God and many worlds. So, if I lose this world, I am sure to proceed to a better one."

A little boy in a race found himself falling further and further behind his competitors. Suddenly his lips began to move with great regularity, his legs picked up speed, and he won. Afterwards, when someone asked what he was mumbling about, he replied: "Oh, I've been talking to God. I told Him, 'Lord, you pick 'em up and I'll put them down. . . . You pick 'em up and I'll put them down. . . .'"

It is told that during one of Napoleon's conquests, he entered a certain town on a day which happened to be *Tisha B'av*—which commemorates the destruction of the Temple in Jerusalem. He found hundreds of Jews sitting on the floor of the synagogue intoning tearful prayers. When he was told the cause of these lamentations, he is said to have remarked: "A people who, after so many centuries, can still shed tears over the loss of its land and the destruction of its Temple, is bound to regain it some day."

150

A grocer complained to a friend that one of his neighbors had opened a grocery store on the same block and was ruining his business.

The friend said to him: "If you have ever seen a horse drink water from a pool, you must have noticed that he stamps with his hoof in the water. He does this because when he bends his head to drink, he sees his shadow in the water. He thinks that his image is another horse drinking and because he fears that there will not be sufficient water for him, he chases the other horse by stamping his foot. The horse is actually afraid of his own shadow, and if he had more sense he would know that there was enough water for many horses."

As the grocer listened, the man continued: "You are behaving like the horse. You, too, are afraid of a rival. Be assured that God will provide every man with a livelihood in accordance with His will and the man's merits."

A learned man was once asked to quote the most meaningful verse that he had found in the entire Bible. He thought for a moment and then replied:"And it came to pass." Those who heard his reply were startled. Other learned men in history had been asked this same question and had picked verses like: "Thou shalt love thy neighbor as thyself," or, "Have we not all one father?"

"Why did you pick such a simple statement like, 'And it came to pass?' " asked one of his friends.

"I picked it," answered the learned man, "because whenever I am in trouble, whenever sadness enters my life, I think of this phrase and it helps me. It encourages me to believe that my trouble came only to pass; it didn't come to stay. And this gives me hope to carry on. It helps me take the bad in life with the good. It helps me pick out the good parts of life and enjoy them even when I am surrounded by sorrow.

"I know that the sorrow came, but I also know that it will pass, and that I will still be here then, and must continue to live."

A man was hurrying to catch a train. On the way, he met his minister leisurely strolling along towards the railroad station.

"Aren't you taking the 5:11 to Chicago?" the speeding one called.

"Plenty of time, plenty of time," counseled the minister. He pulled out his watch. "See? We have 20 minutes."

So the two proceeded at a calm pace and arrived at the station to learn that their train had already pulled out. The minister shook his head. "I had the greatest faith in that watch," he replied sadly.

"Yes," replied the other man, "but what use is faith without works?"

⁓

Two boys were conversing about Elijah's ascent in the chariot of fire.

"Wouldn't you be afraid to ride in such a chariot?" asked the first boy.

"No," was the immediate reply, "not if God drove."

⁓

A story is told of a famous preacher who met one of his followers unexpectedly in the market place. The disciple, who was a moderately successful businessman, was rather embarrassed by this chance encounter. His rapid steps had shortened his breath and covered his face with prominent beads of perspiration. He seemed to be deeply upset by disturbing business matters, and was hardly in a mood for leisurely conversation. When the clergyman asked him where and why he was running so breathlessly, he haltingly replied, "To make a living, of course."

The preacher philosophically retorted, "How do you know, my dear man, that your living lies in the direction toward which you are running? Perhaps, it is in the opposite direction, and you are actually running away from it."

⁓

One evening, a father and his young daughter were returning from a neighbor's house. This was the first time that the girl had ever been outdoors in the night, and she was afraid. "I can't seem to see our house, Papa. I don't know the way. Where are we going?" she asked anxiously.

"I see the road and I know the way," he replied. "If you hold my hand, I will take care of you."

Comforting herself, she said, "Yes, you know the way. You will take care of me because you love me."

After this, with a new-found faith, she grasped her father's hand a little tighter and trudged cheerfully onward to wherever he led her.

⁓

All of us try to get as much out of life as we can. William Allen White once said: "I have never been bored an hour in my life. I get up every morning wondering what new strange glamorous thing is going to happen and it happens at fairly regular intervals. Lady luck has been good to me and I fancy she has been good to every one. Only some people are dour, and when she gives them the 'come hither' with her eyes, they look down or turn away and lift an eyebrow. But me, I give her the wink and away we go."

In the days of sailing ships, a young, inexperienced sailor was sent aloft in a storm to disentangle a broken sail. In spite of the raging wind, the young man climbed up swiftly and did the job. When it was time to descend, he looked down and saw the vessel tossing and rolling in the angry sea.

Suddenly, he was drained of courage. He felt dizzy and faint. Looking down to the mate below he yelled, "I'm going to fall."

The mate, who had spent many years at sea, yelled above the storm, "Don't look down boy! Look up!"

The young sailor did just that and, with renewed courage, came down safely.

FALSEHOOD

A man approached a group of boys sitting in a circle with a small dog in the center. When he came up to them, he asked, "What are you doing to the dog?"

One little fellow answered, "Whoever tells the biggest lie, wins the dog."

"Oh," said the man, "I am surprised at you boys, for when I was young like you I never told a lie."

There was a silence for a while, until one of the boys shouted, "Hand him the dog!"

When Aristotle was asked what a man could gain by telling a falsehood, he replied, "Never to be credited when he speaks the truth."

A prominent politician once said: "The greatest struggle within me is to overcome the tendency to give false facts, to color stories to suit my own purposes. I find it increasingly difficult to carry the weight of the guilt I feel over having turned fact into

153

fable. The worst of it is that the truth must be locked within yourself; the truth that you have been living with untruth. I promise myself that henceforth I shall not barter my soul for glory."

A sage once stated: "When the human being will have purged his very soul of falsehood, he will discover a paved road where he will find it simple enough to resist all other evil temptations.

"The first lie paves the necessary way for further lies. The first lie gives mental anguish, but an accumulation of falsehoods leads to emotional gastritis and fear of discovery. The liar forgets the meaning of truth and soon enough gets to believe that the entire universe lives by standards comparable only to his. Since he cannot believe anything or anyone, his greatest frustration is the belief that everyone is deceiving him. This is a ridiculous contradiction on the part of one who can deny the existence of the sun when it is blazing in its awesome splendor at noon.

"The saddest thing of all is the spiritual myopia suffered by liars. They live in fear of discovery by man today but seldom, if ever, fear inevitable discovery by God."

A preacher once spoke quite sharply about the sin of false weights and measures. There was a simple milkman in the crowd, and the preacher's words made a strong impression on him. He made up his mind that from that moment on he would not put a drop of water into the milk he sold.

Some time later, the same milkman approached the preacher and complained that people had stopped buying his milk with the complaint that the milk was not as good as before.

"You see," said the preacher, "the world is so full of falsehood that men and women can hardly recall what truth is like."

FAME

A friend once said to Cato the Elder, "It's a scandal and disgrace that no statue has been erected to you in Rome! I am going to form a committee to see that this is done."

"No," said Cato, "I would rather have people ask, 'Why isn't there a statue to Cato?' than 'Why is there one?' "

Once, at a dinner, a woman said to Lord Northcliffe, "Thackery awoke one morning and found himself famous."

"When that morning dawned," Lord Northcliffe answered, "Thackery had been writing eight hours a day for fifteen years. The man who wakes up and finds himself famous, madam, has not been asleep."

The heights by great men reached and kept
Were not attained by sudden flight,
But they while their companions slept
Were toiling upward in the night.

—Henry W. Longfellow

FAMILY

An active communal worker once described a unique personal experience. He said: "I finally hit a jackpot last night, something I have been trying to do for weeks. I was just lucky, I guess. There was no meeting to attend, so I stayed home. For those who are not so fortunate, I can report that it is a great experience. You get to play with the children, listen to the radio, talk with your wife, read, and fall asleep in your favorite chair. I repeat: "It's great. Someday I hope to have enough time to take up membership in the organization known as *The Home*."

Evelyn Millis Duval, author and family-life counselor, writes: "Our families are built much as a good orchestra is built, not with every member playing the same instrument or the same notes, but with every member knowing his own instrument and blending it with the others, achieving a harmony that is based upon difference. This is the kind of harmony that is our crying need today in the modern world."

"What do you think makes a happy family?" asked a teacher of a young teen-ager.

"A happy family," he replied, "reminds me of a big league baseball team, with Mom pitching, Dad catching, and the children fielding, with everyone taking a turn at bat."

A man who shows no pity for his fellow man gives ample reason to question his parental lineage. Character-building is the greatest part of our education and begins from the moment a mother entwines her arms around her baby. Till the day we die, we must continue to polish and groom this part of us, our character. And when a person is evil, it is not uncommon for others to say, "What kind of upbringing did this man have?" It is also the usual thing to hear people say about a good person, "He must come from a very nice family."

FASTING

The wealthy do not know the pangs of hunger that share the daily lives of the poor. Once a year, on the Day of Atonement, when fasting is required, the well-fed wealthy Jew experiences the hunger pains which a poor man feels during the entire year.

On the morning of the Day of Atonement, a wealthy man went to services. Before the morning was over, he began to feel ill, and by the afternoon the man, a complete wreck, bellowed for a doctor to be summoned, and pleaded with the people around him to help him, for he was dying.

A poor man in the congregation walked over to the rich man and asked him to describe the symptoms he felt. Between groans, the wealthy man managed to explain what he felt, and then the poor man said: "The symptoms you describe are nothing more than hunger pains; a malady to the rich but a companion to the poor."

FATE

The German-Jewish philosopher, Moses Mendelssohn, was an intimate friend of Frederick the Great.

Once, while strolling aimlessly on Unter den Linden, the chief thoroughfare of Berlin, the king met his learned friend. After saluting each other in an amiable fashion, the monarch asked his Jewish subject where he was going.

"I don't know," Mendelssohn replied quite truthfully.

The eyes of the mighty ruler flashed with quick anger. Friend or not, this man could not trifle with His Majesty. "I will ask you just once more," he growled ominously. "Where are you going?"

"I'm sorry, Your Highness, but I don't know."

The king at once ordered his guards to arrest the "insolent" man, but before the day was over, he relented. He visited the eminent philosopher in his cell.

"Look here, Mendelssohn," he scolded, "what was the idea of trifling with your king in such a frivolous manner?"

"I didn't mean to trifle with you, Your Majesty," explained the scholar ruefully. "I really did not know where I was going. It certainly must be clear to you by this time. Earlier today I set out for a simple stroll and I landed in jail. What more proof do you need?"

FATHER

"What is it," asked the teacher who had been discussing the weather in different seasons, "that comes in like a lion and goes out like a lamb?"

A small girl raised her hand and volunteered, "Father."

Joey had asked his father a few questions from his history homework which his father could not answer. The father, wanting to get back to his newspaper, said, "Joey, I'd like to know what would have happened if I'd asked as many questions when I was a boy."

"Perhaps," answered Joey, "you'd have been able to answer some of mine."

A little child looked up at the starry heavens as he was saying goodnight to his mother. "Mama, will I go to heaven some time?"

"Yes," she replied, "if you will be a good boy."

"And will you be there?" he asked.

"I hope so, and Daddy'll be there too."

The young child thought for a moment and then replied: "He can't be there because he won't leave the store."

FAULTS

An elderly woman selected two very fine-looking sweaters and mailed them to her son-in-law as a birthday present. Some weeks later, the mother-in-law paid a visit. Being a dutiful man, the son-in-law was wearing one of the sweaters when his mother-in-law arrived.

157

She looked him up and down and barked: "What's the matter, didn't you like the other one?"

—·—

Every man, so a very ancient legend goes, is born into the world with two bags hanging around his neck. The bag in front is small and full of his neighbor's fault, while behind him is a large bag filled with his own. This is why men are quick to see the faults in others and yet are so often blind to their own shortcomings.

—·—

FAVORS

There was once a sage who spent his lifetime studying the Torah. Though he was financially distraught, he always refused financial assistance.

His wife once chided him, saying: "You are a family man and are not equipped to earn a better livelihood. Why do you frown at the favors good friends wish to bestow upon you?"

The sage smiled at his wife and said: "People are friends as long as you do not take advantage of their proposed favors. When you are willing to receive their help and exploit their generosity to any degree, all who seem to be 'friends' will slowly vanish."

—·—

A wise and pious man was once riding in a wagon together with some peasants in the Carpathian Mountains. This particular countryside was all hills and vales, and the unpaved road was extremely bumpy. The wagon shook and rattled terribly, and the peasants were very frightened. Only the pious man sat quietly and showed no fear.

"How can you maintain such composure while we travel over such dangerous terrain?" queried the peasants of the wise man.

"Life the world over is full of ups and downs, hills and vales. Such danger is ever present, and one must grow accustomed to it or conquer it; otherwise it may defeat you."

—·—

In Family Court, a woman once complained tearfully and bitterly that her husband gave all he had to charity. At the same time somebody else complained that he and his wife were starving and his wealthy brother refused to help them at all.

The judge summoned both men: the rich alms-giver and the

rich miser. "Why do you give away everything you have?" asked the judge of the first one.

"Because, your Honor," the rich man answered, "I am only a poor sinner, and death may come at any moment and take me away. I therefore give to charity to ensure eternity."

"And why don't you help your brother?" asked the judge of the miser.

"Your Honor," the latter replied, "one never knows. Perhaps I will live to be a hundred and I must provide for my old age."

"Each of you is overly concerned about the unpredictable future, and that is how you are permitting the present, which is the only life we can be sure of, elude you. May God spare you from what each of you fears," said the judge sadly.

A famous trapeze artist was once instructing his pupils as to how to perform on the high trapeze bar. After giving them full explanations and instruction in this skill, he asked the students to demonstrate their ability. One student looked up at the insecure perch upon which he was to perform, and was suddenly filled with fear. He froze completely. He had a terrifying vision of falling to the ground. He was in such a deep fright that he could not move a muscle. "I can't do it! I can't do it," he cried.

The instructor put his arm around the boy's shoulder, and said, "Son, you can do it, and I will tell you how. Just throw your heart over the bar and your body will follow."

A woman was in mortal fear of high places. Her son was annoyed at her inability to look into the Grand Canyon, and her stubborn refusal to travel by air.

The boy was taken into the army. From a remote training camp, he sent his mother an honest confession that he was "afraid of being afraid." On receipt of the letter, his mother boarded a plane and flew to her son.

"I thought you were afraid to fly," the boy said.

"I am," replied the mother, "but I flew to prove to you that fear can be conquered if the reason is important enough. A brave man is not a man who is not afraid, but one whose will is stronger than his fear."

An Indian fable tells of a mouse who was in constant distress because of its fear of the cat. A magician took pity on it, and turned it into a cat. Immediately, it became afraid of the dog. So the magician turned it into a tiger. Immediately it began to fear the hunter. Then the magician said: "Be a mouse again. You have only the heart of a mouse and I cannot help you."

A legend tells of Abraham, the elderly patriarch, who was traveling in Mesopotamia and approached a group that remained standing some distance from the crossroads. He asked the people: "Why do you tarry here and not continue to the crossroads?"

They answered in fear: "The man standing yonder at the crossroads is a brigand and we fear his strong-arm methods."

Abraham then said: "I will approach him and reprimand him in the name of God in order that he mend his ways!"

As the Patriarch came closer to the crossroads, he noticed to his surprise that the brigand was only a stuffed scarecrow dressed as a robber. Abraham feared no man—a mere scarecrow—because his heart and mind were filled with reverence and love for God.

A little girl was once riding in a train that was traveling at breakneck speed. The ticket collector passed by, and noticed that she was sitting alone in the car, tranquil and happy. He leaned over to her and said, "My little girl, aren't you afraid of riding all alone in this speeding train?"

Her eyes opened wide. "Oh," she said, "why should I be afraid? My father is the conductor."

There was once a wicked king who enjoyed nothing more than the wanton use of his powers as head of his kingdom. He liked to "make" or "break" people without a thought of justice or consequence. Of course this aroused much hate and made him many enemies. The king was so blinded with power and self-righteousness that when his ministers advised him that his subjects despised him and were plotting to do away with him, he suspected them of disloyalty and sedition and had them put to death. Each time he would appoint new ministers. They would, after a time, report the same situation to the king—that his life was in danger because of the discontent that existed among his subjects. When he finally realized that these reports were true, everyone became suspect— ministers, counselors, servants. He even suspected his own sons, and when they objected to being sent away to distant lands, he had them bound in chains.

The king managed to maintain his outward composure, though he was inwardly being destroyed by fear. He was afraid to sleep and always had a servant taste his food before he ate it. He trembled at any unusual sounds or the sight of unfamiliar faces. In defiance, however, he issued even more stringent edicts, gained more enemies and grew ever more fearful. In the end, a crazed subject killed the crazed king.

Had he only put love in his heart, kind words on his lips, and extended his hand in friendship to his people, the love would have been returned with more love, the kind words would have been rewarded with appreciation, and the friendship would have been met by undying loyalty. What was actually a nightmare might have been a long, happy life.

There is an old folk tale that the Angel of Death appeared in a vision to a sainted man, and revealed to him that he was going to take away five hundred lives by a plague. After the terror of the plague swept through the community, the Angel of Death appeared again to the man.

The man berated him, "You lied to me. Instead of five hundred lives, you took five thousand lives."

"No," said the Angel of Death, "I took five hundred, and not one more. It was fear that destroyed the rest."

A certain man loved to boast about his courage. "I am prepared to fight for my rights, even if it costs my life," he stated.

One day a burglar broke into his place of business, flashed a gun, and ordered him to raise his hands. The man didn't hesitate for a second. The next day his friends learned about this incident and they poked fun at him. "What kind of a hero are you?" they demanded. "He told you to raise your hands and you obeyed like a frightened kitten."

"True," the man replied, "but you didn't see how my fists were clenched when they were raised."

FIRST-AID

The woman was describing an accident she had witnessed. "It was a good thing I remembered my first-aid lesson," she proudly related. "I was crossing the street when I heard a crash. I turned 'round and saw the poor man lying there. He had been hit by the cab and was in a bad way. Then all my first-aid came back to me, and I stooped right down and put my head between my knees to keep from fainting."

FLOWERS

George Bernard Shaw was known for his sharp tongue. One day, a distinguished visitor was at the home of the famous author and expressed some surprise that no flowers were on display. "I thought," he declared, "that you were exceedingly fond of flowers."

"I am," answered Shaw abruptly, "I am very fond of children, too. But I don't cut their heads off and stick them in pots all over the house."

FOOD

Alfred Hitchcock is a lover of good food. He was once an invited guest at a sparsely furnished dinner table which did not even begin to satisfy his appetite. As the coffee was being served, his host said, "I do hope that you will soon dine here again."

"By all means," said Hitchcock. "Let's start now."

FOOLS

A certain nobleman kept a fool, to whom one day he gave a rod with an order to keep it till he met a person who was a greater fool than himself. Not many years later, the nobleman fell deathly ill.

The fool came to see him and was told by the nobleman that soon he was going to leave for another world.

"When will you return?" asked the fool.

"Never! Never!" replied the nobleman.

"Never?" asked the fool. "And what provision have you made for your stay when you go?"

"None at all."

"None at all!" echoed the fool. "Here, then, take the rod; for with all my foolishness I am not guilty of a folly as great as yours."

FORBEARANCE

There was once a man who was well known as a great scholar and holy man. He was also a great humanitarian and loved every human being without exception. If someone had a joyous occasion, he shared his joy, and if anyone suffered a misfortune, he genuinely suffered along with him.

Once the keeper of the bathhouse of Leipnik became seriously ill and the humanitarian, as was to be expected, suffered much grief. He returned home one day to find his daughter and maid laughing together. He censured them both and said: "How can you have fun and laugh while our bathkeeper and friend is so gravely ill at his home?"

FORESIGHT

Two friends decided to go out and explore the world. One took along a torch, the other decided that he would find his way without a light. The latter, upon his return, said, "Everywhere I went I found nothing but darkness." The first man replied: "Everywhere I went I found light."

FORGIVENESS

A wise man once said that when a person undresses for bed at night, he should also undress his mind from the mistakes and failures of the day. The art of forgetting is a virtue we ought to acquire. Forgetting makes life possible. The person who remembers hurts and frustrations carries a burden of the past that becomes a terrible affliction.

"I can forgive, but I cannot forget" is only another way of saying "I will not forgive." Forgiveness ought to be like a cancelled note: torn in two, and burned up, so that it never can be shown against anyone.

A man strikes me with a sword, and inflicts a wound. Suppose, instead of binding up the wound, I show it to everybody; and after it has been bound up, I take off the bandages constantly, and examine the depth of the wound, making it fester. Is there a person in the world who would not call me a fool? Such a fool is he, who, by dwelling upon little insults, causes them to infect his mind. How much better were it to put a bandage on the wound, and never look at it again!

Judaism was very well explained in a poem by Whittier. He tells of two religious Jews who prayed on the Day of Atonement to be forgiven their sins. After praying for some time, one said, "Oh Lord, if it be Thy will not to forgive my sins, do Thou forgive the sins of my brother who writhes in the agony of his soul." Just then he felt that he himself had been forgiven.

A great theologian once taught that a crime against a fellow human being is far worse than a sin against the Almighty. "If you hurt a human being," he said, "you may be unable to locate him to beg his forgiveness. The Creator, however, is omnipresent; He is everywhere and always available for consultation."

A Piece of String, written by Guy de Maupassant, describes a man who ruined his life because he could not forget. While walking through a busy marketplace one morning, he spied a piece of string on the ground. Thinking that it might come in handy some day, he bent down and picked it up. Some time later, he was accused of having found a wallet lost at that same spot. Though he protested his innocence, he was taken to the station-house.

Fortunately, the lost wallet was found the next day. But the man felt that he had been insulted. He could not forget it, brooded about it daily. The piece of string had become an obsession. He neglected his work, his family, and even himself. He went from person to person telling them how he had been wrongly arrested. He died of a broken heart, mumbling, "The Piece of String."

When Mr. Wesley was on his voyage to Georgia with General Oglethorpe, the general threatened revenge upon an offending servant, saying, "I will never forgive."

"Then I hope, sir," said Mr. Wesley, "that you never sin." The general felt the force of the rebuke, and modified his attitude towards the servant."

As the spiritual leader of a congregation looked around the house of worship, he noticed that the people were conversing during their prayers. He was affectionately called "The Defender" because he always found reasons to forgive his people. And so, on this occasion, instead of rebuking the congregation, he lifted his hands heavenward and said to the Almighty: "Dear God, look how zealous Your people are. Even when they are busy talking, they are not too busy to worship You."

The man was obviously dying. He had been ailing for some time and his end was near.

"You cannot die with hatred in your heart," said the priest who stood nearby. "Forgive Joe, erase the thought of murder and revenge from your heart."

"All right," said the sick man at last. "I'll forgive him. But if I should recover, he'd better watch out."

FRANKNESS

A foreign diplomat unexpectedly walked in on Abraham Lincoln while the President was shining his shoes.

"I am astonished, Mr. President," he finally said, "to find you blacking your own shoes."

"Whose shoes do you shine?" asked Lincoln.

One of the guests at a dinner listened attentively as the hostess played the piano after the meal. As the hostess began to play a second selection, the guest leaned over to a charming woman seated next to him, and said, "What do you think of her execution?" The lady turned to him and whispered, "I am in favor of it!"

FREEDOM

A liberated slave met his former master in the street: "Are you as well off as you were before you were free?" The Negro admitted that his clothes were frayed, that his house leaked, and that his meals were nothing like the food on the old plantation.

"Well, wouldn't you rather be a slave again?"

"No, massa," was the positive reply, "there's a sort of looseness about this here freedom that I like."

Felix Frankfurter, who died on Feb. 22, 1965 at the age of 82, and served on the Harvard Law School faculty and on the Supreme

Court of the U.S. (1939-1963), did a job, performed a service, that no one else could have done.

His biographers tell us that he was a bit of an enigma. When he was a private citizen, he acted one way; when he became Associate Justice of the Supreme Court, he acted in another way. As a judge, he did not always vote on the side of the interests he had championed as a private citizen.

In private practice, he had been strong for labor unions, yet as Associate Justice he voted to restrict their activity if it was socially undesirable. In 1940 (Thornhill vs. Alabama), he joined Justice Frank Murphy in holding that picketing was a form of free speech and that a state could not interfere with this constitutional right of the individual. Yet, one year later, in 1941, he wrote in a decision (Meadowmoor Dairies Case), that a state could prevent picketing even if it was peaceful, if it could lead to violence. He held this opinion because it would enable the government to keep the upper hand over the Communist Party that was menacing our freedom.

Frankfurter was criticized for talking out of both sides of his mouth when, what he was really doing was defending those rights that were most precious at a given moment.

FRIENDSHIP

Two men were employed by the same firm for many years. They appeared to be very close. After many years, one of them was transferred to another city. People came over to commiserate with the remaining man on his losing a friend. The answer that came back is an interesting commentary on friendship.

"He was not my friend, only an acquaintance," was the reply.

"But," they interrupted, "you laughed together, shared so many good times."

The man pondered for a moment and answered, "But we never cried together."

Joseph Addison, brilliant English author, enjoyed one particular friendship because the man argued so spiritedly with him when they disagreed. Ignoring the advice of Shakespeare—"neither a borrower nor a lender be"—Addison loaned his friend a sum of money. Now that the friend was in debt to Addison, he found it difficult to talk on equal terms and began to agree with him on every controversial subject. Exasperated, Addison one day

166

demanded: "Either start contradicting me again, sir, or pay me my money!"

~~~~

Abraham Lincoln received thousands of appeals for pardon from soldiers involved in military discipline. Each appeal was supported by letters from influential people. One day a single sheet came before him, an appeal from a soldier without any supporting documents.

"What!" exclaimed Lincoln. "Has this man no friends, no one to speak for him? I will be his friend."

~~~~

A weary traveler was making his way along a lonely path when he noticed a dry, shrivelled leaf in his path. Picking it up, he was amazed at the delightful perfume it exuded.

"Oh, you poor withered leaf," he exclaimed, "where did you get this exquisite perfume?"

"For a long time I have lain in the company of a rose," was the reply.

~~~~

An artist painted the portrait of a friend whom he loved deeply. He mixed his colors carefully and lavished the utmost care upon the painting. When it was finished, the friend examined it carefully and remarked, "You have painted my portrait far too beautiful for it to be true."

"It isn't that at all," the artist replied. "I have only painted it with the love I have in my heart for you."

~~~~

We have heard many definitions of a friend, but none is more true than the one offered by a little boy: "A person who knows us—and still likes us."

~~~~

"Who is a friend like me?" said the shadow to the body. "Do I not follow you wherever you go? Sunlight or moonlight, I never forsake you."

"It is true," said the body, "you are with me in sunlight and moonlight, but where are you when neither the sun nor the moon shines upon me? The true friend abides in darkness as well."

~~~~

A young boy was once caught by a hospital guard. The boy was holding a mirror in his hand and reflecting the sun's rays on a third floor window.

"What are you doing?" shouted the guard.

"Nothing!" stammered the frightened boy. "My friend is sick. They won't let me in to see him so I'm sending up some rays of sunshine to make him feel better."

SOMEBODY

Somebody did a golden deed;
Somebody proved a friend in need;
Somebody sang a beautiful song;
Somebody smiled the whole day long;
Somebody thought, " 'Tis sweet to live"
Somebody said, "I'm glad to give"
Somebody fought a valiant fight;
Somebody lived to shield the right;
Was that "somebody" you?

There were once two very good friends. One of them was falsely accused of being a spy. The friend of the accused tried everything in his power to save his life, but in vain. The accused was sentenced to death. When his good friend saw him being brought before the executioner, he ran forward in his despair crying loudly, "It was I who did it, kill me!" But now, the other, seeing what a misfortune his friend was bringing upon himself, called out, "No, don't believe him, it was I who did it."

The judges, all confused, did not know what to do. Ultimately, the matter came before the king. To him, the unhappy friends revealed the truth, that they both were innocent and that they had only tried to save each other's life.

The king exclaimed enthusiastically, "What a wonderful friendship! May I be the third friend, and share your precious friendship."

Asked how she succeeded in always making her guests feel welcome, a clever woman once replied: "Three words suffice. When they arrive, I say 'At Last,' and when they are ready to depart, I say 'Already?' "

168

He who has a thousand friends
Has not a friend to spare.
And he who has one enemy
Shall meet him everywhere.

When a man ain't got a cent, and he's feeling kind o' blue,
An' the clouds hang dark and heavy, an' won't let the sunshine
    through;
It's a great thing, O my brethren, for a feller just to lay
His hand upon your shoulder in a friendly sort of way!
                                —James Whitcomb Riley

Honi Hama'agel, who lived many years ago in ancient Judea,
was the Jewish counterpart of Rip Van Winkle. One day, as Honi
sat down to rest, he fell asleep and slept for a period of seventy
years. Upon awakening he made his way homeward. Everything
seemed strange. He inquired after his son and was shocked to learn
that his son had been dead for many years, and that his grandson
was now the head of the family. He made his way to the synagogue. Many people were engrossed in the study of the Torah
but not a soul did he recognize. Soon a discussion arose and to
his amazement he heard one of the disputants exclaim, "Surely,
it must be so, for in the times of Honi Hama'agel it was thus
accepted." At last he made himself known but alas, no one would
believe him. Soon he felt so bewildered, lost and completely out
of things that he prayed for death saying, "Give me friends or
give me death."

FRUSTRATION

I never have frustrations,
The reason is to wit:
If at first I don't succeed,
I quit!

FULFILLMENT

A Hassidic Jew named Meir once remarked, "If they will ask
me at the Heavenly Court, 'Why were you not like Akiba?' I shall
not be disturbed, for I will tell them, 'I did not have the soul of
Akiba.'

169

"If they will ask me, 'Why were you not like Rashi?' I shall not be alarmed, for I will tell them that I do not possess the mind of a Rashi.

"But when they will ask, 'Why were you not like Meir?' I shall tremble with fear, for to myself, I could have been more true indeed."

There are three rules that should be followed if you are to achieve fulfillment.

1. Learn something new each day.
2. See something beautiful each day.
3. Do something good each day.

GENIUS

A young man once asked Mozart, the great composer, to tell him how to write a symphony. Said Mozart: "You are very young to begin writing symphonies."

"But you composed them when you were only ten years old," the youth replied.

"Yes," Mozart returned, "but I did not ask how."

Once, after Paderewski played before Queen Victoria, the sovereign exclaimed with enthusiasm, "Mr. Paderewski, you are a genius!"

"Ah, your Majesty," he replied, "perhaps. But before I was a genius, I was a drudge."

GIFTS

Artaban, an ancient Persian king, sent a most precious diamond to Judah the Prince. In return, Judah sent him a Mezuzah. The king took offense at the small gift which was worth only a few coins. Judah then explained: "You have sent me something which I need guards to watch, and I have sent you an object which will guard you."

A man who reached his hundredth birthday was asked the secret of long life. "Just using the gifts of the Creator," he answered. "He gave us the night for sleeping and the day for working and relaxing . . . and I use them."

A scholar once remarked: "There are three kinds of givers in the world—the flint, the sponge, and the honeycomb.

"To get anything out of a flint, you must hammer it, and then you get only sparks.

"To get anything out of a sponge you must squeeze, and the more you squeeze the sponge, the more you will get.

"But the honeycomb overflows with its own sweetness.

"Some people are stingy and hard; they give nothing away if they can help it.

"Others are good-natured; they yield to pressure, and the more they are pressed, the more readily and abundantly they give.

"A few delight in giving without being asked at all, and of these, the Bible says: 'The Lord loves a cheerful giver.'"

A wise scholar spent much valuable time selling the books he wrote. He would travel from town to town so that he could be personally involved in the sale of his works.

A friend once reproached him, "Why do you not accept gifts from some of your well-wishers? You would gain more time which you could spend on your studies."

The wise man answered, "Perhaps gifts are offered me only because the donors know I will refuse them. If it were known that I accept gifts, no one would offer them."

A poor woman greatly desired a bunch of grapes from the king's conservatory for her sick child. She took half a crown, and went to the king's gardener, and tried to purchase the grapes, but was rudely repulsed. A second effort, with more money, met like results. However, this time the king's daughter overheard the conversation as well as the crying of the woman. She asked the woman the reason for her unhappiness and was told the entire story. To which the princess replied: "My dear woman, you were mistaken. My father is not a merchant, but a king; his business is not to SELL but to GIVE." With these words, she plucked a bunch of grapes from the vine and gently dropped it into the woman's apron.

GIVING

A rosebush grew near an apple tree. Everybody admired the beauty and the scent of the roses. Basking in the praise, the rosebush became very vain.

"Nothing can compare to me," it said. "My roses are a delight to the eye and the most fragrant among all the flowers."

The apple tree looked down at the rosebush and answered. "You cannot, however, compare to me in kindheartedness."

"How is that?" demanded the rosebush.

The apple tree replied, "You do not give your flowers to people unless you first prick them. I, on the other hand, give my fruit even to those who throw stones at me."

A missionary who was returning from a visit home wanted to take something back to his mission that would be accepted by the natives. He finally selected a large bronze sundial. When he returned he called the tribe together, explained the sundial's purpose, and helped them set it up so that the sun would show the correct time of day. The natives were delighted with their gift and made many trips back and forth from their homes to see this strange sight.

One day, the missionary was astonished to find that the natives had built a shelter over the sundial to protect it from the weather. It took a lot of explaining that this protection would make the sundial unfit for service. To be of service it had to be exposed.

When Alexander Woollcott visited his blind friend, the famous Helen Keller, he never took roses or other flowers. He knew that color meant nothing to the blind woman. Instead, he took great bunches of geranium leaves. They gave out a spicy, fresh fragrance that appealed to her. She could touch them and smell them.

This is the way to give: fit gifts to the recipients.

Vachel Lindsay, the poet, told of his experience one night when tired and hungry. Stopping at a farmhouse, he asked to stay overnight. He had no money, but offered to pay for his lodging by reciting original poetry. The housewife, not interested in poetry, replied, "We cannot keep you, but those people there may," and she pointed to a small house across the field.

Going over to the house the man welcomed him, and said,

"You may stay if you are willing to put up with what we have." There were only two small rooms, the poet observed. Not a rug on the floor, no window shades, not one piece of furnishing worth two dollars. There was a bed, a rickety table, an old stove, and a few broken chairs.

When Lindsay left the next morning, this is what he said to a friend: "That man had nothing, and gave me half, and we both had abundance."

One night a man took a little candle out of a drawer, lit it, and began to ascend a long winding staircase.

"Where are you going?" said the candle.

"Higher than the top of the house where we sleep," was the answer.

"And what are you going to do there?" asked the candle.

"I am going to show the ships out at sea where the harbor is," said the man. "For we stand here at the entrance to the harbor, and some ships far out on the stormy sea may be looking for our light even now."

"No ship will see my light," said the candle. "I'm so very small."

"If your light is small," replied the man, "keep it burning bright, and leave the rest to me."

Then he climbed the stairs to the top of the lighthouse and took the little candle and lighted the great lamps that stood ready there with their polished reflectors behind them. A little light gave and made a greater light possible.

A rich man once asked his friend, "Why is it that everybody is always criticizing me for being miserly, when everyone knows I have made provisions to leave everything I possess to charity when I die?"

"Let me explain," replied the friend. "Take for example the pig and the cow. The pig was lamenting to the cow one day about how unpopular he was. "People are always talking about your gentleness and your kind eyes,' said the pig. 'Sure you give milk and cream, but I give more. I give bacon and ham. . . . I give bristles, and they even pickle my feet! Still nobody likes me. Why is this?'

"The cow thought a minute, and then said, 'Well, maybe it's because I give while I'm still living.' "

The best thing to give your enemy, according to the lamented Grenville Gleiser, is forgiveness; to an opponent, tolerance; to a friend, your heart; to your child, a good example; to a father, reverence; to your mother, conduct that will make her proud of you; to yourself, respect; to all men, charity.

There is a little anecdote told about a horse and a goat: It happened that a goat and a horse once had a debate as to who was more useful to man. During the course of his arguments, the goat mentioned the fact that man used his gut to make the strings for such instruments as the violin. Whereupon, the horse countered, "Yes, but they have to use my tail to make the bow with which to play the instrument. Moreover, they can only use your gut after you are dead, while they can cut my tail, and I go on living."

GOALS

A reporter was once sent out to interview a famous marksman, who, according to all reports, was the most amazingly accurate sharpshooter the world had ever seen. When the newsman arrived at the country home of the sharpshooter, he found that the fences, the trees, the shrubbery, the hedges were all covered with targets. And in the center of the target, in the middle of each bull's eye was a bullet eye.

"How do you do it?" the reporter asked him. "What is the secret of your amazing skill?"

The answer was frank and to the point. "It's really very simple," he said. "You see, all I do is shoot the bullet first, and then I draw the target around the bullet hole."

A pupil once asked his teacher, "I have been wondering why it is that South America, with all its natural advantages, its mines, its rivers, and its waterfalls as great as Niagara, is so far behind America."

The teacher replied after some silence, "I have come to this conclusion. South America was settled by the Spanish who came in search of gold, but North America was settled by the Pilgrims who came in search of God."

A little Japanese boy called at a gentleman's home and offered to sell some pictures for ten cents each.

"What are you going to do with the money?" he was asked.

"I am raising one million dollars for the earthquake relief," he answered gravely, and he was so tiny and the sum he named was so large that everyone laughed.

"One million dollars!" they said. "Do you expect to raise it all by yourself?"

"No," he replied, "there is another little boy helping me."

In an interview, Albert Einstein is reported to have advised young men to follow this bit of wisdom: Do not try to be a man of success, but try to be a man of value. The successful man takes more out of life than he puts into it; while the man of value gives more to life than he takes out of it.

A man once pondered the purpose of man's existence on earth and, dissatisfied with his own conclusions, consulted a sage on this matter. The latter answered him thus:

"The world beyond this life is a beautiful, unmarred place. The souls (which are, in effect, the most important part of the human being) in the world beyond live together so harmoniously, it is almost too difficult to comprehend. It would not do to permit entry into Heaven to untamed, selfish souls, souls inexperienced in doing kindnesses for others. The earth, sometimes a cold, cruel place, is a sort of proving ground where the human being can learn to live not for self alone but for the sake of others as well. A human being who has learned to live successfully on earth has learned to give of himself, and if he has accomplished this, if he has served his term of selflessness on earth, he is ready to take on an eternity in Heaven."

A president of a very small railroad once sent a complimentary pass to the president of a large railroad, and asked him to reciprocate. Thereupon, the recipient returned the pass with the observation, "How dare you, a president of an eleven-mile-long railroad compare yourself to me, the president of a railroad empire whose tracks stretch for thousands of miles?"

The president of the mini-railroad answered, "It's true that the tracks of your railroad are much longer than my railroad, but my tracks are just as wide as yours."

~~~~~

A well-known leader once taught: "You must work with ability and determination as if this was going to be the last day of your life, and you must initiate self-improvement as if you were going to live another hundred years.

~~~~~

In the Talmud, Rabbi Joshua Ben Chananiah tells how he was once walking along the road, seeking his way to town. At the crossroads he met a boy and asked the way.

The boy pointed his finger to the right and answered: "This road is near and far." He then turned to the left, pointed his finger and said, "This road is far and near."

Joshua took the road to the right, thinking that it was the shorter, but found the way blocked by fruit gardens surrounded by fences. He returned and found the boy who had directed him.

"Why did you mislead me?" he remonstrated.

"You did not take heed of my directions," retorted the boy. "Did I not say that the road to the right is near and far? It is the nearer road, but because of the garden barriers it is farther. The other road, although the farther, is the nearer because it is clear and unobstructed."

~~~~~

Matthew Arnold caught the aimlessness in some lives with the following poem:

> We do not what we ought.
> What we ought not, we do,
> And lean upon the thought
> That chance will bring us through.

~~~~~

The snow covered the ground and three young boys were having fun. A man approached them and said, "Would you like to try a new type of race? I'll give the winner a good prize."

The boys quickly agreed and the man told them that his race would be one that required skill. "I will go to the other side of the field," he explained, "and when I give the signal, you will start to run. The one whose footsteps are the straightest in the snow will be declared the winner."

The race began, and the first boy kept looking at his feet to see if his steps were straight. The second fellow kept looking at his companions to see what they were doing. But the third boy just ran on with his eyes steadfastly fixed on the man on the other side of the field.

The third boy was the winner, for his footsteps were straight in the snow. He had kept his eyes firmly on the goal.

An ancient sage wishing to teach a lesson in life told the following story:

There was a man who saddled up his horse to travel to Petrograd to save the imperiled community there. Of necessity, he stopped periodically to feed and rest his horse.

Having told the story, the wise man asked, "Why are they going to Petrograd?"

Various answers were offered but none satisfied the sage. Finally, he said: "The man goes in order to save lives, but the horse goes for the oats!"

The story is told of Witold Malcuzynski, the world-famous Polish pianist who was receiving the praise of admirers after a brilliant concert in which he had displayed his fantastic technical skill.

One woman kept repeating, "Incredible! However in the world do you manage it with only one pair of hands?"

After a minute or two, the young master replied, "It's really not difficult. I simply follow the advice of old Johann Sebastian Bach: 'Put your fingers on the right notes at the right time and let the instrument do the rest.' "

GOD

A French astronomer said, "I have swept the universe with my telescope, and I find no God."

J. W. Hawley responded to him, "That is as unreasonable as for me to say, "I have taken my violin apart, I have examined each piece with my microscope and I find no music."

A five-year-old child once asked his mother what God was like. The mother answered by taking two glasses of water, and putting them on the kitchen table.

"Now," she said, "taste this glass of water," pointing to the one nearest to her. The child drank from the first tumbler, just as he was told. The mother continued, "Take some sugar and put it into the second glass of water, and stir it well." The lad followed his mother's orders. "Now drink the water, and tell me how it tastes." The boy then described the sweetness of the water. "Can you see the sugar?" the mother asked.

"No," said the boy, "but I can taste it."

Then the mother affectionately said to her son, "This is just the way God works in the world. We never see Him, but we taste his sweetness when we see His universe, the heavens and stars above, the good people, and the wonderful things in the world created by a master Craftsman."

A pious man once said: "The love of God should be completely selfless. Nothing can ever influence me to compromise my love of God. I love God for Himself alone and for the infinite, wondrous things about Him, and I need no bribes, no promises of a reward of the 'World to Come.' I rejoice in my love of God, for I know He loves me, too."

"I am first and I am last," says God. A man of the cloth, in delivering a sermon, illustrated this passage with the following parable.

A well-to-do businessman suffered financial reverses. He and his wife studied their problem and decided that they could not cut down on the amount of apparel required, nor could they curtail their amusement or summer vacation expenditures. As one, they agreed that the only place they could cut down their expenses would be in their contributions to various charities. "There, you see," said God, "when there is a matter of reducing expenses, My requirements are the first to be eliminated. I AM FIRST to be cut out."

It happened, the parable continues, that a child belonging to this couple became ill. The child received the best medical and nursing care; not a stone was left unturned, it seemed, but despite everything, the doctors held out very little hope, and said to the parents, "The only thing you can do now is to pray to God." Without a moment's hesitation the parents ran to their house of worship and prayed for the recovery of their child. "You see," said God, "when everything else has failed, they turn to me for help as a last resort. Though I am always close at hand, people habitually take the long way around, and I AM LAST."

～

As no man knows the place of the soul, so no man knows the place of God. As the soul fills the body, God fills the world. The soul carries the body, God carries the world. The soul outlives the body, God outlives the world. The soul is one and alone in the body, and God is one and alone in the world.

～

A learned man once crossed a river in a ferry boat. The crew of the boat consisted of two people—a father and a son. The son was obviously still very young. In fact, he was so young that it was clear that the lad should have been attending school. The scholar went up to the boy and spoke to him: "Why are you working on the river at such an early age, instead of going to school? You could learn about physics, mathematics, geography and history instead of attending to the boat. Half of your life is lost because of your ignorance."

It was now the lad's turn to speak. What he had to say startled the scholar greatly.

"Do you ever find time to notice the sunset?" he asked the professor.

"Not often," was the short reply.

"Do you ever go for walks in the country, and see and hear the birds singing, the waters rushing, or the buds bursting?"

Again the reply was, "No."

"Then," the lad continued, "your whole life is lost and wasted. For if you have no time for the more beautiful things in life, you cannot be close to Almighty God. And without being near to God your whole life is of little use."

～

A little girl was busy with her crayons. Her mother asked her whose picture she was drawing.

"God," the young girl replied.

"But my darling child," replied the mother, "nobody knows how he looks."

"They will when I'm finished," said the girl.

～

A group of disbelievers had gathered to burn up the old church. "We will burn or tear down anything that could remind you people of God," said the leader.

"If that is the case," replied the old preacher, "you'd better tear down the stars from the sky, extinguish the light from the sun, and put out the moon. For all of these will remind our people of the glory and power of God."

Little Jimmy, aged five, was very proud of the fact that he could say his prayers by himself without any coaching. This didn't stop his parents from checking up on him, however, to see that he didn't forget anything.

One night, while listening at the bedroom door, they heard him add one or two thoughts of his own. He had just finished his "God bless Mom . . . God bless Dad . . . God bless Grandma," and normally would have hopped right into bed.

This particular night, however, he stayed on his knees a moment longer. Finally, he looked up and said earnestly: "And please take care of yourself, God, 'cause if anything happens to You, we're all sunk."

The other day a minister walked out of his church study onto the street. Leaning against a lamppost he noticed a man not too well dressed, with a hat slouched over his right eye, as if ashamed to have the world see his face. The minister reached into his pocket and took out two crisp dollar bills and handed them to the man. "Godspeed," said the minister in a kindly tone, and he walked on.

A few days later, much to the minister's surprise, the same man to whom he had given the money walked into his study and placed twenty one-dollar bills on the desk. "You picked a good one," he said. "Godspeed was a 10 to 1 shot and he came in first."

A member of the board of education was testing one of the classes in religious instruction. He turned to one of the students in the class and asked: "Tell me where God is and I will give you an apple."

The boy looked up directly into the eyes of the examiner and replied: "Tell me where He isn't and I'll give you a bushel of apples."

An old man had a dream in which an angel said to him that God would appear to him on Passover. He waited breathlessly for the great moment to arrive and in the meantime busied himself with a number of things. He saw a famished child dying of hunger and nursed it back to life. He made peace between two people on the verge of striking each other. He distributed Passover food to the needy of the community.

Passover night came and passed, but God did not appear. On the last night of the holiday, however, the angel appeared. In dismay the old man confronted him: "What happened to your promise?" Whereupon the angel retorted: "God was with you when you succored the famished child; God was with you when you made peace between neighbors; and God was with you when you distributed *matzos to* the poor. Indeed, God is always with you when you serve your fellow men."

The famous Rabbi Akiba once started out on a long journey. He rode on a donkey, carried a rooster to awaken him in the morning, and a candle to dispel the darkness. At the end of the first day's journey he sought shelter at an inn, but was turned away. Without complaint he continued on his way, stopping only long enough to say, "All that God does is for the best." As he made ready to spend the night in a nearby field, his donkey and rooster strayed off and a gust of wind blew out his candle.

In the morning he was informed that during the night a band of robbers had attacked the people at the inn. After a moment's thought he replied, "See how narrowly I escaped death! At the inn I would have been attacked. Also, the braying of the donkey, the crowing of the rooster or the light of the candle might have attracted the band of robbers to my sleeping place in the field. Have I not always contended that all that God does is for the best?"

"How do you know there is a God?" a small boy asked his friend, who was flying a kite so high that it was completely out of sight. The lad looked up at the sky for a moment and replied: "In the same way that I know there is a kite up there. I feel the pull of it."

Meier ben Isaac Nehorai, 11th century poet described the Almighty with these words:

> Could we with ink the ocean fill,
> Were every blade of grass a quill,
> Were the world of parchment made,

181

And every man a scribe by trade,
    To write the love
    Of God above
Would drain the ocean dry;
    Nor would the scroll
    Contain the whole,
Though stretched from sky to sky.

Following God cost Abraham the willingness to yield his only son. It cost Esther the risk of her life. It cost Daniel being cast into the den of lions. It cost Moses years of family life. What does it cost you?

A youngster was playing hide-and-seek with his friends, but for some reason they stopped playing when it was his turn to hide. When he learned what had happened, he broke into tears. His old grandfather came out of the house to see what was troubling him and to comfort him.

"Do not weep because your friends left and did not come to find you," he said. "Perhaps you can learn a lesson from this disappointment. All of life is like a game of hide-and-seek between God and man. But it is God who weeps, because man does not play the game fairly. God is waiting to be found and man has gone off to search after other things."

An old preacher in a tiny village found a very distinguished international statesman in his congregation one day. He conducted his service as usual, and delivered a short sermon, but took no notice of the visitor.

After the service, several members of the congregation gathered about him and said, "We had a distinguished visitor today, but you did not seem at all embarrassed or even impressed."

The elderly preacher looked at the circle of men around him and replied, "I have been praying and preaching in the presence of Almighty God for fifty years. Do you think, with Him as one of my regular listeners, any man can impress me by his presence?"

A French scientist was traveling in the desert and sat outside his tent in the cool of the evening talking with his young Bedouin guide about religion. "Nobody knows," said the Frenchman, "nobody knows for certain that God exists."

The lad pointed to a smooth stretch of sand across which extended a track of footprints.

"When I see those footprints in the sand," he said, "I know for certain that some man has passed this way. Only a man could have made them."

He pointed to the fading colors of a glorious sunset in the west, and then overhead, to the dark blue sky in which the great stars were coming out one by one. "And when I see the sun, and the moon, and the starry heavens in their beauty, I know for certain that the Creator has passed this way."

A learned atheist once met a laborer going to church. He asked him, "Where are you going?"

"I'm going to church, sir."

"What will you do there?" was the next question.

"I will worship God."

"Is your God, a great God or a small God?" was the next question.

"He is both sir," was the reply. "He is so great that the heavens cannot contain Him, and He is so small, that He can dwell in my poor heart."

Lord Moynihan, the great British surgeon, had just finished operating before a gallery full of distinguished visiting doctors. He was asked how he could work with such a crowd present.

He replied: "You see, there are just three people in the operating room when I operate—the patient and myself."

"But that is only two," his questioner commented. "Who is the third?"

Moynihan responded: "The third is God."

A woman in Manhattan died and willed her estate to God. To settle the estate a case was filed, naming God as a party thereto. A summons was issued and the court went through the motions of trying to serve it. The final report stated: "After due and diligent search, God cannot be found in the City of New York."

"Let me see this God of yours," a Roman emperor said to Rabbi Joshua. The rabbi pointed upwards: "Lift your eyes to the sky; God is there." The emperor looked up, but the sun was shining so strongly that he covered his eyes and looked away.

"What?" said the rabbi. "You ask to see the Master, when you cannot even look His servant straight in the face?"

—⁓—

A little girl asked her mother on the way home from their house of worship, "Mommy, is God poor?"

The question surprised her mother who quickly answered, "No, dear. God is not poor; everything belongs to Him."

The child looked perplexed and then asked, "Isn't the religious school I attend God's house?"

"Yes," said the mother, "why do you ask?"

"Because it is so broken down," replied the child.

—⁓—

A young, brilliant scholar had just been ordained a minister and with high hopes left for his birthplace. As he was happily riding along on his donkey, his heart was filled with song. The future seemed bright and inviting, and proudly he thought of the joyous reception awaiting him. Suddenly, he was roused by a voice which called, "Master, master." He beheld a dwarf, begging for alms.

Resentful of the interruption of his reverie, he rudely replied, "Tell me, are all the people in your town as ugly and misshapen as you are?"

The dwarf, hurt, replied, "I do not know. Ask the Artist, who fashioned me."

The young scholar was repentant. "Forgive me, my brother," he pleaded. "I am ashamed of my words. Please grant me another chance to make amends for my rudeness." But all the bitterness which had accumulated through the years combined to make the dwarf adamant.

Mile after mile the young scholar followed the dwarf, begging for forgiveness. Soon they approached the town, where the young scholar was greeted by a rousing welcome.

"Why all this excitement?" asked the dwarf. "Has the Messiah come?"

"Why, don't you know," replied the people, "that he, our townsman is now accounted one of the greatest scholars in all the land of Israel?"

"May there be no more like him," exclaimed the dwarf. "For of what avail is all his learning if it has failed to teach him kindness and consideration, especially for the less fortunate?" The people were amazed.

"My friends," said the scholar, "all this man says is true. Will you please intercede with him in my behalf, and urge him to forgive me?" His townspeople finally prevailed upon the dwarf to forgive the scholar.

The following morning, the young minister was invited to preach his first sermon, and with new understanding he chose as his text: "Let a person be as pliant as a reed, and not as unbending as a cedar."

There is a story of a mother who once overheard her young son praying. As she eaversdropped more intently, she heard him telling God what he planned to do, and asking God to help him. The mother rebuked the offspring with these words: "Son, don't bother to give God instructions, just report for duty."

A farmer inscribed on his weather vane the following statement: "God is Love." He was constantly asked why he had put that statement on a weather vane. Did it indicate that he felt God's love was changeable?

"No, a thousand times no," was his usual reply. "I mean to point out that whichever way the wind blows, God is still love."

Joseph Haydn, the composer, was once accused by an over-pious critic of writing religious music that lacked seriousness. Haydn straightened his shoulders and answered firmly, "Sir, I can compose in no other way. When I think of God, my heart is so full of happiness that the notes run ahead of me. And since God gave me a joyous heart, I think He will forgive me if I serve Him joyously."

A little boy, whose parents were not devout, spent his vacation period with his grandparents who were very pious. Before going to sleep on the last day of his visit, he recited the prayer which the old folks had lovingly taught him. At the end, placing his head in his hands, he sobbed, "And now, goodbye, God, goodbye. Tomorrow, I am going home to my mommy and daddy."

185

Emerson put it well when he said:

There is no great and no small,
To the Soul that maketh all.

~~~

James Russell Lowell tells an instructive parable of a dissatisfied pilgrim who went out to discover the mountain of God. He travelled a long and weary road until he reached the object of his quest. He made his way up to the very top of the mountain, but even there he found no sign of God's presence. And so he prayed that God might show him some visible token of His divine presence. Thereupon, a rock broke open and he saw a beautiful white flower. When he picked it up, he saw to his surprise that it was the same flower that his own child had picked from his own back yard and had given to him as he started on his pilgrimage. The point of the parable is clear. We search for God over distant horizons and far away places, forgetting that God is present in our own back yard.

~~~

A king was proclaimed "immortal," that he was the greatest in all the world. A clergyman asked him to test his claim and the king agreed. His throne was placed at the seaside. The tide began rolling in, and threatened to drown him. He commanded the waves to stop but of course, they did not. Then the king acknowledged to his followers, "Behold, how small is the might of kings compared to the might of God's creations."

~~~

The Baron de Rothschild was once approached by a man who needed a loan of $1,000. The Baron agreed to grant the loan, if only the client would provide an endorser. The man could not think of a single individual who would accept that responsibility. Finally, he told the Baron that the only one who trusts him is God Almighty. The Baron looked puzzled for a moment, but then replied, "He will be fine. I'll accept Him as an endorser." He asked the man to sign the note, and on the back he wrote, "Endorsed by God Almighty."

Six months later the client returned to repay the loan, but the Baron refused payment. When the debtor begged for an explanation, the Baron, with a smile, replied, "My dear friend, the Endorser has already repaid the loan."

~~~

GOLD

In the Temple in Jerusalem, there was an old flute, fashioned out of reeds, that had been handed down from the days of Moses. The sound of the flute was sweet and beautiful, capturing the soul of the worshippers. But one day the priests of the sanctuary decided to decorate the flute, and they covered it with gold. The flute was never the same again. Its sweet, clear tones were now harsh, metallic, and jarring. Gold had coarsened its melody.

The Chinese tell of a man who loved gold and even dreamt of it. One day, he dressed in his finest garments and went into the crowded market place. He stepped directly up to the booth of a gold dealer, snatched a bag full of gold coins, and walked calmly away. The officials who arrested him were puzzled: "Why did you rob the gold dealer in broad daylight," they asked, "and in the presence of so many people?"

"I did not see any people," the man replied. "I saw only gold."

A story is told of a man whose back was bent and who walked in a stooped position. A boyhood chum who had not seen him for many years was puzzled about the physical deformity. He remembered his friend as a strapping young man, tall and straight. He learned the cause of the affliction. His friend had once found a gold coin in the street. This made him very happy. In his desire to find more and more money, he walked in a stooped position, his eyes fixed on the ground. He did manage to find a few more pennies, a watch, and some screws and buttons, but in the process of his lifetime searching, his back was bent and his eyes grew dim. What a price to pay for gold!

GOODNESS

A sage once said: A truly good person who, in the manner of a saint, is completely devoid of evil, can see no evil in others. He looks upon the sins of others as human errors which are to be forgiven. He can always find an apology for the hurt one man inflicts upon another. He cannot comprehend the desire to do evil unto another, for he has not ever felt the urge to commit evil himself. A truly good person sees the world through his own eyes, and from his point of view, since he can do only good, he feels this way about the rest of the world.

~

I once heard a wise man say that there are no people who are born bad. All babies are good and pure. When we encounter a seemingly bad person we must realize that badness is not an integral part of him; it is something that has happened to him along the way. Badness is a stranger that has stealthily crept into his behavior, against his will and against his nature. There are people who do bad things, but a bad man does not exist at all.

~

John Wesley had this rule of life:

> Do all the good you can,
> By all the means you can,
> In all the ways you can,
> In all the places you can,
> At all the times you can,
> To all the people you can,
> As long as ever you can.

~

Abraham Lincoln used to say that he always plucked a thorn and planted a rose wherever he thought a rose would grow.

~

A man suffering from an unusual and severe streptococcus infection had to have a transfusion of blood from a man who had recovered from an identical spinal infection. For several days the sick man's wife repeated an appeal for a blood donor over the radio. Finally, a response came from a distant city, from an army officer who had been stricken with the same disease some years earlier.

The transfusion proved successful, and the donor said: "I am just beginning to understand why it is that I was punished with that terrible disease. I suffered 15 years ago so that I might perform a good deed, and help this man now."

~

In the Metropolitan Museum of Art in New York, there is a beautiful, white statue called "The Struggle Between the Two Natures" by George Gray Barnard. It depicts two identical male figures. One figure is lying on the ground while the other stands over him with one foot on his thigh and the other foot on his neck. They look like wrestlers with every muscle clearly visible.

The statue portrays the perennial struggle which takes place between our natural instinct for physical survival and our spirit. Which one is victorious? The sculptor, instead of labeling the two figures, leaves it to the judgment of the viewer.

Sometimes the physical symbol triumphs, and sometimes the spirit emerges the victor. It is not the sculptor's task to render the final decision. He merely depicts the struggle between seemingly irreconcilable forces.

~~~

A pious man said: "Evil, too, possesses a small amount of good. It is the lowest degree of perfect goodness. The broom, for example, though low in station, has some goodness in it, for does it not clean up dirty things?"

~~~

GOSSIP

The great philosopher Maimonides, who lived some 800 years ago, wrote, "The sin of the man with the evil tongue is worse than the murderer, since the slanderer destroys a man's reputation which is more precious than life. He kills with his tongue three victims: himself, the man listening to his slander, and the innocent subject."

~~~

Constance Cameron tells of a lesson her mother taught her. One day, when she was about eight, she was playing beside an open window, while Mrs. Brown confided to her mother a personal problem concerning her son. When Mrs. Brown had gone, her mother realized that the little girl had heard everything. She called her in and said, "If Mrs. Brown had left her purse here today, would we give it to anyone else?"

"Of course not," the child replied.

Her mother continued: "Mrs. Brown left something more precious than her pocketbook today. She left a story that could make many people unhappy. That story is not ours to give to anyone. It is still hers, even though she left it here. So we shall not give it to anyone. Do you understand?"

She did. And ever since that time a confidence or a bit of care-

189

less gossip which a friend left at her house was considered personal—not hers to give to anyone.

~~~~~

During Aaron Burr's long life, he tasted the cup of honor and distinction and also drained the dregs of bitterness and humiliation. As he lay dying, a friend who was waiting upon him reported some rumor, and began, "They say." Burr interrupted her and said, "My dear, never use that phrase. It has broken more hearts than any other."

~~~~~

Franklin D. Roosevelt was asked by his secretary whether he had heard that one of his old friends was saying very nasty things about him. Roosevelt said, "Is that so? When did this happen?"

His secretary said, "Oh, the past few weeks."

Roosevelt leaned back in his chair, took a puff from the long cigarette holder which he always carried, blew out a thoughtful ring or two, and said, "That is strange. I don't recall ever doing him any favor."

~~~~~

It takes an enemy and a friend, working together, to hurt you to the heart. The one to slander you, and the other to get the news to you.

—Mark Twain

~~~~~

Two women were having an afternoon cup of coffee in the kitchen. One of the women started to complain about her neighbor: The children were always dirty. The house was never clean.

Then she pointed to the backyard and exclaimed, "Just look at the clothes on the line, gray and streaked."

The friend went to look at the sight outdoors and then observed, "Why, it looks to me as if the clothes are very clean. It is your window that is dirty."

~~~~~

It is said that "He who tosses dirt on the street can never find a good enough apology for the portion of the dirt which clings tenaciously to him. . . ."

There is never a bit of gossip that doesn't hurt someone. It is for this reason that those of us who like to consider ourselves as good people must never repeat idle gossip, no matter how spicy

190

it may be. No matter how nicely you may word it, gossip is still gossip, and "One cannot fling dirt with clean hands."

A young minister complained that his sermons did not seem to accomplish much. His senior colleague replied, "If during the time of your preaching you have prevented them from indulging in gossip and slanderous remarks, you have already accomplished a great deal."

A lady, known to be a gossip, was standing in the street conversing with a second woman when the latter dropped her handkerchief. The gossip bent down to pick it up and said, "What a beautiful handkerchief. May I have it?"

"Please return it to me," replied the woman. "I want to have one thing into which you have never put your nose."

The founder of a religious sect once taught: "A gossip can be compared to a broom which can sweep the whole place clean but itself remains dirty."

The Chinese tell the following fable concerning three monkeys. . . .

There was once a wise old mother monkey. She wanted to teach her children a useful lesson. So she made three small clay monkeys and placed them on a limb of a tree where her offspring could constantly see them. One had his hands over his eyes. The second had his hands over his ears, while the third had his hands over his mouth.

This is the lesson she was teaching the children: First, to see no evil thing. Second, to hear no evil thing. Third, to speak no evil thing. If you want to have a happy life, free from disagreeable happenings, you must not permit evil things to be a source of pleasure to you.

Mrs. Horowitz was talking to Mrs. Pomerantz, her neighbor. "I just can't stand that woman across the street . . . you know, the one who just moved in."

"Oh yes, the one who's always complaining about her husband."

"Believe me, it's worse than only complaining. She's terrible, the way she talks about him. Now take my husband; he drinks too much, he gambles, he stays out late—a worse husband you never saw in your life—he should drop dead! But do I ever say anything to anybody?"

⁓

A man once became very angry with an article which defamed his character. A friend, noticing his wrath, observed: "Don't let it annoy you. Half of the people who receive the paper never see the article. Half read it, but do not understand it. Half who understand it do not believe it. And half of those who believe, are not important in this town anyway."

⁓

There was a woman to whom gossip was so utterly distasteful that whenever a visitor brought up any gossip, she would say, "Come, we will go and ask if this is true." The tale-bearer was always so taken aback that she would beg to be excused. But the determined woman insisted on escorting the reluctant tale-bearer to the subject of his tale to verify its truth or falsity. It is said that no one ever repeated the offense of tale-bearing to this insistent woman.

⁓

A trumpeter was captured by the enemy. He pleaded with his captors: "Spare me. I have no gun. I am not guilty of any crime. I have not slain a single man. I only carry this poor brass trumpet with which I lead the men to action."

"That is the reason for putting you to death," was the reply. "For, while you do not fight yourself, your trumpet stirs up all the others to battle. It causes many others to kill."

⁓

GOVERNMENT

The wife of the congressman sat up abruptly in bed, with a startled look. "Henry," she whispered, "there's a robber in the house!"

"Impossible!" was his reply. "In the Senate, perhaps yes; but in the House, never!"

⁓

Frederick the Great, King of Prussia, had a difficult time balancing his country's budget. On one occasion he tendered a

192

banquet, inviting important people to discuss his problem. He told them that despite the high taxes there was not enough money on hand to meet expenses.

A wise sage stood up at the table, took a lump of ice in his hand and held it there for a moment. He then passed it to his neighbor, asking that it be passed from hand to hand until it reached the king. This was done but when it came to Frederick, it was reduced to the size of a walnut.

The general then sat down. The lesson was obvious; there were too many hands and too much waste in the government.

~~~

GRATITUDE

A gifted artist, standing on the summit of a craggy mountain, was intently painting the landscape before him. In order to attain a better perspective, he continued to move backward, unknowingly reaching the very edge of the precipice. A friend, standing nearby, noticed the imminent peril, and knowing that it was too late to shout a warning, reached over to the canvas and slashed it. The artist, in speechless anger, rushed forward, thereby saving himself. When he realized the circumstances, he was most grateful.

~~~

The story is told about the parents of a young man killed in the war, who gave their house of worship a generous donation as a memorial. When the presentation was made, another war mother whispered to her husband, "Let's give the same for our boy."

"What are you talking about?" asked the father. "Our boy didn't lose his life."

"That's just the point," replied the mother. "Let's give it because he was spared."

~~~

There was a lady who had been single for very many years. One day, a friend met her on the street and said, "Congratulations! I hear you are going to be married."

"Not a word of truth in it," replied the single girl, "but thank heavens for the rumor!"

~~~

Two angels flew to earth. Each carried a basket, and wherever anyone stood in prayer, the angels stopped and went in. Schools, cottages and castles were visited. Very soon the basket carried by one of the angels grew heavy with the weight of what he had collected, but that of the other remained almost empty. Into the first were put prayers of petition. "Please give me this. . . . Please I want that." Into the other went the "Thank you" prayers.

"Your basket seems very light," said one angel to the other.

"Yes," replied the one who carried the "Thank you's." "People are usually ready enough to pray for what they want, but very few remember to thank the good God when He grants their requests."

⁓

The pupil of a great teacher had ventured forth from the school, gone to a distant town, and prospered in the business world. Some years later, the famous sage was passing through this town and naturally the businessman came to visit his former teacher.

"What are you doing?" the teacher asked solicitously.

"Thank you," his pupil answered. "I'm doing quite well. My business has grown, I have many employees, my financial rating is excellent."

The conversation turned to other matters. In a few minutes the teacher asked again: "What are you doing?"

It seemed odd that the teacher should repeat the question, but perhaps he had forgotten.

"Thank you," replied the pupil a second time. "I have a nice family, a lovely wife and fine children."

Again the conversation took different turns and again the teacher asked, "What are you doing?"

This time the pupil could not contain himself. "Honored teacher," he protested, "you have already asked this very question three times!"

"Yes, I know," the teacher said in mild rebuke. "I have asked three times but you have not answered the question even once. I asked you, 'What are you doing?' You tell me of your prosperity, your family. That's not your doing. That is God's doing. I asked you, 'What are you doing?' How much charity are you giving? What are you accomplishing for your people? Now *tell* me, my son, what are you *doing*?"

⁓

A patronizing young dandy was seated opposite the famous James McNeill Whistler at a dinner one evening. During a lull in the conversation he adjusted his monocle and leaned forward toward the artist.

"You know, Mr. Whistler," he drawled, "I passed your house this morning."

"Thank you," said Whistler abruptly. "In fact, thank you very much."

Two ministers called on a man who had been ill for two years. The man's three-year-old nephew, who was blind, lived in the same house. As they left, one of the ministers put his arm around the young boy, and said: "Good-bye son. We prayed for you too."

"Why me?" he asked. "I can walk."

Hyman Edelson, the well-to-do grocer, was a pleasant sort of chap, but he hated to pay the asking price for anything.

One day, while eating herring, a bone became lodged in his throat. He could neither swallow nor disgorge it, and within moments he could scarcely breathe. His wife hurriedly called the family doctor, who arrived just as the patient's face was turning blue. The physician quickly removed the bone with a pair of forceps.

When Edelson recovered and was again breathing normally, he was overwhelmed with gratitude, but he cautiously asked, "How much do I owe you for this little two-minutes' work?"

The doctor was well acquainted with the grocer's miserly nature. "I'll tell you what," he said, "Just pay me half of what you would have given when the bone was still stuck in your throat."

A charitable lady once approached a celebrated philanthropist on behalf of a very young orphan-child. "I'll draw a check for $5,000," said the philanthropist, "and when you need more, call on me."

The lady was thrilled. "As soon as the child is old enough, I will teach him to thank you," she said.

"Stop!" said the good man. "You are mistaken. We do not thank the clouds for the rain. Teach the child to look higher and to thank God who gives both the clouds and the rain."

Matthew Henry, the famous scholar, was once accosted by some thieves and robbed of his purse. He wrote these words in his diary: "Let me be thankful; first, because I was never robbed

195

before; second, because although they took my all, it was not much; and third, because it was I who was robbed, not I who robbed."

GREED

"What is wrong with your sons?" asked a neighbor of Abraham Lincoln. "They seem to be fighting and crying."

"What is wrong with the world," replied the President, "is wrong with my two sons. I have three walnuts and each of my sons is envious. Each one wants two of them."

While Alexander the Great was traveling in the East, he wandered to the gate of Paradise. He knocked, and the guardian angel asked, "Who is there?"

"Alexander," was the answer.

"Who is Alexander?"

"Alexander, you know—*the* Alexander—Alexander the Great —conqueror of the world."

"We know him not—he cannot enter here. This is the Lord's gate; only the righteous enter here."

Alexander then humbly begged for some token to take with him, to show that he had reached the heavenly gate. A small fragment of a human skull was thrown to him, with the words, "Weigh it."

Alexander took it away, and showed it to his Wise Men, who brought a pair of scales. Placing the bone in one scale, Alexander poured some of his silver and gold in the other; but the small bone outweighed it. More and more silver and gold were heaped into the scale, and at last his crown jewels and diadems were put in; but the scale flew upwards as if filled with feathers, as against the weight of the bone. Then one of the Wise Men placed a few grains of dust on the bone. Up flew the scale on which it rested. The bone was part of the skull which surrounded the eye, and nothing will ever satisfy the eye until covered by the dust of the grave.

There is an old fable about a beggar who chanced to meet Fortune one day. Fortune agreed to empty her golden horn into the beggar's purse on condition that any of the gold falling on the ground would turn to dust. The beggar kept demanding more and more, until his worn-out wallet burst, and all the gold fell to the ground. Too many of us are forever grasping just like this greedy beggar until our lives are filled with needless struggle, tremendous worry, and final defeat.

An old saint overtook two travelers. One was a greedy man; the other was of a jealous nature.

When they came to the parting of the ways, the saint said he would give them a parting gift. Whoever made a wish first would have his wish fulfilled; and the other would get a double portion of what the first had asked for.

The greedy man knew what he wanted, but was afraid to make his wish because he wanted a double portion and could not bear the thought of his companion getting twice as much as he had. The envious man was also unwilling to wish first, because he could not bear the thought of his companion getting twice as much as he would get. So each waited for the other to wish first.

Finally the greedy man took his fellow by the throat and said he would choke him to death unless he made his wish first. At that the envious man said, "Very well; I will make my wish. I wish to be made blind in one eye."

A hungry fox was eyeing some luscious fruit in a garden, but to his dismay, he could find no way to enter. At last he discovered an opening through which, he thought, he might possibly get in, but he soon found that the hole was too small to admit his body.

"Well," he thought, "if I fast for three days I will be able to squeeze through." He did so, entered the garden, and then proceeded to eat to his heart's content from the fruit in the orchard. But lo! When he wanted to escape so that the owner of the garden would not find him, he discovered to his distress that the opening had again become too small for him.

Again he had to fast for three days, and as he escaped, he cast a farewell glance upon the scene of his latest joy, saying: "O beautiful orchard, how delicious are your fruits. But what have I now for all my labor and all my cunning?"

Prior to his death, a man called in his best friend and said, "I give you all my possessions. Give my wife whatever you want; keep the rest for yourself."

197

When the man died, the friend took 90% of the estate for himself, and gave the widow ten percent. She was shocked. Her husband loved her, surely he would not leave her so little!

She called the friend before the judge. He heard the arguments and ruled: "The husband meant that you give the wife whatever you want, and the rest you keep yourself. You wanted 90%, then give it to her. Ten percent is for you."

Mar Ukba was a very kind and charitable man. There was a poor man in his neighborhood whom he wished to help, but he desired to do so in such a manner that the poor man would not know who his benefactor was.

Very early each morning, Mar Ukba would go to the poor man's home, slide four coins under his door, and leave stealthily before anyone could see him.

One day the poor man said to himself, "I will arise early and see who it is that is so kind to me, and perhaps I can induce him to give me more."

The next day, when Mar Ukba approached the house, the poor man opened the door. Mar Ukba, rather than put him to shame by dispensing charity to him in public, turned and ran and never approached that house again. Hence was the poor man punished because he was not content to accept what was given him.

A very poor Chinese had his small laundry next door to a more prosperous Chinese restaurant. Every day he would take his bowl of rice, put his chair as close as he dared to the restaurant, and sniff the appetizing aromas.

One day, he received a bill from his neighbor for "the smell of his food." The poor man promptly went indoors and appeared with a small money box, and rattled it in the ears of his "creditor," saying, "I hereby pay for the smell of your food with the sound of my money."

A miser sold all his property for gold. This he buried in a hole in the ground near his home. Every day he dug up the hole to look at his wealth. One man, who noticed his daily visits to that spot, determined to discover the reason for these visits. When he learned the secret, he went to the hole, dug up the wealth and disappeared. On his next visit, the miser found the hole empty. He began to tear his hair and cry out in anguish. A neighbor, who knew the habits of the miser, sought to console him with these words: "Do not grieve so much. Take a pile of stones and bury them in the hole. Make believe that the gold is still there. It will do you the same service; for when the gold was there you did not make the slightest use of it."

Leo Tolstoy tells of a land-hungry man who went to a distant country where the chief of a tribe offered to give him all the land he could walk around in a day. The man was told to put his money down on a certain spot and then walk till sunset. When he returned to his money, all lands enclosed by the path of his steps were to be his. The man started out, hurrying as fast as possible, and returned only after great exertion to the point of his departure. But the task had been too great for him, and he fell dead at the spot from which he had begun. In the end, six feet of ground was all he needed.

GROWTH

The late Jerome P. Fleishman, editor and publicist, once wrote the following pithy statements: "I believe there is more satisfaction in patting a man on the back than in standing on his neck. I believe there is more fun in lifting a man up than in holding him down. I believe happiness is bound up with helpfulness. I believe our job is to reach out for bigger things rather than to curl up in our own little shells and snarl at the world."

A young boy was being examined by a panel of teachers. One of them asked him: "What great man was born in your city?"

The young boy, truly a genius, replied: "Great men are not born, they develop. Only infants are born."

The older men were astounded at this unexpected reply, for many years of experience had taught them that wisdom is produced only by adding the proper ingredients. Thus an infant must be taught to walk, talk, to love, to share, and as it gets older it must receive an education. Only then is a person ready to do great things.

Two physicians were once discussing a colleague of theirs who was giving the profession a bad name because of his incompetence.

"You'd imagine," remarked the first doctor, "that, after twenty-seven years of experience, he would know better."

To this, his friend answered, "You've got that all wrong. He hasn't had twenty-seven years of experience. He has had one year of experience, twenty-seven times."

The one who thinks little thoughts is little; the one who does little things is little. A little person who associates only with little people lives a little life and is little mourned when he leaves his little world.

When Longfellow was well along in years, his hair was white as snow, but his cheeks were as red as a rose. An admirer asked him how he was able to keep so vigorous and yet have time to write so beautifully. Pointing to a blossoming apple tree, the poet said, "That tree is very old, but I never saw prettier blossoms on it than those which it now bears. That tree grows new wood each year. Like that apple tree, I try to grow a little new wood each year."

GUIDANCE

The story is told of a young boy who was attempting to lift a heavy stone out of the way of his mini-automobile. His father, happening by and noticing the son's failing efforts, said to him, "Son, are you using all your strength?"

"I sure am," the boy exclaimed impatiently.

"No you are not," replied the father, "You haven't asked me to help."

"My boy," said a father to his son, "treat everybody with politeness, even those who are rude to you; for remember, you show courtesy to others, not because they are gentlemen, but because you are one."

Preacher Billy Sunday once visited a strange city. He met a boy in the street and asked him how to get to the post office. The boy answered rather rudely. "Do you know who I am?" inquired the preacher. "I am Billy Sunday. If you come to my house tomorrow I can show you the way to heaven."

The boy laughed, "Look who's going to show me the way to heaven! Why, you don't even know the way to the Post Office!"

"When my child annoys me," said a woman, "I quiet him by brushing his hair. . . . If this doesn't work, I use the other side of the brush on the other end of my child. That always works."

HABIT

There are four good habits—punctuality, accuracy, steadiness, and dispatch. Without the first of these, time is wasted; without the second, mistakes occur; without the third, nothing can be well done; and without the fourth, opportunities of great advantage are lost.

A pig once made its way into the courtyard of a beautiful mansion. He soon found his way to the stables and kitchens, wallowed in filth, crammed itself full of garbage, and then returned to his home.

"What have you seen?" asked the owner. "They do say that the homes of the rich are filled with pearls and diamonds, and everything of the finest."

The pig grunted, "What nonsense that is. I saw no splendor at all—nothing but dirt and garbage."

Guha was an Arab philosopher. One day, he sold his house on condition that one particular nail should remain his property. Every day, he was habitually admitted to the house to check upon his nail. The house became accessible to him, and it was as if he had never sold it.

A rich but very tight-fisted merchant had one habitual answer whenever anyone came to him for some charitable purpose, even for the most worthy ones: "I cannot give."

One day this same person unfortunately fell into a nearby river. A young man who happened to be passing by called out to him: "Give me your hand and I will pull you out."

But instinctively, and as a result of many repetitions, the miser promptly called out: "I cannot give."

The reader can supply the conclusion to the story.

———

At roundup time, they like to tell about the cowboy, who, hanging on to a running steer's tail, was dragged across the hard ground and through brush until he was cut, battered and bruised. Fearing he would be killed, the other cowboys who were watching, shouted wildly at him: "Let go! Let go!"

"Let go, nothing!" he yelled back. "I'm doing all I can to hold on."

———

There is a story about a miller and a camel. One winter day, when the miller was sleeping in the house, he was awakened by a noise. Looking up, he saw a camel that had thrust his nose through the door.

"It's very cold out here," said the camel. "Please let me warm my nose a little."

"Very well," said the miller, "but just the nose."

A little later, the camel asked to put his forehead in; then his neck. Bit by bit he kept crowding in, until at last his whole body was in the miller's room.

Then the camel began to walk about the room, knocking things over and doing whatever he pleased. The miller asked that he leave.

"If you don't like the room, you can leave it whenever you wish," replied the camel. "As for myself, I am very comfortable and mean to remain."

The same goes for a habit that comes knocking and then takes over.

———

A wise old man was once taking a walk through a forest with an idle, careless youth by his side. The man suddenly stopped and pointed to four plants. The first was a tiny sprout, just coming up out of the earth. The second had rooted itself quite firmly in the soil. The third was a small shrub. And the fourth had grown into a well-developed tree.

The old man said, "Pull up this first plant."

The youth pulled it up easily with his fingers.

"Now pull the second," said the old man.

With slight effort the plant came up, roots and all.

202

"And now the third," continued the old man.

The boy pulled with one hand, then the other, but it would not come. Then he took both hands, and the plant yielded to his strength.

"And now," said the man, "try the fourth."

The young boy grasped the trunk with all his might, but as could be expected, not even a leaf shook. "I cannot move it," he exclaimed.

"I didn't expect that you would," commented the wise man. "You see, it is the same with the habits you have acquired. When they are young and small, you can get rid of them, but when they are full grown, they cannot be uprooted."

It is believed that the young man took the visual demonstration and changed his way of life.

~

HANDICAP

A beautiful story is told of the king who owned a valuable diamond, that was the most pure and perfect diamond in the entire world. One day the diamond fell and a deep scratch covered the face of it.

The king summoned the best diamond experts to correct the blemish, but they could not remove the blemish without cutting away a good part of the surface, thus reducing the weight and value of the diamond.

Finally, one expert appeared and assured him that he could fix the diamond without reducing its value. The self-confidence of this expert was convincing and the king gave the diamond to this man. In a few days this artistic expert returned the diamond and the king was amazed to behold that the ugly scratch had disappeared and in its place was etched a beautiful rose. The old ugly scratch had become the stem of an exquisite flower.

~

HAPPINESS

A poor man went to a banker one day and saw a pile of banknotes which the banker was busy counting. The poor man thought of his poverty-stricken home, and the wants of his family, and almost without thinking, he said half aloud, "How happy some of this money would make me."

The banker overheard him. "What did you just say, my good man?" he asked. The poor man was a bit frightened, claiming that he had really not intended saying anything. However, the banker persisted. "How much of this money would it take to make you happy?" he asked.

"I don't really know," stammered the poor man, "but the weather is cold, my wife is ill, the family is hungry, and I am sick. But I don't want much; about $25 would get us all we need."

"Bill," said the banker to his clerk. "Give this man $25."

The poor man's heart raced with joy. He could not get home fast enough to tell his wife the good news. At the close of the day, the clerk asked the banker how he should enter the money spent. The books had to be kept in balance. The banker thought a moment, and said: "Write, for making a man and his family happy—$25."

A sage once counseled: "A person must always make himself lighthearted and happy. Even when things are clouded by sadness, one must fight to smile. Somewhere among all sad thoughts there must be some recollection of better days which may curve your lips into a smile. No matter how faint the smile, it will warm your heart which will, in turn, brighten your spirit; and a bright spirit cannot be defeated by sadness."

"The happiest people are those who think the most interesting thoughts," commented William Lyon Phelps. "Those who decide to use leisure as a means of mental development, who love good music, good books, good pictures, good company, good conversation, what are they? They are the happiest people in the world; and they are not only happy in themselves, they are the cause of happiness in others."

A wealthy and very unhappy man went to his spiritual adviser and begged to be taught the art of being happy.

"I cannot sleep at night, nor can I rest during the day. I am tense, nervous, and always depressed. What can you do to help me?" cried the "poor" rich man.

"Well," said the holy man, "there is nothing that I can do for you, but I know of a man who may be able to help you. Jonathan, the handyman, lives near the outskirts of town. Go to him, and tell him that I have sent you. I know he will surely help you."

The rich man went to the outskirts of town and found the place where Jonathan, the handyman, lived. Jonathan's home was

very humble indeed. It was a hut containing only one room, a scant amount of furniture, and poverty shared every corner of this room with him. But as he answered the rich man's knock on his ramshackle door, Jonathan's face glowed with contentment. "I have been sent to you by the spiritual leader of our congregation who said that you can cure my mind of the unrest and depression with which it has been afflicted."

"He sent you to me?" cried the amazed Jonathan. "I wonder why? Before I can help you I must know what unhappiness means, and I have never been unhappy."

One may be happy, though humble and poor; and one may be perfectly wretched, though powerful and rich.

A group of men were having coffee together, and during the conversation one witty fellow told some jokes. Everyone enjoyed the humor, but one man in particular laughed louder than the rest. The other men stared at the man in disbelief because he was known to be a man of very serious mien.

The fellow who had livened the party with his jokes explained to his bewildered friends: "I told the jokes mostly for the benefit of the man whom you heard laugh so heartily. He is burdened with so many problems and is often very depressed. It is an act of mercy to draw him out of himself and to put a smile on his unhappy face."

William Blake's description of a happy man might be adopted by many of us if we are to find happiness in life:

> I have mental joys and mental health,
> Mental friends and mental wealth,
> I've a wife that I love and that loves me;
> I've all but riches bodily.

"Which part of the body helps the others?" asked a boy of his father.

"Son," replied the father, "I think it is the eye. A beautiful eye makes silence eloquent; a kind eye makes contradiction an assent; an understanding eye brings happiness to the heart."

Happiness does not come from possession, but rather from our appreciation of them. It does not come from our work, but from our attitude toward that work. It does not come from success, but from the spiritual growth we attain in achieving that success.

About 100 years ago, Robert Louis Stevenson wrote in his book, *An Apology for Idlers*: "There is no duty we so much underrate, as the duty of being happy."

A very practical definition of happiness was given by Dr. Albert Schweitzer. "Happiness," he said, "is nothing more than good health and a bad memory."

A large dog saw a little puppy chasing its tail and asked, "Why are you chasing your tail?"

The puppy replied: "I have mastered philosophy; I have solved the problems of the universe which no dog before me accomplished; I have learned that the best thing for a dog is happiness, and that happiness is my tail. Therefore I am chasing it; and when I catch it, I shall have happiness."

The older dog took only a minute to reply: "My son, I, too, have paid attention to the problems of the universe in my weak way, and have formed some opinions. I, too, have judged that happiness is a fine thing for a dog, and that happiness is in my tail. But I have noticed that when I chase it, it keeps running away from me; but when I go about my business, it comes after me."

HATRED

Charles Lamb once said, in his own whimsical way: "Don't introduce me to that man. I want to go on hating him, and I can't hate a man whom I know."

There is such a destructive reflex action in the soul of any man who allows himself to hate another that it is surprising any sensible person would allow himself to be subjected to it. Hate is a poison which vitiates all character, and brings about the degeneration of personality.

This story was told of General Robert E. Lee: Hearing General Lee speak in the highest terms to President Davis about a certain officer, another officer, greatly astonished, said to him, "General, do you not know that the man of whom you speak so highly to the President is one of your bitterest enemies and misses no opportunity to malign you?"

"Yes," replied General Lee, "but the President asked my opinion of him; he did not ask for his opinion of me."

HEALTH

Three friends agreed that they would separate, and each would master a particular field of learning by going to a special school. At an agreed upon time, they were to meet and compare their experiences.

When they met, one had perfected a telescope through which he could see what was happening in distant parts of the world.

The second had perfected a vehicle that could cover great distances in the briefest time.

The third had prepared a tonic that could cure all diseases.

As the first friend was demonstrating his telescope, he saw a distant country terribly distressed because the king's daughter was critically ill and no physician could cure her.

Said the second friend: "Hop into my speed carriage and let us go to help her!"

Said the third friend: "Take me along. I have the perfect tonic."

In minutes they were in the city. The tonic was administered and the princess recovered. The king had promised his daughter to the person who saved her life.

Said the first friend: "She is mine; I saw her in my telescope."

Said the second friend: "She is mine; my carriage brought us here."

Said the third friend: "She is mine; my tonic saved her life."

The king asked his daughter to decide who was entitled to her hand. She reflected for a while and answered: "You have all had a hand in saving my life. But I do want to look into the future. What will serve my welfare best? It will not be the telescope nor will it be the carriage. Only the tonic can best serve me and so I will marry the person who perfected the health-giving medicine."

When Jim collapsed in the doctor's office, the doctor who had known him well confided to a mutual friend: "Jim sacrificed his life for his beliefs."

"What beliefs did he cherish?" the friend wanted to know.

"Jim believed," answered the doctor, "that he could live a 30 year old life with a 55 year old body."

———

A nice old gentleman of 75 went to a physician and requested a general checkup. After looking him over thoroughly, the doctor reported, smilingly, that everything was fine.

"Tell me," said the doctor, as the old patient paid his fee, "have you followed any regular regimen which would account for your excellent condition?"

"Well, it's this way," the patient replied. "When I was married some fifty years ago, I entered into an agreement with my wife to the effect that whenever I lost my temper and began to blow off steam, she was to remain silent. When she, on the other hand, lost her temper, I agreed to leave the house. Well, for over fifty years I have enjoyed a fine outdoor life."

———

Billie Burke, the famous actress, was enjoying a trans-Atlantic ocean trip when she noticed that a gentleman at the next table was suffering from a very bad cold.

"Are you very uncomfortable?" she asked sympathetically.

The man nodded.

"I'll tell you just what to do for it," she offered. "Go back to your stateroom, and drink lots of orange juice. Take five aspirin tablets. Cover yourself with all the blankets you can find. Sweat the cold out. I know just what I am talking about. I am Billie Burke of Hollywood."

The man smiled warmly, and introduced himself in return: "Thanks, I am Dr. Mayo, of the Mayo Clinic."

———

To get his wealth, he spent his health,
And then with might and main
He turned around and spent his wealth
To get his health again.

———

Three men were talking one day about the frailties of people. The conversation was lively, with each of the three people giving his interpretation.

Said the first man: "The trouble with most people is that they eat too much."

The second man objected, and said, "It isn't how much you eat, but what you eat that counts."

The third man, a very wise person, commented, "It's neither what you eat or how much you eat. It's what's eating you that is important."

HEART

"You must have a good heart," said one man to another, "if you are going to act right in this world. Suppose my watch were not going well: would it do any good if I went to the townclock, and made the hands of the watch to point the same as those of the clock? You know it would do no good; for the hand would, before long, be as inaccurate as ever. I must send my watch to a watchmaker, that he may put its heart right, and then the hands will go right."

A teacher asked a little girl in her class: "Do you think you have a new heart?"

"Yes, teacher, I hope so," replied the child.

"What makes you hope so?"

"Because I love the things which I used to hate, and hate what I used to love."

The Chinese recite a beautiful verse about the heart which reads:

> If there is righteousness in the heart,
> There will be beauty in the character.
> If there is beauty in the character,
> There will be harmony in the home.
> If there is harmony in the home,
> There will be order in the nation.
> If there will be order in the nation,
> There will be peace in the world.

The understanding of fellow man was beautifully expressed in a poem by Edna St. Vincent Millay:

> The world stands out on either side
> No wider than the heart is wide;
> Above the world is stretched the sky—
> No higher than the soul is high.

> The heart can push the sea and land
> Farther away on either hand;
> The soul can split the sky in two,
> And let the face of God shine through.

HEAVEN

"I know the way to heaven," said a young girl to her brother, who stood by her side, looking at a picture-book.

"You do?" asked the brother. "Please tell me how to get there."

"Just commence going up," she replied, "and keep on going up all the time and you'll get there. But remember, you must never turn back."

There will be three things which will surprise us when we get to heaven:

> One, to find many there whom we did not expect;
> Another, to find some not there whom we had expected;
> A third, and perhaps the greatest wonder, will be to find
>   ourselves there.

A man had a striking dream. He dreamed he had ascended the ladder from earth to heaven. Expectantly, he knocked on the door. Someone responded and demanded, "Who is that knocking?"

Proudly, the man called his name.

"Who is with you?" came the reply.

"No one," answered the man, "I am alone."

"Sorry," said the angel, "but we are instructed never to open these gates for a single individual. Bring another soul with you and both of you will gain entrance."

I. L. Peretz, the great Yiddish writer, described the true holy man, the true *tzadik,* when he told the story of the Rebbe of Nemirov who disappeared every Friday morning during the *Selichot* (penitential) period before the High Holidays. He didn't appear in synagogue for the *Selichot* service, and whenever people asked: 'Where is the holy rebbe?"—his *hasidim* would answer: "He is in heaven making preparations with God for the coming year."

One Litvak, a learned Talmudist who did not believe in the rebbe, and who refused to be taken in by all these fanciful tales about the holy rebbe and his exploits in heaven, decided to find out for himself. Can you guess what this Litvak did?

On a Thursday night, he crept under the rebbe's bed so he would see exactly what the rebbe does on Friday morning when he is supposed to be in the synagogue.

Early on Friday morning, the Litvak was up. He peeked out from under the bed and watched the rebbe as he started to dress. From his closet, the rebbe took a bundle of clothes—the kind the peasants wore—linen trousers, high boots, a heavy mackinaw, a big felt hat and a wide leather belt studded with brass nails. Then he reached under the bed and drew out a long-handled axe.

The Litvak watched all this and trembled, especially when the sharp axe passed so close to his nose.

He followed the rebbe to the outskirts of the town and watched as he chopped down a tree, and then converted the tree into logs and the logs into sticks. He watched as the rebbe tied them into a bundle and made his way to a small broken down shack where a sick, frightened woman lived all alone.

He knocked at the window, and the woman asked in a frightened voice: "Who is there?"

"It is I, Vassil," answered the rebbe in a Russian-peasant accent.

"Who is Vassil? What do you want?" she asked.

"I have wood to sell, very cheap."

"I have no money," she answered. "Go away."

"You don't need money, I'll trust you."

"But who will make the fire?" she asked.

"I'll make the fire," answered the rebbe.

Then Peretz continues with the story. The rebbe goes into the house and, as he puts the wood in the fireplace, he recites in a soft voice the first part of the *Selichot* prayers.

Then he kindles the fire and recites in a more joyous voice the second part of the penitential prayers. When the fire is fully ablaze, he recites the third and final section of the *Selichot*.

The Litvak watches all this through the shack window and he is dumb-struck.

From that time on, whenever anyone asks a disciple of the

rebbe where the holy rebbe of Nemirov is on Friday morning when the penitential prayers are recited, and why the rebbe is not in the synagogue—*and* a disciple of the rebbe answers: "He is up in heaven making preparations," the Litvak does not laugh or mock anymore. He only adds quietly, "Yes, he is up in heaven— if not higher!"

Voltaire never missed an opportunity to scoff at religion. One day during a formal dinner party, he said, "I would sell my place in heaven for a Prussian dollar."

"Monsieur Voltaire," observed another person who was present, "in Prussia we never buy costly goods without making certain of the owner's title. If you can prove your right to a place in heaven, I will buy it for ten thousand dollars."

Joe McCarthy, former manager of the New York Yankees, was fond of telling this story:

McCarthy had a dream. He was called to heaven. There he was requested by St. Peter to assemble a baseball team. What a pleasure it was for him, for all the old-time great men of baseball were there for him to choose from: Babe Ruth, Lou Gehrig, Christy Matthewson, Walter Johnson and a host of others. McCarthy rubbed his hands together in delight. What a lineup!

Then the phone rang. It was Satan challenging him to a ball game. "What!" cried McCarthy. "You haven't got a chance! I've got all the good players!"

"Yes," answered Satan. "But I've got all the umpires."

An old rabbi lived over a grocery store on the lower East Side of New York. In front of the grocery was a sign reading: *RABBI RABINOWITZ IS UPSTAIRS*. When the old rabbi died, after a long dedicated life, he left no money even for his burial. He had never demanded payment for any service he had rendered to the members of his tiny congregation. When he was buried, his friends wanted to put up a memorial or stone on his grave. They had no money for an expensive tomb-stone so they set up over his grave the very same sign that hung in front of the grocery. It served as a beautiful epitaph: *RABBI RABINOWITZ IS UP-STAIRS.*

A minister became seriously ill and would see no visitors. However, when an agnostic friend of his came to see him, he ordered that he be admitted.

"I appreciate this very much," said the agnostic, "but why do you see me when you deny yourself to all your friends?"

"I'll tell you why," said the minister. "I feel confident of seeing my friends in the next world, but this may very well be the last chance I have to see you."

HEAVEN AND HELL

A philosopher was once asked to describe the basic difference between heaven and hell. He replied: "In hell there are thousands of souls, all standing together, their arms bound by splints and heavy ropes so that they cannot bend their elbows. Overhead hang quantities of food: fruit, bread and vegetables. The inhabitants of hell are all starving and emaciated. True, there is plenty of food hanging overhead, and they can reach it with their hands. They can touch it, but they cannot bend their elbows to bring the food to their mouths."

"And now, heaven," continued the philosopher. "Here, we see the same thousands of people, their arms bound by splints and heavy ropes. The same quantities of food hang overhead. But there is a vast difference. In heaven, they are not at all hungry because they have eaten; they are happy because they are satisfied. True, their arms are bound at the elbow. They can reach up to the food hanging overhead; they can touch it and pluck it; but, as in hell, they cannot bring the food to their own mouths. But in heaven the difference is this: here each one conveys the food to his neighbor's mouth! And that," said the philosopher, "is the basic difference between heaven and hell—a helping hand."

A man of unsavory character died and was admitted to Hell. He found the place not at all to his liking. His quarters were hot, hotter than he had anticipated. His bed was most uncomfortable. He griped and complained continuously. In great desperation, he finally cried out, "Please get me out of this place!"

An angel heard his cry and asked him what he had ever done to merit a better resting place. After much pondering and soul-searching the man replied, "I remember once giving a carrot to a half-starved donkey."

"Good," replied the angel, "I believe I can now help you." No sooner were these words out of the angel's mouth than an immense carrot was lowered from Heaven and a Voice cried out, "Take hold of the carrot and you will be saved."

The man needed no second invitation. He seized the carrot, which began to carry him heavenwards. Hundreds of souls saw this miracle. They, too, wanted to be saved, so they hurried to take hold of the carrot, and began to rise with him. Suddenly, the man's true nature asserted itself and he shouted, "Let go there! This is my carrot. Go get your own carrot if you wish to be saved!" Immediately, the carrot dropped and the man returned to his original destination.

HECKLERS

Charles Lamb, the essayist, was giving a talk to a mixed gathering when someone in the audience hissed. A stunned silence followed, for this was totally unexpected in this very proper group. The speaker paused for a few moments and then calmly said: "There are only three things that hiss—a goose, a snake, and a fool. Come forth and be identified."

HELPING

There wasn't a person who showed any compassion for the poor man as he went begging for a job so that he could have a meal and a bed to sleep in. He was growing more and more discouraged as the weeks passed by. One wintry day, he slipped on the icy street and broke his leg. A crowd gathered; an ambulance came, and soon he was in the hospital. There, he was bathed, new clothing was given him, and he was placed in a bed to recuperate. Now that he was clean and fed and had a bed to sleep in, he wrote to his wife, "Thank God I broke a leg."

John Galsworthy, the noted English author, had a framed motto which for years hung over his writing table. These were its words: "I shall pass through this world but once; any good thing, therefore, that I can do, or any kindness that I can show to any human being, or dumb animal, let me do it now. Let me not defer it or neglect it, for I shall not pass this way again."

214

An old Quaker, passing along the street, saw a cartman's horse suddenly fall dead. It was a serious loss, for the horse was the man's livelihood.

The bystanders shook their heads and clucked sympathetically. The Quaker took off his broad-brimmed hat, placed a bank-note in it, and said: "Friends, I am sorry for this man ten dollars worth. How sorry are you?"

A holy man was once visited by a poor man who impressed him as a man of quality. The saintly man received him cordially and with great respect. It turned out later, however, that the guest was an impostor. This unpleasant incident upset the family, but the holy man reassured them and told them that they must not be disturbed by it. He cited the following example:

"When God decided to delight our Father Abraham with the blessing of hospitality, He often sent him guests who were not really in need of his hospitality, for angels are not in need of food at all. Our Bible has thus indicated that it is incumbent upon every individual to fill his heart with goodness and a sincere desire to serve humanity, never doubting that the one who puts his hand out to you is really in need. It behooves us to do our duty and not to sit in judgment of others."

There is a story of an old man who went about carrying an oil can, and whenever he went through a door that creaked, he would pour a little oil on the hinges. If the gate was hard to open, he would oil the latch. And so he passed through life lubricating the hard places, and making it easier for those who came after him.

HEREAFTER

Two unborn babies in their mother's womb are aware only of life as they then know it. Imagine that the two are able to discuss the possibilities that await them in the future. One baby is an optimist; the other, a pessimist. The optimist believes that life lies ahead; the other thinks that death is in store for them.

"Nature has been working on us for nine months and nature isn't crazy," says the optimist. "It must mean something; something is coming of all this. We're not just going to die."

The pessimist would reply: "What are you talking about? There's no such thing as our going on living outside of this matrix in the womb. We will be cut off from all nutrition and we will die."

It would be difficult for the optimist to describe breathing, eating, drinking, freedom to move about. And if the optimist was the first to leave the womb, the pessimist might hear the first cries of his brother and believe that the end had come. He would not in any way hear the congratulations of the parents or see the smiles of joy on their faces.

How foolish it is to deny the possibility of a different kind of existence after death simply because we cannot describe it in detail.

Every man has the following three friends: his children, his money, and the good deeds he accomplishes in this world. When the time comes for him to leave this world he calls upon his children to save him and the children reply, "Don't you know that no one can conquer death?"

The dying man then calls upon his money, saying: "Day and night I have worked for you, save me now." But the money replies, "Wealth cannot deliver you from death."

The expiring man next calls upon his good deeds and they reply, "Go in peace. By the time you arrive in the next world we will be there before you to offer you help."

—Talmud

HEREDITY

Two seeds befriended each other, one a flower seed, the other the seed of a thorn. They lived together and were proud to consider themselves brothers. One day they both felt a hand grasp and place them in plowed earth. They understood that they had been sown. Both agreed that they would spring from the earth as identical plants.

How amazed they were when they discovered that the flower seed had become a colorful flower whose fragrance filled the air, while the thorn seed grew to be a prickly thorn bush, repulsive to the eye and painfully injurious to those who dared approach or touch it.

"It is obvious," lamented the thorn, "that naught avails, for the plant depends upon the seed that is sown."

She had given birth to her first-born, a boy, and both she and her husband wrangled about what to name him. The husband wanted the new-born boy named after *his* father. She wanted the boy named after *her* father. Interestingly enough, the names of both grandparents were the same: NATHAN.

They came before the wise man who was going to settle the issue. "You see," claimed the wife, "my father was a pious man, a great scholar, but my husband's father was a plain ordinary thief. How can I name my son after a thief?"

"My decision," said the wise man, "is to name the boy Nathan. If he turns out to be a scholar, then you'll know that he was named after his mother's father. If he turns out to be a thief, you'll know that he was named after his father's father."

The principal had entered the Sunday School classroom. The boys and girls had just finished reading a Bible story. Smiling broadly, the principal asked the class, "Why do you believe in God?"

Many answers were given, but the one that really stunned the official came from the youngest in the group. He merely answered, "I guess it runs in the family."

A teacher noticed how courteous and polite one of her students was. Wishing to praise the girl and, at the same time, teach a lesson to the class, she asked: "Who taught you to be so polite?" Quickly, the girl answered: "No one, really, it just runs in our family."

HERITAGE

English history recounts that when Queen Anne elevated John Churchill to become the first Duke of Marlborough, some of the members of the established nobility would not readily accept the newcomer because of his humble parentage. They taunted the new Duke whenever the opportunity presented itself.

On one occasion, one of them said, mockingly, "Tell me, whose descendant are you?"

To which the Duke of Marlborough replied, "Sir, I am not a descendant; I am an ancestor."

217

"What can we wish for in a heritage that is not to be found in God?" asks author Sinclair Lewis. And he answers the query with these words: "Would we have large possessions? He is immensity. Would we have a sure estate? He is immutability. Would we have a term of long continuance? He is eternity itself."

~~~

During a formal dinner, a snobbish lady turned to Rabbi Stephen S. Wise and stated that she was a member of the Daughters of the American Revolution. "And my ancestors," she said, "witnessed the signing of the Declaration of Independence."

The rabbi replied: "That is all very well, Madam, but I do want you to know that my ancestors witnessed the signing of the Ten Commandments."

~~~

HOARDING

A youth was leaving his aunt's house after a visit. Looking out of the window, he saw it was beginning to rain so he took an umbrella that was standing in a corner, and was proceeding to open it, when the old lady sprang toward him, exclaiming: "No, no! I have had that umbrella twenty-three years, and it has never been wet yet; do not wet it now."

~~~

HOME

Because of the housing shortage near the military base where he was stationed, a young doctor and his wife and three children had to live in cramped quarters in a hotel. A friend said to the doctor's six-year-old daughter, "Isn't it too bad that you don't have a home?"

To which the philosophic young girl replied, "Oh, we have a home, we just don't have a house to put it in."

~~~

A young girl watched her mother dust the furniture, wash the dishes, and vacuum the rugs, and thinking of how many times she did this type of work, she asked, "Mother, don't you ever get tired cleaning the house?"

The mother replied, "I'm not cleaning the house. I'm building a home."

~~~

A woman once came to a real estate agent with the intention of buying a house. The salesman showed her a variety of dwellings, but she was not satisfied. One was too large, another too small; one had the wrong design and another was in the wrong neighborhood. Finally, in complete exasperation, the agent said, "Madam, why do you need a home? You were born in a hospital, educated in a school building, courted in an automobile and married in a House of God. You live at hamburger stands and eat out of freezers and cans. You spend your mornings at the golf course, your afternoons at the bridge table and your evenings at the movies. All you really need is a garage."

An artist who wanted to paint the most beautiful picture in the world, asked a pastor, "What is the most beautiful thing in the world?"

"Faith," answered the pastor. "You can feel it in every house of worship, find it at every altar."

The artist asked a young bride the same question. "Love," she replied. "Love builds poverty into riches, sweetens tears, makes much of little. Without it there is no beauty."

A weary soldier said: "Peace is the most beautiful thing in the world. War is the most ugly. Wherever you find peace, you find beauty."

"Faith, love and peace! How can I paint them?" thought the artist. Entering his door he saw faith in the eyes of his children, and love in the eyes of his wife. And there in his home was the peace that love and faith had built. So he painted the picture of the most beautiful thing in the world. And, when he finished, he called it "HOME."

HONESTY

A king of Prussia once visited a prison and interviewed the prisoners one by one. He asked each of them what crime they had committed. They all declared themselves innocent of any misdeed whatsoever, except one man who owned up to the evil he had done, and admitted he was getting what he deserved. The king ordered his immediate release saying, "This man obviously has no business here among all the innocent people."

219

"Joe," said a customer to the clerk, "you must give me a good measure, you know, your master is not in." With this, he gave him a sly wink.

Joe looked sharply at the customer and replied: "My Master is always in."

⁓

Two businessmen asked their minister to give them his blessing, since they were going into partnership.

"I'll do more than that," replied the wise minister. "I'll draw up the partnership agreement."

With these words he took pen and paper and wrote the letters A B C D. When he noticed their questioning glance, he explained:

A   stands for Agreement
B   stands for Blessing
C   stands for Cheating
D   stands for Disaster

"If you will agree between yourselves, there will be blessing. But if you cheat one another, then there will be disaster."

⁓

It was a cozy set-up. The father was relaxing in his favorite chair after having eaten an excellent dinner. His young son entered the room and showed him a new penknife, which he said he had found in the street.

"Are you sure it was lost?" inquired the father.

"Of course, it was lost!" his son answered. "I saw the man looking for it myself."

⁓

The little girl was seven years of age. She was watching her mother smooth cold cream over her face, and asked, "What's that for, Mother?"

The mother answered, "Why, this is to make me beautiful."

The mother then proceeded to remove the cold cream with tissues. The girl looked up at her mother and remarked, "Didn't work, did it?"

⁓

HONOR

The Talmud says that when a man appears before the Throne of Judgment, the first question he will be asked is not "Have you

220

believed in God?" or "Have you prayed?" or "Have you performed the rituals properly?" He will be asked, "Have you been honorable and faithful in all your deaings with your fellow man?"

HOPE

When John Adams asked his old friend Thomas Jefferson if he would agree to live his seventy-three years over again, Jefferson replied, "Yea, I think, with you, that it is a good world on the whole. My temperament is sanguine. I steer my bark with hope in the head, leaving fear astern."

Ella Wheeler Wilcox, who was known as the feminine Eddie Guest of her day, once emphasized, in poetic form, her idea of hope in the future.

> "Has some misfortune fallen to your lot?
> This, too, will pass away; absorb the thought,
> And wait—your waiting will not be in vain,
> Time gilds with gold the iron links of pain.
> The dark today leads into light tomorrow;
> There is no endless joy, no endless sorrow."

A mighty king condemned one of his subjects to die. The poor wretch offered to teach the king's horse to fly if the king would only postpone the execution for one year.

"Why delay the inevitable?" a friend asked the condemned man.

"It's not inevitable," he replied. "The odds are 4-to-1 in my favor:

1. The king might die.
2. I might die.
3. The horse might die.
4. I might teach the horse to fly.

In the Louvre there is a beautiful painting of Goethe's *Faust*. It depicts Mephistopheles and Faust, with a chessboard between them on the table. Mephistopheles points with a leer; and Faust sits there dejected. Mephistopheles says, "Checkmate."

One day a great chess player was admiring the painting when

221

suddenly he lunged forward and exclaimed, "Satan, one minute; Faust has one more move!"

Let us say to the devil who threatens our civilization with doom, "Wait Satan, one minute; we have one more move."

A sole survivor of a shipwreck was cast upon an uninhabited island. After much trouble, he built a rude hut in which he placed the little belongings he had saved. Each day he prayed to God for deliverance, and anxiously scanned the horizon to hail any ship that might chance to pass. One day, upon returning from a hunt for food, he was horrified to find that his hut was in flames. All that he had was gone. To his limited vision, it was the worst that could happen, and he even cursed God. Yet, the very next day a ship arrived. "We saw your smoke signal," the captain said.

HOSPITALITY

There was once a hotel keeper who was known for the goodness of his heart. Some merchants once arrived late on the Sabbath eve, and the inn keeper, who was also a pious man, received them very cordially.

As the merchants were preparing for the Sabbath services, he entered their room and told them: "Since you are strangers, here, I should like to acquaint you with the rates at my hotel. It will cost you $25.00 per person for two nights and the day. You may think this price is rather steep, but for that price you can eat and drink of the best during the entire Sabbath, including the late evening meal on Saturday."

The merchants agreed and remained in the inn for the entire Sabbath, partaking of the finest in food and drink. On Sunday morning, when they asked for a bill, the hotel keeper laughed and said: "Do you think that I would sell a good deed as valuable as hospitality for $25.00?"

The merchants paid nothing and went away enriched in pocket and in heart.

The *Proverbs* state that the virtuous man shall eat until he is satisfied, while the wicked shall suffer hunger. A bright scholar once explained this as follows:

"When a virtuous man invites a poor man to his home and asks him to dine with him at the same table, he tries to eat as much as possible in order to encourage the poor man to eat a great deal without feeling embarrassment. On the other hand, when a wicked man invites a poor man to dinner, he gorges himself beforehand, and when he sits down to the table with the poor man, he eats as little as possible so that the poor man may follow his example and consume very little."

HUMILITY

The Talmud, in describing the Temple that King Solomon built in Jerusalem, tells us that Solomon imported the finest wood and stone from all parts of the world so that the edifice he was to erect would be a symbol of beauty and goodness for all time. He decorated the interior with handsome tapestries and adorned it with vessels of gold and silver. The raw wood and the lifeless stone now radiated warmth and life.

But there was one room in this glamorous and complex structure that King Solomon left unadorned. And that room was called "The Chamber of the Silent."

The only pieces of furniture in this room were its charity boxes. People entered and left the room in silence. In this room only their hearts spoke. How much of their worldly good they dropped into the boxes nobody knew, nobody cared, nobody inquired. And with the same, quiet anonymity by which the charity was collected, it was dispensed. No one knew who entered the room to give; no one knew who entered to receive. Man's mark in that society was measured by the modesty, the humility, with which he was able to share his life and the fruit of his hands with others.

There was once a man, a student of character, who had great disdain for people who disregarded the rights of others in their own frantic scramble to be noticed. On the other hand, he looked up to the truly humble. In one short sentence, he made his feelings clear: "There is always a place reserved for the person who doesn't knock anyone over while grabbing a place for himself."

A preacher once prayed: "I beseech, Almighty God, that You heed the prayers of those who stand in need of Your help so that

223

they may be spared the necessity of humbling themselves to ask me to pray for them."

⁓

A well-known holy man was on a mission to collect contributions for an important cause. Since it was winter-time, he was wearing rubbers.

As he entered the well-apportioned house of a notorious miser in town, he removed his rubbers in the hall. The miser, at once suspecting that the other had come for a donation, was not exactly exalted over the prospect and greeted him with a sarcastic barb:

"In the olden days," he said, "one would hardly see a man in your position wearing rubbers."

Without hesitation, the saintly man replied: "That is because in the olden days people like myself did not have to crawl through the mud as I have had to do today."

⁓

Ernie Pyle, the war correspondent, was in the Pacific Theatre of Operations during World War II, covering the invasion of one of the islands. There he met a soldier who was busily reading the Pacific edition of *Stars and Stripes,* the armed forces newspaper. Suddenly the soldier turned to the journalist and showed him an article describing the courage, devotion, and heroism that was being shown by American troops on the beachhead, and asked to which beachhead the article referred.

Mr. Pyle answered, "The one which you now occupy."

⁓

A friend once asked the famous conductor of a great symphony orchestra which instrument in the orchestra he considered the most difficult to play. Without a moment's hesitation the leader answered, "The second fiddle. I can get plenty of first violinists. But to find one who can play second fiddle with enthusiasm—that's the problem. And if we have no second fiddle, we have no harmony."

⁓

A farmer went with his son into a wheat field to see if it was ready for harvest. "See, father," exclaimed the boy, "how straight these stems hold up their heads! They must be the best ones. Those that hang their heads down I am sure cannot be too good."

The farmer plucked a stalk of each kind, and said, "See here, my son. This stalk that stood so straight is light-headed and almost

224

good for nothing, while this that hung its head so modestly is full of the most beautiful grain."

A story is told of a king who once wanted to learn the secret of humility. To achieve humility he wore old clothes on his body, ate very little food, left his beautiful palace to live in a hovel, and employed men to revile him. All this did not help, for he felt more proud than ever before. A wise man then showed him the path to true humility when he advised: "Dress like a king, dine like a king, act like a king; but inside, let your heart be humble."

Carlos Romulo tells of an interesting experience in his youth:

"I had just won an oratorical contest in the Manila High School. Flushed with exultation over my victory, I ignored the congratulations of one of the other contestants. As we left the auditorium, my old father asked, 'Why didn't you shake hands with Julio?'

"I told father that I had no use for Julio, for he had been speaking ill of me before the contest.

"I can still see my dignified, gray-haired father, as he put his arm around my shoulder, and said, 'Your grandfather used to tell me that the taller the bamboo grows, the lower it bends. Remember that always, my boy.'

" 'The taller the bamboo grows, the lower it bends.' Throughout these many years this homespun advice on humility has helped to guide my life."

After Chaim Weizman died, Ben-Zvi was called to the presidency of Israel. On the day he became president, he returned home at night and found a sentry marching up and down in front of his dwelling. He asked the soldier what he was doing there. The young officer replied that he had been sent by the Chief of Staff as an honor guard before the home of the President. Ben-Zvi was truly amazed. He entered his home but in a few minutes he went out again into the cold, wintry, night air.

"Look here," he said to the soldier on duty, "it's cold outside. Come in and have a cup of hot tea."

The soldier indicated that he could not leave his post. "Orders are orders," he informed Ben-Zvi.

The President entered his home again. "Make some hot tea,

please," he said to his wife, "I am going out once again to speak to the sentry."

Once again he walked out and addressing the soldier said, "Look, I have an idea. You go in and have a cup of tea. I will stand outside with your gun and take your post."

Toscanini was so humble that when his orchestra burst into applause at a rehearsal because they realized the heights to which he had lifted them, he said with tears in his eyes, "It is not me. It is Beethoven."

When Thomas Mann was visiting America for the first time, one of Hollywood's famous writers abased himself before the novelist, emphasizing that he was nothing, a mere hack; that his work was not worth mentioning in the same breath with that of the master.

Mann listened with infinite patience and courtesy. But when the party was over, he turned to his host, an old friend, and said, "That man has no right to make himself so small. He is not that big."

Paul Cezanne never knew that he was called the "father of modern painting." Having struggled for 35 years without recognition, the shy old man was living in oblivion in Aix, giving away masterpieces to indifferent neighbors.

Then, a discerning Paris dealer gathered several of these canvases and presented the first Cezanne exhibit. The great of the art world were tremendously impressed and they saluted the master.

Cezanne arrived at the gallery on his son's arm. He gazed wonderingly at his paintings. Tears came to his eyes. "Look," he whispered to his son, "they have framed them!"

A reporter once asked Billy Graham: "How do you explain your success?"

"The only explanation I know is God."

"But why," asked the reporter, "did God choose you?"

"When I get to Heaven," said Billy, "that's the first question I am going to ask Him."

In ancient Greece, there were a few politicians who decided to downgrade one of their number, as he had met with disfavor among them. In order to take their vengeance upon him, they used their influence to have him appointed as public scavenger.

However, the man, instead of being outraged and humiliated, took his new job with all seriousness, and set out to show one and all what could be done with this humble assignment. He corrected the city's unsanitary conditions, promoted civic cleanliness, stimulated civic pride, and made the city a healthier place to live in.

It later turned out that the post of public scavenger became a position of honor and responsibility, sought by the best of men.

Humility has the delicious and delicate taste of a rare vintage wine, but it takes an expert to discern its extraordinary quality and unique refinement. Moses possessed all the virtues and fine traits that any human being can possibly possess. The fact that the holy Bible chose to praise him specifically for his humility is the best proof that humility is the greatest, noblest trait.

There are those who say that neither they nor anyone else amount to anything worthwhile. According to these people, the world is filled with nothing but nonentities. This is false humility.

To be truly humble is to look up to others as if they were better and greater than you.

HUSBANDS

The bookstore looked attractive so the man entered. "Have you a book entitled *Man, Master of the Home?*"

The saleswoman looked at him for a moment and replied, "Try the fiction department, please."

A father who was hesitating whether to give his daughter in marriage to a worthy man having little money, or to a rich man who had no other recommendation, went to consult a counselor on the subject. "I would bestow my daughter," advised the counselor, "upon a man without money, rather than upon money without a man."

227

HYPOCRISY

There is the story of the old woman who was about to walk across an old, rickety bridge. She said: "O God, if I get across safely, I'll give five dollars to charity." When she was a quarter of the way across and all seemed well, she said, "Oh, God, I don't have so much. You will not mind, I know. Three dollars are also enough." As she walked a little further, the bridge suddenly began to shake underneath her feet. "Oh," she said, "I was only joking, God. Don't take me seriously!"

A monarch of old once invited his subjects to a celebration in the palace. Each was requested to bring a bottle of his finest wine which would be poured into a common vat. Now it happened that if he brought a bottle of water and poured it in, no one would be able to discern the difference. This he did. After all the subjects had emptied their bottles into the vat, the king invited the people to drink. To the startled king came the realization that all his subjects had brought water!

A wise man, sensitive to the frailties of humanity, once said: "I can understand and find excuses for many human weaknesses. What I cannot comprehend or forgive is the unmitigated gall of supposed friends who can hardly wait for your back to be turned before they launch a smear campaign."

IDEALS

The Talmud relates that the Roman government issued a decree forbidding the Jews to study and practice the Torah. A certain Pappus ben Judah came and found Rabbi Akiba publicly studying and teaching the Torah, and asked him: "Akiba, are you not afraid of the government?" Not long afterward, Rabbi Akiba was arrested and thrown into prison, and Pappus ben Judah was also arrested and imprisoned with him. When Pappus saw the rabbi in the cell, he exclaimed: "Happy are you, Rabbi Akiba, that you have been seized for studying and teaching the Torah! Woe unto Pappus who has been seized for busying himself with nonsense."

228

As a mother once sat by the cradle of her child, five spirits approached her and offered her a gift for the child.

The first said, "I am health, and whom I touch shall never know pain or sickness."

The second said, "I am wealth, and whom I touch shall never know poverty or want."

The third said, "I am fame, and whom I touch shall have immortal fame."

The fourth said, "I am love, and whom I touch shall have a friend in life's darkest hour." But the fifth said, "Whom I touch shall be forever faithful to his dreams and his ideals."

When the wise mother heard the fifth spirit, she took hold of his garment and besought him to touch her child.

~~~~~

Solomon did not ask for a long life, but for a good life. Philip James Bailey expressed a similar thought in *Festus*:

> We live in deeds, not years; in thoughts, not breaths;
> In feelings, not in figures on a dial.
> We should count time by heart-throbs. He most lives
> Who thinks most, feels the noblest, acts the best.

~~~~~

G. Linnaeus Banks summarized, in his oft-quoted verse, what may well serve as our goal in life.

> I live for those who love me,
>   For those who know me true,
> For the Heaven that smiles above me,
>   And awaits my spirit too;
>
> For the cause that lacks assistance,
>   For the wrong that needs resistance,
> For the future in the distance,
>   And the good that I can do.

~~~~~

IMAGINATION

"What is an actor, Dad?" asked a son of his father.

"An actor," replied the father. "Why an actor, son, is a man who can walk to the side of a stage, peer into the wings filled with theatrical props, dirty and dusty, and other actors, stagehands, old

229

clothes, and a mess of claptrap, and say: 'What a lovely view there is from this window!' "

A well-known American sculptor had in his studio a large block of marble. It had neither shape nor form; it was no more than a slab of stone. During spare hours, the sculptor chipped at it and cut from it, and soon there began to emerge the fine features of Abraham Lincoln. In fact, it looked as if this would be one of the finest representations of our great president.

One day while the sculptor was working, a young child happened to enter the studio. He saw the emerging bust of Lincoln and, with genuine astonishment, said to the sculptor: "How did you know that Lincoln was in that block of marble?"

The sculptor turned to the child and with a warm smile replied, "I saw the features of Abraham Lincoln in this block of marble and I am putting away all the marble that hides it.

IMITATION

The idea that a child aims to imitate a parent is best illustrated in the following poem:

> His little arms crept 'round my neck,
> And then I heard him say
> Four simple words I shan't forget,
> Four words that made me pray. . . .
>
> They turned a mirror on my soul,
> On secrets no one knew;
> They startled me, I hear them yet,
> He said, "I'll be like you!"

A man had a Chinese plate which he valued very much. One day it fell and cracked down the middle. He ordered six duplicates and, to be sure that he would receive the exact pattern, he sent his broken plate to the craftsman, as a sample. When he received the package from China, six months later, he was astonished to find the Chinese craftsman had so faithfully followed his copy that each new plate had a crack right down the middle.

A dinner was held in Hollywood to celebrate Charlie Chaplin's birthday. Chaplin entertained the guests throughout the evening by imitating people with whom they were familiar: friends, his chauffeur, his servants, his secretaries. Finally he sang at the top of his voice an aria from an Italian opera and sang it superbly.

"Why Charlie, I never knew you could sing so beautifully," a guest exclaimed.

"I can't sing at all," Chaplin rejoined. "I was only imitating Caruso."

A father warned his son not to go to the burlesque show because he would see things he should not see.

Naturally the young man sneaked off at the first opportunity and went to the show where, sure enough, he saw something he should never have seen: his father!

Some hunters are reported to have captured a number of monkeys by having small boots made for them, which they filled with pitch. The hunters sat down in sight of the monkeys, and pulled off and on their own boots; then retired, leaving the small ones. As soon as they were out of sight, the monkeys descended from the trees, and began doing as they had seen the hunters do. The boots stuck to their feet, they could not escape, and were easily caught.

A French naturalist once performed an experiment with insects called "processionary caterpillars." He led them onto the rim of a large flower pot, so that the leader found itself nose-to-tail with the last caterpillar in the procession.

Through force of instinct, the ring of insects circled the rim for seven days and nights. Then they all died of exhaustion and starvation in spite of a visible supply of food nearby.

Thoughtlessly following the beaten path can prove disastrous for people, too.

Every morning the worker in charge of blowing the noon factory whistle would check his watch with the clock in the jeweler's window as he passed on his way to work. After a number of years of doing this, he met the jeweler one day and asked him,

"Your clock in the window . . . is that set by Western Union Time or Naval Observatory Time . . . just how do you check it?"

"Oh," replied the jeweler, "I just check it every noon by your factory whistle."

Some people remind me of an incident which took place while I was detouring on my way to a meeting. I saw a car with this sign on it: "DON'T FOLLOW ME—I'M LOST, TOO."

IMMORTALITY

In the Gallery of the Louvre, Napoleon once turned from a fine picture to a nobleman standing beside him, and said, "That is a fine picture!"

"Yes, immortal," was the reply.

"How long will this picture and that statue last?" asked Napoleon.

"The picture five hundred years, and the statue a thousand years, sire."

"And this you call immortality?" Napoleon replied, turning away.

IMPATIENCE

A merchant was riding home with a knapsack full of gold behind him. It rained heavily, and he was wet through and through. He complained bitterly that God gave him such bad weather for his journey.

As he was riding through a dense forest, he saw a robber, who pointed a gun at him, and pulled the trigger. He would have been killed without a chance of escape but, owing to the rain, the powder had become damp, and the gun did not go off. The merchant escaped with both his gold and his life. "How foolish I was," he reflected, "to be impatient with God."

IMPRESSION

There was a shopkeeper in the city of Grodno whose knowledge of Hebrew was rather inferior and whose Talmudic knowledge was quite deficient. Yet, his majestic figure, his long, well-kept beard, his immaculate clothes, and his proud bearing gave him the appearance of being a great scholar. One day, when a group of Talmudic students was debating the interpretation of a difficult passage in the Talmud, this scholarly-looking gentleman entered the academy. The loud conflict subsided at once. "Sh-sh," one said to the other. "Let us ask that gentleman."

"In a moment, this impressive stranger was surrounded by a score of eager students who set forth their various opinions as to the exact meaning of the passage, and begged him to tell them what the right interpretation really was. The bearded, well-dressed, stately gentleman was shaken. Of course he did not know the interpretation of the passage, but to admit his lack of learning was not in his makeup.

"Look here, gentlemen," he said. "Never do this again. Fortunately, you happened to approach a scholar. But suppose you had asked this question of an untutored man, you surely would have embarrassed him. Therefore, I am not going to give you my opinion, so that you will be careful not to embarrass anyone in the future."

As a tourist in Italy, I walked through the magnificent ruins of ancient Pompeii. On the main street is a drinking fountain that stood in the middle of the thoroughfare centuries before the Common era. The guide pointed out where the water had gushed forth, and, amazingly, the spot on the marble where people placed the four fingers of their hand to lean over for a drink. There, etched in the marble, are the deep indentations of a human palm and four fingers. Incredible? It is hard to imagine that a hand leaning on a piece of marble would leave a mark. But when done for 400 years the hand might as well be a chisel.

IMPROVEMENT

A businessman was being interviewed by a newspaper reporter. The reporter commented, "I understand that you are a self-made man."

The man turned to face the reporter and said, "Yes, I guess you might call me a self-made man." Then a bit ruefully he added, "But if I had to do it over again I think I'd call in a little help."

233

A poet once described the goal of man in these few lines:

"Your task . . . to build a better world," God said.
I answered, "How . . . ?
This world is such a large vast place,
So complicated now,
And I so small and useless am.
There's nothing I can do."
But God in all His wisdom said,
"Just build a better you."

INDECISION

A hunter set out on a day's hunt and soon struck the trail of a deer and followed it for hours. Then he came upon the trail of a fox and decided that he would leave the deer and catch the fox. Then he came to where the trail of the fox was crossed by that of a rabbit. Since it was getting dark, he decided that he would pursue the rabbit. As dark fell, he discovered the trail of a mouse. He decided that it was too dark to catch anything but this mouse. So he followed its trail until it was so dark that he could not see. He went home that night empty-handed.

Lincoln used to tell the story of a blacksmith who heated a piece of iron in the forge, but did not know just what he was going to make out of it. At first he thought he would make a horseshoe; then he changed his mind and thought he would make a trivet. After he had hammered on the piece of iron for a little while, he changed his mind again and started on something new. By this time, he had hammered the iron so much that it was not good for much of anything. Holding it up with his tongs and looking at it in disgust, the blacksmith thrust it into a tub of water and listened to it hiss. "Well, at least I can make a fizzle out of it!" he exclaimed.

IDENTITY

On the third day of Creation, when God created the herbs and flowers of the field, He gave a suitable name to each of these lovely things. Later on, when they passed in review before the Throne of the Almighty, each one identified itself by repeating its own name. Every flower remembered its name, with the exception of one. This embarrassed little flower lowered its pretty head, and in a trembling voice declared that it had forgotten its name. Wishing to impress on his creations the importance of knowing who they were, God immediately renamed the flower and called it "Forget-me-not."

~~~

IDLENESS

Among the disciples of Hillel, the wise teacher, was one named Saboth, who submitted to idleness. Hillel was grieved, and resolved to cure him of his fault. He took him to the Valley of Hinnom near Jerusalem, where there was a stagnant pool, full of snakes and vermin and covered with muddy weeds.

"Here," said Hillel, "let us rest."

"Not here," cautioned the youth. "Do you not see what poisonous vapors it exhales?"

"You are right, my son; this bog is like the soul of a slothful man."

Hillel then took the youth to a waste field of thorns and thistles. "This," he said, "has good soil to produce all that is good and pleasant; but it is forgotten and neglected. A little while ago, you saw the soul; now behold the life of an idle man."

Saboth was so impressed by the lesson that he began to lead a new life.

Then Hillel took him into a fertile valley, where a clear brook flowed between fruitful trees and flowery meadows. "This is the picture of your new industrious life," said Hillel. "Nature, which warned you, will now reward you. Her beauty and grace can only give joy to him who sees in her life a picture of his own."

~~~

INDIVIDUALITY

Progress depends on those who dare to be different.

Woolworth conceived the idea of the five-and-ten-cent store. That was different. His fortune was measured by millions when he passed away.

Wanamaker conceived the idea of one-price to everybody in his retail stores. That was different, for at the time he put this policy into effect it was directly contrary to the accepted practice throughout the country.

Ford determined to build a light, cheap car for the millions.

That was different. His reward came in the greatest automobile output in the world.

Human progress has often depended on the courage of a man who dared to be different.

INFANT

Israel Zangwill, the brilliant novelist, says that a baby is a joy to its mother, an heir to its father, a charge to its nurse, a soul to the clergyman, a new biological specimen to the physician, a new customer to the shopkeeper, and a nuisance to the neighbors.

INFERIORITY

Advised Eleanor Roosevelt: "No one can make you feel inferior without your consent."

When Arturo Toscanini was a young man, he played the cello. He was extremely nearsighted, and in order to avoid bending close to the music, he memorized his part as well as the parts for every instrument in the orchestra.

One night, the conductor of the orchestra took ill. Fellow musicians suggested that he do the conducting. The audience was amused at the poise of the nineteen-year-old boy and was most interested to see what he could do.

He closed the score book and conducted the entire program from memory, receiving a tumultuous ovation.

A wise man once said: "A truly great person, a person of quality and accomplishment, need never downgrade others so that he may be noticed. If he is really superior, he will stand out because of his achievements. Those who have little to commend them often resort to looking down at others as a means of feeling their own importance. When an individual is singing his own praises while damning others, I always wonder what the other side of the picture looks like. I feel that the surest way to display one's inferiority is to belittle the greatness of another."

INFLUENCE

Two parrots lived near each other. One parrot had learned to sing hymns, and sang them all day long. The second parrot had learned to curse and swear, which he could be heard doing throughout the day. The owner of the second parrot obtained permission for his parrot to live with the first parrot in the hope that he would break the habit of swearing and that he might learn to sing hymns. However, the very opposite resulted. After a short time, both parrots became masters at swearing.

An elementary school teacher found an apple on her desk wrapped in a paper containing the legend, "From Bobby and Jimmie." Turning to the youngsters, she expressed her thanks and then asked: "How is it that two of you happen to bring me one apple?"

Jimmie's reply is worth noting: "This is what happened," he said. "Bobby was about to eat his apple when I told him that we ought to give it to you. So, you see, it was his apple but my thought."

INGENUITY

A traveler in China, wishing to test the reputed ingenuity of the Chinese people, arrived at an inn and, throwing down a hunk of copper, said to the innkeeper, "For this copper I want food, drink and entertainment."

The innkeeper returned with a slice of watermelon. Placing it before the traveler, he said: "You asked for food, drink and entertainment. Here it is. Eat the pulp, drink the juice, and play with the seeds."

During the construction of one of the bridges over the East River in New York, the engineers were baffled by an old sunken barge which lay embedded in the river bottom. Powerful engines, steel cables, derricks, and tugs were powerless to remove the obstruction.

A young man, fresh from technical school, thought he could solve the problem. At low tide, he had a large barge towed out to the spot and had cables attached to either side and fastened to the sunken derelict. As the tide came in from the Atlantic, the

237

barge rose, bringing with it the submerged wreck. The young engineer had linked to his task the limitless power of the ocean tides.

INGRATITUDE

Two men worn out by the heat of the summer's sun, lay down at noon under the shade of a tree. As they rested under its cool shade, one of the men said to the other:

"What a useless tree this is! It bears no fruit, and is not of the slightest use to man."

The tree interrupted him, saying: "How ungrateful can you be? While you rest under my shade, you berate me, claiming I am useless and unprofitable."

A miser was once traveling on a lonely road. The day was hot, and he soon became fatigued and hungry, but there was no food nor drink to be had in this forsaken spot. So he prayed: "Dear God, I am hungry and tired. Please help me to find something to eat, and in return I will offer half of what I find as a sacrifice to you.

In a little while, he stumbled upon a bag in the road. "This is surely a bag of gold," the miser thought to himself, as he bent down and picked it up. However, when he opened the bag, he found, instead of gold, dates and almonds. He sat down, and while he rested, he refreshed himself with these delicious fruits.

When he had eaten sufficiently, he took the pits of the dates and the shells of the almonds and made a sacrificial pyre of them and said: "Dear God, accept my offering You can see I have kept my promise. I have shared with you both the inner and outer parts of my find."

INITIATIVE

Long ago, a shipload of people were wrecked on an island in the Pacific. They found neither food nor fresh water, and their bones were soon bleaching on the sands.

Years later, a second ship was wrecked on the same coral reef. This shipload found springs of fresh water. But they could find no food on the island; so they too, after a while, perished from hunger.

238

Many years later, still a third ship was wrecked on the same spot. But these people had initiative. They found the springs of fresh water. They found too, that by diving deep among the coral reefs, there were quantities of fresh oysters. And they discovered that an amazing number of oysters contained pearls. When they were finally rescued, they were not only well-fed but enormously wealthy.

Three men were confined to a dark dungeon. Their greatest problem was how to cut the meat served to them once a week as invariably, each cut his finger in the process. Their respective solutions to the dilemma are truly enlightening.

One simply stopped eating meat.

The second abandoned the niceties of society, took the meat in hand, and, animal-like, devoured it.

The third used his knife and fork to burrow a tiny hole in the ceiling, allowing just enough sunlight into the dungeon to enable him to eat properly.

After a sign reading, *"BOY WANTED"* was hung in a store window, a long line of applicants queued up at the door. One especially anxious fellow scribbled a note which he handed quietly to the owner. It read: "Don't do anything till you've seen me. I'm last in the line, but I've got the goods."

A biologist was observing an ant carrying a piece of straw which seemed too big a burden for it. The ant came to a crack in the earth which was too wide for it to cross. It stood for a time, as though pondering the situation. Then it put the straw across the crack and walked over it.

INSECURITY

An African king wanted his portrait painted and went to the studio of a famous painter. The artist noticed that the king was extremely anxious to observe the work in progress, and that he was not too happy with the painting.

"If there is anything you wish me to do with this painting," said the painter, "tell me and I will try to oblige."

Somewhat abashed, the African king replied, "Yes, there is something you can do. Could you paint my features white instead of black?"

INSIGHT

Just before the outbreak of the Revolution in Russia, Prince Koniev, one of the closest advisers of the Czar, and one of the leading generals of the land, was blown to bits by the bomb of the revolutionary assassins. The wonderful carriage in which he was riding was completely demolished and the magnificent horses which drew it were ripped to pieces.

A few minutes after the terrible explosion, a huge crowd gathered at the scene of the tragedy. Among them were members of the Imperial Guard who lamented the death of the great military leader. A coach-builder was heard to express his profound regrets at the destruction of one of the most lovely carriages in Russia. A great horseman was almost in tears, because of the loss of one of the finest breed of horses of the land. But a *New York Times* correspondent, who witnessed the scene, cabled to his home office the story with the following comment: "The old regime is dead; a new order was born!"

A man best known for his ability at fundraising was once asked why it was that rich men willingly came to the aid of the blind, the lame, and the incurably ill, but turned a cold shoulder to the needs of impoverished scholars and schools.

The reply was simple: "The rich man can easily identify with the blind, the lame, or the infirm, being well aware that the possibility of his being stricken in any of these ways is not too remote an idea. He forms a mental picture of himself in these adverse circumstances and is moved to compassion which opens his hand. There is little danger, however, that the rich man will ever become a man of great learning, and he can hardly see the necessity of having scholars around at all. And why support an 'unnecessary evil?' "

INSPIRATION

A young man who had been apprenticed to a blacksmith, learned during the course of his training how to hold the tongs,

240

how to lift the hammer, how to smite the anvil, and how to blow the fire with the bellows. Having finished his apprenticeship, he was employed at the royal smithery. But the young man's delight at his appointment soon turned to despair, when he discovered that he had failed to learn how to kindle a spark.

～～

Jacques Lipschitz, the sculptor, spent his youth in Paris, where he was a close friend of Soutine, Modigliani and Chagall. One day, a friend complained that he was dissatisfied with the light he painted on his canvasses, and went off to Morocco, seeking a change in light. He found, however, that the light in the Moroccan canvasses was no different. Lipschitz then advised him, "An artist's light comes from within, not from without."

～～

A group of students sought to discover the secret of the inspiration behind the poetry of a writer. They requested permission to visit his residence so that they might watch him at work. He invited them to his tiny apartment and pointed to his "patch of green," the backyard where he sat and composed his verse. It was a small splash of grass, hemmed in on all sides by concrete walks."

"Is this where you find the music for your poetry?" asked one of the students. "Your poems have such grandeur and majesty in them — and yet, your working space is so confining."

"Inspiration is in the heart and eyes," was the comment of the poet.

～～

In a little village, there was a cobbler who lived a very humble and modest life. Nobody ever found it of interest to communicate with him about anything but shoe repairs, for he was naught but a mere cobbler. When his customers thought that he had not done his job properly, they did not hesitate to scold him to their hearts' content. In their eyes he was but a lowly bootmaker, and they thought nothing of abusing him freely.

One day, the villagers were greatly surprised when they learned that this modest, unassuming, insignificant cobbler had published a book of poetry. They could not reconcile the cobbler with the poet, so the village turned its surprise into ridicule and mockery. "What kind of poetry could this be, coming from a cobbler?" they asked each other. Although they had never seen his work nor read a single line of his writing, they teased and mocked him unceasingly. The cobbler paid no heed to his tormentors and continued in his unassuming manner. To their increasing amazement, the people soon learned that not only was the cobbler a poet but that his work was widely acclaimed. Men of letters and critics of art and literature agreed that his work was outstanding. Eventually, even the most outspoken of all scoffers could no longer defy the opinions of learned people who knew how to judge poetry. The fame of the cobbler was even more widely acclaimed and universally acknowledged.

The puzzle, however, remained. Where did a cobbler find inspiration to write great and profound poetry? His more trusted and intimate friends put the question to him directly.

The bookmaker explained: "The rhythm of my hammer knocking nails into leather, the gradual formation of a shoe from shapeless material, the turning of dilapidated and worn boots into shapely, useful articles, are quite enough to inspire a person in whom there is a sense of beauty and poetry."

INSULTS

A man cuts me with a knife and inflicts a wound. Suppose, instead of bandaging the wound, I began to show it to everybody. And even after it was bandaged, I would constantly remove the bandage and show the wound to all, examining its depth and leaving it open to infection. If I did this I would be called a fool.

However, a man who dwells upon injuries and insults, causing him great unhappiness, is equally a fool. How much better off he would be were he to put a bandage on that wound as well, and never examine it again.

On hearing insults, one should consider how insignificant it will appear after twelve months have elapsed. If this consideration were applied to most of the minor vexations of life, by which our quiet is too often disturbed, it would prevent many painful sensations.

INTEGRITY

A man's integrity can be discerned by the questions he asks. Upon arriving in a strange city, the erudite will ask where the libraries and universities are; the drunkard will inquire about the nearest saloons and taverns; the cultured man will ask about the art galleries and museums; and the religious man will ask for the houses of worship.

~~~~

Two candidates applied to George Washington for a certain office. One was a dear friend, a life-long associate of Washington; the other, rather hostile to the policies of Washington. In fact, he could be found in the ranks of the opposition.

Washington, to the surprise of everyone, appointed the latter to the post. "My friend," he said "I receive with a cordial welcome but, with all his good qualities, he is not a man of business. His opponent is, with all his hostility to me, a man of business. I am not George Washington, but the President of the United States. As George Washington, I would do this man any kindness in my power but, as President, I can do nothing."

~~~~

In the city of Bagdad lived Hakeem, the Wise One. A great many people went to him for counsel which he gave freely to all, asking nothing in return.

A young spendthrift came to him and said: "Tell me, Wise One, what shall I do to receive the most for that which I spend?"

Hakeem answered: "A thing that is bought or sold has no value unless it contains that which cannot be bought or sold. Look for the Priceless Ingredient."

"But what is that Priceless Ingredient?" asked the young man.

Spoke the Wise One: "My son, the Priceless Ingredient of every product in the marketplace is the honor and integrity of him who makes it. Consider his name before you buy."

~~~~

INTELLIGENCE

Someone has said that the world's greatest area of undeveloped territory lies under people's hats.

~~~~

Confucius said, "Mankind differs from the animals only by a little thing, and most people throw that away."

When asked, "What is that little thing by which they differ from the animal?" he said, "Intelligence."

Descartes put it better. Descartes said, "There is only one good

243

thing in the world of which everyone thinks he has enough, and
that is intelligence."

—Dr. Will Durant

INTENTIONS

There was once a thief who would steal from everyone; but
was of the opinion that it was a sacrilege to steal from a church.
He would never commit such a crime. One cold winter night, he
went forth to seek his illicit livelihood. He was desperate. Too
many people were in the streets, and he feared that he might be
seen. The temptation was great; but he promised himself that he
would not go near a church. He would not start up with God.

As his strength was slowly sapped by the cold night and he
still saw no prospect of gain, he thought that perhaps there might
be something valuable on the roof of the church. Surely that
would be no concern of God. It would not be stealing from the
church. He climbed up and began to feel around in the dark. Suddenly, he felt a chunk of rusty iron, a screw and a bolt. Thinking
to sell the screw and bolt for scrap metal, he unscrewed it slowly,
when suddenly, there was a loud crash. The giant golden chan-
delier in the church, suspended from the ceiling by this rusty
screw, had fallen and shattered into a million pieces.

"But I only intended to take the screw," he said as he was led
to jail.

INTERDEPENDENCE

Harry Emerson Fosdick wrote: "We ask the leaf, 'Are you
complete in yourself?' And the leaf answers, 'No, my life is in the
branches.' We ask the branch, and the branch answers, 'No, my
life is in the root.' We ask the root, and it answers, 'No, my life
is in the trunk and branches and leaves. Keep the branches strip-
ped of leaves, and I shall die.' "

A group of men were traveling on a boat. Suddenly, one of
them took a drill and began to bore a hole under his seat. The
other passengers were worried, and shouted at him: "What are
you doing?"

He replied, "What has that to do with you? Am I not making
the hole under *my* seat?"

"Yes," they retorted, "but the water will enter and drown us all."

※

Before electric lights were installed in the City of Vilna, there was a problem keeping the synagogues lighted through the long winter Friday nights for worship and study. Many synagogues used large sectional candelabras with many successive rows of candlesticks lined one below the other. Each candlestick had a narrow opening in the bottom. Each row connected to the candles of the lower row by means of wicks drawn through these openings. When one row of candles would burn out, the candles of the other row would catch on fire. Thus, there was an automatic succession of kindling lights. This enabled the pious to recite the Psalms and other prayers, and the diligent student to study the Bible.

The scheme worked well as long as the candelabra were kept clean. The wax did not clog, and the connecting wicks were properly prepared. When the one in charge of the lamps was derelict in his duties, and permitted the openings to be stopped up, or if he used faulty wicks, there was trouble ahead. The succeeding candles would not ignite, and the light would grow dim and die out.

※

INTOLERANCE

"Why did the Puritans come to this country?" asked the teacher of her class in American history.

The answer was not long in coming: "To worship in their own way, and make other people do the same."

※

INVESTMENT

"My son," said a banker to his son, "I want to give you a lesson in business. Here is a half-dollar. Now, if you can find any boy whom you can trust, who will take this money, and pay you interest for it, you may lend it to him and, if you invest this wisely, I'll increase your capital."

When evening came, the banker asked, "My son, how did you invest your money today?"

"Well father," replied the son, "I saw a boy on the street without any shoes, and he had not eaten, so I gave him my fifty cents to buy something to eat."

"You'll never make a successful business man," replied the father. "In this world, business is business."

"But I am preparing for the next world as well," was the reply of the son."

~~~

In a famous Boston church, a group of tourists were being guided by the janitor of the institution. He pointed out to the visitors the outstanding features of the church: the beautiful hand carved pews; the expensive, ornate altar; the handsome vestments; exquisite paintings and furnishings. He explained the history of each article and sang its praises. Then he took his visitors to the steeple, and there, with pride, pointed to the beautiful organ with its shining gold pipes. "This organ," he said, "was presented to the church in 1925. It cost me $50,000 at that time." The visitors gasped, and looked at each other in disbelief.

"I wasn't always a janitor," he said, as if to answer their unexpressed doubts. "Before 1929, I was a millionaire. Then I lost all my money in the crash. This organ is all I can see and enjoy today of all my wealth."

~~~

IRRITATION

"Why didn't you tell her she was taking more than her share of room and encroaching upon your rights?" This question was asked of a young girl who was merrily describing an old woman who had taken a seat beside her in a crowded railway car, and crammed a bird-cage, a basket of apples, and various bundles and packages into the small space.

"It wasn't worthwhile to argue about it; we had such a little way to go together," was the girl's reply.

What a beautiful motto for those of us on our life-journey!

~~~

JEALOUSY

A boy who dwelled in the mountains was fascinated by a house on the opposite side of the valley. Each evening its windows were sheets of shining gold. Drawn to this seeming treasure, he made his way across the valley toward the house. But the path was rough and, exhausted, he lay down and slept.

Early the next morning he hurried to the house. Instead of sheets of gold, the windows were but ordinary glass. Disappointed

246

and bitter, he turned toward home, then stopped in surprise. Across the valley, he saw his own home, and it was agleam with windows of gold.

The famous opera star had just finished an aria. The audience applauded with great fervor. One man turned to his friend and said, "What wonderful singing!"

"What's so wonderful about it?" said the other. "If I had his voice, I'd sing just as well."

JEWS

Aimé Pallière, a French Catholic studying for the priesthood, once entered a synagogue on Yom Kippur during a period of silent devotion. He described his reaction to the first Jewish service he attended as follows:

"That which revealed itself to me at that moment was not the Jewish faith. It was the Jewish people. The spectacle of that large number of Jewish men assembled, their shoulders covered by the *talit* (prayer shawl), suddenly disclosed to my eyes a far-off past. The Hebrews of the Bible were there on their feet before me. Two details struck me particularly about the faithful, bent over their ritual. At first, on seeing the prayer shawl worn uniformly by all the participants in the service, I thought that in a way they were all officiating. In the second place, it seemed to me that this silent assembly was expecting something to happen.

"Here were revealed to me two characteristics of this misunderstood people and its great faith: the form of collective priesthood which characterizes Judaism, and the spirit of expectancy and of faith in the future which stamps its entire cult with a special zeal."

Clarence Darrow, famous criminal lawyer, was once asked what he thought of Jews. Were they inferior to the common run of human beings?

"You must understand," answered the trial lawyer, "that when yours and my ancestors were sitting on trees cracking nuts with bare paws, the Jews came around and sold us nutcrackers."

JUDGMENT

> In men whom men condemn as ill
> I find so much of goodness still;
> In men whom men pronounce divine
> I find so much of sin and blot,
> I hesitate to draw the line
> Between the two, when God has not.

Man was created with two eyes. With one eye, he must see the virtues and good qualities of others, and with the other he must see his own faults and failings. We must judge others as we would judge ourselves.

I once heard a sage say that "He who is a party to something in which he has a personal interest is worse off and can see less than a blind man.

"A blind man sees nothing, accepts this fact, and does not offer opinions on things he cannot see. A person passing judgment in his own court sees everything, but brings on temporary blindness by his personal interest in the matter and his desire to twist things to his own satisfaction. He can see nothing but that which is favorable to him."

He who says that "the whole world is crazy," and ridicules everything must remember that this "whole crazy world" is made up of people like himself, and others are judging him as severely as he is judging them.

A sage once said: "Only two can rightfully judge whether a person is a truly devoted, God-fearing man: God Himself and the man's wife. God is all-knowing and surely knows who among us pays homage to Him, and a man's wife (the other half of his soul) also surely must know how her other half lives. This is truly a case of the right hand knowing what the left hand is doing."

A very pious man once returned home from the marketplace. His children surrounded him and asked, "Father, what did you bring home from the market?"

The man stood with tears in his eyes as he replied: "Some day when I will return from the marketplace called 'life' to the Supreme Court of Judgment in Heaven they, too, will ask me, 'What did you bring?'" He was silent for a moment and then continued, "Woe is me! What will my answer be then?"

A wise man wished to discourage his four sons from making rash judgments. At his command, the eldest made a winter journey to see a mango tree. During the spring he sent the next oldest son on the same errand. Summer followed and the third son went. When the youngest boy had returned from his autumn visit, the wise man called them together.

"Describe the tree," he said to them.

The first said it looked like a burnt stump.

The second disagreed, describing it as lovely in lacy green.

The third declared its blossoms were as beautiful as the rose.

The fourth said all were wrong, "Its fruit was like a pear."

"Each one of you is right," said the wise father, "for each of you saw it in a different season."

So it must be when we view another's actions. We should withhold judgment until we are certain we've seen "the tree in all its seasons."

JUSTICE

A clergyman had a very strict sense of justice. One day his own wife raised an outcry because she believed the maid had stolen an object of value. The servant, an orphan, tearfully denied the accusation. "We will let the court settle this," declared the mistress of the house.

When the husband saw his wife preparing to go to court, he immediately put on his best suit.

"Why do you do that?" she asked in surprise. "You know it is undignified for a man of your position to come to court with me. I can very well plead my own case."

"Of that I am sure," he answered, "but who will plead the case of your maid, the poor orphan? I must see that she gets complete justice."

Two men came to a sage with a dispute about cemetery plots they had bought. Each claimed the better plot of ground. They argued the question before the wise man who listened intently and gave the following verdict: "He who dies first will get the better grave." From then on the dispute ceased.

A college position was open and two teachers were invited to present sample lectures so that the authorities could decide who deserved the position. Both men lived quite a distance from the college, and having to spend the night in the town, they were given adjoining rooms in the same hotel.

During the evening one teacher decided that he would run over his lecture. As he pictured himself on the college platform, his voice thundered out so that the entire lecture was quite audible to the second teacher. The speech was impressive, and when morning came there were two teachers who knew the same lecture, the one who had prepared it and the one who had overheard it all through the night.

When morning came, both left for the college. As luck would have it, the first teacher to be called upon was the one who had overheard the lecture and had decided to make it his own.

He mounted the platform and began. The other teacher was bewildered. There went his lecture, every word, every idea, every thought. He now realized what had happened.

Finally, the speech was over and the second teacher was called upon to deliver his lecture. "Ladies and gentlemen," he began, "you have heard a wonderful talk, full of original ideas and penetrating thoughts. I believe it is worthy of repetition and so I will deliver it once again verbatim." And this he did.

When the authorities heard the delivery, they decided to give him the job because they felt that anyone who could remember a speech after hearing it once, was brilliant and certainly deserved the preference.

The frail, old grandfather, lonely and unwanted, was given his meals from a wooden bowl with a wooden spoon. Shaking with the palsy of old age, he eats with the servants lest he spill soup on the spotless damask, or shatter a priceless plate. Next morning, the father goes off to the city and returns late in the day to discover that his son has spent the entire day whittling from wood a crude bowl and spoon.

"How nice!" the proud father exclaims, patting his son on the head. "A new bowl and spoon for poor old Grandfather."

"Oh, no," says the innocent child, "not for Grandfather. For you, dear Father, when you become old."

※

A devout Negro clergyman was asked by one of his parishioners to explain the doctrine of election. His reply was: "You know what an election is when we elect the President and the Governor. In the Kingdom of God there is always an election going on. Only three votes are cast. The Lord always votes for you. The devil always votes against you. And you have the deciding vote."

※

A fox, who possessed a great deal of cunning, had a stork for a neighbor. He desired to keep on friendly terms with her. He therefore always treated the stork with attention, and when he met her abroad he paid her many compliments. But, in order to maintain the acquaintance, it was necessary that he should now and then invite her to dinner.

This he did, but being very stingy, and also wanting to tease her, he had nothing but soup; and this was served on a plate. The fox lapped it up easily with his broad tongue, but the stork, with her long narrow bill, could hardly get a drop.

The fox laughed to himself, but when the stork gave a dinner, and invited the fox, she had her soup served in a bottle, so that the greedy fox could not so much as moisten his lips with it; and thus he learned that his meanness was fully appreciated, and that, in a game of sharps, he who begins is very likely to get well punished.

※

A poor man was complaining to his grocer. "There is no justice in this world," he wailed. "The rich, who have the money, can buy all they want on credit, while the poor must pay for everything in cash. If there was any justice on earth, the rich should pay cash, and the poor should buy on credit."

"It all sounds very well in theory," was the grocer's retort. "But if I were to extend credit to all the unfortunates in the neighborhood, I would soon be poor myself."

"Why, then you would have nothing to worry about," beamed the poor man. "You would be able to get everything on credit!"

※

Though the heel of the strong oppressor
  May grind the weak to dust,
And the voices of fame with one acclaim
  May call him great and just,
Let those who applaud take warning,
  And keep this motto in sight,—
No question is ever settled
  Until it is settled right.

—Ella Wheeler Wilcox

KINDNESS

"What is real good?"
I asked in a musing mood;
"Order," said the law court;
"Knowledge," said the school;
"Truth," said the wise man;
"Pleasure," said the fool;
"Love," said the maiden;
"Beauty," said the page;
"Freedom," said the dreamer;
"Home," said the sage;
"Fame," said the soldier;
"Equity," said the seer.
Spake my heart full sadly:
"The answer is not here";
Then, within my bosom,
Softly, this I heard:
"Each heart holds the secret—
Kindness is the word."

—John Boyle O'Reilly

A little girl paid a visit to relatives who lived in the country. She found a land terrapin and started to examine him, but the terrapin closed his shell like a vise. Seeing her trying to pry him open with a stick, her uncle said, "No, no. That is not the way."

Her uncle took the creature into the house and set him on the hearth. In a few minutes he began to get warm, stuck out his head and feet, and calmly crawled toward the girl.

"People are sort of like terrapins," her uncle said. "Never try

252

to force a fellow into anything. Just warm him up with a little kindness, and more than likely he'll come your way."

A boy was asked by his mother what he wanted for breakfast. He replied, "Cereal, an egg, and a kind word."

It is told of Rabbi Levi Yitzhok of Berditchev that he transformed many lives. And why? Because he could always see the bright side of a person's character. Once, on Yom Kippur, while going to synagogue, he saw a young man of the Jewish community sitting on a porch and eating.

"What are you doing?" the rabbi exclaimed. "Surely you must have forgotten that today is the Day of Atonement and that Jews are forbidden to eat!"

"No, I haven't forgotten," the young man replied.

"Oh, well then, I guess you must not be well, and the doctor suggested that you eat."

"No, I feel perfectly fine," came the answer.

And so it went on. Soon a number of people had gathered, and they were about to denounce this rascal. But Rabbi Levi Yitzhok turned his eyes to heaven, and declared: "O God, see what a sterling character this young man has. Even at the cost of incriminating himself, he still insists on telling the truth!"

KNOWLEDGE

Three men, two wise and one foolish, were cast into a filthy, black dungeon. Every day food and eating utensils were lowered to them. The misery of imprisonment deprived the fool of his little sense, and in the darkness he did not know how to use the utensils. His companion showed him how on the first night, and then had to repeat the instructions on the subsequent nights. However, the third man was silent and made no effort to teach the fool. This aroused the curiosity of the second prisoner, who asked why he had never helped.

The answer came quickly: "You take so much trouble to teach him, but you do not achieve your goal because every day destroys your work. The fool forgets yesterday's lessons. But I am devoting all my time to boring a hole in the wall to bring in the light of the sun then he will be able to see everything."

253

Out of his many years of study and experience, a sage once said: "He who speaks much knows little, and he who says little knows much. A person of little knowledge does not even know enough to hide his ignorance, but a truly great and learned person knows that humility will enhance his wisdom."

~~~

Whistler was in court trying to collect his fee for a painting which he had sold. The purchaser thought it was overpriced and refused to pay the full amount. Whistler was asked how long it had taken him to complete the canvas.

"About two days," he said.

"And for this you ask two hundred guineas?" asked the lawyer, in an attempt to embarrass him.

"Not at all," replied the artist with asperity. "I ask it for the knowledge of a lifetime."

~~~

LANGUAGE

A Chinese sage was once asked by his pupils what he would do first if he had the power to arrange the affairs of the country. He answered: "I should certainly see to it that language is used correctly.

The pupils looked puzzled. "Surely," they said, "this is a small matter. Why do you say it is so important?"

The wise man replied: "If language is not used correctly, then what is said is not meant; if what is said is not what is meant, then what ought to be done remains undone; if this remains undone, morals and art will be corrupted; if morals and art are corrupted, justice will go astray and the people will stand about in helpless confusion."

~~~

LAWYERS

A diminutive lawyer, appearing as a witness in a court, was asked by a gigantic counselor what his profession was, and replied that he was an attorney.

"You a lawyer!" said the giant counselor. "Why, I could put you in my pocket!"

"Very likely you could," rejoined the other, "and if you did you would have more law in your pocket than you ever had in your head."

⁓

LAZINESS

The man had entered the doctor's office. After the examination he asked, "Now, Doc, tell me in plain words exactly what's wrong with me."

"In plain words," replied the doctor, "you're lazy."

"Now, Doctor," inquired the patient, "give me the medical terms to tell my friends."

⁓

A mother-bird sought to instruct her young in the important maxim "The early bird gets the worm." She impressed upon them the importance of striving hard and laboring diligently in order to survive. All her young were quite impressed with her instructions. But, after a few days, one of the young birds, tired of the struggle for existence, chanced upon a farmer who suggested a novel idea. "If you give me one of your bright feathers, I'll give you a worm for it."

"What a wonderful way to get my daily food!" the smart bird thought. "Let all the other birds get up early and seek their worms. I'll just relax in the sun, and, whenever I become hungry, I'll fly to the farmer and exchange a feather from my plumage for a worm."

But before too many days passed, the smart bird lost his beautiful plumage, so that not even his family could recognize him.

⁓

LEADERSHIP

The snake was crossing a road. It was then that the tail complained to the head. "How long will you insist on leading, while I drag behind you? Let's change places at once. I will lead and you will follow."

"Very well, go first," replied the head.

And so the tail became the leader and the head the follower. They soon came to a water hole, and the tail, having no eyes, slipped directly into the hole, dragging the head along.

The question now is: Who is to blame: the head or the tail?

At least a moral can be learned and that is never allow yourself to be led by a brainless tail.

A small town had just had its first railroad tracks laid, and the first locomotive had just pulled into the station. The Hasidim decided to point out this tremendous advance in scientific and mechanical genius to their Rebbe. As the Rebbe neared the station to inspect this modern means of transportation, he saw a long line of black, cold, somber-looking cars attached to each other behind the locomotive which was belching fire. The boiler was getting hotter and smoke was rising from its short chimney. Suddenly, with a tremendous roar, black clouds of smoke rose heavenward, the engine started moving, and the long line of trains moved along with it.

"Rebbe, Rebbe, what do you say to this wonderful sight?"

The Rebbe appeared to be lost in thought for a moment and then replied softly, "Look how one, hot, fiery creation can pull along so many cold ones!"

A poor half-wit was befriended by a millionaire lover of music who happened to have a private orchestra. One day the half wit came to his benefactor and asked for a position in his orchestra. Astonished, the rich man said, "I had no idea you could play an instrument."

"I can't," was the answer. "But I see you have a man there who does nothing but wave a stick around while the others play. His job I can handle."

A famous conductor was rehearsing a great symphony orchestra. Everything seemed to be going well; 150 skilled performers were responding to the conductor's guidance.

Suddenly, in the middle of a fortissimo passage, the conductor rapped on the music stand. There was sudden silence. "Where is the piccolo?" demanded the conductor.

The piccolo player had missed his entry, and the trained ear of the conductor, even in that glorious volume of sound which filled the hall, had noted its absence.

Leaders are never men who stress their hardships. The explorers who opened this country to development did their work against heart-breaking odds. They had to fight the wilderness, storms, and Indian enemies, and often saw all their supplies swept away when their ships went on the rocks, or their canoes hurtled down rapids, or their storehouses burned. They wasted none of their time and energy complaining. They were too busy creating something.

—Anonymous

One of the world's largest department stores in London was built up by H. Gordon Selfridge. He achieved success by being a leader, not a boss. Here is his own comparison of the two types of executives:

The boss drives his men; the leader coaches them.

The boss depends upon authority; the leader on good-will.

The boss inspires fear; the leader inspires enthusiasm.

The boss says "I"; the leader, "we."

The boss fixes the blame for the breakdown; the leader fixes the breakdown.

The boss says "Go"; the leader says "Let's go!"

LEARNING

A philosopher once wrote: "There are three classes of people in the world. The first learn from their own experiences — these are the wise; the second learn from the experiences of others — these are the happy; the third group learn neither from their own experiences nor from the experiences of others — these are the fools."

The Rebbe of Sadagora once said to his followers, "Not only can we learn from all that God created, but we can also learn from everything that man has made."

"What can we learn from a train?" one student asked.

"In one second, we can miss everything."

"From the telegraph?" was the next question.

"Every word is counted and charged."

"From the telephone?"

"What we say here, is heard there."

A religious scholar once explained: In the sayings of the fathers we are told that "a wise man is one who learns from all

257

men." The meaning is that we can learn and draw lessons not only from professional teachers, but also from an ignorant or wicked person.

1) Everyone has something good within him.

2) By observing evil, we often learn to do good, the evil appearing so obnoxious to us.

3) Who among us is so perfect that we cannot learn something new every day from every contact!

⚘

A famous mathematician was seated next to a 17-year-old girl. No sooner were they seated when she turned to him and asked: "What do you do for a living?"

"I study math," he replied.

"Really?" gasped the wide-eyed young lady. "I finished math last semester."

⚘

A wise man once remarked: A man can learn a lesson in life from a child, and even from a thief.

From a child he can learn three things:

1) To be happy and of good disposition.

2) If he lacks something, he cries and makes his wishes known.

3) A child is never idle. He is always lively and active.

From a thief he can learn six things:

1) He works late at night.

2) If he doesn't succeed the first time, he tries again.

3) He is proud of his "profession," and improves upon his "art."

4) He respects his fellow thief.

5) He is willing to sacrifice his life even for a small thing.

6) He holds his own and insists that he doesn't know anything, even when they try to beat a confession out of him.

⚘

"A person can learn from observing those who do wrong," said a sage. "I have learned some facts of life from the gossip, the impatient, and the evil people. I have learned the art of silence and its advantages from listening to the useless, endless prattling of some men and women. I have learned the art of being patient and its advantages from observing the impracticality of those who were impatient. I have learned good ethical behavior and its advantages from observing how foolish, inadequate, and unworthy are the sinful and the evil-hearted."

George Gershwin did not sit around, waiting for inspiration to bring him good ideas. Oscar Levant, who lived with him, says Gershwin got more of his ideas just by playing. Whenever he sat down to the piano to amuse himself, something came of it. He looked upon his work as play. Creating his career was his way of having fun. His life was clear proof of the theory that the way to learn how to do anything is to do it.

LECTURES

A speech that's full of sparkling wit
　　Will keep its hearers grinning,
Provided that the end of it
　　Is close to the beginning!

A man bought a ticket to a lecture. Before the lecture was half over, he hurried out of the hall and stood at the box office asking that his money be returned.

"Don't you like the talk?" asked the ticket seller.

"Oh, I like it enough," was the answer.

"Well, is your seat a poor one?" was the next question.

"No, I have a good seat," was the answer.

"Well, then what is the trouble?" the ticket seller inquired.

"I am frightened to sit alone in that large hall," answered the sole occupant.

LEGACY

A priest tried to reach one of his leading parishioners. The man, however, was either out or busy whenever he called. After many futile attempts, the priest finally left this message with the man's secretary: "Please call me. A mutual relative of ours died and left us a large inheritance."

No sooner had the priest put down the receiver when a call came through from the very excited man, demanding to know the details.

259

"Well," exclaimed the priest, "our mutual relative is Moses. He left us the Ten Commandments, and I know you will want to share in this great inheritance."

━━━

There was once a man whose last wish it was that all his belongings be bequeathed to only one of his ten sons. As he did not live long enough to speak the son's name, they were in a quandry as to which one was to get the inheritance. The matter was finally brought to an arbitrator who, while discussing the matter with the boys, mused half aloud: "How am I to decide which one the father had in mind? I can only suggest that they go to their father's grave, knock on the tombstone and stomp on his grave till he rouses and tells them which son he meant."

The sons all heard this muttering, but only one son jumped up and shouted indignantly: "Never will I desecrate the grave of my father, not even for the entire inheritance! The love and respect I feel for the memory of my father cannot be measured in worldly goods."

Immediately, the arbitrator knew that this was beyond a doubt the son to whom the father wished to leave his wealth. He was the only truly devoted son.

━━━

An elderly farmer and his wife lived on a small farm. They were too poor to hire any help and did all the hard work themselves.

One day the old man received a letter, but his eyes had grown very weak from age, and he was unable to read it. His wife, who had never learned to read, was of no help to him in this instance, so they laid the letter aside until someone should come by who could read the letter to them. Time passed, nobody came to call on the old people, and the letter lay unopened and eventually forgotten in its hiding place.

The old man continued with his toil until he was overcome by ill health. It was then that relatives came to spend some time with the aged couple; to bolster their spirits, as well as to help with farm and house chores. It was while cleaning the house that a relative came across the hitherto forgotten letter. Upon the farmer's request the letter was read and revealed the astounding news that he was the legatee of a large fortune. How sad that he had not known of this years earlier, so that he would not have had to struggle so hard in his old age.

Meekly the farmer remarked: "I always prayed and hoped that

260

I might be 'given' a gift, but I should have asked that I be worthy to 'receive' it. Indeed, though I had been given the legacy, I did not receive it until now when my time is near, and it is too late for me to enjoy it."

LEISURE

A man once dreamt that he died and found himself in the Great Beyond. He was exceedingly comfortable and rested for a while, then, becoming somewhat bored, he shouted out, "Is anyone here?"

In a moment a white-robed attendant appeared and asked, "What do you want?"

"What can I have?" was the answer.

"You can have whatever you want," replied the attendant.

"Well, then, bring me something to eat."

"What do you want to eat?" asked the attendant, "You can have anything you want."

And so they brought him just what he wanted, and he went on eating and sleeping and having a glorious time. He asked for entertainment, and this too was granted. Soon he was bored once again and summoned the attendant.

"I want something to do," he demanded.

"I am sorry, but that is the only thing we cannot give you here," the attendant replied.

"I'm sick and tired of this. I'd rather be in hell," shouted the man.

"And where do you think you are?" exclaimed the attendant.

"Tell me, of what did your brother die?"
"He died, sir, of having nothing to do."

An Italian, being shown around an American home listened patiently to explanations about each time-saving gadget. At the end of the tour he asked, "And what do you do with all the time you save?"

Two men were on their way to work. One man said, "Last night our TV set broke down."

His friend asked, "Well, how did you spend the evening?"

261

"It was terrible," replied the first man. "We did absolutely nothing. My wife and I just talked."

LIFE

At a gathering of men and women the other day, some began to tell the strange, odd, difficult things in their lives. When many had had their say, a man spoke up, and told them a story about a sower who was sowing seed. Some seeds fell on pieces of rock, which had a little earth spread over them. The seed began to grow, but the roots soon hit the rocks, and the green blades dried up and died.

Some of the seeds fell on nice, soft soil, where the roots could drink up moisture as they went down. Up shot the fine green blades, and they looked as if they would bear a lot of grain. But up with the green blades came also some strong weeds which choked off the blades of green, and so they soon died.

But most of the seeds the sower threw around him fell on good, deep soil that was free from hard rocks and ugly weeds. It grew quickly and became strong, and soon covered the whole field with beautiful golden ears of corn.

This is the story of man. Some hearts are like the stony ground, who wish to do well, but the wishes last only for a little while. There are others who really mean to do good, but they will not root out of their hearts the weeds of anger and selfishness and disobedience. These weeds grow so rapidly that they choke the little seeds of good deeds as they try to grow.

Dr. William James, world-renowned philosopher and psychologist, was asked, "Is life worth living?" He replied: "It all depends on the liver."

POINT OF VIEW

If you have a well-developed sense of humor, you will find this world full of absurdities.

If you are a realist, you will find it a world of cold, hard facts.

If you are a money-maker, you will find it a world of opportunities.

If you are a pessimist, you will find it just a climb up a sand dune.

And if you are a poet, you will find it a realm of inspiration.

—Anonymous

Two friends once became involved in a quarrel over a piece of land. They decided to take their dispute to the sage of the town.

When they reached the sage, each of the men argued, "The land is mine."

The sage thought for a moment and then said, "Why don't you come back and ask me the same question 100 years from now?"

In one of his stories, James Barrie writes:

"The life of every man is a diary in which he means to write one story and writes another; and his humblest hour is when he compares the volume as it is with what he vowed to make it."

There is always a difference between the reach and the grasp.

A man's life is full of trouble. He comes into the world without his consent and goes out usually against his will, and the trip between his coming and going is exceedingly rocky. The rule of contraries is one of the features of this journey.

When he is little, the big girls kiss him; but when he is big, only little girls kiss him.

If he is poor, he's said to be a bad manager; if he's rich, they'll claim he's dishonest.

If he needs credit, he can't get it; if he is prosperous, everybody wants to do him a favor.

If he is in politics, they say he takes graft; if he's out of politics, he's not patriotic. If he gives to charity, it's for show. If he doesn't, he's stingy.

When he's actively religious, some will say he's a hypocrite; if he doesn't take a deep interest in religion, they'll call him a sinner.

If he gives affection, he's a soft specimen; if he cares for nobody, he's cold blooded.

If he dies young, there was a great future for him. If he lives to be old, he missed his calling.

If he saves money, he's a grouch; if he spends it, he's a squand-

263

erer. If he works very hard, they say he's crazy; if he doesn't work, he's a bum . . . so what's the use?

—Anonymous

The Talmud tells the story of a pious man who disguised himself as an itinerant vendor of herbs and spices, and going into the market place, proclaimed his wares, crying, "The spice of life! The elixir of life! Who wishes to buy the secret of eternal life?"

Attracted by his cry, a large crowd gathered around him asking for the secret. The commotion reached the ears of Rabbi Yannai who was studying a difficult passage of the Torah. He opened his window and called to the vendor, "Tell me the secret!"

The man took from his sack the Book of Psalms and opening it to Psalm 34, said: "Here is my merchandise." Then he read from the open book. "Who is the man who desires life? Guard thy tongue from evil and thy lips from speaking deceit; do good, seek peace."

Yannai thanked him for the interpretation and quoted the verse from Proverbs: "Whoso guardeth his mouth and his tongue keeps his soul from trouble."

John Wesley had this for his rule of life:

> Do all the good you can,
> By all the means you can,
> In all the ways you can,
> In all the places you can,
> At all the times you can,
> To all the people you can,
> As long as ever you can.

A middle-aged man was asked why he was working so hard. He replied, "My candle is almost burned out, and I don't have another."

Life is a candle constantly burning.

Geraldine Farrar, the former opera star, was recently interviewed on her 80th birthday. In the course of her remarks she made an observation which had the clear, sharp ring of truth: "So much is pressing on humans today, that no one has time to stand still long enough to evaluate it. They gulp life and taste nothing. They eat life and have no savor."

⚬⚬⚬

The pupils of an elementary school were listening to a lecture on plant life. "All living organisms," said the teacher, "are developed from a substance called protoplasm, which is made of oxygen, hydrogen, carbon, and nitrogen. This we know. But from where does the protoplasm derive its power of life and growth? Does anybody know that?"

"I know," said a boy at the back.

"You know what makes protoplasm grow? Then you are wiser than all the biologists. You must tell us."

"God does," said the boy.

The answer was beyond physical science, but it was right, for, as far as we can see, the gulf between dead matter and living matter can be bridged only by the intervention of God.

⚬⚬⚬

An anonymous poet once described the measure of a man's life with these lines:

> Not—How did he die? But—How did he live?
> Not—Where did he gain? But—What did he give?
> These are the units to measure the worth
> Of a man as a man, regardless of birth.
> Not—What was his station? But—Had he a heart?
> And—How did he play his God-given part?
> Was he ever ready with a word of good cheer,
> To bring back a smile, to banish a tear?
> Not—What was his shrine? Nor—What was his creed?
> But—Had he befriended those really in need?
> Not—What did the sketch in the newspaper say?
> But—How many were sorry when he passed away?

⚬⚬⚬

On the wall of an ancient temple is a painting of a king forging a chain from his crown, and nearby another scene of a slave converting his chain into a crown. Underneath, this legend was inscribed: "Life is what one makes it, no matter of what it is made."

⚬⚬⚬

Many years ago, Walt Whitman wrote "Crossing Brooklyn Ferry" in which he poetically describes two different approaches

265

to life. One way of crossing a river, he explained, is to await impatiently our arrival on the other side. We are oblivious to everything about us. The other way is to enjoy the scene and our fellow-passengers. In either case, we reach the other side of the river, but it is obvious that in the second case, our trip is made more enjoyable.

A great sage showed a great deal of perception when he expressed this thought: "Life is like crossing a frozen river. We must not remain too long in one spot, for the ice may break through. We certainly cannot dance, but we must keep moving forward, because the pitfalls of standing still are ever present.

An actor was once asked about his philosophy of life. "I look upon life as a party," he said. "One arrives long after it's started, and one's going to leave before it's over, and it's as well, perhaps, not to try and be the life and soul of it, and not to try and take too much responsibility for it."

A ship was driven off course and sailed in unknown waters until it reached an island where the captain dropped anchor. The passengers on the ship broke up into five parties; the first party decided not to leave the ship, claiming, "A fair wind may cause the captain to sail immediately and leave us behind." The second party went ashore for a brief spell and returned to the ship happy and refreshed. The third party also visited the island but they stayed so long that they only returned to the ship as the anchor was being raised. The fourth party stayed even longer, saying, "We will enjoy ourselves until the last minute. When we hear the ship's bells ringing, we will return. The captain will not leave without us." When they saw the ship leaving, they leaped into the water and swam to it, injuring themselves. The fifth party did not hear the bell. They ate and drank and were left behind to die later when winter arrived.

The island represents this world. The ship refers to our deeds here on earth. People can be divided into the groups above. Some enjoy the pleasures of the world but always remember that they must live in moderation and not neglect good deeds, so that they may reach their ultimate destination in safety.

A middle-aged couple from the country went on a railway journey of about fifty miles to visit with a married daughter for the first time. The train ran through an interesting and scenic region. The wife had looked forward with keen anticipation to the trip. She was going to enjoy, not only the visit with her family but the ride. However, once on the train, it took considerable time to get all her packages and parcels adjusted. She wanted her seat comfortably arranged, the shades pulled just right; everything had to be in order.

Her husband asked her to stop fussing and look out of the window. She replied that she would enjoy the scenery as soon as she was comfortable. Just about the time she had settled down to enjoy the ride, she heard the conductor call out the name of her station, and she had to get up to leave.

"Oh, my!" she said. "If I had only known that the ride would be so short, I would not have wasted so much time fussing!"

A minister once asked a businessman how things were going with him. The man replied, "Things are very, very bad."

"Never say things are bad, my son," said the sage. "Say, rather, that they are bitter. A doctor's prescription may be bitter, but it cures the malady, so it is not bad, it is good. So it is with life. The bitterness in life has its therapeutic value. After we have overcome the bitterness, we know that it has served to help us to better enjoy the sweet."

"Preacher," complained an aggravated young wagoner, "I am at my wits' end about my horses. They don't eat anything but hamburgers and french fries. Already they're so skinny I'm afraid they won't last much longer."

"Let me ask you something," said the preacher. "Do you pray every day?"

"Why, er—uh—not usually," the driver stammered.

"Do you wash your hands before every meal?"

"Not always."

"And do you ask God's blessing before you eat?"

"No!" the driver answered tersely.

"Then all is perfectly clear," said the preacher. "It is irrevocably intertwined with the divine law of compensation. Since you eat like a horse, your horses eat like humans."

267

St. Francis of Assisi was busy working in his garden. A visitor asked him what he would do if he were suddenly to learn that he was to die at the end of the day.

The saint answered, "I would finish working in my garden."

The two men had been walking along the country road discussing life and values. Suddenly, one turned to the other and asked: "What is better than God and worse than the devil?"

The second man was dumbfounded at the question and indicated his inability to answer it.

"One word can be the answer to both questions," remarked the first man, "NOTHING."

A professor of English prescribed a set of rules for adequate living, which he called "The Grammar of Life." He said:

"Live in the active voice, not the passive. Think more about what you make happen than what happens to you.

"Live in the indicative mood, rather than the subjunctive. Be concerned with things as they are, rather than as they might be.

"Live in the present tense, facing the duty at hand without regret for the past or worry for the future.

"Live in the first person, criticizing yourself rather than finding fault with others.

"Live in the singular number, caring more for the approval of your own conscience than for the applause of the crowd.

"And, if you want a verb to conjugate, you cannot do better than to take the verb *to love.*"

During the period of the French Revolution, King Louis XVI reigned over France. When he entered the courtyard amidst the heralding blares of bugles and unfurled flags, all of his subjects and soldiers snapped to attention. When complete silence reigned, the loudspeakers pronounced the king's schedule for the day: *Le roi ne fera rien!* "Today the king will do nothing." And so we find that King Louis XVI is referred to in the histories of the French Revolution as the *Roi Fainéant,* "the magnificent do-nothing king."

This is one pattern of life.

A sage once said: "We can always hear some people complain that they can't make a living. They just don't know what they are going to live on. I haven't yet heard a person complain that he doesn't have a sufficient quantity of good deeds and blessings stored to prepare him for the World to Come."

He further remarked: "All my life I have known that I must some day die, but I have not yet learned to be prepared for it."

A man once came to his spiritual leader and asked, "Tell me, how can I die as a good person should?"

The man of God answered, "Don't worry about how to die; just live as a good person and you will die as a good person!"

LIGHT

There is the story of the followers of a great sage, who approached him with the complaint about the prevalence of overpowering darkness in the world. Intent on driving out the forces of evil, they implored him to advise them. At first he suggested that they take brooms and attempt to experiment in a nearby cellar by sweeping the darkness which filled the atmosphere. The bewildered disciples proceeded to this curious task, but to no avail. Then he suggested that they take sticks and beat vigorously at the darkness to drive out the evil. When this too failed to bring the expected results, he said, "My children, one can readily overwhelm the challenge of darkness by simply lighting a candle. Thereupon, his followers descended to the cellar and kindled each his candle, and the darkness vanished.

There is a famous passage in Cicero in which he writes of a prisoner who, having spent his life in a dark dungeon, knew of the existence of light only from what he experienced coming through a small fissure in the rock. He inferred, if the walls were removed the light would cease to exist because the fissure would be destroyed.

Many people live in a similar dungeon and draw the same inference. They think that if the walls they have built to safeguard the truth were destroyed, truth itself would perish.

Abraham Lincoln, the quiet man of few words, was fond of telling the story of a man lost in a dark, dense forest. Thunder crashed on all sides and occasionally a streak of lightning would illuminate his way. Being very much disconcerted over the infrequency of the lightning and the intensity of the thunder, he turned to heaven and prayed: "If it's all the same with you, O Lord, give us a little more light and a little less noise."

LIKENESS

A scoffer once thought it a good idea to send a New Year's card to a preacher. He chose one with a picture of a hog, to show his opposition to religion. The preacher immediately dispatched a New Year's card in return and enclosed a picture of himself. When the two met later, the scoffer asked, "I was surprised to receive your New Year's card. I didn't deserve it."

"You certainly did," was the reply. "Since you sent me a likeness of yourself, I returned to you a likeness of myself."

LIMITS

A student of philosophy was once invited to a celebration by a rich, pious man. The host asked the philosopher to have a drink with him and to make a toast, explaining that he felt this was the way to bring people closer to one another. When they finished drinking one glass, he suggested they take a second. The scholar was not used to drinking, yet he was kind enough not to refuse the host and had a second drink. But when the host insisted that he have a third drink, the guest said to him:

"I agree to drink a third glass, but only on the condition that you fill the glass to the very brim." The host did so. When the glass was filled to almost overflowing, the guest said: "Please pour some more," to which the host replied: "You are poking fun at me. Don't you see that the glass is so full that it cannot take even one drop more?"

To this the philosopher replied: "Let this be a moral lesson to you. The glass is an inanimate object and yet it contains a certain measure. It should be an example to a human being who is full of life and dynamic will-power to control himself in all fields of life, to know his limitations, and not to over-indulge his desires. . . ."

LISTENING

A small boy sitting in the rear of a classroom appeared to be day-dreaming. The teacher was curious.

"Do you have trouble hearing, David?" she asked.

"No, ma'am," the boy replied politely, "I have trouble listening."

~~~

The young child returned home with a crayon drawing she had done at school. She almost danced into the kitchen where her busy mother was preparing dinner.

"Mother," she cried in glee, "you'll never guess what!"

"Right," replied the mother not looking up, "I don't know what."

"Mother, you're not listening."

"Yes, I am, darling," said the mother as she attended to her pots.

"But, Mother, you're not listening with your eyes."

~~~

A story is told of the psychiatrist who was approached by a friend with this question. "Tell me," the friend asked, "how can you listen, hour after hour, day after day, to people pouring out their distress and troubles?" To which question the psychiatrist is supposed to have replied, "Who listens?"

~~~

LIVELIHOOD

A businessman once confided to a friend that while he was struggling, his competitor was tremendously successful.

His friend smiled sympathetically and advised: "With one small head you are trying to manage two establishments—yours and that of your competitor. Tomorrow, when you go to your place of business, start a concentrated campaign on building up your business. But before you do anything, you must stop wasting precious time and energy on envy. Use that energy to improve your business, and then you will see how it will flourish."

~~~

A well known philosopher once noticed a man hurrying along the street. The philosopher asked him: Why do you run like this? What is this great urgency?"

271

"I am seeking my livelihood," the man replied.

"How do you know," asked the philosopher, "that your livelihood has run ahead of you and that you must pursue it? Maybe it is behind you and you must just stand still until it catches up with you? Perhaps in this way you are running away from your livelihood."

LOGIC

We aspire to be logical. We rule ourselves and want to be ruled by logical leaders and logical laws. But is life logical and are people's lives governed by pure logic? Often, by the use of sheer logic, we arrive at very illogical conclusions.

One story, reflecting this observation concerns a man who had an obsession that he was dead. He went to a psychiatrist for help. The psychiatrist used all the known techniques at his command but to no avail. Finally, the psychiatrist tried appealing to the patient's logic.

"Do dead men bleed?" asked the doctor.

"No, of course not," answered the patient.

"All right," said the doctor, "now let us try an experiment."

The doctor took a sharp needle and pricked the man's skin, and the patient began to bleed profusely.

"There! What do you say now?" asked the psychiatrist.

"Well I'll be darned!" answered the patient. "By gosh! Dead people do bleed!"

Abraham Lincoln won many arguments through sheer force of logic. On one occasion, having failed to make a stubborn opponent see the error of his reasoning, Lincoln said, "Well, let's see. How many legs has a cow?"

"Four, of course," was the ready answer.

"That's right," said Lincoln. "Now supposed we call the cow's tail a leg, how many legs would the cow have?"

"Why, five, of course."

"That's where you make an error," said Lincoln. "Simply calling a cow's tail a leg doesn't make it a leg."

In H. Allen Smith's book, *The Pig in the Barber Shop,* which deals with his experiences in Mexico, an interesting new theory

272

in economics is advanced by the Head Man of a small Mexican Indian tribe.

It seems that this tribe was very adept at making a straw mat that had great sales potential in the United Staes. The representative of an American firm went down to visit the tribe and tried to make a good business deal. He spoke to the Head Man and said that his company would like to order several thousand pieces. The Head Man agreed, but stipulated that the price per unit would be *higher* on such a large order than it would be if only a smaller order were placed.

The American was more than a little shocked at the business sense of the Indian and maintained that the price should be lower, because of the large volume, and certainly not higher.

"No," replied the Indian.

"And why not?" asked the American.

"Because it is so tiresome to make the same article over and over," answered the Head Man.

A man of fifty married a woman of thirty. The marriage caused quite a bit of talk in their circles. Once, when someone asked the newly married man about the great difference in age, he replied, "It's not bad at all. When she looks at me she feels ten years older and when I look at her I feel ten years younger. So what's wrong? We're both forty!"

He had gone bathing in the lake and almost drowned. Luckily, his outcry brought a crowd and one of the men dived in and rescued him. When he came to, he looked at his rescuer and said, "I swear never to go into the water again until I learn how to swim!"

Two men were walking; one was holding a closed umbrella. Suddenly it began to rain.

"Open your umbrella quickly," said one man to the other.

"It won't help at all," came the answer.

"What do you mean it won't help? It will protect us from the rain."

"It's no use, the umbrella is full of holes like a sieve."

"Then why did you take it in the first place?"

"Because I didn't think it was going to rain."

273

"Which is more important, the sun or the moon?" asked one man of another.

"The moon without a question," was the reply. "It shines at night when it is needed. The sun shines only during the day when there is enough light already."

LOSS

A businessman sent word to his minister that he had lost everything. It was during a time of great financial stress. The minister went to see him and the following conversation took place:

"I regret to hear that your wife died," said the minister.

"You are mistaken," replied the businessman. "My wife is well and has helped me in this disaster."

"Then, I regret the disloyalty of your sons," continued the minister.

"You are mistaken again," said the businessman. "Every one of my sons has come home and offered me all their money to help me out."

"Too bad that your health has taken a turn for the worse," said the minister.

"Again you're wrong," said the businessman. "My health is perfect."

"Then," demanded the minister, "what do you mean by saying that you have lost everything? You lost money, it is true, but you have your wife, your sons, and your health. What more can you wish for?"

A little girl who had just moved to a large city, became lost. She went to the corner policeman who began plying her with questions, but she was unable to give him her address. Then the little girl interrupted: "Officer, if you will take me to the church, I can find my own way home."

LOVE

Three men were courting the same woman. She did not know which one to accept, so she decided to go on a trip to another continent to think things over. The suitors were asked to furnish her with an expression of their love before she went away. One brought her a gold charm, inscribed with her name; another presented her with a rich garland of fragrant roses. The third appeared before her, and said, "My love, I have neither a gold charm nor a fragrant bouquet; but I have a heart, here your name is engraved; here your memory is precious. And this heart, full of affection, will follow you wherever you travel, and remain with you wherever you will be."

A handclasp is an outward sign of warmth. Some might also consider it a gauge that measures, to a degree, the affection in a friend's heart. The handclasp has become a custom, but then some might say that so has a kiss. To what degree a friend will understand the meaning of your handshake or embrace depends entirely on how it is given. The person who is merely following custom slips you a limp, cold, clammy hand. But something warm is definitely generated from the other hand to yours when it is definitely given. The affection is taken from the heart and put into the hand, and one can feel the leap of the other's heart.

There was once a man who was the essence of goodness. He literally did not know the meaning of the word "hate."

A friend once asked him: "How come you are beloved by all, even your enemies?"

"Enemies?" queried the saintly man. "I do not have enemies, for I have loved them so long and so sincerely that they have become my friends. Now they have begun to love me in return."

A worried father once asked a psychologist for advice about his young son. If one could apply the word "wicked" to a child, that is what this youngster was. It seemed as if his only occupation and purpose in life was to give his parents Hell-on-earth.

After the psychologist had listened to the father, he replied: "The medicine you seek for your son cannot be manufactured in a test tube. It can only come straight from your heart, and you must keep on increasing the dosage. Never fear any ill-effects, for there is no such thing as an overdose of *love*. The worst reaction I can caution you about is that the little child's heart will love you back."

A man found frost on his windows and tried to scrape it off. A neighbor saw him. "What are you doing?" he asked.

275

"Getting rid of the frost," said the other, "for I can't see out."

His friend, realizing that the work was slow, advised him: "Why don't you just light a fire inside and the frost will disappear of itself?"

⁓

I love you, not only for what you are, but for what I am when I am with you.

I love you, not only for what you have made of yourself, but for what you are making of me.

I love you for ignoring the possibilities of the fool in me and for laying firm hold of the possibilities of the good in me.

I love you for closing your eyes to the discords in me, and for adding to the music in me by worshipful listening.

I love you because you are helping me to make of the lumber of my life, not a tavern, but a temple, and of the words of my every day, not a reproach, but a song.

I love you because you have done more than any creed to make me happy.

You have done it without a word, without a touch, without a sign.

You have done it by just being yourself.

Perhaps, after all, that is what love means.

—Anonymous

⁓

The man went to the bookstore to purchase a book for his daughter. He looked around and finally selected one which he thought fitting. Timidly, he asked the salesman: "No sex in it, I hope?" The salesman replied: "No, sir, it's a love story."

⁓

There was once a very sick little boy. His father loved him dearly and sat vigil day and night at the child's bed. With tenderness in his heart and a constant prayer on his lips, the father scrutinized the boy with bated breath, looking for a sign of improvement.

One night, as the father thus sat watching, the boy rose from his bed, and in his sleep walked into the kitchen where he destroyed everything within his reach. When there was nothing left for him to break, the boy, still asleep, went back to his bed. The father painfully observed this tragic procedure but did not waken the boy for fear of causing him harm.

The next night, while the father still kept vigil at his son's bedside, the child again sleep-walked, but this time he went to the library. In a short time, the boy was on his way back to his bed, leaving nothing but destruction in his wake. Again the father was struck dumb with distress.

On the third night, the father sat near his son and prayed for divine help. The boy got out of his bed, went to the kitchen where he picked up a knife, and proceeded to his brother's room. The father, speechless with terror, watched all this. Just as the sick child raised the knife to plunge it into his brother's chest, the father shouted: "Stop! You must not kill my child!"

The father was fearful of hurting his sick child, but he loved his other son as well.

HEART SONG

Unless you can feel when left by one
That all men else go with him;
Unless you can muse in a crowd all day
On the absent face that fixed you;
Unless you can love as the Angels may
With the breath of Heaven betwixt you;
Unless you can dream that his faith is fast,
Unless you can die when the dream is past,
Oh, never call it loving.

—Elizabeth Barrett Browning

An eminent pediatrician had a standard treatment for frail newborn infants who failed to gain weight.

When he came to such a baby's chart during his rounds in the hospital, he invariably scrawled the following directive to the nurse in attendance: "This baby to be loved every three hours."

A four-year-old boy taught his neighbors a lesson.

Toward evening one fall day, his mother placed him and his three-month-old brother out on the porch of their modest home to catch the last rays of sunshine. The young boy was impressed with the fact that he was acting as a guard over his baby brother. Nestled near his side was his fluffy collie puppy who seemed to be perfectly content to be pressed up against his master's body. The three of them formed quite a picture in the afternoon sun. A passerby saw the beauty of the scene and paused, walked across to the little boy and said softly, "What are you doing, sonny?" The little boy looked at the stranger for a moment and then replied, "I am loving them."

⁓

God sent an angel down from heaven to look for the most beautiful thing on earth. When the angel saw the flowers at springtime, he said, "These must be the most beautiful things on earth," and he gathered them up to take them back to heaven.

Then he met a child of wondrous beauty and lovely smile. When he saw the child he said, "This must be the most wonderful thing on earth. Nothing could be sweeter than the smile of that innocent child."

Before long, in a remote valley, he came upon a humble cottage where a mother sat in the doorway with her little baby on her lap. As he watched her care for the child with love and tenderness, he said, "This must be the fairest thing on earth. I will take that mother's love back with me to heaven."

When he reached the portals of heaven the flowers had faded and were dead, the smile on the child's face had changed into a scrowl—but the mother's love was unchanged.

⁓

Tennessee Ernie Ford was reading an article by a psychiatrist in which he explained how two young married people could determine whether they loved each other.

"Things have changed," said Ernie. "A few years ago people were so busy raising a family they did not even have time to take the test."

⁓

Said one friend to another:
"Tell me, do you love me?"
The other replied: "I love you deeply."
The first asked, "Do you know what gives me pain?"
The other responded: "How can I know what gives you pain?"
"If you do not know what gives me pain," was the reply, "how can you say that you truly love me?"

⁓

A young girl was showing off her collection of dolls. Although she had many fine dolls, her favorite was the oldest one—torn, tattered and limp. When she was asked why she preferred this one, she replied, "I love her most because if I didn't love her, no one else would."

⁓

The old gardener, engaged in breaking apart and re-setting rhubarb crowns, looked up as a little girl approached.

"How is your baby brother?"

Tears emerged at these words, for Mary was painfully jealous of the new baby. The old man talked as though he had not noticed.

"I suppose your Mom and Dad are very busy with him now. Might even seem as though they'd be too busy to love you as much as they did, but love is like rhubarb. If it's divided, it grows better. Yes, sir," he continued, "I loved my mother a lot; then I met and loved a girl and married her. We had a baby pretty soon, and another one came along. But each time loving the new one did not take a mite away from the old. Yes, love is like rhubarb; when it's divided, it grows."

People give attention in their wills to the distribution of their wealth and property. But one of the most meaningful testaments we know of is that of a New York woman who left her children a valuable piece of advice in addition to her worldly goods. These are the last lines of her will:

"Love one another. Hold fast to that, whether you understand one another or not, and remember nothing really matters except being kind to one another, and to all the world as far as you can reach."

"It is love in old age, no longer blind, that is true love. For love's highest intensity doesn't necessarily mean its highest quality. Glamour and jealousy are gone; and the ardent caress, no longer needed, is valueless compared to the reassuring touch of a trembling hand. Passersby commonly see little beauty in the embrace of young lovers on a park bench, but the understanding smile of an old wife to her husband is one of the loveliest things in the world."

—Booth Tarkington

There was once a man and wife. As will sometimes happen, the man at one time became very ill and required complete physical rest and nursing care. His wife, who was a very good woman and loved him as much as her own life, took over the management of his business, fearing that a stranger hired to do the job might not give it the necessary attention. In addition to running the business, she decided to nurse her husband as well.

"It isn't enough," she said to herself, "to have a nurse give him a pill and go back to her reading. He is very ill; he feels badly that he cannot work; he needs to be encouraged and made to understand that he is not a burden. With every dose of medicine that I give him, I can assure him of my love and my need for him, in spite of his illness. I can kiss his brow and make him feel like a loved little boy instead of an inadequate sick man. I can hold his hand when the pain is bad and share it with him so he'll only feel the half of it. Only I can nurse him back to health because I can administer love."

And the husband, weak in his bed, said to himself: "I must get well. I must fight to live. I cannot leave her alone, and for her sake, to take care of her again, I must live. But for her devotion and loving care, I would perhaps not care if I lived or not. I could not bear the pain alone. Since she is, in fact, my life, I must do what I can to preserve it."

And he did get well, and he did dedicate the rest of his life to her who cared so selflessly and so well for him.

> If you don't feel just right,
> If you can't sleep at night,
> If you moan and you sigh,
> If your throat feels dry,
> If you don't care to smoke,
> If your food makes you choke,
> If your heart doesn't beat,
> If you're getting cold feet,
> If your head's in a whirl—
> Why not marry the girl?
>
> —Bagolo

LOVING-KINDNESS

The teacher, turning to his class, asked, "Who knows what is meant by loving-kindness?" One youngster replied, "If I were hungry and my mother gave me a slice of bread, that would be kindness. If she put lots of peanut butter on it, that would be loving-kindness."

LUCK

Two middle-aged men who had attended school together in their youth met by chance. They began to tell each other of their lives during the intervening years since their last meeting, and during the course of their conversation one of the men complained bitterly about the way his only son had turned out.

"I had no luck with my Paul," he lamented. "I had hoped that he would study at the Academy, as we had, and become a learned man of faith. But he went, instead, to an out-of-town university where he quickly became 'emancipated.' Now he ridicules our traditional way of life and worship and has no respect for his mother or me. I just had no luck with my boy."

"Luck had nothing to do with it," replied the other man. "Place the blame correctly—on yourself. When your son was still too young to decide for himself, you simply put him on the wrong train, and he has been on the wrong track ever since."

LYING

A teacher, who believed in cooperating with the parents of her pupils, called at the home of a small boy whom she had caught in a number of falsehoods.

"I cannot see how you can say that," the boy's mother objected. "John never lies. I am mighty particular about it myself. He is out in the yard now."

"Annie," she said to the boy's small sister, "you go out and tell him to come in this minute."

Annie went, but in a few minutes returned without her brother. "He will not come," she announced proudly.

"He won't come. Did you tell him who was here?" inquired the mother.

"I did," said Annie.

"All right," said the mother. "Go back and tell him his grandmother is here and that she has some candy for him. That will bring him!"

A liar is worse than a thief. A thief gets into your pockets and steals nothing more than your money. The liar creeps into your mind and steals your thoughts, your ideas, and your trust. The liar steals your heart and depresses your spirit. The wound inflicted by the thief is superficial, for you will soon get over the loss of money, but one sometimes never gets over the loss of those intangibles which are taken under false pretenses.

A merchant once sought to obtain character references about a man with whom he was about to do business. The source he went to knew that the man was not reliable but did not wish to say so openly. His answer accomplished both ends: "There are people who have the ability to remember things which happened a year ago. A person of much better memory is able to remember things that took place two years ago and even before. But the person you ask about has such a fantastic memory, he remembers things that have never taken place."

MAN

Dr. Harry Emerson Fosdick spoke about a conversation between an astronomer and a philosopher. Said the astronomer, "Astronomically speaking, what is man?" The question is understandable. When we think of the staggering dimensions of the universe; when we contemplate the number of stars and galaxies, it is understandable to ask, "Astronomically speaking, what is man?"

The philosopher thought for a moment and answered, "Astronomically speaking, man is the astronomer."

"Why women join the Lib movement is a puzzle to me," exclaimed a talkative man at his club.

"Life isn't fair to us men. When we are born, our mothers get the compliments and the flowers. When we are married, our brides get the presents and the publicity. When we die, our widows get the life insurance and the winters in Florida. What do they want to be liberated from?"

When Woodrow Wilson became President of the United States, he remarked, "When a man takes office in Washington he either grows or swells." There is a world of difference between the two.

The famous dramatist and critic, Alfred Polgar, emphasized the importance of the individual through the following story:

A sergeant said of a soldier in a foxhole: "Never mind him, so long as we can save our squadron." The lieutenant said: "Never mind that squadron, as long as we can save our platoon." The captain said: "The platoon doesn't matter, as long as we can save the rest of the company." the colonel said: "Never mind the com-

pany, as long as we can save the rest of the regiment." The briga-
dier was interested only in saving the rest of the brigade, while
the general wanted only to save his army.

"The army doesn't matter," said the leader of the country,
"as long as we can save the world." And God said: "The world
doesn't matter, as long as the universe isn't destroyed, too." . . .
"The universe doesn't matter," said the mother of the soldier in
the foxhole, "as long as I get my son safely home."

When Professor Eliot was president of Harvard University, he
had occasion to dedicate a new hall of philosophy and searched for
an appropriate inscription to place above its entrance. He called
his faculty members together and after much deliberation, they
suggested the well-known Greek maxim: "Man is the measure of
all things." With that, they adjourned for their summer vacation.
When school reopened in the fall, they were surprised to find that
the president had decided upon his own inscription. Instead of
"Man is the measure of all things," he had seen fit to have inscribed, "What is man that Thou art mindful of him?"

Francis Bacon, the English philosopher of the sixteenth century said: "It is not what men eat, but what they digest, that makes
them strong; not what we gain, but what we save, that makes us
rich; not what we read, but what we absorb, that makes us learned;
not what we preach, but what we practice, that makes us lovable."

Man can be divided into three categories: fits, misfits, and
counterfeits.

Fits are those people who fit into society and do the job they
have set out to do.

Misfits are those who are trying to do a job they do not know
how to do.

Counterfeits are those who try to give the impression they are
doing a job when in truth they are doing nothing.

MANNERS

A sage was questioned, "Master, what is the test of good manners?"

He answered: "It is being able to put up pleasantly with bad ones."

~~~~~

MARRIAGE

A young girl was anxious to marry someone with a lot of money. Unfortunately, her boy friend only had $45.00 to his name.

So he decided to leave town with his $45.00 to seek his fortune in the big city. His girl kissed him goodbye and said: "You can return when you have $50,000!"

Seven years later the boy returned. The girl who had been waiting impatiently all through the years, rushed into his arms. "How much money do you have now?" she asked breathlessly.

"$55.00," he replied.

"That's close enough," she said.

~~~~~

"I am the head of my house," remarked one recently-wed husband to another. "After all, I should be; I am the one who earns the money."

"Well," said the other, "my wife and I have a different arrangement. We have agreed that I should decide all the major problems and she the minor ones."

"And how is it working out?" asked the first.

"Well, so far, no problems of major importance have come up."

~~~~~

The Talmud reports the wise counsel given by a mother to her daughter who was about to be wed. "My daughter," she advised, "if you will respect your husband, he will treat you like a queen. If you will serve him like a slave-girl, he will serve you like a slave. But if you will be too proud to serve him, he will treat you like a maid-servant. . . . If his friends come to his home, welcome them heartily. . . . Watch well your home and your husband's possessions. He will be delighted with you and you will be the crown of his head."

~~~~~

It was just an everyday fur coat that her husband had given her for her birthday. She looked at it with wonder. Finally, she turned to her husband and remarked: "I just don't understand

284

how such a beautiful coat can come from such a stinking little beast."

With a hurt look, her husband replied, "I'm not asking for gratitude, but a little respect I can surely expect."

⚉

Henry Ford, founder of the Ford empire, was a hard-working simple man. At his fiftieth wedding anniversary he was asked by a reporter, "How do you account for your happy marriage?"

The Ford king did not hesitate for a moment before he replied, "By sticking to one model."

⚉

Two men were discussing married life. Said one to the other: "I have an excellent wife. She is at home in literature, at home in music, at home in art, at home in science. In fact she is at home everywhere except. . . ."

"Except what?" questioned the second man.

"Except at home," was the sad reply.

⚉

She had announced her engagement and the family was delighted. One afternoon, a friend came to call and was met at the door by the maid who announced, "No, madam, Miss Irene is not home this afternoon, she went down to the class."

"What class is she attending?" inquired the friend.

"You know Miss Irene is going to be married in the fall," explained the maid, "and she is taking courses in domestic silence."

⚉

A reporter covering a golden wedding anniversary celebration asked the husband the inevitable question: "To what do you attribute your longevity and apparent good health?"

"When my wife and I were first married," answered the old man, "we made a pact that would ensure harmony. We decided that if we ever became involved in an argument I would leave the house and go for a walk to give us both an opportunity to cool off." With a sigh the man continued, "And I've been living an outdoor life ever since."

⚉

"Help your wife," advises one marital counselor. "When she washes the dishes, wash the dishes with her; when she mops the floor, mop up the floor with her."

⚉

"We are the ideal married couple," boasted Mrs. Lawrence to her friends. "We have never had a harsh word between us because of one simple arrangement. In the morning I do as I want, and in the afternoon, my husband does as I want."

He was angry and quite disgusted with his wife's actions. He had had it, and so he addressed her with these words, "Believe me, I'll never know why God made women so beautiful and so dumb."

"I'll give you the answer," replied the wife. "God made women beautiful so you men would love us, and He made us dumb so we could love you." The husband's answer was never recorded.

A young married couple, raised in the city, moved to a farm of their own. They were appalled at all the unanticipated expenses. One day they acquired a cow. She was a heavy financial burden, and they made up their minds to be mighty careful with her. They decided not to milk her very often, and took only one quart at a milking. The cow died soon thereafter. Apparently they had confused the animal's true nature with thriftiness.

"When my husband speaks in public," said the woman proudly, "I tremble."

The husband, sitting nearby, commented, "And when my wife speaks in private, I tremble."

The chairman rose to congratulate the last speaker. "Congratulations on your typical married man's speech," he said humorously as he slapped him on his back.

"But I said only a few words," replied the speaker.

"Exactly, exactly!" replied the chairman.

My first day back at the office after my honeymoon was a hard one. I came home tired and hungry. I sat down for supper and dug right in, finishing in no time. As I looked up I saw that my bride was crying. "What's wrong, dear?" I asked.

286

"The hours I spent slaving over our first dinner," she said, wiping away her tears, "and all you do is sit there and eat it!"

⁓

At a golden wedding anniversary, to which both young and old were invited, the question was raised, "Which season of life was the most happy?" After being freely discussed by the guests, it was referred for answer to the mature groom, who was seventy years of age.

He was silent for a moment or two and then asked if they had noticed a grove of trees in front of his dwelling. When they nodded assent, he continued: "When the spring comes, and in the soft air the buds swell on the trees, and they are covered with blossoms, I think 'How beautiful is spring.' And when summer comes and covers the trees with heavy foliage, and singing birds are all among the branches, I think 'How beautiful is summer!' When autumn loads them with golden fruit, and their leaves bear the gorgeous tints of frost, I think, 'How beautiful is autumn.' And when it is winter, and there is neither foliage nor fruit, then I look up through the leafless branches and see, as I could never until now, the stars as they shine through."

⁓

The old couple, so obviously devoted to each other, were celebrating their golden wedding anniversary. The affair was attended by the usual newspaper reporter looking for a human interest story, who asked the usual questions: "Are you still in love with your wife?" "More than ever; I adore her," was the immediate answer.

"You mean," persisted the obviously doubtful reporter, "that despite fifty years of being married to the same woman, you are more in love with her than ever before?"

"No, son," was the slow reply, "not despite the fifty years, but because of them."

⁓

Matters couldn't get much worse and so she decided to visit a marriage counselor. "My husband has no outstanding vices," she said to the counselor, "but I'm going to divorce him."

"Remember," the counselor advised, "when you married this man it was for life."

"I know, I know," she replied, "but for the past five years he hasn't shown any signs of life."

⁓

A lecturer before a woman's club, talking about Iran, was telling how careless men over there are with their wives. It was no uncommon sight, he said, to see a woman and a donkey hitched up together.

A lady in the audience piped up: "That's nothing—you can see that here, too."

A married couple went to the parish priest for marital counseling. In the course of the conversation, which was serious at first, the priest commented on the number of good-looking girls in the parish.

"Father," said the husband, "you surprise me."

"Why?" he asked. "Just because I'm on a diet doesn't mean I can't look at the menu."

"It is important if you want to have a successful marriage," said the woman, "to make your husband the boss. I believe in letting the man make all the important decisions."

"Who made the decision that he was to be The Boss?" she was asked.

"Naturally, I did," was the reply.

"If you want to make your marriage a happy one," said the lecturer, "you must have a realistic attitude. You must be patient with your wives. When you are going out together, don't worry if your wife is not ready on time. The thing for you to do is to have a book handy so that you can read it while you wait. I assure you that you will be absolutely astonished at the amount of culture you will acquire."

Evidently she had been doing some reading on her own. When her husband returned from his office that evening, she asked him, "Dear, what is meant by the expression, 'the average man?'"

He thought for a minute and then answered, "An average man is one who isn't as good as his wife thinks he is before she marries him, and not as bad as she thinks he is afterward."

André Maurois has suggested that this vow be made a part of every marriage ceremony: "I bind myself for life! I have chosen;

from now on my aim will be, not to search for someone who may please me, but to please the one I have chosen."

⌘

Socrates was unhappily married. When asked for his advice about marriage, he commented: "By all means marry. If you get a good wife, you will become very happy; if you get a bad one you will become a philosopher—and that is good for every man."

⌘

Joshua was an aesthetic youth with a great love for music, as well as the other arts. A rather shy fellow, he had never proposed to a girl, and his father decided to find him a suitable wife. After much discussion with two of his best friends, each of whom had a daughter, he gave his son a choice: He might marry a beautiful girl with no talent for music and little education, but with a fine cooking ability, or he might marry the daughter of his other friend. This one had a face that could curdle milk; her eyes were set too close together, she had no neck, her head seemed to be fastened to her shoulders with concrete, her nose could hold two dollars in nickels. But she had one virtue—a gorgeous voice. In fact, she adored all forms of music. The father showed his son a poster announcing the ugly girl's coming appearance at the Metropolitan Opera.

The youth's artistic sense overcame his attraction toward the beautiful girl, so he married the homely opera singer.

On the first morning after the wedding, he awoke, took one look at that face sharing his pillow and shook her. "For heaven's sake," he cried, "*sing* a little something!"

⌘

A solicitor for a Home for the Aged called upon a well-to-do young couple for a donation. Hearing a commotion inside, he knocked extra-loudly on the door.

A somewhat disheveled man admitted him. "What can I do for you?" he growled, clearly upset about something.

"I would like to speak to the master of the house," said the solicitor politely.

"Then you're just in time," barked the young man. "My wife and I are settling that very question right now!"

⌘

Asked to write a brief essay on the life of Benjamin Franklin, one little girl wrote this gem of a paragraph:

"He was born in Boston, traveled to Philadelphia, met a lady on the street, she laughed at him, he married her, and discovered electricity."

~~~~~

Two former college friends met on a downtown street one evening. They had not seen one another for years, and so, decided to sit in a hotel lobby and exchange stories of the past. They became engrossed in one another and did not realize the lateness of the hour.

They left for home, but both of them were a little fearful of what their wives would say about their coming in so late. The next day they met again. One asked, "How did your wife take your coming in so late?" "Oh," replied the other, "I explained it to her and it was all right. What about your wife?"

"Well," he replied, "when I came in my wife got historical."

"You mean 'hysterical,' don't you?" his friend asked.

"No," he replied, "I mean 'historical.' She brought up everything that has happened in the past thirty years."

~~~~~

MARRIAGE-BROKERS

The marriage-broker had gotten him a blind date and they went to call on her together. When the man saw the girl, he was furious. He pulled the marriage-broker aside and whispered to him: "Some girl you got me! She's too fat, her nose is broken, her hair is bleached, she's knock-kneed, and she's missing two front teeth."

"You don't have to whisper," answered the marriage-broker, "She's deaf, too."

~~~~~

MATURITY

A preacher, leaving his church one day, noticed three small boys sitting on the steps. One had a toy airplane, one a miniature racing car, and the third a copy of *Newsweek* magazine.

"What would you like to be, son?" the preacher asked the first boy.

"A pilot," was the quick retort.

"And you?" he asked of the second.

"A racing driver."

"What would you like to be?" he asked the youngster with the magazine.

The boy looked straight at the preacher and answered, "Grown up, sir, grown up."

⁓

Freud was once asked for a definition of genuine maturity. Freud's reply was brief and pointed: *"Lieben und arbeiten,"* he said. To be truly mature one must be able to love and to work.

⁓

At the very start of his legal career, Darrow faced, in court, a veteran lawyer who kept referring to Darrow's beardless face.

Finally Darrow replied: "My opponent condemns me for not having a beard. Let me tell him a story. A king once sent a youthful nobleman to the court of a neighboring king, who received the visitor with the comment, 'Does the king lack men that he sends me a beardless boy?' To which the ambassador replied, 'Sir, if my king had supposed you imputed wisdom to a beard he would have sent you a goat.' " Darrow won the case.

⁓

MEMORY

In Maeterlinck's beautiful play, *The Blue Bird,* the children Tyltyl and Mytil are about to begin to search for the fabled blue bird of happiness. The fairy tells them that on their journey they will come to the land of memory whereupon turning the magic diamond in Tyltyl's hat, they will see all their departed loved ones—their grandparents, brothers and sisters.

"But how can we see them when they are dead?" asks Tyltyl in amazement.

The fairy looks intently, and kindly, at the youngster and replies softly: "How can they be dead, when they live in your memory?"

⁓

MERIT

A rich person, who was generous and kind to anybody who called on him for his assistance, decided one day that he would, in the future, not be so generous to people whom he hardly knew. He made up his mind that he would examine the merits of every person before he helped them, in order to make sure that the person really deserved his assistance.

Suddenly the wealthy man lost all his business and became

291

very poor. He went to the priest and asked for an explanation. "I have always been ready to help others," he said to the priest, "and more recently I have examined the merits of every person carefully, in order to make sure that I would assist those who were really worthy. Why have I now been punished with poverty?"

"That is the answer," said the priest. "As long as you were willing to help anybody who asked for assistance, the Almighty did not examine whether you were really worthy of all the riches He had bestowed upon you. But once you started to search for the worthier person before you offered help, God, too, examined you to see whether you were really deserving of all these riches. He must have found a person of greater merit, and therefore took away from you all the riches and gave them to another."

MESSIAH

A pious man who had an infinite amount of faith was discussing the coming of the Messiah with some students.

"Believe me," he said, "if we had reached sundown of the last day before the earth was to be destroyed, I still would not give up hope. I would continue to wait for his arrival."

When we cease to permit ourselves to be wooed by falsehoods; when we shall become blind to the beckoning hand of untruths; when we cease to fall for the flirtatious wink of guile and learn to give a welcome smile to truth and sincerity, then shall the Messiah be willing to tread on our hitherto unworthy soil.

A wealthy landowner burst into his home one day and, in a voice filled with despair, cried to his startled wife, "Marushka, there is a terrible rumor in town—the Messiah is coming!"

"So what's terrible?" asked the wife. "I think it's wonderful! Why are you frightened?"

"I have good reason to be afraid," he whimpered. "We have a fine dairy herd, a barn full of grain, and our orchards are laden with fruit. Now we will have to give up everything and follow Him."

"Compose yourself," said the wife soothingly. "The Lord our God is good. He knows how much suffering we Jews have had to endure. We had a Pharaoh, a Haman—always somebody; but our dear Lord got rid of them all. Just have faith, my dear husband. He will get rid of the Messiah also!"

～～～

MINORITY

William Jennings Bryan, one-time candidate for president, was not afraid to pick up the cause of the minority and fight for it with all his might. He taught: "Never be afraid to stand with the minority when you feel the minority is right, for the minority which is right will one day be the majority; always be afraid to stand with the majority which is wrong, for the majority which is wrong will one day be the minority."

～～～

A certain rabbi of Prague, reputedly able to work miracles, was in his study when the quiet afternoon was shattered by a frantic pounding on the door. The sexton admitted a distraught woman.

"My husband has left me," she sobbed, handing the *shammes* the deserter's farewell letter.

"Hmmm, I'd better show this note to the rabbi," said the sexton. "Just wait here—I'll be right back."

He returned in a few moments and consoled the woman. "Be at ease, madam. The rabbi sends good news. Seventy-six hours, eighteen minutes and thirty-four seconds from now, your husband will return."

When the relieved woman had departed the *shammes* went back into the study.

"Why do you look so glum?" asked the rabbi.

"It's that woman; I feel sorry for her."

"What's the matter? Don't you believe I can work miracles?"

"That's not the point," answered the sexton. "You only saw her note. I saw her face!"

～～～

MISERS

He was an old miser and it was apparent that he was near the end. He was dictating his last will: "And to each of my employees who has been with me for five or more years, I bequeath the sum of $1,000."

"That's very generous," commented the lawyer, in admiration.

"Not at all," said the sick man. "There is not one of them who has been with me for more than a year, but it will certainly make me look good in the papers."

~~~~

There was once a man who lived in seeming poverty. He never married because he "could not afford" to support a wife and, perhaps, a family. When he got older, he was taken ill, and his kindly, sympathetic neighbors cared for him and tried everything they could to nurse him back to health. But it was all in vain; his time had run out, and the poor man died. He did not even have money enough to pay for burial clothes and a funeral. Again his kind neighbors got together and gave him a simple burial.

Some time later, when the dead man's apartment was being renovated for a new occupant, the men who were working in the apartment came across an odd-looking box in the closet. They had no key for the lock, so they broke it open and to everyone's amazement discovered thousands of dollars in the cache.

Because he lived in poverty, the man felt poor; because he was known to be penniless he was treated like a pauper and was buried in a poor grave. Only when he was gone did his wealth become a fact, and people were heard to say, "That poor *rich* man."

~~~~

There was a rich tightwad in a town who refused to give his contribution even for those in need of bread. The head of the community persisted, however, until the miser finally came across with a donation. Then the head of the community said: "I can almost boast that I am a greater man than Moses. Moses merely drew *water* from a stone, but I drew *money* from a stone."

~~~~

A rich old miser became critically ill and the doctor prescribed a medicine with the following warning: "If after taking the medicine, you perspire, it is a sign that you will recover. If you don't perspire, only God can help."

The miser took the medicine, but failed to perspire. If seemed that the rich man was about to die.

"Let us call on him," said the mayor to the elders of the town. "Perhaps he will now repent his ways and leave something for the church."

They visited him, and found him in a repentant mood. They brought paper and ink and the mayor got ready to write. "The church," he said, "is badly in need of repairs."

294

"A hundred dollars for the church," said the miser, and groaned.

"The widows and orphans fund is depleted," said the mayor.

"A hundred—wait a minute, wait a minute!" the miser cried suddenly. "Cross it out! I am perspiring! I am perspiring!"

A stingy, rich man once invited a wayfarer to dinner. The latter became ill from the spoiled food the miser offered him and died shortly thereafter. The host made the funeral arrangements.

In his eulogy at the interment, the spiritual leader of the community said: "Our wealthy citizen performed three blessings at one time: Hospitality to guests, visiting the sick, and attending the dead to the grave."

A miser was once asked for a contribution to a charitable cause. Of course the miser found some excuse for turning down the request. As he was leaving, the representative of the charity turned to the miser and said: "Happy holiday to you."

"As far as I know, today is no holiday!" replied the astonished miser.

"Well," replied the other smilingly, "when I leave here without getting your contribution, it surely must feel like a holiday to you."

A young reporter called one evening on a rich, old farmer to learn the farmer's secret. He too, wanted to become rich.

"It's a long story," said the old man, "and while I'm telling it, we might as well save the candle." And he blew it out.

"You need not go on," interrupted the youth. "I understand."

The miser never enjoys his money. He hoards and worries about it as if it were his own, but he is as afraid to spend it as if it belonged to someone else.

MISTAKES

Dr. William Arthur Ward listed the following as ten mistakes to avoid:

1. Remorse over yesterday's failure.
2. Anxiety over today's problems.

295

3. Worry over tomorrow's uncertainty.
4. Waste of the moment's opportunity.
5. Procrastination with one's present duty.
6. Resentment of another's success.
7. Criticism of a neighbor's imperfection.
8. Impatience with youth's immaturity.
9. Skepticism of our nation's future.
10. Disbelief in God's providence.

—————

"I told you so," a parent once said to his fourteen-year-old son. "You would not have made that foolish mistake if you had used good judgment."

The boy said, "Well, how do you get good judgment?"

And the parent answered, rather slowly, "By making mistakes, of course."

—————

MODERATION

A preacher once said: "I am afraid that because of the ordinary people we shall have to wait to achieve our 'World to Come.' They are always too joyful."

"Anything to the extreme," he continued, "is unhealthy—too much joy, too much sadness, too much wisdom, or too much complacency. If we are to be too joyful, we will not be ready for the shock of disappointment. If we are too sad, we will despair of ever being happy. If one is too wise, one may not be able to meet the challenges confronting the very prudent. If one is too complacent, he will mark time and never get anywhere."

—————

Before King David died, he called on his son, Solomon, and said to him: "My advice for a successful living is never to be too exalted in moments of success and never to fall into a state of depression in times of stress and adversity."

King David then took a golden ring and put it on the hand of his young son. "Here," he said, "are engraved Hebrew letters. When you feel boundlessly happy, look at the engraving on the ring, *This Too Shall Pass.* In time of sadness or despair, remember the inscription on the ring again: *This Too Shall Pass.*"

—————

In the same way that evil tempts the human being to commit sin, it likewise tempts him to become too saintly. A sinful person

makes life difficult for others while a person who is overly righteous will find life difficult for himself.

MODESTY

"Every man should have two pockets in his garments," I remember hearing a wise man say. "In one pocket he should have
a piece of paper saying, "The entire world was created for my
sake," and in the other pocket should be the reminder, "I am but
dust and ashes."

As the mayor of a mountain village was being sworn into office, honored and surrounded by thousands of followers, he turned
and looked out of the window, directing his gaze at the highest
mountain peak. A friend, noticing his absorbed stare, commented,
"This is such a solemn, meaningful moment; can you find nothing
better to do than to stare at the mountains? Surely this is not the
first time you have seen a mountain."

The mayor replied, "I have often looked at the mountains, but
I think I see them for the first time now, and I cannot understand
how a mere lump of earth can make so much ado about itself
before it becomes a mountain."

The famous sage seemed to be fast asleep. Nearby sat some of
his followers. They carried on a whispered conversation about the
sage's unparalleled virtues.

"What generosity!" exclaimed one. "There isn't another one
like him in all the land."

"And his piety is without limit!" exclaimed a second.

"And his education!" cried a third. "He's a real genius."

"And his patience! He never gets excited."

They fell silent for a minute. Whereupon the sage slowly
opened one eye and said, "And my modesty you don't even mention?"

MONEY

When Bernard Baruch made his first million, he went to tell
his father about it. His father, however, did not seem to be im-

pressed. "I am not even thirty," said Bernard, "and already I have made my first million—and you are not even happy?"

"No, my son," replied his father, "I am not impressed. What I want to know is—how will you spend the money you have earned?"

———

A man paid a dollar to a miser for a look at his treasures. He stared at the piles of gold, then said, "Now I am as rich as you. All the fun you get from your money lies in looking at it. You do not use it. Others derive no benefit from it. Of its real value you are really not aware."

———

A wealthy businessman once offered $4,000 to anyone who could convincingly name four things which money could not buy.

He was positive that no one would be able to meet the challenge. He smiled skeptically when one man took a pad and pencil, wrote four short lines and passed the note to the challenger. He glanced at it, then gave it a more studied look. Without a word, he got out his checkbook and made good his promise. The list of the four things money could not buy read:

1. A baby's smile.
2. Youth after it is gone.
3. The love of a good woman.
4. Entrance into Heaven.

———

A small boy had swallowed a dime, and his mother was frantic. "Quick, quick," she yelled to her husband, "Send for the doctor!"

"No," replied the man cooly, "I think we ought to send for the minister."

"Why the minister?" exclaimed the wife, "Is our boy dying?"

"Oh, no," was the quick answer, "but our minister can get money out of anyone."

———

Henrik Ibsen wrote, "Money may be the husk of many things, but not the kernel. It brings you food, but not appetite; medicine, but not health; acquaintances, but not friends; days of joy, but not of peace or happiness." It is good to have money and the things that money will buy. It is also good to check up and make certain that we have not lost the things that money will not buy.

———

298

When man digs too deeply for money, it will often bury him. The more he becomes engrossed in his feverish search for money, the further he withdraws from friends. He has so little time for unimportant things. The deeper he becomes engulfed in the madness of amassing an enormous sum of money, the further he withdraws from sunlight and the beautiful things that cost nothing. There is no time for trivia—for a romp in the park, a ride in the car, a walk in the sun. Money becomes the sole object of his life!

When he finally has the time to take a ride, it is no longer at his own request. Nor can he enjoy it, for the time has come for him to die. Now his harassed search is over and just a little of the money which buried him while he was alive will be used to bury him now that he is dead.

But those who will inherit it will be so much the wiser; they'll spend it much more freely than their benefactor, the miser.

The president of an organization made several attempts to call upon a rather tightfisted millionaire, to ask him for a donation to a very important cause. But the wealthy man always refused to see him, with the excuse that he was very busy and had no time to talk.

When the millionaire died, the president of the organization was asked to deliver the eulogy, and he commenced by saying: "Woe be unto us, Mr. Jones. When you had money you never had time, and now when you have plenty of time on your hands, unfortunately you do not have any money."

If a man runs after money, he's money-mad; if he keeps it, he's a capitalist; if he spends it, he's a playboy; if he doesn't get it, he's a ne'er-do-well; if he doesn't try to get it, he lacks ambition. If he gets it without working for it, he's a parasite; and if he accumulates it after a lifetime of hard work, people call him a fool who got very little out of life.

People are funny. They spend money they don't have, to buy things they don't need, to impress folks they don't like.

299

MORALE

Robert Louis Stevenson was ill the greater part of his life. One day his wife went into his room when he had been compelled to put aside his manuscript to stanch the life blood that he was coughing away.

"I suppose you will tell me that it is a glorious day," she said.

"Yes," he replied as he looked at the sunlight streaming through his window. "I refuse to permit a row of medicine bottles to block the horizon."

MOTHER

If you had to place an advertisement for a mother, it would probably read as follows:

WANTED: A woman to cook, shop and sew; to clean house; to wash clothing and do all odd jobs. Must know something about medicine, psychology, and business management. Must be at home with illness, adversity and crisis of every kind. No salary, no vacation, long hours, and no opportunity for advancement.

A child speaking of his home to a friend, was asked, "Where is your home?"

Looking with loving eyes at his mother, he replied, "Where mother is!"

Two women sat talking in a public park. One had three healthy children tumbling about in play; the other woman had none. The woman who had no children watched wistfully while the little ones romped like puppies on the grass. "I would give ten years of my life to have three such wonderful children as yours," she said enviously. "Well," the mother answered, after a few moments, "three children cost just about that."

She was the mother of thirteen children. At a P.T.A. meeting she was asked, "How in the world do you have time to care for thirteen children?"

"Well," she replied, "when I had only one child it took all my time; what more can thirteen do?"

MOTIVATION

A preacher took his first trip in a railroad train. Thousands of his followers came to meet him at the depot. When he was questioned about his experiences, he related that he had learned a grand moral lesson from the locomotive. When pressed for an explanation, he pointed to the locomotive and said: "When the boiler is hot and the steam is going full blast, the locomotive is capable of moving hundreds of passengers and freight cars as well. But when the boiler is cold, it cannot move an inch. So it is with a human being. A warm and sympathetic heart can carry the burdens of his community and his people. But a cold heart, no matter what you will do to it, will never be moved."

The young salesman was perturbed. He had lost an important sale he had thought was in the bag. While discussing the matter with his supervisor, the salesman shrugged his shoulders and said, "You can lead a horse to water but you can't make him drink."

"For Pete's sake!" shouted the supervisor. "Who told you to make him drink? Your job was to make him THIRSTY."

Two music students were discussing their part-time jobs. Said one, "I work in the opera at night and carry a spear in one act."

His friend asked, "How do you manage to keep awake so late at night?"

"It's simple," replied the first. "The man behind me carries a spear, too."

MUSIC

There is a legend which says that after God created the world, He called the angels to Him and asked them what they thought of it; and one of them said, "One thing is lacking: the sound of praise to the Creator." So God created music, and it was heard in the whisper of the wind, and in the song of the birds; and to man also was given the gift of song. And all down the ages this gift of song has indeed proved a blessing to multitudes of souls.

A man was reminiscing about his late father. He described the man's sensitive soul, his love of music, and his deep feeling and

301

perception. "When my father listened to violin music, he not only *heard* the instrument talk; he could *tell* you what it said."

NAIVETE

A small-town resident went to the big city for the first time, to visit his brother.

As he sat in his brother's modern apartment, he heard a siren blow and bells begin to ring. He was startled and asked, "What is that?"

"Why, it is nothing," answered the brother. "There is probably a fire somewhere and it is being extinguished."

"Ah," thought the small-towner. "So this is how fires are extinguished in the city."

When he returned to his small town, he said: "Gentlemen, I have come back with a marvelous new idea. We no longer have to worry about fires. We will buy a siren and bells and when a fire breaks out, we will ring the bells and sound the siren and the fire will be extinguished."

Everybody in town purchased a bell. Soon a fire broke out. Everybody ran out into the street and rang their bells, but it did not help, and the property was completely destroyed.

The small-towner appealed to his brother. "What have you done? Why did you mislead me? Why did you tell me that fires could be extinguished with bells?"

"Foolish man," replied the brother, "the bells are not enough. With the bells you need equipment, fire-hoses, chemicals, water and labor. The bells are only a call to action."

NAMES

Alexander the Great had a soldier in his army who bore his own name, but was a great coward. The emperor, enraged at his conduct, justly said to him, "Either change your name, or learn to live up to it."

NEED

Owen D. Young, American financier and lawyer, once said: "We need today inspiration, not irritation. We need education, not deduction or coercion. We need appreciation of the good that is, not assumption that all is evil. We need research so that we may know more. We need respect, not cynicism. We need faith, not hopelessness. We need stability to make homes and keep them. We need expansion, not mere restoration of resources, so that more than the upper third of our population may have homes. We need more things, more widely distributed, with good manners.

~~~~~~

Rossini, the Italian composer, was visiting in France. There he learned that a group of wealthy admirers planned to have a statue erected in his honor.

At the time the composer was quite poor. "How much will it cost?" he inquired.

"Ten million francs," was the answer.

Rossini chuckled, as he replied: "How extravagant they are. For five million I'll stand on the pedestal myself."

~~~~~~

NEGLECT

Charles Dickens, in one of his classics, tells of a man who dug in his yard and suddenly broke through the earth's crust and fell headlong into the world inside. There he discovered an odd and unique state of affairs. Every person in this mysterious country was born a perfect human being. No person was born lame. No person was born blind. No one was born with any deformity.

But this state of perfection was not lasting. It all depended on the individual, for upon reaching a certain age, each person was deprived of the parts of his body he never used. In this strange land, Dickens discovered a cab driver with only a pair of hands. A lawyer had lost everything but his massive jaw. Two society girls were just a bundle of nerves and blazing eyes. An old schoolmaster had nothing left but his heart.

It is rather difficult for us to judge whether Dickens was only playing in the realm of fantasy or attempting to point out the frailties of human beings. No matter what his intentions were, his story expresses a psychological truth.

~~~~~~

NERVE

Whistler, the famous artist, was very fond of his French poodle. When the poodle came down with a throat infection, Whistler had the audacity to send for the great throat specialist, Mackenzie.

303

When the specialist came and saw that he had been called to treat a dog, he was incensed but said nothing.

The next day he sent for Whistler. The artist felt he was being summoned on some matter connected with the health of his dog and went immediately.

When he arrived, the specialist asked, "How do you do, Mr. Whistler? I need your advice about having the front door painted."

OBSERVATION

After Billroth, the Viennese surgeon, had told his students that a doctor needed two gifts: freedom from nausea and power of observation, he dipped his fingers into a bitterly nauseating fluid and licked it off, requesting them to do the same. They did it without flinching. With a grin, Billroth said, "You have passed the first test well, but not the second, for none of you noticed that I dipped my first finger in but licked the second."

OBVIOUS

A king wanted to pick the wisest man among his subjects to be his prime minister. When the search finally narrowed down to three men, he decided to put them to the supreme test.

Accordingly, he placed them in a room in his palace, and installed a lock which was the last word in mechanical ingenuity. The candidates were informed that whoever was able to open the door first would be appointed to the post of honor. The three men immediately set themselves to the task. Two of them at once began to work out complicated mathematical formulas to discover the proper lock combination. The third man, however, just sat in his chair, lost in thought. Finally, without bothering to put pen to paper, he got up, walked to the door, turned the knob, and the door opened. It had been unlocked all the time!

An ocean vessel, limping in from sea after a difficult passage, dropped anchor at some distance from the mouth of a river and signaled to shore for fresh water. Back came the answer, "Drop your buckets!"

The captain became angry, thinking it hardly the time or place for a joke. Again he signaled for water, adding, "Let's be serious about this."

Again came the answer: "Drop your buckets."

The captain signaled a third time. When he received the same answer, he ordered the buckets lowered into the water. When they were pulled up, the captain was amazed to find fresh drinking water in the buckets.

OCCUPATIONS

Columbus was the son of a weaver. Cervantes was a common soldier. Homer was the son of a poor farmer. Molière was the son of a tapestry-maker. Demosthenes was the son of a cutler. Terence was a slave. Oliver Cromwell was the son of a London brewer. Howard was an apprentice to a grocer. Franklin was a journeyman printer, and son of a tallow-chandler and soap-boiler. Daniel Defoe was a hostler, and son of a butcher. Virgil was the son of a porter. Horace was the son of a shopkeeper. Shakespeare was the son of a wood-stapler. Milton was the son of a money-scrivener. Robert Burns was a ploughman. Mohammed was a driver of asses. Napoleon, descendant of an obscure family, was a major when he married Josephine, the daughter of a tobacconist. Bolivar was a druggist. Vasco da Gama was a sailor. John Jacob Astor sold apples in the city streets. Abraham Lincoln was a rail-splitter. General Grant was a tanner. Com. Vanderbilt was a ferryman. Alfred Smith, Governor of the State of New York, worked in the Fulton Fish Market.

OPPORTUNITY

Many people have wonderful opportunities surrounding them but do not see them. They are like Ali Hafed, the Persian farmer, who sold his fertile farm and traveled over the world in an unsuccessful search for diamonds. He finally died in poverty and despair in a distant land while, in the meantime, the famed diamond beds of Golconda had been discovered on his abandoned farm.

An Indian princess, upon coming of age, was given a basket and told she might fill her basket with the finest ears of corn in a given row. There was only one condition: she was to choose as she went along. She could not retrace her steps.

The princess admired the fine quality of the corn before her but, as she examined one ear after another, she left them on the stalk, always thinking that better ears lay ahead. Suddenly, and to her dismay, she came to the end of the row—and she had gathered none.

Once, a wild boar of the jungle was whetting his tusks against the trunk of a tree. A fox passing by asking him why he did this, seeing that neither hunter nor hound was near. "True," replied the boar, "but, when that danger arises, I shall have something else to do than to sharpen my weapons!"

A poor man once complained to a loaf of bread: "Why do you always grace the table of the rich and avoid my family and me?"

"My dear man," the loaf replied. "When I come to the rich man he treats me with great respect and pomp. He spreads butter, jam, and other goodies on me. In short, I am honored. But, when I come to you, your wife and children attack me, tear me to pieces, and swallow me dry. In but a few moments, nothing remains of me. That is why I don't like to come to you. I may be a mere loaf of bread, but I know a good opportunity when I see it."

OPTIMISM

The story goes that Napoleon's marshals came to him one day and told him that the enemy is very close, and that the danger of defeat is imminent. He replied, "Bring me larger maps."

Grover Cleveland preached optimism all of his life. His lectures breathed the spirit of hoping for the best and of looking at the bright side of things. When he was once praised for his optimism, he replied, "I am what you call an optimist but I hope never to be an 'ifist.'"

When he was asked to explain the meaning of an "ifist," he replied, "An ifist is a slave to the little word 'if,' whereas an optimist hopes for the best in a sane manner. There was once an 'ifist' who was lost in the woods. When night came, they were all quite hungry but had nothing to eat. With a perfectly serious face one of the group turned to the rest and said, "If we only had some onions, we'd have onions and eggs, if we only had some eggs."

PARENTS

Once there was a little boy. When he was three weeks old, his parents turned him over to a baby-sitter.

When he was two years old, they dressed him up like a cowboy, and gave him a gun.

When he was three, everybody said, "Ain't he cute!" when he lisped a beer commercial.

When he was six, his father occasionally dropped him off at Sunday school on his way to the golf course across town.

When he was eight, they bought him a bee bee gun, and taught him to shoot sparrows. He learned to shoot windshields by himself.

When he was ten, he spent his afternoon time squatting at the drugstore newsstand, reading comics. His mother wasn't home, and his father was too busy.

When he was thirteen, he told his parents that other boys stayed out as late as they wanted to, so they said that he could, too. It was easier that way.

When he was fifteen, the police called his home one night. "We have your boy. He's in serious trouble."

"In serious trouble?" screamed his father. "It can't be my boy!" But it was.

PATIENCE

A very young boy was given a lantern on a dark night and told by his father to go to the woodshed and bring an armful of wood into the house. The boy told his father, "Daddy, I can't see." The father then asked, "How far can you see?" "Only three steps," was the reply. "Take them," advised the father. "How far can you see now, son?" "Three more steps," was the answer.

Finally, by going forward three steps at a time, the boy reached the woodshed and brought in the wood.

An admirer once asked pianist Ignace Paderewski: "Is it true that you still practice every day?"

"Yes," said the pianist. "At least eight hours a day."

"You must have a world of patience," said the other.

"I have no more patience than the next fellow," said Paderewski. "I just use mine."

The Chinese tell of a student who was disheartened by his difficult studies and decided to throw away his books in despair. Then, one day, upon seeing a woman rubbing a crowbar on a stone, he inquired the reason. He was told that she needed a needle and decided to rub down a crowbar until it became small enough to serve as a needle. Inspired by this example of patience and determination, he resumed his studies and became one of the foremost scholars of the empire.

A drunkard once knocked on the door of a scholar who was studying the Bible late at night. The scholar, at first somewhat annoyed at this disturbance, hesitated to admit the man; his presence would prevent him from continuing with his studies. However, after a moment's reflection, he said to himself: "If God tolerates the existence of a drunkard in the world, perhaps it is meant that I, too, ought to put up with him for a little while in my own small world." And he opened the door to the stranger.

A man once came to his priest and said, "Father, things are so bad. My life is completely hopeless."

"Never say that life is bad or life is hopeless, my son," said the priest. "When one is ill and the doctor prescribes a medicine, the medicine may be bitter, but it is not bad. It is meant to cure the sick. Life may sometimes be very bitter, but it is never bad."

This prayer was written by the famous theologian, Reinhold Niebuhr in 1934, just before he entered the pulpit of the little church near his summer home in Heath, Massachusetts:

O God, give us—
Serenity to accept what cannot be changed
Courage to change what should be changed
And the wisdom to distinguish the one from the other.

Harry Emerson Fosdick once used this homily: Most of us can afford to take a lesson from the oyster. The most extraordinary thing about the oyster is this: Irritations get into his shell. He does not like them. But when he cannot get rid of them, he settles down to make of them one of the most beautiful things in the world: he makes his irritation into a lovely pearl. There are irritations in our lives today—and there is only one prescription: make a pearl. It may have to be a pearl of patience, but anyhow, make a pearl. And it takes faith and love to do it.

At a crowded intersection, while waiting for the traffic light to change, a car stalled, holding up a line of other vehicles behind it. Obviously flustered, the man who was driving the car hurriedly got out and lifted the hood of the engine to investigate. As he did, the driver of the car behind began honking his horn.

The honking continued until the driver of the stalled car, still unsuccessful in discovering the trouble, straightened up and spoke to the impatient motorist behind him. "If you will fix my car," he said calmly, "I'll be glad to keep blowing your horn for you."

PEACE

A Chinese sage was asked by a farmer when the world would truly know peace. The sage replied, "Follow me."

He then brought him to the side of a brook, put his hand on the farmer's head, and pressed it into the water until the farmer came up gasping for breath. The sage then said: "This is your answer. When man wants peace, when he wants peace as much as you just wanted air, when he comes up gasping for peace, when he is ready to give everything in himself to have peace, as you have given to have air, he will have peace."

On his departure from America, a visiting English philosopher said, "In 1776, you Americans conquered your father. In 1861, you conquered your brother. In 1918, and again in 1945 you conquered your neighbors. Now all that remains is for you to conquer yourselves."

PEOPLE

There are four kinds of people:
There is the kind that does not know when things are wrong.
There is the kind that knows when things are wrong, but does not care.
There is the kind that knows when things are wrong and does care, but does not care enough to try to make them right.

There is the kind that knows when things are wrong, and strives intelligently to make them right, and to keep them right.

⁓

A man once presented a Roman emperor with a gift of three small dolls. The emperor was infuriated at so insignificant a gift.

"You are mistaken as to its value," advised the man. "This is a most unusual gift." With these words he handed the emperor a string and advised him that it went with the present. "There is a hole in the ear of each doll," he said. "Put the thread through the hole and see what happens."

The emperor was intrigued. He quickly picked up the first doll and put the string into the ear. It went into one ear and quickly out the other.

"This is one type of person," said the man. "Whatever you say to him goes in one ear and out the other."

The emperor picked up the second doll and put the thread into the ear. This time it came out of the mouth.

"This is a second type of person," explained the man. "Whatever you tell him, he spreads through the neighborhood."

The emperor picked up the third doll and repeated the process. This time the thread did not appear anywhere.

"This is a third type of person," advised the man. "Whatever you tell him he keeps to himself."

"Tell me," questioned the emperor, "which type of person is best?"

"None of them," was the immediate reply. At this point, the man gave the emperor a fourth doll and asked that he again put the thread through the ear. He tried several times and each time the thread reappeared in different places. It came out through another ear, through the mouth, and once it did not come out at all.

"This is the best type of person. A person must possess all three traits," explained the man. "He must know when to forget, when to remain silent, and when to speak out."

⁓

A man may be compared to a house. His fine character needs no advertising; it speaks for itself—loud and clear. He is a finished product; and all his fine characteristics and the honors they have brought him, as well as the good they have caused him to do for others, are there for all to see. His actions will always shout down any verbal self-praise.

If one sells a finished building, one need not enumerate

310

minute details in the contract. But, if one is selling a house that is yet to be built, one must list exactly what it will consist of: number of apartments, doors, windows, etc.

There is so much good in the worst of us, and so much bad in the best of us, that it's hard to tell which one of us ought to reform the rest of us.

William Saroyan has a delightful story that he tells of the poor, little orphan boy standing amidst a long line of men and women queued up in front of a movie house. A friend passed and asked: "Why are you standing here? You haven't got the fifty cents admission charge."

"I'm not going to the movies," the boy replied.

"Then why are you standing in line?" asked the friend.

"I'm standing in line," answered the boy, "because I'm lonely, and I like people."

There are three kinds of people in the world. They are: The Wills, the Won'ts, and the Can'ts. The first accomplish everything; the second oppose everything; the third fail in everything.

Psychologists have attempted to divide people into various categories. Ella Wheeler Wilcox has also made an observation, and this is what she has to say:

> There are two kinds of people on earth today,
> Just two kinds of people, no more, I say.
> Not the good and the bad, for 'tis well understood
> That the good are half-bad and the bad half-good. . . .
> No! the two kinds of people on earth I mean
> Are the people who lift and the people who lean.

A wise man once said: There are three kinds of people: rowboat people, sailboat people, and steamboat people. Rowboat people need to be pushed. Sailboat people move when a favorable wind is blowing. Steamboat people move continuously, through calm or storm. They are usually masters of themselves, their surroundings, and their fate.

311

In Lewis Carroll's fantasies there is an incident of a padlock with arms and legs that says to everyone it meets, "I am looking for a key to unlock myself." Most of us are locked up in ourselves. We go through life looking for the key to unlock life. And we never find it because we look for it in ourselves, and we should be looking for it *beyond* ourselves. If the I—the Me is always and forever at the center of things, we can never find the key. It is our fellow man who has the key to unlock our lives, as we have the key to his.

~~~~~

PERFECTION

Plato, in one of his parables, relates that before a soul comes down to this world, an angel leads it through a large, brilliantly lit hall where it glimpses perfection and beholds the highest form of ideas. Finally, an angel hands it a candle to light its way in the darkness of the world. But some souls linger for a while and take a few candles with them. As they enter a human form, they blend the various lights into one flame, and these souls become the torch-bearers of mankind.

~~~~~

Michelangelo was working on a statue one afternoon when some friends visited him. A month later they returned and found him still working on the same statue.

"What have you done since our last visit?" one asked.

"Oh, I've smoothed a line here, and polished an arm, taken a few flakes of marble from the forehead, and so on," replied the great artist.

"But those are only trifles! Is that all you've done?"

"True, they are but trifles," Michelangelo responded, "but trifles make perfection, and perfection is no trifle."

~~~~~

When Phidias was carving the statue of Diana to be placed in the Acropolis and was working on the back side of the head, he was careful to bring out, with his chisel, every strand of hair, as far as was possible. Someone watching remarked: "That figure is to stand a hundred feet high, with its back to the marble wall. Who will ever know what details you are putting there?"

Phidias replied, "I will know." And he continued with his detailed chiseling.

~~~~~

PERSEVERANCE

Rafael Solano, discouraged and physically exhausted, sat on a boulder in a dry river bed and announced to his two companions, "I'm through. There's no use going on any longer. See this pebble? It makes about 999,999 I've picked up and not a diamond so far. If I pick up another, it will be a million—but what's the use? I'm quitting."

This occurred in 1942, when the three men had spent months prospecting for diamonds in a Venezuelan water course. They had worked, stooping, gathering pebbles, hoping for a single sign of a diamond. But they never thought of quitting until Solano said, "I'm through."

Glumly, one of the other men said, "Pick up another and make it a million."

"All right," Solano said, and stooped, put his hand on a pile of pebbles, and pulled one forth. It was almost the size of a hen's egg. "Here it is," he declared, "the last one."

For that millionth pebble, Harry Winston, the New York jeweler, paid Rafael Solano $200,000. Named The Liberator, it was the largest diamond ever found.

The Emperor Tamerlane, on one occasion, had everything against him. His armed forces had been defeated, routed, and dispersed by the enemy. Opposing troops were searching the countryside for Tamerlane himself, who sought security by hiding in an old deserted barn in a hidden valley. Amid his dejection, he noticed an ant busily trying to carry a large grain of corn up a perpendicular wall—a grain much larger than the ant itself.

Repeatedly, the ant tried and fell back—sixty-nine times! Tamerlane watched, fascinated as the creature tried for the seventieth time. This made the Emperor leap to his feet, having learned a lesson in perseverance from the humble ant, who succeeded on the seventieth time. Tamerlane reorganized his army and put his enemies to flight.

A man owned a store which was destroyed in the Chicago fire. He arrived at the smoking ruins the next morning, carrying a table. He set this up amid the charred debris, and above it placed this optimistic sign, "Everything lost except wife, children, and hope. Business will be resumed as usual tomorrow morning."

Jacob Riis, in his drive against slums, never passed up a chance to tell his fellow citizens about these evils. It took a lot of telling, and he sometimes grew discouraged. "But," he said, "when nothing seems to help I go and look at a stonecutter hammering away at his rock perhaps one hundred times, without as much as a crack showing in it. Yet the one-hundred-and-first time will split it in two, and I know that it was not that blow that did it, but all that had gone before."

Fritz Kreisler had just finished a concert and was going backstage when an enthusiastic music fan cried out: "Mr. Kreisler, I'd give my life to play as you do!"

Quietly, the master musician replied, "Madam, I did."

After a great snowstorm, a little fellow began to shovel a path through a large snowbank in front of his grandmother's door. He had only a small shovel to use. "How do you expect to get through that drift with that shovel?" asked a passerby. "By keeping at it," was the boy's cheerful reply.

A laboratory assistant found Thomas Edison one morning at two o'clock, wreathed in smiles. Expecting that Edison had solved a problem in research that he had been carrying on for years, the assistant said: "You've solved it! You've found the answer?"

Edison replied: "Not a blamed thing works; now I can start over again."

When Arago, the astronomer, was young, he became thoroughly discouraged over mathematics. One day he found on the fly-leaf of a textbook a few words from the famous D'Alembert to a student who had been discouraged like himself. D'Alembert's advice was very short; it was, "Go on, sir, go on!"

Arago said afterwards that that sentence was the best teacher of mathematics he had ever had. Following it doggedly, he went on until he became the leading mathematician of his day.

No man has ever exhausted the power that lies in the words, "Go on."

A man went west during the gold rush days. He planned to grow rich. Eventually, he discovered a rich "strike." Machinery was quickly purchased, and when the first car of ore had been mined and shipped, returns proved that he had one of the richest mines in Colorado.

And then, just when it appeared that he was on top of the world, the vein of gold ore disappeared. His desperate efforts to pick up the vein again were of no avail. So he decided to quit. Everything was sold to a junk dealer for one hundred dollars. Before junking everything, the junk dealer consulted an engineer who discovered that the vein of gold continued just *three feet* from where the first man had stopped drilling!

PERSPECTIVE

Have you ever wondered about the "superiority" of man?

A wise man who had evidently given this some thought, bent down to the earth while walking one day and said: "Earth, oh earth, it is within your nature to be productive, to give so much more to mankind than I. Why, then, do I tread on thee? But my day will finally come, and I shall be dust, and then will I be buried within thee to be a part of thee."

Two friends once visited a spa in the Carpathian mountains. Looking down from a high mountain to the town below, one of the men, a wise fellow, remarked to his friend: "See how small and insignificant all the large things down there seem when looking down from up above?"

An old teacher often spoke to his students about his garden. He described it so vividly that they came to visualize the place as a large area filled with many flowers. One evening, they visited him and found him seated in a tiny space, shut in by walls.

"Your garden is very narrow!" exclaimed a disappointed student.

"Yes," smiled the professor as he looked upward into a bright sky, "but see how high it is!"

PLAGIARISM

Nicholas Murray Butler and Professor Brander Matthews of Columbia University were having a conversation, and Professor Matthews was expounding his ideas on plagiarism.

"In the case of the first man, to use an anecdote," he said, "there is originality; in the case of the second, there is plagiarism; with the third, it is lack of originality; and with the fourth, it is drawing from a common stock."

PLEDGES

The millionaire was being questioned by the local minister. "Do you give much to charity?" asked the preacher.

"I give enough," was the quick reply, "but I'm a modest man. I don't say much about it."

"Say more and give more!" admonished the minister.

POINT OF VIEW

An American and a British shoe salesman traveled on the same boat to West Africa, each representing different shoe companies. Their first impression after landing was that all the natives were barefooted.

The Briton cabled his head office: "Nobody here wearing shoes. Coming home by next ship."

The American salesman, seeing the situation differently, cabled his chief "Nobody here wearing shoes. Send one million on consignment. Market wide open."

Someone asked a savage: "What is evil?"

The savage replied: "Evil is if someone should steal my wife and cattle."

The questioner then asked: "What is good?"

The savage replied: "Good is if I will steal someone else's wife and cattle."

POLITICIAN

A politician who had changed his views rather radically was congratulated by a colleague who said, "I'm glad you've seen the light!"

"I didn't see the light!" came the terse reply. "I felt the heat!"

POLLUTION

Many years ago, an oriental king became nauseated with the stench of the town in which his castle was located. He decided that he would saturate every room in the castle with the finest perfumes money could buy.

He traveled for miles to consult a noted perfume-maker. This artist agreed to scent a number of rooms in the king's palace. It was agreed that the king would walk about in darkness, so that he would not be influenced by the drabness of one room or the beauty of another.

That night, with a candle in his hand, the king moved from room to room. The first room delighted him. It had the lingering scent of a rose garden. Each succeeding room brought him delightful fragrances, so much so that the king's olfactory sense was so satiated that he hardly knew which fragrance he liked best.

In total darkness, the perfume-maker led the king out of doors onto a broad terrace. The moment they were outside, the king exclaimed, "Oh, what splendid fragrance is this? This is the finest of them all. I must have this glorious perfume in every room of my palace!"

"Your majesty," replied the perfume-maker with some dismay, "that is no perfume at all. That is only clean, fresh air. Nothing more."

POWER

A powerful king was annoyed by the flattery shown him by his courtiers. He ordered his throne to be placed by the seaside. When the tide rolled in and threatened to drown him, he commanded the waves to stop. Of course, they did not. Then he said to his flatterers, "Behold how small is the might of kings!"

PRACTICE

Some time ago, a minister and a soap manufacturer went for a walk. Suddenly the manufacturer turned to his companion and said, "Of what good is religion? After thousands of years of preaching truth, honesty and goodness, there is still trouble, misery and dishonesty in this world. Religion has failed."

Soon they reached a crowded street where girls and boys were playing. "Look," said the minister, pointing to a dirty child, "just look at that boy. He is about the dirtiest youngster I've ever seen.

You say that soap keeps people clean, but you can almost peel the dirt off that boy. Soap is a failure."

The manufacturer protested, saying, "This is not fair. You cannot expect the boy to be clean if he doesn't use the soap."

"This is my point," answered the other. "So it is with religion. It is not effective unless used."

PRAISE

A Broadway producer decided he was fed up with the extravagant ballyhoo in the advertising of so many shows. He decided that he would insert a clause in his contract giving him the right to approve all advertising for the new play he was producing.

Writer after writer prepared ads embodying the honesty and sincerity he said he wanted in his ads. He turned them all down.

Finally, one brought in a piece of copy which read like this:

> "Here is a play which combines the drama of Shakespeare, the wit of Rostand, the strength of Tennessee Williams, the intellect of Marlowe, and the plot mystery of Dickens. Greater than Hamlet, more moving than the Bible. This is a play destined to live forever."

"That's it," shouted the producer. "No exaggeration! Just the simple truth."

A judge in a court of domestic relations tells the story of a middle-aged couple who were seeking a divorce and whose differences he was trying to reconcile.

"Are you sure you want this divorce?" he asked the woman.

"Yes," she replied.

"Why?" the judge persisted.

"We have been married fifteen years," she replied. "All that time I've kept his house and got his meals and mended his clothes and. . . ."

As she paused tearfully at the recollection, the judge prompted, "And did he find fault with you?"

"No," she said, "it's not that, but in all that time he has never once said, 'You've done a good job.' "

PRAYER

There was once an irreligious seaman who was in a boat fishing with some friends. A sudden storm broke out which threatened

318

to sink the ship. His companions pleaded with him to offer a prayer, but he hesitated, saying it was years since he had prayed or entered a house of worship.

When they continued to insist, he finally made this prayer: "O Lord, I have not asked you for anything for fifteen years, and if you deliver us out of this storm, and bring us safely to land again, I promise that I will not bother you again for another fifteen years!"

Loretta Young once stated that she has a simple formula for everything she does. "Every day, no matter what I'm doing, I say, 'Lord, I'll do the best I can, and You do the rest.' "

A little girl who was on her way to school was afraid of being late. She turned to her sister and said: "Let's stop running and pray that we won't be late."

Her sister was wiser, for she replied, "Let's pray while we run."

A young child, the son of irreligious parents was visiting his religious grandfather in Albany. While there, his mother noticed the boy praying and said, "Sonny, what are you doing?"

He answered, "O, mamma! We must pray all we can here in Albany because there's no God in Brooklyn."

A minister once compared prayer to a pump. He said, "When a pump is used frequently, the water pours out at the first stroke, because it is high; but if the pump has not been used for a long time, the water gets low, and you must pump a long while before water shoots forth. It comes only after great effort. So it is with prayer. If we neglect our prayers, it is difficult for us to recapture the mood."

A farmer whose barns were full of corn was accustomed to pray that the wants of the needy might be supplied; but when anyone in needy circumstances asked for a little of his corn, he said that he had none to spare. One day, after hearing his father pray for the poor and needy, his little son said to him, "Father, I wish I had your corn."

"Why, my son, what would you do with it?" asked the father. The child replied, "I would answer your prayers."

～～

In the White House, Abraham Lincoln was pacing up and down, lonely and troubled, as the battle reports poured in from Gettysburg and the fate of the United States hung in the balance. At that tense moment, Lincoln went to his room, locked the door, and prayed.

Later, Lincoln described that moment to a friend. "I told God that I had done all that I could; now the result was in his hands; if this country was to be saved, it was because He so willed it. The burden fell off my shoulders, my intense anxiety was relieved, and in its place came a great trustfulness!"

～～

An old man was walking in his garden when he heard his young granddaughter intoning the alphabet in a melody that sounded like a sacred prayer.

"What are you doing?" he asked her.

The little girl explained: "I'm praying, but I cannot think of exactly the right words to use, so I am just saying all the letters, and God, who knows what is in my heart, will put them together for me."

～～

A wealthy farmer prayed with his family that his unfortunate neighbor might not starve. When they arose from their prayers, his young daughter remarked: "Daddy, you needn't have bothered God with that. You can easily keep him from starving."

～～

The girl's doll was broken. Her brother laughed as she prayed to God to put the pieces together again. "Do you expect God to answer your prayers?" he scoffed.

"You will see that God will answer," was her reply.

A few hours later, when the brother returned and the doll still lay broken on the floor, he demanded, "Well, has God answered?"

"Yes," was her reply. "He said no."

～～

A young farm lad, orphaned in infancy, had never been taught to read, but he had inherited a large, heavy prayerbook from his grandfather. On Christmas morning, he brought it into church, laid it on the reading stand, and cried out tearfully: "Lord of Creation! I do not know how to pray, so here I give Thee the entire prayerbook. Select the prayers for me that You know are in my heart."

A World War II chaplain noticed that after each enemy bombing raid the attendance at his chapel increased. It became so obvious, that, when the chapel attendance dropped, the men would joke, "Chaplain, we need another raid."

Letters that are not addressed properly are sent to the dead-letter office. They are never to be read by the right party, nor ever to be answered. The prayer that has power with God must be a prepaid prayer, otherwise it goes to a dead-prayer office, where unfortunately no answers will be sent out.

"What do you do before you pray?" asked a man of his spiritual advisor.

"I pray that when I pray it should be with all my heart," was the immediate answer.

A friend of a condemned man went to plead before the Roman Emperor Vespasian, hoping that the man's life would be spared. When he was led into the presence of the Emperor, the man bowed and said: "Peace unto thee, O King; Peace unto thee, O King." The Emperor replied: "If I am your king, why is it that you have not come to see me before?"

A construction company was doing some work in front of a church. During the week a large sign was displayed which read, "Spraying machine at work." On Saturday night it rained heavily and the first letter on the sign was obliterated, so that when the people came to the church on Sunday morning they were amused to see the sign read: "Praying machine at work."

Alas, how close this reading comes to the true characterization of the condition that exists in many of our houses of worship today.

An extremely pious man hired a wagon and horses to take him to an appointment in a distant city. During the journey he realized that he would not get to his destination soon enough, so he prayed to God to speed him on his journey. Miraculously, the horses got renewed strength and sped along the roads at an unbelievably rapid pace. Having traveled this route hundreds of times previously, the road and all its routine stops where they were fed hay and water were very familiar to them. But they literally flew, bypassing all stops; never feeling the need for rest or refreshment.

The horses said to themselves, "This holy man performs wonders through prayer and his wisdom. By now we have probably been transformed into human beings, and just like them we will eat when we reach the hostelry at night." They winged their way past one hotel after another; and still no food. They said to themselves: "We probably are no longer human beings; we must surely be angels by now, and angels don't eat."

But when they arrived at their destination and they stood before the troughs of hay, they dug in and gorged themselves, truly like horses.

<hr>

A grandfather asked his little grandson if he said his prayers every night. "Oh, yes," was the little boy's reply.

"And every morning?" his grandfather asked.

"Why should I?" asked the child. "I'm not scared in the daytime."

<hr>

A priest visiting a family noticed one of the sons feeding his dog. "How often do you feed him?" asked the priest.

"Several times a day," was the immediate answer.

"He certainly looks well-cared for," remarked the priest.

"He gets wonderful attention," said the young man. "I see that he is fed and washed regularly. It pays to be careful."

"It must take you four or five hours a week to care for him," observed the priest.

"At least that," was the proud answer.

"How long does it take you to pray each night?" was the priest's next question.

"About two or three minutes," was the answer.

"It seems to me," said the priest, "that you take better care of your dog than you do of your soul."

<hr>

A passenger was once critically injured in a train wreck. One of the first witnesses on the scene was a physician. The doctor examined the patient while some onlookers wept and others stared with hope in their eyes and a prayer on their lips.

After examining the patient, the doctor stood up straight and seemed to be staring down at the patient while his lips moved almost imperceptibly. The spectators became furious with the doctor for his apparent lack of activity, and demanded that he do something for the injured man who seemed to be dying.

The doctor replied in an almost inaudible whisper: "I have done all I can do with the instruments in my bag. The only instrument left for me to use now is *prayer*. Kind people, won't you assist me in asking my Teacher for His help?"

When Dwight D. Eisenhower was Supreme Commander of the Allied invasion of Europe, he was faced with the responsibility of making one of the most far-reaching decisions ever forced upon one man's conscience: the decision to change the date of D-Day almost at the last moment.

The consequences of being wrong in his decision, he said, were so overwhelming that he felt absolutely crushed by it. In his extremity, he sought for someone to help him make his decision. But he was the Supreme Commander and in the last analysis, this lonely man had to make the decision that would affect millions of lives, alone. He said later:

> I knew I did not have the required wisdom. But I turned to God. I asked God to give me the wisdom. I yielded myself to Him. I surrendered myself. And He gave me clear guidance. He gave me insight to see what was right, and He endowed me with courage to make my decision. And finally He gave me peace of mind in the knowledge that, having been guided by God to the decision, I could leave the results to Him.

There was a little girl who really believed in prayer. Her brother had made a trap that caught little sparrows, and she prayed that it might fail.

Suddenly her face became radiant, and for three days she prayed hard, and her faith was so absolute that her mother asked one morning, "Jane, why are you so sure your prayer will be answered?"

323

Jane smiled. "I know that my prayer will be answered, because I went out there three days ago and kicked the trap to pieces!"

~~~

PREACHING

The newly-appointed bishop to the court of Queen Victoria was anxious to make a favorable impression with his first sermon, and sought out Disraeli for advice.

"How long, Mr. Prime Minister, do you think my first sermon should last?" he inquired.

"Well," answered the Prime Minister, "if you preach for forty minutes, Her Majesty will be satisfied; for thirty minutes, she will be delighted; if you preach for only fifteen minutes, Her Majesty will be enthusiastic!"

~~~

PREJUDICE

There was a little girl who could not dust the furniture to suit her grandmother. Again and again her grandmother examined the furniture and was dissatisfied. The girl did it again—once, twice, three times, and still the grandmother was not satisfied. Finally, the child looked up and said, "Grandmother, that dust is not on the furniture; it must be on your glasses!"

~~~

A Negro who wanted to join a fashionable church was told by the minister to go home and think it over. "Perhaps," said the minister, "you will be happier among your own people."

When the Negro returned a week later, he said, "You were right. I've decided not to join. I talked it over with God and He told me: 'John, give up the notion of joining that church. I've been trying to get into that church for five years myself.' "

~~~

A survey was once conducted of people's attitudes toward other groups. Participants were given a list of various races, religions and cultures, and were asked to check each item with a plus (if the attitude was favorable), a minus (if unfavorable), or zero (for neutral or unknown). Among the many groups listed were some fictitious names: Melonians and Waluvians.

It was amazing how many reacted negatively to these. They

could have put "zero" but they did not. Apparently they thought: "Here are some strange names—thumbs down on them, whoever they are!" That is prejudice—pure and simple—and we are all guilty of it to some extent.

~~~~~

PREPARATION

According to an old legend a woman went to heaven and looked about the streets for her mansion. She saw many beautiful homes, but hers was not among them. At last, on a small side street, she saw a tiny cottage. She was told it belonged to her. She was indignant, but an angel said, "When you were on earth you built a beautiful and expensive home, but you sent very little material here for your heavenly home. Here we can only use virtue, charitable deeds and kindly thoughts as building materials. You failed to send much of it up ahead of you."

~~~~~

Henry was a poverty-stricken man who seldom made a living for his family. One day he decided to leave for the city in order to make his fortune. As luck would have it, he arrived just as the wealthiest man in the city was making a wedding. Because he was a visitor, he too was invited to attend.

When Henry arrived at the banquet hall, he was impressed by the dazzling settings on the table. At the far end of the room, the host sat on a raised dais. All eyes were upon him.

Suddenly, the host rang a bell and waiters responded by bringing in trays of food. Later, the host rang a second time and more delicacies appeared. Henry was thrilled. Now that he had learned how things were done in the big city, he too would buy such a bell.

A few days later Henry was on his way home, with the bell he had purchased. It was a duplicate of the one owned by the rich man. When he arrived home, he asked that his wife and children get into their best clothing. "Set the table as if it were a holiday," he ordered, "and seat yourselves."

They all sat at the table. Henry seated himself at the head and immediately rang the bell. Nothing happened. He rang again and again with absolutely no results. Dejected, he left, advising his family that he had been fooled and that he was returning to the city.

The next morning he arrived at the store, and with a harried look cried out, "Why did you not give me the same bell? You made me the laughing stock of my family!"

325

When he explained what had happened, the storekeeper said, "Did you not understand that the wealthy man had prepared all the delicacies before he rang the bell? The bell was merely a signal to bring in the tasty dishes he had prepared ahead of time."

A wealthy man died and was being escorted to the Heavenly Tribunal. On the way, with his guide, they passed through a gorgeous hall where many souls appeared to be enjoying divine bliss.

"Here is where I would like to remain," said the man.

"Only if you have the price of admission," replied the guide.

"I have plenty of gold," replied the millionaire.

"Gold has no value here," explained the guide. "Here we use receipts from charitable institutions."

"If you will grant me a few minutes on earth again," said the man, "I shall descend and exchange my gold into charitable receipts."

"Sorry, it's too late for that," said the angel. "Here you must come prepared."

A king wanted to test the devotion of his subjects and thought of an interesting way of doing it. He sent word to a number of towns that he was coming to visit with many of his ministers and servants. Would the people of the town make the necessary preparations for the projected visit? When the message arrived, the councilors of the various cities sat down to consider what to do about it. They did not know how many persons were due to arrive, nor did they understand what kind of preparations they were expected to make. The result was that many cities did not do anything in the matter. The councilors of other towns, on the other hand, listened to the various opinions offered in explanation of the message, and then they complied with every opinion offered, so as to be sure that the king would be pleased.

There was once a musician who, with great care, practiced his trumpet many hours each day. Every evening he dressed in his tuxedo, drove to the concert hall, took his place on stage, arranged his music on the stand, and set his instrument carefully upon his knees. But as the rest of the orchestra played he sat motionless. The violins carried the melody through the hall; the oboes, flutes, and horns gave depth to the rich composition, and the drums

326

gave it rhythm, but this man sat with his trumpet on his knees and played nothing.

Suddenly, the moment for which he had prepared came. He straightened himself, placed his instrument to his lips, and then the conductor brought him in. Clear and true, a trumpet note rang out—just one note, and no more. Then he relaxed. His contribution had been made. He had rendered his *one* note in time and in tone. When the orchestra leader finally called on him, he was ready.

PRESENT

A young girl was tacking up a new wall calendar, containing the unfamiliar figures of the new year which was about to begin.

"It's going to be a beautiful year!" she exclaimed.

Someone, who heard the girl's prediction, asked, "How do you know it is going to be a beautiful year? A year is a long time, and you never know what will happen."

"Well," she replied, "a day isn't a long time, I know, because I'm going to take a day at a time, and make it beautiful. Years are only days put together, and I'm going to see that every day in the new year gets something beautiful into it."

"If you do this, then it will be a beautiful year," the friend said.

PRIDE

A wise old man counseled a pompous individual with these words: "The peacock, beholding only its gay feathers, may be inflamed with pride; but a look at its ugly feet will soon decrease this feeling. So with men. If there is beauty, wealth, fame, success, or any other thing that will engender pride, there is also some counterpart to it to keep us humble."

The president of a large firm one day decided to visit its many departments and their supervisors. The head of one department did not greet the executive cordially and was, as a matter of fact, rather arrogant. Later on, speaking at a luncheon meeting, the executive made a subtle reference to the undignified behavior of the head of one small department.

"I always wondered why, when the king removes his crown,

he puts it on a nail on the wall and not on a human head on which it would fit better. It is because a person, seeing that the crown fits his head, would strut, start to feel he is fit to be king, and on further thought become convinced that he is actually more fit to be the king and should really be in the king's place. But a nail remains a nail. . . ."

PROCRASTINATION

Satan wanted to destroy the world. He called his chief assistants for advice. First came Anger, who said, "Let me destroy man. I will set brother against brother." Next came Lust: "I will defile men's minds." Greed followed with "Allow me to go and I will instill in men's hearts the most destructive of all passions: Man's own uncontrolled desires." The twins, Gluttony and Drunkenness came, and told how they could make men's bodies diseased and their minds cloudy. Envy, Jealousy, and Hate each told how he could destroy man. Idleness claimed he could do the job.

Satan was not satisfied with any of these plans. Finally, his last assistant entered. This one said, "I shall tell him how fine his plans are to be honest, clean and brave. However, I shall tell man there is no hurry; he can do all of those things tomorrow. I shall advise him to wait until conditions become more favorable."

"You are the one who shall go on earth to destroy man," commented Satan. It was Procrastination. "Just put it off a while longer."

A prince in command of a company of soldiers in Zululand was told that it was not safe for him to remain where he was, in a camp which the Zulus had surrounded.

"Oh, let us stay ten minutes longer and drink our coffee!" the prince answered.

In that ten minutes they might have made their escape, but the enemy attacked and the prince was killed.

"That was his great mistake, even when he was a little boy," the sad-hearted mother said afterwards. "He was always asking for ten minutes more."

PROGRESS

A railway bridge had been destroyed by fire and it was necessary to replace it. The bridge engineer and his staff were ordered to the scene. Two days later, the superintendent of the division arrived.

"Bill," said the superintendent to the engineer, "I want this job rushed. Every hour of delay is costing the company money. Have you got the plans for the new bridge?"

"I don't know," said the engineer, "whether the architect has completed his sketches, but the bridge is up and trains are passing over it."

A young lawyer was asked by his former teacher at the university what he had accomplished for justice during his first five years of practice. The young man replied that he had not yet done much.

The teacher was displeased with the answer, and asked, "When you light a candle do you expect it to give light after it is half burned, or when you first light it?" "As soon as I light it," was the quick reply, and with his answer the young man understood the point that was being made.

An old Princetonian who had been a member of the rowing squad maintained interest in Princeton crew affairs throughout his life. When he retired, someone said to him: "Rowing must mean more to you than mere exercise. It must have some symbolic meaning. What is it?"

"Yes," he answered, "I had rather be a member of a society of eight men facing backward and going forward than a member of a crowd facing forward and going nowhere."

The little girl was put to bed. She had said her prayers and was ready to go to sleep. During the night she fell out of bed. The next morning, she related this to her mother.

"How did it happen?" asked the concerned mother.

"I don't know, mama," she replied, "unless I stayed too near the place where I got in."

PSYCHOLOGY

A woman was in the habit of placing her child in a large outdoor playpen every morning. As soon as she closed the gate, the child would begin to cry bitterly. This would irritate the neighbors.

One morning, a neighbor asked that he be permitted to put the child in the playpen. As he closed the gate, he leaned down and whispered something into the child's ear. As if by magic, the child remained calm and quiet.

Later, the neighbors asked how he had achieved this miracle. He answered, "I merely told the tot I was locking the gate to keep the mother out!"

~~~

PUNISHMENT

A young Jewish man called on a Catholic priest and informed him that he wished to join the Church.

"My son," the priest said, beaming, "I am indeed happy that the light of the new day has finally dawned for you. I cannot see you until the day after tomorrow, but at that time I will be only too glad to instruct you in the true and holy faith."

"But that will be too late, Father," insisted the young man. "I want to change my religion at once."

"Why the hurry? A great faith like ours cannot be imparted in a few minutes."

"Well it's like this, Father," explained the young man. "I just had a terrible fight with my wife and, before I cool off, I want to do something immediately to disgrace her."

~~~

RATIONALIZATION

The woman was weighing herself while her husband looked on. She made a wry face.

Puzzled, he asked, "What's the matter? Are you overweight?"

"No, not that," she replied, "but according to this chart, I should be six inches taller."

~~~

The mate of a sailing vessel took a drop too much and became drunk for the first time in his life. The captain recorded in the ship's log: "Mate drunk today."

When the mate read this entry he implored the captain to erase it from the record, saying that when it was read by the owners of the ship it would cost him his post, and that the captain well knew that this was his first offense.

But the captain refused to change the record and said to the mate, "This is the fact, and into the log it goes."

Some days afterwards, the mate was keeping the log, and he made this entry: "Captain sober today." The indignant captain protested when he read the record, declaring that it would leave an altogether false impression in the minds of the owners of the vessel. It would appear as though it were an unusual thing for him to be sober. But the mate answered in the captain's words: "This is the fact, and into the log it goes."

A small boy was standing on his cat's tail. The mother, hearing the terrible outburst, called from an adjoining room, "Tommy, stop pulling the cat's tail!"

Tommy yelled back, "I'm not pulling the cat's tail. I'm only standing on it. He's the one who's doing the pulling."

"I'm one dollar short in my pay envelope," cried an irate employee as he carefully placed it in front of the paymaster.

The paymaster checked the record and, smiling, replied, "Last week we overpaid you a dollar. You didn't complain about that mistake, now did you?"

"I can overlook a mistake once in a while," answered the angry man, "but not two in a row."

READING

Reading serves for delight, for ornament, and for ability. The crafty condemn it; the simple admire it; the wise use it. Reading makes a full man; conference, a ready man; and writing, an exact man. He that writes little needs a great memory; he that confers little, a present wit; and he that reads little, much cunning to seem to know that which he does not.

REALITY

In the past he had been a simple man, when suddenly he became wealthy. He had long noticed that the rich owned yachts, that owning a boat was a badge of wealth. He went out and bought a boat and a captain's uniform for himself. No sooner did he put on his uniform than he went to his parents' home.

"Look at me now," he said proudly. "I'm a regular captain you know."

His mother did not look enthusiastic, though she did say, "Fine, fine."

"But Mom," protested the son, "You don't look proud at all. Why?"

"Listen my son," said the mother, "to papa you're a captain, to mama, you're a captain. . . . But I ask you, to captains are you a captain?"

~~~

"Well," said the examining psychiatrist, "you can go now and lead a normal life with your friends and family." As the confused man stared at his "release papers," he replied, "Gee, for three years I was Napoleon, now I'm a nobody!"

~~~

An astrologer who spent his time gazing at the heavens, once fell into a hole full of mud and water. When he was rescued by one of the villagers, he was told: "This will teach you a lesson to look at what's right in front of you. What's the use of reaching for the stars when you can't see what's right here on earth?"

~~~

REFLECTION

There was a very ugly man, with a face so distorted, that he could not even bear to look at himself in the mirror. He removed all the mirrors in his home, to spare himself the anguish they caused him. Even his friends, after a while, removed the mirrors from their walls on the day of his visit. One day he visited a friend's store. To his amazement, wherever he turned, he was confronted by a shining mirror that reflected his ugly features.

He became apoplectic with fury and rushed over to his friend, exclaiming, "What do you mean by this outrage? Why did you leave the mirrors here when you knew I would visit you?"

The friend replied, "In my home you are my guest, so I must suit your taste. Here, this is my business. Can I help it if I sell mirrors?"

~~~

An explorer was making his way deep into Africa. Among the trinkets he took along with him for the natives were two full-size mirrors. One day, deep in the jungle, while in camp, he placed these two mirrors against two different trees and then sat down to talk to some of his men.

The explorer noticed that a strange savage approached one of the mirrors with a spear in his hand. As he looked into the mirror he saw his reflection. He began to jab his opponent in the mirror as though it were a real savage and broke the mirror into bits.

When asked why he had smashed the mirror he replied, "He kill me, I kill him first." The explorer led the savage to the second mirror and explained to him, "See, the mirror is something which shows you how strong you are." Only then was the savage quieted.

RELIGION

A man who had travelled far into the world went back to visit his native village. Everything was changed; there was not a street, store, or house which he could recognize. Even the fields and the trees were different. Only one thing was just the same—and that was the spring out of which, as a thirsty, barefoot boy, he used to drink.

A man met his pastor one day on the street, and after the usual exchange of pleasantries, the congregant told his spiritual advisor of his despair at the sad state of the world. He wound up by saying, "I tell you Reverend, it's enough to make a man lose his religion."

After a moment's reflection, the pastor replied, "Seems to me, it's enough to make a man *use* his religion."

Samuel Tyler Coleridge, the great English poet of the Romantic Period, was once talking with a man who did not believe in giving children any religious instruction whatever. His theory was that the child's mind should not be prejudiced in any direction, but, when he came to years of discretion, he should be permitted to choose his religious opinions for himself.

Coleridge said nothing, but after a while he took his visitor to see his garden. The man looked at Coleridge in surprise, and said, "Why, this is not a garden! There is nothing here but weeds!"

"Well, you see," answered Coleridge, "I did not wish to infringe upon the liberty of the garden in any way. I was just giving the garden a chance to express itself and to choose its own production."

"How is it," asked a man of his preacher, "that your religion has been going on for thousands of years and has not influenced more people than it has done?"

The preacher thought for a moment and replied, "How is it that water has been flowing for even more than thousands of years and many people are still dirty?"

A non-believer once went to his minister and said, "I know that you are a man of common sense and frankness. I have read your sermons and I know that you will give a man a straightforward answer. Do you beieve that I have a soul?"

The minister replied, "Yes, I do."

"Well," answered the man, "that is an extraordinary thing for a man of your ability to think. If you go to a museum, you can see exactly what the component parts of a man are—so much lime, so much sugar, so much phosphorous, so much carbon, and so much starch." He went on to enumerate sixteen ingredients which make up a man. "You can see them all," he said, "in bottles in a museum. Where, then, does the soul come in?"

The minister looked at him and replied, "Excuse me, but I must decline to continue the argument any further."

The man said, "That was just what I expected. When you cannot meet an argument, you throw in the sponge and will have nothing more to do with it."

"But," said the minister, "I am a reasonable man, and as such, I must decline to hold any argument with so many quarts of water, so much phosphorous, so much lime, and so much carbon."

Thus the minister answered a fool according to his folly.

A man had just returned from the Far East and was asked by a friend what articles he had brought back with him and what customs he had been compelled to pay. "Did you bring back a new religion?" asked the friend facetiously.

"No, I didn't bring back a new religion," he replied. "But had I done so, there would have been no difficulty about customs duties, for any country would be happy to import a religion without any *duties*."

Eddie Cantor once said: "Religion is not a soothing syrup. It offers no glib, easy answers to life's problems. You cannot go to church or synagogue and pray, and expect to find the road smooth and easy when you come out. Prayer will give you a new outlook, a sense of unity with your fellowmen, the courage to stand up straight on your own two feet and fight a good fight. It gives you the kind of confidence no lesser force can take away."

⁕

The author was entertaining several guests and wanted to give each a copy of his latest book, *Seekers After God*. He called the local book dealer and ordered six copies. Within a few days he received this reply by wire:

"No seekers after God in New York; try Philadelphia."

⁕

A student of religion was known to be somewhat of a free thinker. In spite of the fact that he was immersed in the study of the Bible, he had little faith in the existence of God.

"You see," apologized the teacher to his other pupils, "that man is so engrossed in his religious studies, he forgot there is a Creator in Heaven."

⁕

The famous artist, James Whistler, is best known for his portrait of a mother. Perhaps even greater than Whistler's "Mother" is the portrait depicted in this little story about Whistler's respect for his mother.

Whistler was once asked if he attended church with his mother on Sundays, to which he replied with pride that he never failed to take his mother to church on Sunday. She went in and he remained outside. The tribute Whistler paid to mothers by his great work of art would lead one to believe that he worshipped his mother and that he would follow her way of life and religious tradition. His actions, however, are a most poignant expression of the greatest tragedy of our times: complete emancipation, rejection of tradition, and neglect of our duty to God.

⁕

The college students were being addressed by an outstanding physicist. His theme was Positive Religion. During the question and answer period, a young student arose and said, "Sir, how can you really prove to me what religion offers. I want definite proof."

The physicist asked for an orange and proceeded to peel it and eat it while everyone watched curiously. When he finished, he asked the young student, "Do you know what this orange tastes like?"

335

"No, I do not," came the terse reply. "Only the one who eats it can know."

"So it is with religion," their physicist said. "You must taste it for yourself."

❧

Some people trade in their religious beliefs for gold and silver, though they do not believe this is the case. A preacher was once trying to prove this point with a rich man who had given up his belief in God. The preacher took out a sheet of paper and wrote the word GOD on it. "Do you see that?" he asked.

"Yes, I do," was the reply.

The preacher now covered the word with a half-dollar he took from his pocket. "Do you see it now?" he asked.

"No, but I know it is still there."

"That's the point," replied the preacher. "Don't let money come between you and God. Always remember that God is here."

❧

Above the door of a church was engraved a message which read: THIS IS THE DOORWAY TO HEAVEN. Below was a carefully painted sign which stated CLOSED DURING JULY AND AUGUST.

❧

A minister was very concerned about the drop in attendance at religious services. He pleaded with his membership, asking them to come. However, his attendance did not improve.

He conceived a plan which he put into immediate operation. He placed an ad in the local newspapers stating that since the church was dead, it was only proper that it be given a decent burial on Sunday.

His congregants, not knowing what to expect, arrived in the place of worship. They noticed a coffin near the pulpit. The minister read the obituary and delivered a eulogy. He then invited his congregants to step forward and pay their last respects to the elderly departed. The line filed by. Each mourner peeped into the coffin and quickly turned away with a guilty look. In the coffin, tilted at the correct angle, was a large mirror. Everyone who looked into the coffin saw himself.

❧

A bulletin board in front of a church read: COME TO PRAY DAILY AND AVOID THE HOLIDAY RUSH.

❧

William James gives us the following beautiful illustration: Religion may be compared to a light that is put on in a dark room. When the light is put on for the first time, you suddenly find that you are limited. There are walls which you did not see before; there is furniture which you had not noticed. In the darkness, before there was light, you were not aware of these limitations and felt no sense of being enclosed or confined.

REMORSE

A father, in guiding his son, told him to drive one nail into a post every time he did an evil thing, and to withdraw one nail each time he did a good act. The son did as he was told, but regretted he could not pull out the nail holes as well. So, with the record of every life. We may amend, change our program, turn over a new leaf—but some flaws remain. The nail holes stay, and they remind us of unwise decisions.

REPENTANCE

While addressing his congregation, a preacher once stated that a sinner could be absolved of his sins if he sincerely repented. In fact, his act of genuine penitence would turn his sins into good deeds.

A sinner, who had a great deal of audacity, heard this and quite disrespectfully said to the preacher: "If this is true, then I shall hasten to increase my sins so that when I do repent, I will have many good deeds in my favor."

"You brash young man," replied the preacher. "Your suggestion would be excellent if you knew your appointed time of death. Your day of reckoning may come before you have a chance to free your soul."

A prince was exiled by his father because he could not be disciplined. Unaccustomed to the hardships of just being a vagabond, he decided to become an apprentice to a blacksmith. In time, the prince's face became blackened by the soot, until he looked like a typical smith. No one would believe that he was of royal blood.

One day, the king passed through the village where his son, unknown to him, worked. The prince ran before the chariot of the king and shouted that he was his son. Unceremoniously, he

337

was pushed away by the king's soldiers, but he held on to the chariot with all his strength, weeping and shouting wildly that he was the prince. The many tears washed away the soot, dirt and blackness from his face, and then the king recognized him as his son, exiled long ago, but since forgiven.

A very pious man somehow became bewitched by the allurements of lust and passion and strayed from the path of his religious life. He realized one day that the licentious, wild life he had been leading was very unreal. His soul could no longer carry the ever-increasing burden of his sin, and in his earnest search for penance he turned to the mountains and said, "Oh, ye majestic mountains and lofty hills, plead for me," and the mountains said, "No." Whereupon he beseeched heaven and earth, sun and moon, to plead on his behalf and these, too, refused. He now did the only thing left him to do. . . . He took a long, hard look inside himself, and in the final reckoning he realized that there need be no go-between. Nobody else could express the regret and remorse he felt; only if he pleaded his own case would it be true penitence.

A man once came to confession with the following story:

"Father," said he, "a friend of mine has committed some very bad sins," and he went on to describe the ways in which his friend had sinned. "However," he continued, "my friend now regrets having sinned and wishes to do penance. But because he was too ashamed to come in person, he asked me to confess his sins for him and to find out what his penance must be in order to be absolved."

The priest, well aware that the messenger was the sinner himself, said to him, "Your friend is a foolish man! He did not have to reveal his sins to you. He could have come to me by himself, and said that he was inquiring on behalf of someone else."

RESOURCEFULNESS

"Now, boys," said the teacher, "suppose in a family there are five children, and the mother has only four potatoes to divide among them. She wants to give each child an equal share. What is she to do?"

Silence reigned in the room. Everybody was calculating diligently. Finally, one little boy put up his hand.

338

"Well, Johnny, what would you do?" asked the teacher.
"Mash the potatoes, sir."

___

RESPECT

A young man named Dama owned a very precious stone. Some priests offered him a large sum of money for it, and he agreed to sell it. Going into the next room to get the jewel, he found his father fast asleep, his feet resting on the box where the jewel was kept. Without waking his father, he returned to the priests and told them he could not sell the jewel. They offered him twice as much for it, and then three times as much. "No," he answered them. "I would not disturb my father's rest, even if I could obtain all the treasures in the world."

The priests waited until the father awoke. When Dama brought the jewel to them, they counted out their money in the amount of the last offer they had made. But Dama refused it. He would not take more than the amount of their first offer, for he did not want to profit from what he regarded as his duty in honoring his father.

___

RESPONSIBILITY

The boy had brought a very bad report card home to his father. As his father was getting more and more indignant, the boy said to him, "Dad, what do you think is responsible for this report card—heredity or environment?"

___

An itinerant umbrella-mender sat on a box in an alley, mending broken and torn umbrellas. He seemed to take unusual care, testing the cloth, carefully measuring and sewing. A young man who was watching in fascination turned to him and said:

"You seem extra careful."

"Yes," he replied, without stopping his work. "I have always tried to do good work."

"Your customers would not know the difference until you were gone."

"No, I suppose not."

"Do you ever expect to come back here?"

"No."

339

"Then why are you so particular?"

"So that it will be easier for the next fellow who comes along," answered the worker firmly. "If I put on shoddy cloth or do bad work, the people will find it out before long, and the next mender who comes along will never get any work."

A suburban train was stalled by a blizzard one winter's night, and so deep was the snow that its passengers were afraid to leave the car not knowing how far they were from shelter. The next morning the 150 half-frozen commuters were startled to see a signal tower only a few hundred yards away. The signal station attendant had seen the stalled train the night before, an investigation revealed, but when asked why he'd done nothing about it, he answered, "It is not part of my job."

RETRACTION

A peasant had a troubled conscience and sought the help of the village sage. The peasant had repeated some slander about a friend and later he had found that his words were untrue. He asked the sage what he could do to make amends. The sage advised: "If you want to make peace with your conscience, you must fill a bag with goose feathers and go to every door in the village and drop a feather on each porch."

The peasant took a bag, filled it with goose feathers, and did as he had been told. Then he returned and asked: "Is this all that I have to do?"

"No, that is not all," was the answer. "There is one thing more. Take your bag and gather up every feather." The peasant left. After a long period he returned, saying, "I could not find all the feathers, for the wind had blown them away."

The sage retorted, "So it is with gossip. Unkind words are easily dropped, but are difficult to take back again."

RETRIBUTION

There was once a king who derived great pleasure from listening to violin music. There was one violinist in particular whose beautiful playing delighted him so that the king appointed him court musician.

The musician was a man of unscrupulous morals, and com-

340

plaints frequently came to the king's ears about his offenses. No matter how terrible the crime, the king would not have the violinist punished, for he felt he could not relinquish a diversion which had become a necessity to him. One day, an irate husband surprised the evil musician, pounced upon him with a sword and cut off his right arm. The agonized musician appealed to the king to mete out just punishment to the man who had maimed him.

The hitherto pampered musician was stunned to hear the king shout to his guards, "Seize this man! He is to be hanged."

"Why do you want to kill me?" exclaimed the musician. "Why do you not punish the man who made an attempt on my life?"

The king replied, "If it were possible to do so, you should be hanged again and again for all your evil deeds of the past. However, with two hands you could make your violin sing for me and bring some beauty into the world, and I could find some reasonable explanation for your existence. But now that you are minus one arm, the part of you that created beauty is gone, and all that is left of you is evil. Your usefulness in this world is over, and it is apparent that the day of reckoning has come. You must now pay for your sins."

REVENGE

When Tasso, the Italian poet, attained the height of his career, he was informed that he was in a position to take revenge upon a man who had hurt him greatly in the past.

"I do not desire to plunder him," the poet replied, "yet there is one thing I would like to take from him."

"His honor, his wealth, his life?" the poet was asked.

"No," came the gentle reply. "What I desire to take from him I will try to gain by kindness, patience, and forbearance. You see, I want to try to take away his ill-will!"

As you read the Bible, you note that God calls himself a jealous God. Many years ago, this thought captured the imagination of a philosopher who turned for advice to one of his friends, a clergyman.

"Your God, in His Book, calls Himself a jealous God who can endure no other god besides Himself, and on all occasions makes known his abhorrence of idolatry. Why, then, does He threaten and seem to hate the worshippers of false gods, more than the false gods themselves?"

341

Peering over his glasses, the clergyman replied: "A certain king had a disobedient son. Among other worthless tricks of various kinds, he had the baseness to give his father's name and titles to his dogs. To whom should the king show his anger, the prince or the dogs?"

"Well said," rejoined the philosopher, "but if your God destroyed the objects of idolatry, He would take away the temptation to worship them."

"Yes, if the fools only worshipped things that were of no use. But they worship the sun, the moon, the hosts of heaven; the rivers, the sea; fire, air and what not. Would you have the Creator, for the sake of these fools, ruin His own works and disturb the laws appointed to nature by His own wisdom? If a man steals grain and sows it, should the seed not shoot out of the earth because it was stolen? Oh, no, the wise Creator lets nature run her own course, for her course is His own appointment. And what if the children of folly abuse it to do evil? The day of reckoning is not far off."

~~~

REWARD

A self-righteous man went to see a philosopher. "I was taught once," he complained, "that they who learned to do the right things are happy. I have not found it so. I am tired of doing the right things when I do not get rewarded for my sacrifices."

"I see your difficulty," replied the wise man. "There is something yet for you to learn. It is not enough just to do the right things. If you would be happy, you must learn to enjoy doing them."

~~~

A rich man hired laborers to work in his orchard. He set them to pruning and caring for a variety of trees. Each laborer was permitted to select the tree which appealed to him the most.

When the work was completed, the rich man gathered the laborers together and asked each one, "At which tree did you work?" One pointed out a pepper tree; he was given a small gold coin. Another, who had worked on a white-blossom tree was given two small gold coins. A third, who had worked on an olive tree, was given 200 gold pieces.

The laborers who had received the smaller sums were perplexed and disgruntled. "If you had told us in the beginning," they

342

complained, "for which tree there would be the higher reward each of us might have chosen to work on it."

The rich man replied: "Had I done that, my whole orchard would never have been properly pruned and cared for."

～～～

A sage once argued with a wealthy but tight-fisted man:

"See here," said the sage. "You work day and night, you run hither and thither, and you are always overworked and over-wrought. Stop and reflect sometimes. Imagine that you are already a millionaire. Don't you know that you are merely the guardian of your property? Why don't you deduct something for your labor of guardianship? Have some sense and give alms to needy people and let that be your wages for guarding the property. The little you give will bring you riches that cannot be counted."

～～～

RUMOR

A speculator in oil leases died and went to heaven, only to find the place so crowded that he could barely find room inside the door. The speculator hit upon a trick which he hoped would relieve the congestion. He produced a scrap of paper and a pencil from his pocket and scribbled a note, *"oil discovered in Hell,"* which he dropped on the floor. Soon the note was picked up and read. The man who read it whispered to a few other persons and slipped away. Those in whom he had confided similarly whispered to others and followed him. There was a regular exodus in the direction of the reported strike. Watching the procession, the man who started the rumor grew more and more restive. At length he could stand it no longer. "There may be something in this thing—I guess I'd better look it over," he said as he joined the stampede.

～～～

SABBATH

A preacher, speaking of robbing God, used this illustration: "It came to pass that a man went to market with seven coins. Seeing a beggar asking for alms, he gave the poor man six coins and kept one for himself. The beggar, instead of being thankful, followed the good man and stole the seventh coin also. What an abominable wretch! But then, don't we steal a seventh day after being given six?"

～～～

SACRIFICE

A young man saved some men from drowning. His father asked: "How did you dare do it? Didn't you know that you might lose your own life?"

The brave young man replied: "I was not thinking of my life, father. I was thinking of saving those men."

Little Joey's five-year-old sister had undergone an operation and had lost so much blood that a transfusion was necessary. A test made of the boy's blood indicated that it was the same type as his sister's.

"Will you give your little sister some of your blood, Joey?" asked the doctor.

Joey turned pale but said that he would.

As the blood was being drawn from his veins, the doctor noticed that the boy was growing paler and paler, and knowing that this was not normal he asked, "Are you sick, Joey?"

"No, sir, but I was just wondering when I will die." The doctor was stunned but said, "Do you think people die when they give a little blood?"

"Yes, sir," replied Joey.

"And you are going to give your life for your sister?"

"Yes, sir," he said quietly.

An SOS had been received from a ship that had been wrecked on the rocks and was sinking very rapidly. The skipper of the Coast Guard boat that went to the rescue found himself with a very new crew. When he gave the order, "Launch the boat," one of the crew members came forward and objected, "We're not going out on a night like this, are we? Why, we'll never get back!"

The skipper quietly faced the novice seaman and repeated his command, "Launch the boat! We have to go out, but we don't have to come back."

A young woman came to a priest, distressed by her failure to fulfill the religious duties of life. The priest was aware that she was living a life of sacrificial devotion to her blind father. She cared for his every need.

"Don't you think," asked the priest, "that your service to your father is fulfilling the performance of a religious duty?"

344

"No, no," answered the woman, "it cannot be so, because helping my father brings me joy. It is the delight of my heart to serve him."

SAINTLINESS

A preacher once spoke to a very pious man. "It is not difficult," he told him, "to be a saint when one is secluded in his own home, shut up in his own study, insulated against the problems and temptations of life. Go out into the world; mix with people," he continued, "and if you can still remain pure and lofty, as holy as a saint, you will indeed have proven true greatness."

A very righteous man once said: "A real saint is one whose spirituality is greater than that of the average person and whose deeds reach the highest point of perfection. A college degree and an illustrious grandfather are wonderful things to hold on to and take pride in, but one cannot spend an entire lifetime coasting along on one's good heritage. Sooner or later, we must each stand up and answer for ourselves."

SATISFACTION

A youngster was once observed skiing with one ski. When asked to explain this unusual procedure, the lad looked up and with a happy grin on his face replied, "I know that I ought to be skiing on two skis, but I ain't got 'em. But Mister, you can have a lot of fun with one ski if you ain't got two!"

SCIENCE

One of the television networks put on a documentary about the Kentucky mountain folks, and they brought to New York a man who had spent his entire life in the mountains. The visitor was absolutely amazed at all he saw around him.

His eyes popped as he saw a little old lady enter an elevator in the lobby of the R.C.A. building. The door closed, the little red light blinked, and she was gone. Then, he almost dropped dead in surprise when, a minute later, the same door opened and out stepped a gorgeous young blonde.

"You just can't beat science," he said. "If I'd a known about that contraption, I'd have brung along my old woman."

～～～

SECURITY

A little boy, five years old, was very unhappy and he decided to run away from home. He packed a small suitcase and sneaked out of his house through the back door.

An hour later a neighbor approached him and asked, "What are you doing with the suitcase?"

The little fellow explained that he was running away from home. He was angry with his mother!

"Then why do you keep walking around the block?" the neighbor asked.

To which the boy replied: "Because I am not allowed to cross the street without my MOMMIE."

～～～

SELF-APPRECIATION

Matthew Arnold wrote:

> Resolve to be thyself: and
> know that he
> Who finds himself, loses
> his misery.

～～～

It might be wise to acknowledge the fact that when man was created by God, his joints were so arranged that he could not pat himself on the back.

～～～

SELF-CONTROL

An emperor was walking along a road on the outskirts of the city, when he accidentally brushed against an old man whose steps were slow and uncertain.

As the monarch's walk came to an abrupt end with an apology to the old man, the king asked, out of curiosity, "Who are you?"

"I am a king," the old man answered, much to the monarch's surprise.

"A king?" he asked, "Over what do you reign?"

"Over myself," answered the old man. "I rule myself because I control myself. I am my own subject to command."

~~~

Abraham Lincoln used this illustration to show how some people lacked emotional control. "Some people are like a boat I know that has a six-foot boiler and a nine-foot whistle. Every time they blow the whistle, it takes so much steam the engine stops."

~~~

Franklin Delano Roosevelt was fond of telling the story of two Chinese coolies who were arguing heatedly in the midst of a crowd. A stranger expressed surprise that no blows were being struck. His Chinese friend replied, "The man who strikes first admits that his ideas have given out."

~~~

A man carrying a pitch fork on his shoulder was walking along the road when a dog came running out of a farm and bit him. The man, in self-defense, struck the dog with a prong of the pitch fork and killed him.

"I did it in self-defense," said the man.

"Why didn't you strike the dog with the other end?" queried the farmer.

"Why didn't your dog come at me with the other end?" replied the man.

~~~

SELF-CONSCIOUSNESS

A grandchild once turned to his elderly grandfather and asked him what he did with his long white beard when he went to bed. Did he sleep with it outside the covers or inside the covers?

The old man answered that he had never really paid any attention to it, but when he went to bed that night he was determined to find out the answer. First, he put the beard over the sheet but was uncomfortable. Then he put it under the sheet but was still uncomfortable.

He kept alternating the process all night without any comfort. Finally, in sheer desperation, he exclaimed, "Here, I've had this beard for sixty years and it never gave me any trouble. Now one question about it has caused me such great disturbance."

~~~

347

SELF-DECEIT

An old Arab was sitting under a tree in his little village, looking only for peace and quiet. Suddenly a group of noisy children started to play nearby.

This annoyed the old Arab, and he tried to chase them away, but they wouldn't leave. Then he called one of the smaller boys and whispered a secret into his ear. The other boys rushed over and begged to be told the secret. The old Arab finally agreed to tell it to them.

"In the nearby village," he said, "just two kilometers away—they are giving away free melons today. And you can have all you can carry!"

All the children scrambled to their feet and ran like mad towards the neighboring village.

Again it was quiet and peaceful.

In fact, it was too peaceful; and this worried the old Arab. And he began to chastise himself.

"Why am I such a fool!" he thought. "If they are giving away free melons in the next village, why am I lying here under this tree?"

Quickly, he picked himself up, and rushed to the next village to get his share of free melons.

SELF-DESTRUCTION

One bright summer afternoon, an artist was standing atop a rocky mountain cliff, painting the beautiful panorama. He was deeply absorbed in his work. With every stroke of the brush, he paused to regard his painting from various angles.

When he placed the last stroke upon his masterpiece, the artist began stepping backwards in order to obtain a better view of the completed painting, not realizing that each step was bringing him nearer to the edge of the cliff. One more move would be disastrous. His friend, standing nearby, noticed the artist's danger. Knowing that a shouted warning would be too late, he dashed over to the easel, seized a brush, and smeared the face of the painting. The artist, furious at his friend's behavior, rushed forward to protect his work.

When the friend explained the precarious position from which he had saved him, the artist was overwhelmed with gratitude.

When the trees in the forest heard the clanging of the iron implements, they began to tremble with fear. "Woe is us," they moaned in distress. "They are preparing to cut off our young lives."

"It is only the iron we hear," counseled one tree. "From iron alone we have nothing to fear. It only becomes dangerous when the piece of iron is attached to something which comes from our own kind—a wooden handle."

SELF-IMAGE

A well-known, young businessman fell in love with an equally well-known actress who was greatly respected. For months, he courted her, taking her to all the right places. Finally, he decided that he would marry her.

However, being prudent and careful, he hired a private investigator to file a report. The agent hired for this job did not know the identity of his client, the businessman.

After some weeks, the report reached the desk of the love-smitten executive. It read: "Miss —— has an excellent reputation. Her past is spotless and her friends are of the highest calibre. The only hint of scandal is that in the last few months she has been seen in the company of a businessman of doubtful reputation."

SELF-IMPROVEMENT

A man possessed of great wisdom once said: "Often, when the occasion arises for a person to look into that mirror that may reveal some part of his 'self,' we find him staring with his eyes shut tight. I am afraid he fears the revelation that he has not risen above the common-place. Those who steal a glance at themselves and face facts honestly are motivated to seeking some self-improvement. Truthfully, one must keep one's person as up-to-date as the fashions in one's wardrobe. It is even easier to get by unnoticed with an outmoded garment than with old-fashioned ideas. If you wish to live happily with yourself, alter decadent points of view, refurbish your soul, renovate your heart to make room for love to thrive."

A wise man once said: "In my younger years, I decided to correct and to improve the entire world. When I grew older, I

349

came to the realization that this was an impossible task, so I said to myself: 'I will try to improve the short-comings of my own city.' Again I failed, and in the meantime I grew old. Feeling a pressing need to do something to correct existing evils, I attempted to set my own family, my household, straight. Again I was confronted with failure. But when I grew very old, I realized that had I begun at the outset to improve myself alone, I might have enjoyed a reasonable amount of success."

SELFISHNESS

There was a king who would spend hours in his dress uniform, admiring himself before a large mirror in his room. He would keep parading in front of the mirror, not realizing that his subjects were starving to death. One night, a wise member of the king's court gathered a group of palace attendants, and, while the king slept, cut a window in the wall where the king's mirror had hung.

The next morning, when the king dressed himself in his uniform, he walked to where the mirror had been and saw to his amazement the unending procession of his people passing on the street. He saw starving children reaching into garbage cans for bread crusts. He saw the sick and the maimed. He saw sufferings and wrongs he had not known existed.

He tore off his medals, called for simple clothes, and went out to mingle with his people. His outlook on life changed when he stopped looking into a mirror at only himself.

When King Solomon sat on his throne, he was given an emerald cup, full of the water of life. The waters were sufficient for him only, and if he drank of it, he would be young forever.

Solomon called before him representatives of all created things and asked their advice. All advised him, "Drink, O King! Live forever."

Then Solomon inquired if all creatures were present, and learned that the dove had not yet appeared. When he asked the dove why she hadn't come, she said, "O King, if my mate should die, I would want to die too. What good is immortal youth, if you see everything which you love perish?"

Taught by the voice of devotion, Solomon poured out, untasted, the water of endless life intended for himself alone.

A wealthy woman was once asked to help the people in the slums of her city. She refused, saying that she did not want to set foot in such filthy places. One day, she dropped her diamond wedding band in the mud. Without a moment's hesitation, she put her hand into the mud and picked up her ring. "It is not fear of filth," said her friend, "that prevented you from helping the unfortunate in our city, but rather an unwillingness to put yourself out for anyone but yourself."

A parable often related in the eastern countries indicates how destructive selfishness can be. It concerns a selfish man who was bequeathed a rice field. The first season the irrigation water ran through his field and made it productive and fruitful, then overflowed into the neighbor's field and gave him blessings as well. His field, too, was greatly aided by the flowing waters.

When the next season arrived, the selfish fool said to himself, "Why should I permit all the waters to flow through my field into his? Water is wealth, and I must keep it all for myself." He then built a dam which prevented the water from flowing into his neighbor's fields. The result was that he had no crop that year. The irrigation water brought blessing only as it flowed. When it became stagnant it bred a marsh and a swamp.

A tutor was once engaged by a wealthy man, who wanted his son tutored. One day, the rich man purchased a golden candelabra and had it hung in the dining room. The man enjoyed the light. The tutor also admired the unusual brilliance of the candelabra and an expression of joy and satisfaction was on his face.

The host was a selfish man and, noticing the happiness on the tutor's face, was angered. He pointed a finger at the tutor and demanded, "Tell me, why are you so happy? The candelabra is mine."

"It doesn't make any difference to whom it belongs. It is standing above us and gives us all light. I, too, can admire its artistry."

"Yes," the merchant said, "but you must never forget that you are only here for one semester. Soon you will leave this house and never see the candelabra again. But I will always have it because it is mine."

"You are mistaken," answered the young tutor. "You forget that you are also here for a single term, and that when it will end, you will also leave the house and the candelabra."

SELF-PITY

When Victor Hugo was being persecuted by France, his heart almost broken, in enforced exile, he would climb a cliff overlooking the harbor at sunset, select a pebble, and stand in deep meditation before throwing it down into the water. He seemed to derive great satisfaction in performing this simple ritual each evening. Some children watched him throw these pebbles into the water, and one of the children grew bold enough to ask, "Why do you come here to throw these stones?"

Victor Hugo smiled gravely. He was silent a moment, and then answered quietly, "Not stones, my child. I am throwing self-pity into the sea."

SELF-UNDERSTANDING

A man awoke one day, with the idea that he would try to improve all the people living in the city. "I will go from door to door, from person to person, from neighborhood to neighborhood, spreading my ideas and good will," he thought. "I will preach cooperation and understanding. I will demonstrate the value of honesty and social living. I will bring out the best character traits in all individuals. I will make this city a model city for the rest of the world to study and follow," he said to himself.

As he continued to ponder over this Herculean project, he decided that improving the entire city was too enormous an undertaking. He felt that perhaps he ought to concentrate on his immediate neighborhood first. The more he thought about it, the more he was convinced that even the task of improving his own neighborhood was too difficult. Perhaps he ought to begin by improving the people residing on his own street, or better yet, in his own apartment house.

"If I am going to improve the people living in my house, I ought to begin with the members of my own family," was the next thought that came into his mind. Finally, he concluded that before he could improve the character of his family, he ought to begin by improving his own actions.

SERMONS

A large crowd had turned out to hear the speaker, including one man who was reputed to be a great scholar. The following morning the speaker met the man on the street. "How did you like my sermon?" he asked.

"Your sermon made it impossible for me to sleep all night," was the reply.

"Was the subject matter so deep, or was it my delivery?" was the next question.

"Neither," was the answer, "but when I sleep during the day I can't sleep at night."

⁓

A noted clergyman was asked by a colleague why the loud, vehement preaching of his early career had given way to a more quiet, persuasive manner of speech. The preacher laughed and responded: "When I was young, I thought it was the thunder that killed people, but when I grew up I discovered it was the lightning. So I determined that in the future I would thunder less and lighten more."

⁓

Rev. Norman Vincent Peale, pastor of New York's Marble Collegiate Church, gave an example of the strain and tension of modern life. "We've become so keyed up and nervous," he said, "that it is almost impossible to put people to sleep with a sermon. I haven't seen anyone sleeping in church in years, and that's a sure sign."

⁓

The renowned evangelist, Billy Graham, had come to town and the auditorium was packed. For the better part of an hour, Dr. Graham denounced the evil of drink, his impassioned denunciations taking in the distillers and sellers, as well as the imbibers.

The vast audience was enthralled with the fiery speech, but no one was as fascinated as Hymie Kaplan who had entered the hall only to get out of the rain, and who was hearing him for the first time.

Now the evangelist was winding up his lecture. "Who has the largest bank account?" he thundered. "I'll tell you who—the liquor store owner, that's who! And who lives in the finest house and in the most exclusive neighborhood? Again, the liquor store owner! Who buys his wife mink coats, Cadillacs and jewels? The liquor store owner! And who is keeping him in all this luxury? You, the working man who spends his hard-earned money for all that whiskey, wine and beer!"

At the close of the sermon, the audience rose as one and accorded him the most enthusiastic ovation he had ever received.

Hymie rushed up to the platform and grasped Rev. Graham's hand. "Thank you! Oh, thank you!" he cried. "You are indeed an inspiring man!"

"Then you are saved?" asked the good minister. "You've decided to give up drinking?"

"Well, no, not that," explained Hymie. "But I'm going right out and buy a liquor store!"

~~~

A famous clergyman once remarked to his congregation that "every blade of grass is a sermon."

A few days later, he was engaged in mowing his lawn when a witty member of his congregation passed by, and remarked, "That's right, Reverend, cut your sermons short."

~~~

SERVICE

According to Roman law, a soldier had the right to ask any passerby to carry his pack for one mile. A tired soldier once asked an old man to carry his pack. At the end of the mile the old man refused to put down his burden.

"You have carried it for a mile," said the soldier. "Why don't you put it down now so that I can relieve you?"

"Why don't I put it down?" replied the old man. "It is simple to see. The first mile constitutes my duty to the country. If I am to be of real service I must go beyond my duty. And so I want to carry it a second mile so that I will be giving real service."

~~~

An itinerant preacher related the following parable: "I once met a rather stout man who smoked furiously. When I asked him why he smoked so much, he replied that he did it in order to better digest the rich foods on which he had overeaten. A little later, I met a very lean man who also smoked to excess. When I asked him why he smoked so much, he answered that he was always very hungry and when he smoked, his hunger was somewhat appeased. "I then thought to myself," the preacher concluded, "that if the stout man would give up some of his fat to the lean man, neither would have to smoke."

~~~

Sir Moses Montefiore, the British philanthropist, was once asked how much he was worth. He replied, "I am worth 40,000 pounds."

"But," the questioner asked in amazement, "people say that you possess millions."

"Very true," rejoined Sir Moses with a smile. "I do possess millions. But you asked me how much I was worth, and since 40,000 pounds represents the sum I distributed during the last year to various charitable institutions, I regard this sum as the barometer of my true worth. For, it is not how much a person possesses, but how much he is willing to share with his less fortunate fellowmen that determines his actual worth."

When God created the world, He also created the insects. The Lord then suggested that they find their own means of sustenance. Each species immediately obtained a suitable job from which to derive individual benefits. The bees were the only ones who were not concerned merely with their personal interests but also expressed a desire to serve mankind. Soon a thundering voice pierced through the heavens, "Those insects who seek only to satisfy their own interests and are unconcerned about the welfare of others shall live in the dust and eat of the rubbish. The unselfish bees, however, shall nourish themselves on the nectar of the flowers and thus fulfill their duty towards man, in providing the world with sweetness and honey."

SHARING

Three men came to the Angel of Fire and asked him to entrust them with his most precious possession, the white fire. The angel gave it to them with the instruction: "Keep it well and use it wisely." Thereupon, the three joyous men departed, each to his own home.

The first one walked into a dark valley where people were groping in total blackness. On all sides, he heard their cries of anguish: "If only someone would bring light and liberate us from this dark prison." The man, deeply moved by their cries, and with the fire which the angel had given him, kindled wood and made a huge fire which led them out of the darkness toward the light of the sun.

The second man's journey took him to a snow-capped mountain where people were freezing. He was so moved by their plight that he used the fire which the angel had given him to light a fire to provide warmth for the people.

The third man thought, "How can I keep my fire safe so that the winds will not blow it out nor the rains extinguish it? I will hide it within my heart where no harm can come to it."

When the three men returned from the journey and appeared before the Angel of Fire, he asked each in turn, "How did you use my gift?" The first one answered that with the fire he made a light for the distressed people in darkness. Thereupon, the angel said, "Your fire will never burn out." The second man replied that by the fire he saved people from freezing to death. "Your fire, too, will never burn out," said the angel. The third one said, "I have brought my fire safely to the end of the journey. See, it is hidden in my heart. "Oh, poor man," exclaimed the angel, as he showed him that the fire had gone out. "My white fire can live only while it serves," he said quietly.

～～

A very poor Scotch mother sent her son off to America, during the last war, to join the U.S. Navy. He travelled to the four corners of the earth, and after the war, decided to stay in America.

He wrote his mother a letter every month and she read each one with pleasure. She glowed with pride at every word. Her son had become successful and wealthy in this new land of his!

Some of the neighbors in Scotland, listening to the pride with which the mother spoke of her son, were very curious. And, one day, one of the neighbors got up enough courage to ask: "If your son is so successful and so wealthy, how is it that he allows you to live in such abject poverty, with so little food to eat and in such a broken-down house? Doesn't your son ever send you any money?"

"No," said the mother reluctantly, "but he does send me beautiful pictures every month, in every letter."

"May I see those pictures?" asked the curious neighbor.

"Why certainly," said the old lady. She pulled herself out of her rocking chair and from the cupboard shelf she took down an old Bible. From its pages she pulled out the beautiful pictures her son had been sending her month after month.

The neighbor looked at them and his blood tingled within him. They were American Bank Notes—enough money for her to satisfy all her needs for the rest of her life—all of this money hidden away there in the Bible.

The old Scotch mother was proud of her son but she didn't

realize what her son was doing for her, and she let the treasure lie buried in the pages of the Bible.

SILENCE

Calvin Coolidge was a man of few words. When someone twitted him for his habitual silence, he replied, "Well, I found out early in my life that you never have to explain something you haven't said."

A tourist was spending the night in a New England town. He joined several men who were sitting on the porch of the general store. They were a quiet group and, after several vain attempts to start a conversation, he finally said, "Is there a law against talking in this town?"

"No law against it," answered one of the men. "But there's an understanding no one's to speak unless he is sure he can improve on silence."

A loquacious young man came to Socrates to learn the art of oratory. Socrates asked him double the price.

"Why charge me double?" asked the youth.

Socrates replied, "Because I must teach you two sciences—the one, how to be silent, and the other, how to speak."

Professor Albert Einstein gave what he considered the best formula for success in life: If "a" is success in life, I should say the formula is $a = x + y + z$, "x" being work and "y" being play.

"And what is 'z'?" inquired the interviewer.

"That," he answered, "is keeping your mouth shut."

SIN

"Have you anything you did not receive from God?" asked a teacher of her Sunday School class.

"No," replied all the pupils but one.

"What is that?" asked the teacher of the young dissenter.

"Sin," was the terse reply.

A preacher once said to his congregation: "I beg you to abstain from sin. If you were to busy yourselves with higher values, then you would find no time to sin. And now, let us begin by filling some time with prayer."

Satan, in his great passion for stirring up evil, one day decided to catch people at their worst. Where could their bad deeds be more obvious than at their houses of worship where they go to confess their sins? So he secreted tape recorders in temples, churches, and synagogues.

Gleefully and impatiently, Satan rubbed his hands together as he slunk stealthily from church, to temple, to synagogue. No sooner was the last person out of sight than he excitedly collected his tape recorders and rushed home with his quarry. Imagine his dismay when his tapes yielded sins like the use of mild profanities, coming late for services, forgetting to say grace occasionally, and the like.

Exasperated, he cried: "What has happened to humanity? Have they become soft and cannot commit 'better' sins?" And suddenly, as he ranted and raved, he realized that he was taping in the wrong "studios." Those who go to confess their sins are the least offenders.

Satan once approached the Almighty and complained that his work on earth was becoming monotonous and boring. "I want you to know," he said, "that I have nothing to do day after day."

"That's hard to understand," replied God. "There's plenty of work to be done, only *you* must display more initiative. Why don't you try to lead people into sin?"

"Lead people into sin!" complained Satan. "Before I can get a chance to do anything, they are sinning already."

SINCERITY

A certain king wanted to build a temple. Because he wanted all the credit, he forbade any person from contributing to its erection. Finally, a tablet was placed on the side of the building and his name was carved on it. But that night the king dreamt that an angel came down and erased his name and substituted the name of a poor widow. This was repeated three times.

The enraged king summoned the woman before him, and demanded, "What have you been doing?" The trembling woman replied, "I love the Lord and longed to do something for His name, and for His temple. I was forbidden to touch it in any way; so, in my poverty, I brought a wisp of hay for the horses that drew the stones."

The king saw that he had labored for his own glory, but the widow for the glory of the Almighty. He commanded that her name be inscribed upon the tablet.

A boy scout, about to go to bed, remembered that he had not done his good deed for the day. He quickly went to his brother's piggy-bank, took out a dime and dropped it into the charity container.

The distance from the human mouth to the human heart, from the word to the thought, is sometimes as far as from Heaven to Earth. . . .

There is a parable told about two balls, one made of solid gold, the other covered with a very thin layer of gold. They were put together in a box without any wrappings to protect them. The gilded ball was very careful of itself. It tried to keep very still because it knew that its slight covering would easily wear off. But the ball that was solid gold did not care how much it rolled around in that box or bumped against its neighbor. It was sure of itself. It needed no precautions to protect itself.

The gilded ball, terrified lest its gilt covering be rubbed off by contact with the other ball, said to the gold one, "You had better be careful how you knock about or that stuff will rub off."

"Rub what off?" asked the solid gold one.

A famous actor was asked to entertain at a dinner party one evening. He rose and recited the 23rd Psalm. When he finished the recitation a thunder of applause greeted him. The crowd knew that they were in the presence of a master performer.

The next speaker was an elderly preacher. "I, too, would like to recite the same Psalm," he said quietly. Turning his face upwards, he closed his eyes and began. When he was through, all were silent. There was no applause, but neither was there a dry eye in the room.

Later, a man approached the actor. "I don't understand it," he said. "You both said the same thing. Your presentation was letter perfect. Yet, when the preacher spoke in his own halting manner, people were moved too deeply for words. What made the difference?"

"I know the 23rd Psalm," replied the actor. "But he knows the Shepherd. That's the difference."

A man was asked to purchase a ticket for a benefit concert. "I'm sorry," he said, "but I'm busy that night. However, I do want you to know that I will be with you in spirit."

"Good," replied the solicitor. "Where would you like your spirit to sit? There are tickets for two, five, and ten dollars."

SORROW

Henry Ward Beecher once said: "There are many fruits that never turn sweet until the frost has lain upon them; there are many nuts that never fall from the bough of the tree of life till the frost has opened and ripened them; and there are many elements of life that never grow sweet and beautiful till sorrow touches them."

There are two kinds of decay. One seed may rot in the sand and it becomes decayed and worthless. This is self-pity. Another seed, on the other hand, may rot in the earth and a tree will grow out of it. This is sorrow with thought and understanding at the controls.

SOUL

"In the soul of every human being there lies something of nobleness which cannot be found elsewhere. . . ." This observation could only have been made by someone with great faith in and a deep love for the human population.

A minister once passed the shop of a parishioner, who was a poor shoemaker. Though it was late at night and the candle was sputtering its way to oblivion, the shoemaker still labored on to repair shoes promised for the next day. Much impressed by the shoemaker's industry and his desire to fulfill his promises to his customers, the minister spoke of the poor man in his sermon the following week.

"Let us take an example from the hard working shoemaker," he said. "As long as the candle's light holds out, he labors on. As long as our life's light continues to glow, so should we be tireless in our efforts to complete our work: fight for self-improvement, fight to keep love alive in our heart, fight to remain industrious, fight to know how to be charitable. And, of course, we must never tire in our efforts to keep alive the glimmer of light in another soul."

A man once provided himself with all things necessary for his wedding, but forgot to prepare a wedding ring.

We have a situation analogous to this in the man who strives to acquire all the worldly pleasures that may satisfy his physical needs, and pays no attention to the deprivation suffered by his soul.

A well-known legend relates how Satan sought to conceal man's soul so that he would be unable to discover it in time to achieve immortality.

The angels advised him to bury it in the ground, and he retorted that men would find it too easily when tilling the soil. Then the angels asked him to conceal it in the bosom of the sea, but he replied that man would find it too easily in his fishing exploits in the deep waters. When the angels finally advised him to hide it behind the heavenly clouds, Satan said that man would find it too easily by lifting himself mechanically into the atmosphere. "Where, then, will you hide man's soul so that he will not find it?" asked the angels.

In his diabolic search Satan thought for a long time and came up with the ultimate solution. He decided that he would conceal man's soul within himself. "I shall implant the festering contagions of jealousy and selfishness within the depths of him, and I can depend on it that he will always look elsewhere to try to capture that which is actually within himself."

SPEAKERS

There is a sign near a speaker's platform for the benefit of press photographers. It reads:

"Do not photograph the speakers while they are addressing the audience. Shoot them as they approach the platform."

After-dinner speeches in Japan used to come before the meal. The custom worked well. It not only relieved the speaker's nervous tension but also limited the length of the speech.

He had been invited to speak at a state university and began his address to the students this way: "Now, I'm not going to talk at great length, but if you get what I'm going to say in your head, you'll have the whole thing in a nutshell."

And he looked astonished when a roar followed his unintentional slam.

A prominent speaker began his lecture at a meeting with the following: "My job as I understand it, is to lecture to you. Your job is to listen. If you finish before I do, just hold up your hand, and if any of you wish to leave before I finish, just go ahead. But if too many leave, I'd appreciate it if you will tell me where you are going, and if it sounds better than here, I'll go along."

A local organization was running its yearly installation exercises. The guest speaker was making a rather lengthy address, and there were ushers on the floor to maintain order. In the audience sat a young bride whose husband was one of the ushers. Becoming terribly worried about a roast she had left in the oven, she wrote a note to her husband, sending it to him via another usher. The latter, thinking it was a note for the speaker, hurried down the aisle and laid it on the lectern. Stopping abruptly in the middle of his speech to read the note, the astonished speaker was met with this written injunction: "Please go home and turn off the gas!"

The late Alexander Woollcott once illustrated how to squelch a bore. When he thought the monologue of a certain actor had gone on long enough, he interrupted the speaker by saying, "Excuse me, my leg has gone to sleep. Do you mind if I join it?"

~~~

Political orators can take a meaningful lesson from the wise old minister, who, years ago, had thousands of followers. It was his custom on the anniversary of his birthday to run a dinner, at which time he would address the gathering, giving them a moral lesson.

On one such occasion, his people gathered in his home. The meal had been served and he was prepared to begin his talk. Standing up in his place, he slowly looked them over, and said, "My good friends, do you know what my text will be today?"

With one voice they chorused back, "No, reverend one, we don't know."

The minister replied, "Then I cannot speak to so shallow a group of people," and he left the room.

The next morning, they gathered again. The minister looked over and said, "My good people, do you know what my text will be today?" Having experienced a rebuff the day before, they answered with one voice, "Yes, beloved teacher, we know."

Then he said, "If you already know, then there is no need for me to tell you," and again he walked away.

On the third day, the people gathered again. As before, he addressed them with the same question. "My good people," he asked, "do you know the text of my speech today?"

A spokesman, who thought to outwit the minister at his own game, replied, "Oh, beloved teacher, half of us know and half of us do not know."

The minister looked amused and replied, "In that case, let those who know tell those who don't know." And once again he retired.

~~~

"Ladies and gentlemen," said the after-dinner speaker, "before I begin my address I have something important to say."

~~~

A wise man reflects before he speaks; a fool speaks, and then reflects on what he has said.

~~~

The man evidently was late in entering the hall where a speech was being delivered. As he walked in, a man was walking out. "Has he spoken already?" he asked of the departing man.

"Yes," replied the man, "he has been speaking for half an hour."

"What is he talking about?" asked the other.

"I don't know," was the reply. "He hasn't said yet."

SPIRITUALITY

A famous explorer, describing a journey to the Belgian Congo, relates that after a forced march of several days, his native bearers refused to go on. The natives said that they had traveled so fast that their spirits were left behind. They were going to remain in camp until their spirits caught up.

STATUS

Those who seek glory believe in great people and admire them highly. They also expect those who are less than they to respect and admire them in turn.

To respect those who are superior to us is highly commendable, but to expect others to pay homage to us shows a complete absence of humility. It is a sad state of affairs when we seek status and forget to be humble. It represents one step down from superiority towards inferiority of character.

A charitable person once asked a wealthy but miserly man, "Tell me, please, what kind of food does your daily menu consist of?"

The miser replied, "I eat very little. A piece of dry bread with salt and a cup of coffee is sufficient for me."

The charitable man then said to him, "This is not right. A man in your position ought to have a proper daily meal consisting of several courses, good meat, and wine. If you will eat correctly, as behooves a human being of your status, then perhaps you will have a piece of bread to spare for the poor. But if your own meager meal consists of bread only, then what can you possibly give to the poor?"

STINGINESS

There is a famous story about the Collyer brothers, that made the headlines several years ago. These two wealthy bachelors had

364

inherited a mansion from their parents and lived in it together. They were both very eccentric people. They believed in saving everything, and they gave nothing away. They saved old newspapers and magazines and bottles and cans until every room in their house was filled with junk from floor to ceiling.

One day both of them took sick. They wanted to call the doctor but they had no telephone. They started to wade through the mountain of junk they had accumulated over the years in order to get to the front door, so they might call for help, but they were too weak to push it away.

When the police finally came and made their way into the house several days later, they found the two brothers dead, heaped together like the rest of the junk they had been accumulating and saving all those years.

STUDENTS

One day, an Eastern university professor visited the expanding campus of the University of California. He watched construction work on a dozen new buildings; he inspected new laboratories, and attended summer classes in modern study rooms; he walked across miles of eucalyptus-lined lawns and athletic fields with one of the deans. He was impressed.

"My," he exclaimed, "just how many students do you have here?"

"Let me see," the dean answered thoughtfully; "I'd say about one in a hundred."

The college prof was approached by one of his students who had been doing no work all term long. "Do you think," asked the student anxiously, "that if I cram for the next two weeks I can pass the final examination?"

Replied the professor: "You make me think of a thermometer in a cold room. You can make it register higher by holding your hand over it, but the room will remain just as cold."

SUCCESS

There is an art to being successful in life that can be learned from the Vermonter who all his life has been catching snakes by hand. He manages to stand a little farther from the snake that its

365

fangs will reach, and before it can strike he grabs it with an iron grip below the head. His art, he explains, lies in being just a second quicker than the snake.

Success lies in being just a second quicker than opportunity.

~

A prominent salesman, now retired, summed up his success in three simple words: "And then some."

"I discovered at an early age," he said, "that most of the difference between average people and top people could be explained in three words. The top people did what was expected of them—and then some. They were thoughtful of others; they were considerate and kind—and then some. They met their obligations and responsibilities fairly and squarely—and then some. They were good friends to their friends—and then some. They could be counted on in an emergency—and then some."

~

An eager young graduate sought the advice of a successful businessman. "Tell me, please," he said, "how I should go about getting a start in the great game of business." The reply was not long in coming: "Sell your wristwatch and buy an alarm clock."

~

President Wilson once remarked that he would rather fail in the service of a cause he knew would ultimately succeed, than succeed in the service of a cause he knew would ultimately fail.

~

A father was counseling his son who had been graduated from college and was now entering a profession. "My boy," he said, "remember there are three bones, and you will never have any trouble."

"How will three bones keep me out of all trouble?" inquired the son.

"There is a wishbone, a jawbone, and a backbone," the father explained. "The wishbone keeps you going after things. The jawbone helps you find out how to go after them if you are in doubt, and the backbone keeps you at it until you get there."

~

John D. Rockefeller was once asked to what he attributed his success. He thought for a moment and replied, "To others."

~

366

This is success: To be able to carry money without spending it; to be able to bear an injustice without retaliating; to be able to do one's duty even when one is not watched; to be able to keep on the job until it is finished; to be able to accept criticism without letting it whip you.

SURVIVAL

After having gone without food for a number of days, a starving fox came to a river where he stopped for a drink. He drooled at the sight of the fish swimming in the river, but since he could not swim, he could not jump into the water to catch any.

But, being a fox, he shrewdly tried to coax the fish out of the water by pointing out the hazards they faced in the river. "In the water there are many fish bigger than you, who pursue and try to swallow you. Then there are the never-ending perils of the fishermen's nets that drag you out of the water in hordes. Why don't you jump out on dry land where you will be quite safe from harm?"

The fish replied in one voice: "You are quite right, Mr. Fox. In the water upon which our very lives depend, we face danger every moment of our lives, but we at least have a fighting chance. Take us out of our natural habitat, and we won't even be able to breathe."

Franz Liszt showed that he had great tact as well as being an excellent musician. A pretty woman demanded his unmerited praise of her singing by saying, "Maestro, do you not think I have a good voice?" Liszt replied, "*Good* is not the word for it!"

A minister was completely carried away by his sermon. As he continued to talk, a well-dressed man rose from his seat and walked slowly out of the Temple. The minister felt hurt, and at the conclusion of the service told the president of the congregation that the gentleman had no right leaving before the end of the speech.

"Don't feel hurt," answered the president. "That man always walks in his sleep."

Benjamin Franklin, discussing the value of tact, remarked: "Remember not only to say the right thing in the right place,

367

but, far more difficult still, to leave unsaid the wrong thing at the tempting moment."

~~~

TALENT

A story has it that a great violinist once stood before an audience and enraptured them with his artistic playing. Suddenly, in the midst of the selection, he paused, took the violin from beneath his chin, and smashed it into a thousand pieces. The audience sat aghast. In the mystified silence, the violinist walked to the front of the platform, and addressed the assemblage. "Don't be alarmed," he said quietly, "the violin I just broke was one that I purchased for a few dollars. I shall now play upon a Stradivarius." He quickly unpacked the valuable instrument from the case, tuned it, and began to play on it. While the music was magnificent, it was virtually indistinguishable from the earlier selection. When the artist concluded the selection, he again spoke to the audience and humbly said, "Friends, so much has been said about the value of this violin in my hands that I wanted to impress you with the fact that the music is not in the instrument; it is in the one who plays upon it."

~~~

A New York socialite came into the salon of Walter Florell, the milliner to movie stars and socialites, and announced that she needed a hat at once for a cocktail party. Florell took a couple of yards of ribbon, twisted it, put it on her head, and said, "There is your hat, madam." The lady looked into the mirror and exclaimed, "It's wonderful."

"Twenty-five dollars," said Florell.

"But that is too much for a couple of yards of ribbon!" she gasped.

"Florell unwound the ribbon and handed it to her saying, "The ribbon, madam, is free."

~~~

Screams for help coming from a house caused a passing pedestrian to rush to the open door and offer his services. A distracted mother explained that her little boy had just swallowed a quarter. The stranger grabbed the child by the feet, lifted him into the air, and shook him vigorously. In a moment the coin dropped out of the child's mouth. The relieved mother was profuse in her thanks.

"Doctor, how lucky it was for us that you happened by just at this instant. You certainly knew how to get it out of him."

"But, madam," replied the stranger, "I am not a doctor. I am with the Internal Revenue Bureau."

TALK

A man was invited to eat dinner with a family. The main dish at the meal consisted of a large fish. The man looked at the fish and told his host that it reminded him of one he had seen mounted in a friend's office. The inscription above the fish read: IF I HAD KEPT MY MOUTH SHUT, I WOULDN'T BE HERE.

"Doctor," complained the new patient, "I am in need of help. I talk to myself."

"Do you suffer any pain?" asked the doctor.

"No, I have no pain."

"Well," said the doctor, "in that case, go home, don't worry. Millions of people talk to themselves."

"But, doctor," replied the patient, "you don't know what kind of a bore I am."

TEACHERS and TEACHING

A young woman once asked a guidance counsellor for advice as to which profession to choose. "Should I become a teacher, or should I be a writer?" she asked.

The counsellor replied: "Select teaching, because if you will have the good fortune to have even one able pupil, you, too, will learn. And there is no greater satisfaction in life than to keep growing."

Thomas Carlyle was once asked the secret of successful teaching. Carlyle replied, "Be what you would have your pupils be. All other teaching is unblessed mockery and apery."

Elbert Hobbard wrote: "He is great who feeds the minds of others. He is great who inspires others to think for themselves. He is great who pulls you out of your mental ruts, lifts you out of the mire of the commonplace, whom you alternately love and hate, but whom you cannot forget."

A teacher described a significant episode which occurred early in her teaching career: When I reached the school one morning I was surprised to see a youngster waiting near the door.

"It's locked," he said, as I tried the knob.

I began to fumble for my keys. Immediately, he brightened.

"You're a teacher!" he announced with both surprise and pleasure.

"What makes you think that?" I asked, amused, and not a little pleased to think that my station in life should be regarded with such delight.

He hesitated not a moment, but said softly and with respect, "You have the key."

I was promptly humbled as well as overwhelmed at the magnitude of that simple statement, of the implication and the responsibility involved by merely having a "key."

This was perhaps the most pertinent statement directed toward me in my entire teaching career. It started me thinking. . . .

Professor Joseph L. Blau summed up his goal as a teacher, with the following three R's:

REVERENCE for the creative achievements of men of the past.
RESPECT for the continued creativity of men of the present.
RESPONSIBILITY for maintaining and improving the conditions of creative achievement for the men of the future. This is the faith I consider worth living for, and working for, and, if need be, dying for.

> How shall we teach
> A child to reach
> The stars,
> We who have stooped so much?
>
> How shall we tell
> A child to dwell
> with honor, live and die
> For truth,
> We who have lived a lie?

How shall we say
To him, "The way
Of life is through the gate
Of love,"
We who have learned to hate?

How shall we dare
To teach him prayer
And turn him toward the way
Of faith,
We who no longer pray?

—Mildred Howland

A wise king once decided that he would set aside a day to give honor to the greatest of his subjects. On the specified day, people from all walks of life gathered in the palace garden.

Amid the cheers of his subjects, the king sat down on his throne and instructed the various groups of citizens to present their candidates.

First to be presented was a man of immense wealth. It was told that he gave much of his wealth to the less fortunate.

A doctor was then presented with the words that he was a faithful servant to all in need.

A famous lawyer was introduced with the words that he was a fair judge and was famous for his wise decisions.

Finally, an old, poorly dressed lady was led to the front. Looking into her eyes one could see love, loyalty, and understanding.

"Who is this?" demanded the king.

"This, O King," was the immediate answer, "is their teacher."

Wanted: Nursery school teachers.

Requirements: Must have four hands, four feet, patience of a saint, medical training, bachelor's degree. Must also be a trained furniture mover, expert carpenter, fine pianist, neat, tidy, expert housekeeper, trained psychiatrist, and an artist. Must be able to see around corners, to fly, to run as fast as a slow gazelle, to move slowly and calmly, to sing and dance, to see each child as an individual and children as a group.

TEMPTATION

Years ago in Russia, when a farmer sold his wheat to the produce store in the village, the calculations of the transaction were

371

recorded in a quaint way. The purchaser would deposit a brass token for each ton of wheat. After the wheat was weighed, the tokens would be added up and the farmer was paid so much for each token. The shopkeeper used the weight tokens because he knew that the minute his back was turned, the farmer would not be able to resist the temptation to steal a few of the tokens. Little did the ignorant peasant realize that if he had resisted the temptation, he would have been paid a hundred-fold for each little token at the end of the weighing. In his anxiety to get something for nothing, he lost a large sum of money.

A reckless man in a zoological garden once playfully seized a venomous serpent by the nape of the neck, and held it up before his companions. The man thought that he had the serpent wholly in his power but it began to coil and slowly tighten its long body about his arm, until, in agony, he was obliged to release his hold on it. At that moment the snake turned and bit him, and the man fell dead.

Many of us think we are strong enough to play with temptation only to find, sooner or later, that temptation has become our master.

Temptation may be compared to a man who stands in a crowd with his fists clenched, so that everyone feels certain that he has something in his hands. Simultaneously, he asks, "Guess what I have in my hand?" When he unclenches his fists, everyone sees that they are empty.

Temptation is very much like this. It too deceives the world with false promises, and all run after it because they think that in its hands is the ultimate satisfaction of their desires. Temptation is not to be trusted, for while its promise is great, it has, in reality, nothing to offer.

At one time the small corner grocery was a friendly place to shop. The grocer was almost a member of the family. Of course, if there were three customers in the store, he became very busy. It once happened that Mr. Burton, the grocer, noticed a small boy standing near an open box of cookies.

"Now, Joey," said the grocer, "what are you up to?"

"Nothing," was the immediate reply.

372

"Nothing? Well, it looks to me as if you were trying to take a cookie," said the grocer.

"You're wrong, Mr. Burton. I am trying my best not to take one."

~~~

TEN COMMANDMENTS

When Franklin D. Roosevelt died, he went to heaven where he was welcomed by Moses. "Are you the Roosevelt that was just President of the United States?"

"The same."

"Ah, Franklin, you have my sympathy. I think it's a shame the way the world ignored your Four Freedoms," said Moses.

"Well, I suppose everything is relative," answered Roosevelt. "Your Ten Commandments aren't faring any better!"

~~~

TESTIMONIAL

A man invented a mousetrap and believed that his fortune would be made if he could get President Lincoln to recommend it. After a long, persistent effort, he secured an audience with the President, and received the following testimonial, which will apply to many things besides mousetraps:

"For the sort of people who want this sort of thing, this is the sort of thing that sort of people will want."

~~~

THOUGHTFULNESS

There was a blind man who always carried a lantern. One day he was asked. "Of what use can a lantern be to a blind man?"

"It is simple to understand," he replied. "I do not carry it to prevent my bumping into someone, but to keep them from stumbling over me."

~~~

There was once an old man who went about carrying an oil can. Whenever he went through a door that creaked, he would pour a little oil on the hinges. If a gate was hard to open, he would oil the latch. And so he passed through life, lubricating with the oil of gladness and thoughtfulness.

373

If man went around with his own oil-can, perhaps the corrosion of his heart and mind would disappear.

THOUGHTS

A patient was wheeled into surgery wrapped in all kinds of surgical linen. The doctors and the surgeon, the nurses, and the anaesthetist gathered around. The surgeon started removing the dressing, and finally got down to the abdomen. As he prepared to operate, he looked down and there was a little piece of tape, a very small piece of tape. On it was written, "Doctor, think!"

In the Washington National Museum, there is an interesting reproduction of one of the most fascinating antediluvian animals, called the Stegosaurus. This creature is interesting because it possessed two brains: a very small one in its head, and a much larger one in its tail. It did its thinking with the smaller brain, but control over its actions was concentrated in the larger. In other words, it had much more power to act than to think. The results were not too good, because there were frequent collisions between its motor apparatus and its intellectual operation. Very often, there was a great deal of motion but little progress.

A man entered a flower shop and selected a bouquet of flowers, saying. "These are my wife's favorite flowers." The florist expressed sympathy at the illness of the wife.

"Ill!" exclaimed the husband, "who said anything about illness? My wife is as healthy as you are."

The florist apologized, saying, "Please forgive me for my error; but, to tell you the truth, husbands rarely buy flowers for their wives unless the wives are hospitalized."

THREAT

Mother and daughter were walking through the museum when they came upon the statue of Venus de Milo. The mother turned to her eight-year-old daughter and said, "There, you see what happens if you keep on biting your nails."

374

THRIFT

Shortly after her wedding, Mrs. Calvin Coolidge was high-pressured into buying a book for eight dollars, entitled *Our Family Physician*. This was a compilation of medical information. Afterward, she was afraid of the effect the price she had paid might have on her husband. So she did not mention the purchase to him at all.

One day some time later, she happened to open the book, and found on the fly leaf the following words: "Don't see any recipes for curing suckers. Calvin Coolidge."

A well-to-do man attributed his success to thrift.

"Surely," said a friend, "you must have been tempted to indulge in extravagances."

"Oh, yes," agreed the wealthy man, "but a long time ago I worked out a four-question formula that has saved me a lot of money."

"First, before I buy, I ask myself, 'Do you really want it?' Usually I can answer 'Yes' to that one!"

"Then I ask, 'But do you need it?' That eliminates a good many proposed purchases."

"The next question is, 'Can you afford it?' That is a real stopper."

"And finally I ask, 'But can't you get along without it?' The few items that survive after that are pretty essential!"

TIME

There is an old Jewish legend concerning two students of the *Kabalah*, of Jewish mysticism. They lived at a time when the plight of Israel was so pitiful that there seemed to be no hope in sight. The two men resolved to intervene on behalf of their unfortunate brethren. They began to fast and pray for the advent of the Messiah. One evening both had an identical dream in which they were told to go to the Holy Land and there, near the city of Jerusalem, they would find a cave in which King David was asleep. On a certain day, precisely at the break of dawn, the old king would stretch forth his hands. If at that exact moment they would pour water on his hands and help him rise, David would leave the cave, redeem his people, and usher in the messianic era of brotherhood and peace.

The next day the two scholars set out on the long trek to the Holy Land. They met countless obstacles on their way. They suffered hunger and privation, but they were not deterred. Finally, on the appointed day, they reached the cave of David at midnight and found the old king asleep. They prepared a pitcher of pure water and placed it at his bedside. But inasmuch as there were still a few hours left before the crack of dawn, the men decided to explore the other chambers of the cave.

As they walked about they beheld many treasures which reminded them of the glories of Israel's past. They saw the sword with which David slew Goliath, and the famous harp upon which he played his prayerful tunes to God.

The two men were dazzled by the precious jewels and the ancient relics—they were so absorbed by the magnificence of the cave and its contents that they forgot about their important mission and the great task at hand. When they reminded themselves, and rushed to David's bedside, it was much too late. Dawn had already broken; David had stretched forth his hands and had waited anxiously for someone to pour water on them and help him rise, but no one had appeared. So, frustrated and utterly discouraged, the old king had dropped his hands and went back to sleep. The two scholars, heartbroken and remorseful, cried out, "Woe unto us! We arrived at his bedside too late!"

A wealthy man neglected his opportunities to help others. When he lay critically ill, he realized his mistake and pleaded. "Oh, if only I could live another year I would never postpone a good deed; I would do all my charitable needs immediately."

Immediately, he heard a voice exclaim, "Because you have become wise and mean to do well, you shall be given not one year, but many."

When he recovered, he forgot his fine resolve. Instead, he said, "I have been granted many more years. Let me enjoy myself for the next five years; after that I shall devote myself completely to acts of kindness and mercy."

The years flew by—ten, fifteen, twenty—but still he kept putting his good deeds off for tomorrow. Once more he was critically ill, and again he pleaded for an extension of time so that he might accomplish the good deeds he had postponed. But this time he heard the voice saying sadly, but finally, "Too late."

Voltaire was a dwarf in body and a giant in intellect. In his book *Zadig, a Mystery of Fate*, the Grand Magi puts the following question to Zadig.

"What, of all things in the world, is longest and shortest, the swiftest and the slowest, the most divisible and the most extended, the most neglected and the most regretted, without which nothing can be done, which devours all that is little, and enlivens all that is great?"

Here is Zadig's answer: "*Time*. Nothing is longer, since it is the measure of eternity. Nothing is shorter, since it is insufficient for the accomplishment of your projects. Nothing is more slow to him that expects; nothing more rapid to him that enjoys. In greatness it extends to infinity, in smallness it is infinitely divisible. All men neglect it; all regret the loss of it; nothing can be done without it. It consigns to oblivion whatever is unworthy of being transmitted to posterity, and immortalizes such actions as are truly great. Time is man's most precious asset."

An Indian student was riding in an auto with one of our modern speed demons. The driver saw a train coming, and said: "Unless we beat that train across we shall be delayed three minutes." He stepped on the gas, and made it, with only seconds to spare. When they were safely across, the Indian asked quietly: "Now what are you going to do with the three minutes?"

One man became angry at another and, removing a pendulum from a big clock, used it as a weapon to beat the life out of his companion. The murderer then took poison, and so the two passed on.

A philosopher who commented on the tragedy said: "What a shame to make violent use of the pendulum! Given time, it would have killed both men peacefully, and decently."

The animals were complaining that human beings were always taking things away from them. The cow complained they took her milk. The hen complained that they took her eggs. The steer complained that they took his meat. The whale complained they took his oil.

And so it went. Then the snail smiled. "I have something they would like to have; something they would certainly take away from me if they could. You see, I have time."

An ignoramus managed to get himself invited to a party attended by world-renowned scientists. Among them was Albert Einstein. The illiterate guest immediately made a nuisance of himself by dogging the illustrious physicist's heels and offering what he thought were very profound observations.

"Tell me, Dr. Einstein," asked the pest. "What, in your opinion, is the difference between time and eternity?"

"Sir," answered Einstein, "if I took the time to explain the difference, it would take an eternity!"

An 80-year-old man kept a detailed record of what he had done during each hour of every day, and then figured out how he used his time during the entire period of his long life. He spent 26 years in sleep, 21 years working, 228 days shaving, and 140 days paying bills. He also spent over 26 days scolding his children, and two days yelling at his dogs. Only 26 hours were spent in laughing.

"Guard well your spare moments," Ralph Waldo Emerson advised. "They are like uncut diamonds. Discard them and their value will never be known; improve them and they will become the brightest gems in a useful life."

Somerset Maugham, the famous writer, recuperating in London from a bout with the flu, was phoned by a female admirer. "Could I send you fruit," she asked, "or would you rather have flowers?"

Replied the 88-year-old Maugham: "It's too late for fruit—too early for flowers."

TODAY

John Dryden cautioned us to be concerned with the present, not the past or future. These beautiful lines illustrate this idea.

Happy the man, and happy he alone,
He who can call today his own;

He who, secure within, can say,
Tomorrow, do thy worst; for I have lived today.

Many people say, "When I will retire from business I will study the history and culture of my people, and attend religious services regularly."

But the poet warns us:

> Thou knowest not tomorrow's sun,
> Tomorrow's light is not thine own.
> And what today is left undone
> May forever become undone.
>
> Whatever it is thou has to do,
> Beneath whatever load to bow,
> Be to thy sphere of duty true—
> Be up and doing—do it now."

TOGETHERNESS

A father, who was lying on his death-bed, called his seven sons to himself. He put seven sticks, bound together, before them. "I will give the major part of my wealth to the one who breaks this bundle," he announced.

Each of the sons, in turn, strained to break the bundle, but in vain. "It is impossible," they protested.

"My sons," said the father, "nothing is easier." He untied the bundle, took the sticks one by one, and broke them with ease. The father then continued, "As it is with these sticks, so it is with you, my sons. So long as you are together and aid one another, you will prosper, and none can injure you. But, if the bond of union be broken, it will happen to you just as it happened to these sticks, which now lie broken here on the ground."

In her first appearance as Queen of The Netherlands, Wilhelmina Helene Pauline Maria stood on the balcony of her palace in Amsterdam and stared with a small child's wonder at her cheering subjects. "Mama," she asked, "do all these people belong to me?"

"No, my child," replied the Queen-Regent. "It is you who belong to all these people."

379

TOLERANCE

Tolerance is the ability to keep your shirt on when you're hot under the collar.

～～～

Carlyle wrote of John Knox:
"Tolerance has to tolerate the unessential and see well what that is. Tolerance has to be noble, measured, and just in its very wrath, when it can tolerate no longer. But on the whole, we are not here altogether to tolerate! We are here to resist, to control and to vanquish withal. We do not tolerate Falsehoods, Thieveries, and Iniquities, when they fasten upon us. We say to them, "Thou art false, thou art not tolerable!'"

～～～

Martin Luther King defined the idea of brotherhood when he said, "We must learn to live together as brothers, or we will perish together like fools."

～～～

TONGUE

A wit once said, "The tongue, being in a wet place, is bound to slip once in a while."

～～～

Gamaliel commanded his slave, Tobi, to buy the best food in the market. The slave brought home a tongue. The next day Gamaliel commanded him to buy the worst thing in the market, and again Tobi brought home a tongue. When asked for an explanation, the wise slave replied: "There is nothing better than a good tongue, and nothing worse than an evil tongue."

～～～

TRANQUILITY

The Israeli author, S. Y. Agnon, tells the story of a neighbor of Moses who had most of the good things in life, with one important exception. He had no tranquility. He was always worried and anxious about the future, so much so that he could not even sleep at night.

When he heard that Moses was going up to see the Almighty on Mount Sinai, he pleaded with him to put in a word for him. He reminded Moses that he had been a good man, that he lived by God's law, that he was generous and faithful to tradition, that he never strayed from the precepts of the Almighty.

"Won't you ask for me," he begged of Moses, "a little tranquility. That would make my life complete."

The story goes on to say that Moses did so. But God refused. "It's impossible," He said. "Moses, I created many things during the six days of creation. But one thing I did not create—tranquility."

TROUBLES

There was once a woman who was always grumbling. Her husband, she thought, made more work for her than other husbands; her children took less care of their clothes than other children did. Her home seemed colder in winter and hotter in summer than everyone else's. In fact, she thought God had given her a heavier burden to bear than He had given to any of her neighbors.

One night, she dreamed that her guardian angel stood by her bed. He told her to rise; he had something he wanted to show her. She got up and followed him down the street. The angel beckoned and she peeped through the windows. In one house, she saw a mother and father sitting by the bedside of a dying child. In another, she saw a poor blind woman huddled beside an empty grate. In another, the breadwinner lay dead. Every house seemed to have some trouble. At last they stopped at another house, and as she looked at it she realized it was her own house. How peaceful it seemed.

Afterwards, when she was inclined to grumble, she thought of all those who were worse off than herself, and instead of grumbling she said gladly and thankfully. "Thy will be done, whatever it is."

One kind of trouble is enough. Some folks take on three kinds at once—All they have now, all they have had, and all they ever expect to have.

TRUST

A poor woman applied to the King of Spain for compensation for the loss of her property.

"How did you lose it?" inquired the king.

"I fell asleep and robbers came and stole it," replied the woman.

"But why did you fall asleep?" he asked.

"I fell asleep because I believed that you were awake and watching," was the honest answer.

The king was so pleased with her trust, it is said that he presented her with a bag of gold.

***

Two men came to see the sage. They wanted a partnership agreement drawn up and desired that the sage help them. He agreed, took pen and paper and wrote four letters:

A

B

C

D

With this he handed the paper back to the men and said the agreement was finished.

"What does this mean?" they asked.

The sage explained, "It is simple and complete. The 'A' stands for Agreement and the 'B' stands for Blessing. If there will be agreement there will be blessing. 'C' stands for connivance and 'D' stands for disaster. If there will be connivance, there will be disaster. It is all as simple as A, B, C, D."

***

TRUTH

A newspaperman once asked Sam Rayburn: "Mr. Speaker, you see at least a hundred people a day. You tell each one 'Yes,' or 'No.' You never seem to make notes on what you have told them, but I have never heard of your forgetting anything you have promised them. What is your secret?"

Rayburn's brown eyes flashed: "If you tell the truth the first time," he replied, "you don't have to remember."

***

A wise man once said: "Truth is the most sought-after thing because it is too often hidden."

***

There are people who are constantly prattling about the truth. They complain that the world is false and that nobody in it is truthful. However, they deviate from the truth about things which concern themselves and often color things to suit the occasion.

That is the interpretation of the saying, "To thine own self be true."

~~~~

There is a saying, "Truth travels around the world." A sage once explained it thus: "The truth is driven out by everyone who does not uphold it, and then it wanders from one place to another, looking for a place where it will be welcome."

~~~~

God has chosen truth as his seal because any other value can have imitations in some form or other. But there is no compromising with, there is no substitution for Truth. An imitation of truth, no matter how slight the deviation, tips the scale in the opposite direction and becomes the beginning of an out-and-out lie.

~~~~

"For twenty-one years I have studied the concept of truth," said a righteous man. "Seven years I studied to understand the real meaning of it, seven years I labored to root out falsehood, and for seven years I disciplined myself to acquire the habit of truthfulness."

~~~~

UNDERSTANDING

During World War II, Brig. Gen. Theodore Roosevelt, Jr., was waiting at an airport for a plane. A sailor stepped up to a ticket window and asked for a seat on the same plane, explaining, "I want to see my mother; I ain't got much time."

The indifferent young woman at the ticket window was not impressed. "There's a war on, you know," she replied curtly.

At this point, Gen. Roosevelt, who had overheard the conversation, stepped to the window and told her to give the sailor his seat. A friend spoke his surprise. "Teddy, aren't you in a hurry, too?"

"It's a matter of rank," came the reply. "I'm only a general; he's a son."

~~~~

UNKNOWN

Two ships were once seen to be sailing near the shore. One of them was leaving the harbor and the other was coming into port. Everyone was cheering the outgoing ship, and giving it a hearty send-off; but the incoming ship was scarely noticed.

A wise man, looking at the two ships, said: "Rejoice not over the ship that is setting out to sea, for you know not what destiny awaits it, what storms it may encounter, what dangers it may have to undergo. Rejoice rather over the ship that has reached port safely and has brought back all its passengers in peace."

And then the wise man continued: "It is the way of the world, that when a human being is born, all rejoice; but when he dies, all sorrow. Rather ought the opposite be the case. No one can tell what troubles await the child on its journey into manhood. But when a man has lived and dies in peace, all should rejoice, seeing that he has completed his journey and is departing this world with the imperishable crown of a good name."

USEFULNESS

A father wanted to teach his son a lesson in life. He took out his watch and asked, "What is this good for?"

"To keep time," was the answer.

"Suppose it won't keep time, and can't be made to keep time, what is it good for?"

"It is good for nothing," was the answer.

He then took out a lead pencil, and asked what it was for.

"It is to write with," was the answer.

"Suppose the lead is out, and it won't write, what is it good for?"

"Nothing," was the answer.

He then took out a pocket knife and asked what was its use.

"To cut with," was the response.

"Suppose it has no blade, what is it good for?"

"It is good for nothing," was the reply.

"Then," replied the father, "a watch, pencil, or knife is good for nothing unless it can do the things for which it is made. You must bear this in mind as you live your life from day to day."

VACATION

The late columnist, Arthur Brisbane, declined to accept William Randolph Hearst's offer of a six months' paid vacation in appreciation for his good work.

"There are two good reasons why I will not accept your generous offer, Mr. Hearst," said Brisbane. "The first is that if I quit writing my column for half a year, it might affect the circulation of your newspapers. The second reason is that it might NOT!"

VALUE

In olden times, the wealthy and charitable Jews of France would prepare tables for indigent Jews on special occasions such as weddings, holidays, etc. Later these tables were turned into coffins in which the charitable owners were laid upon death. The purpose of this custom was to show that nothing remains of a man's work and deeds in this world but a table of kindness and charity. Everything passes, but the table remains.

"What is the value of this estate?" asked one gentleman of another, as they passed a fine mansion surrounded by fertile fields.

"I don't know what it is valued at, but I know what it cost its late possessor."

"How much?"

"His soul. Early in life, he professed faith in God and obtained a minor position in a mercantile establishment. When he became a partner in the firm, he gave less attention to religion, and more to business. He became exceedingly rich in money, but so poor in soul, that none would have suspected that he had ever been religious. At length he purchased the large estate referred to, built a costly mansion, became ill and died. Just before he died, he remarked, 'My prosperity was my ruin.'"

A merchant went to a farmer to get a pound of butter. The farmer insisted on swapping the butter for a pair of woolen socks. When the merchant reported this to his wife, she said, "I'll unravel some wool from our bedspread and knit him a pair of socks." When it was finished, the pair of socks was exchanged for a pound of butter.

When the merchant needed more butter, his wife once again

unraveled more of the bedspread and knit more socks, which was exchanged for butter. Finally, she had only enough wool for one sock. The merchant took the sock to the farmer and asked for a half pound of butter for it.

"Nothing doing," replied the farmer. "I'll give you a full pound. You see, I really don't wear the socks. My wife unravels the wool and uses it for knitting a bedspread, and there's just enough in this one sock to finish it."

A wealthy miser had a vast fortune of gems and precious stones. Fearing that someone might be tempted to rob him, he buried them in the ground, not far from his home.

One day, wanting to make certain that his gems were still safe, he told his servant to go and dig them up. The miser stood at the window, waiting. Finally, he saw the servant approaching, perspiring and grunting, weighted down by a heavy burden. The miser wrung his hands in despair, and cried, "Alas, my treasure is gone —and, in its place, someone has substituted ordinary stones." His son, who was standing nearby, asked how he could be sure that the servant was not carrying the sack which contained the treasure.

"No, my son," said the miser with a cry of anguish. "Were he carrying precious stones, gems and jewels, he would not be grunting so, nor would his load appear so burdensome."

Sometime years ago, Art Buchwald told the story in the New York *Herald Tribune* of a Hollywood producer whose hobby it was to collect rare books. He loved his avocation so much that he spoke about it constantly, boring his friends who were tired of hearing about it. One day, they decided to play a joke on him. They hired a bit actor and brought him to lunch. When, inevitably, the subject came up, the actor said he'd had an old German Bible around the house for years, but it smelled so bad he finally gave it away to an aunt in Santa Barbara.

"Who printed it?" the rare book collector asked.

"I don't know, 'Guten' something," the bit actor said.

The producer dropped his work. "Not Gutenberg?" The actor said he believed that was the name. The producer jumped up from the table. "Let's go!" he screamed. "We'll hire a plane!"

"Go where?' asked the actor.

"To get the Bible, man! Don't you realize you have one of the first books ever printed? It's worth $300,000!"

The actor stood up excitedly. Then, suddenly, he sat down again. "It can't be worth anything," he said.

"Why not?" asked the hysterical producer.

"Because," the actor replied, "somebody named Martin Luther scribbled all over it."

〰〰〰

A lady who had a fine brood of chickens had been shelling corn for them with her own hands, when she realized that a valuable pearl was missing from a ring on her finger. She felt sure it was in the corn, but to find it would be like finding a needle in a haystack; she could only grieve for it as lost. But each morning, before pouring corn for the chickens, she looked for it in the trough from which they fed. Finally, one morning, there it lay in the trough, together with a few pebbles.

The pearl, worth more than all the chickens, was to them as valueless as any common stone.

〰〰〰

Rudyard Kipling, speaking to a McGill University graduating class, advised the graduates not to care too much for money or power or fame; for, he said in effect, "Some day you will meet a man who cares for none of these things . . . and then you will know how poor you are."

〰〰〰

In the early years of the development of the West, two covered wagon trains started out from Omaha to cross the prairie to the Far West. For days and weeks, they went on together and then they parted to go separate ways. The Mormons had written on their wagons, GOD SEEKERS; the others had emblazoned on their wagon trains GOLD SEEKERS. The Mormons built a city and transformed a desert into a veritable paradise; the second group found gold, as they hoped, but left nothing behind as a symbol of memory.

〰〰〰

A poor boy was a student at a small school in Poland. He was the son of an impoverished father, and subsisted on the generosity of the people living in the town. They provided food as well as cast-off clothing.

One day, several of his friends showed him wallets that had been purchased for $3. The wallets were beautiful and the poor boy longed to be the owner of one of them. But whereas his friends

387

had comfortable allowances, this boy had nothing. Nonetheless, by pleading, begging, borrowing, he managed to scrape together $2.50.

He ran to the storekeeper, put the money down on the counter and, with true emotion, said: "Believe me, this is my entire fortune. It represents every cent I have, and in fact, I had to borrow money to get the $2.50. Please, give me the wallet at this price."

"Foolish, foolish boy," the storekeeper replied. "If the $2.50 is every cent you have in the world, of what use is the wallet?"

VALUES

A Chinese legend tells of a group of elderly, cultured gentlemen who met often to exchange wisdom and drink tea. Each host tried to find the finest and most varied teas to create exotic blends that would arouse the admiration of his guests.

One day, when the most venerable and respected of the group entertained, he served his tea with unprecedented ceremony, measuring the leaves from a golden box. The assembled epicures praised the exquisite taste. The host smiled and said, "The tea you have found so delightful is not an exotic variety. It is the same simple tea that peasants drink. I hope the golden box in which I keep it did not mislead you. Let this be a reminder to us all that the good things in life are not necessarily the rarest, nor the most costly."

A prankster once broke into a fashionable store and switched the price tags on the merchandise. On articles of low value he placed high price tags, and on the truly precious things he placed ridiculously low price tags.

An observer who watched the proceedings remarked: "How true to life! So many of us have the wrong price tags on our values; and we are not even aware of it."

A pilot who had crashed was on the hospital critical list. His father was "sweating out" the ordeal. During interminable hours of vigil, the father paced up and down the corridor saying, "If only my boy will live. . . . I'll ask for nothing more. I don't care if he's crippled or incapacitated. I'll take care of him. I'll sacrifice anything for him. How foolish I was yesterday to complain about trivial inconveniences, business difficulties. How trivial they seem today."

Through his tears the father could now see beyond the mountain of insignificant frustrations he had made of his life, to the horizon of love.

*

An artist once made an oil painting of a muddy river. A viewer criticized the picture because it had too much mud in it. When the artist heard the criticism, he replied, "He sees the mud, but I see the peaceful river making its slow way down the countryside, making the land about it fruitful.

*

Next time you go shopping for necessities, you might think of a new list that might aid in living a full life. For instance:

A LARGE BOX OF COOPERATION. This is one thing you just can't do without. It is a basic ingredient in every successful venture.

ONE GALLON OF ENTHUSIASM. This is to be sprinkled liberally on all of the activities of daily life. It is astonishing what a few drops can do.

A LARGE BOX OF COMPROMISE. At first this may appear to be a bitter pill to swallow, but actually it often is a magic catalyst which results in good human relationships.

WRAPPING MATERIAL OF TACT AND TOLERANCE. A wrapping can be as important as the package inside, and you may be surprised to find that just a little of this one will go a long way.

SEVERAL PACKAGES OF PATIENCE. It's always best to keep a good supply on hand. This is such a useful item, and it's so very easy to run out of it at the most inconvenient times.

A MATCHED PAIR OF APPRECIATION AND INTEREST. No matter how these two are used, they are invariably "seasoned to the taste" of everyone.

A SPOOL OF UNDERSTANDING. For mending hurt feelings and patching up torn situations. This spool is absolutely indispensable.

A LITTLE JACKET OF HOPE. Try it on for size. A large size makes for difficulties.

389

TWO ORDERS OF CONFIDENCE AND POISE. Order ahead of time and wait for delivery.

LARGE ECONOMY SIZE OF COMMON SENSE. Be sure to get the largest size because you cannot do without it.

~~~~~~

VICTORY

One of his marshals sought an audience with Napoleon, in order to boast about a great victory which he had just achieved. He talked to his chief at length, giving the details of his brilliant strategy. Of course, what he desired and expected was a few words of deserved praise.

Napoleon, deep, quiet, inscrutable, listened attentively and patiently to the entire recitation. But then, instead of praising the soldier, Napoleon asked him one quesion: "What did you do the next day?"

The marshal did not answer. He understood that a person should never be content to rest on his laurels—that the time to prepare for new victories is the moment when victory is ours.

~~~~~~

When Cortez set out to undertake the conquest of Mexico, he caused his ships to be burned in full view of his men, so that all might feel that there was no hope for them except in victory. Their desperation made them perform admirably.

~~~~~~

VIEWPOINT

A young man was noted for his complete lack of interest in the opposite sex. One summer he was called into the army reserves for a two-month training period. His friends wondered whether this stretch of service would change his outlook. One afternoon, as he was telling about his military life, he suddenly stopped to look with interest at four pretty girls coming down the street. He watched them intently until they were out of sight, then turned back and announced, "One of them is out of step."

~~~~~~

An artist studying a curious work of art became so absorbed as to forget all else about him. A spectator, observing him, asked what pleasure he could take in gazing so long on what seemed so indifferent an object to him. "If you had my eyes," was the reply, "you would be just as fascinated as I am."

A little boy was watching his grandmother embroidering a tablecloth. As he stood at her knee, he looked up to see her needle coming through the cloth in rapid stitches.

"What are you making, Granma?" the little boy asked.

"I am making a picture, my child."

"This is no picture, Granma," objected the youngster. "This is just a jumble of different colors and loose ends of thread. See?" and he pulled hard on a loose thread.

"Now, now, don't do that. Here, I will show you the picture." The old lady turned around her embroidery hoop so that her grandchild could see the right side of the cloth where a beautiful picture was taking shape. "You see, my child, from the wrong side it looks like a mixed up mess of threads and colors, but it is not mixed up at all, if you look at the right side."

VIRTUE

When Seth Low suffered defeat in his campaign for political office, he explained it this way: "In my first campaign, I ran on a platform against vice and won because everybody is interested in vice. In the second campaign, I ran on a platform for virtue and lost; nobody is interested in virtue."

A wealthy man was visiting a very religious but poor scholar. When he was about to depart, the wealthy man handed the scholar a thousand dollars.

"Why are you giving me money, and such a large sum at that?" asked the scholar.

The rich man answered, "It is customary to leave a token of money when visiting a good person, a scholar or man of religion, who is in need."

"You are wrong," remarked the scholar. "The good person is not the one who is accepting the money. On the contrary, the good person is the one who is giving the money."

A famous scholar once visited a parsimonious millionaire and sought a donation to charity. The miser, who was also a coarse and ignorant man, refused to give a donation, and dismissed the learned man with a curt, "I have enough good deeds already."

The scholar thereupon remarked to his companions: "Now I understand the meaning of the saying: 'Ignorant people are always as full of virtues as the pomegranate is full of pits.' No sooner do you ask him for a donation than he immediately counters with the argument that he has already accumulated enough good deeds."

~~~

Diogenes, the Greek philosopher, taught that the virtuous life is the simple life. When he was once asked by Alexander the Great what he might do for him, Diogenes replied, "Just please step out of my sunlight."

~~~

WEALTH

A young man came to a minister, asking that he officiate at the funeral of his brother. "I must ask you a few questions," the minister said. "How old was your brother when he died?"

"Thirty-three," was the answer.

The minister continued: "He worked for twenty years, didn't he?"

"Yes, very hard," was the answer.

"Well, what did he get out of all his hard work?" was the next question.

"He left 150 acres of good farm land, a rather large bank balance, and $50,000 in insurance," the brother responded.

"Wait a minute," said the minister. "That's what you got out of it; but what did *he* get out of it? He's going to be buried in a $125 casket. He takes none of the wealth with him."

~~~

An Arab once lost his way in the desert, and was in danger of dying from hunger. At last, he found one of the cisterns out of which the camels drink, and a little leather bag near it.

"God be thanked," he cried. "Here must be some dates and nuts so that I might refresh my body."

He opened the bag, only to turn away in disappointment. There were only pearls in it, and these, valuable as they were, could not save his life.

~~~

A rich hasid came to his master for a blessing. "What is the conduct of your household, and what table do you set from day to day?" asked the master.

"My household is conducted with great simplicity," said the rich man. "My own meal consists of dry bread with salt."

Full of indignation, the master looked at him and asked, "Why do you not favor yourself with meat and wine, as becomes a man of wealth?" And he then proceeded to berate the rich man until the latter finally promised that, henceforth, he would partake of more luxurious meals.

When the hasid had departed, the pupils asked the master: "What matters it to you whether he eats bread with salt or meat with wine?"

The master answered: "It matters a great deal. If he enjoys good fare and his meal consists of fine viands, then he will understand that the poor man must have at least bread with salt. But if, being wealthy, he renounces all enjoyment of life and lives so stingily, he will believe that it is sufficient for the poor to eat stones."

Every rich man possesses two kinds of stones: ordinary stones and diamonds. Of course, the two kinds of stones are carefully stored apart from each other. There are those who store their diamonds in their hearts and the ordinary stones in their pockets, and there are those who store their ordinary stones in their hearts and their diamonds in their pockets.

"How much did he leave?" asked one of the men at the funeral of the millionaire who had just been buried.

"Every cent," was the terse reply.

Many years ago, a British ship was wrecked in a storm off the coast of Brazil. Packed in barrels, it carried a fortune in Spanish silver coins. Some of the barrels were brought up on deck, but the ship was sinking so rapidly, they were abandoned and everybody took to the lifeboats. As the last boat was about to leave, a hammering noise was heard on board, and one of the officers went back to see if anybody was left behind. To his surprise he found a man sitting on deck surrounded by heaps of silver coins, and engaged in breaking open a second barrel with a hatchet.

The officer tried to pull him away. "The ship is breaking to pieces!" he shouted.

"Let me go," the man replied. "I lived in poverty all my life, but now I am going to die a rich man."

J. P. Morgan was once asked the following question, "When has a man made enough to be happy?"

Morgan replied, with a smile, "When he has made the next million."

A man had just left a friend's house in his Cadillac. The host watched enviously as he departed. "Some day, honey, we'll be rich too," he said to his wife. She reached out, took her husband's hand, and replied: "Darling, we are rich now. Someday we'll have money."

A man was complaining about his poverty to a very dear friend. "It is tiresome to have to do without many things all the time," he said.

The friend listened patiently to this and many more complaints and then asked, "How is your health?"

"I am in excellent health," was the immediate reply.

"And how is your appetite?" was the next question.

"Couldn't be better," came the answer.

"Well," said the friend. "You are a rich man. Just the other day I heard a fellow complain that he had lost his appetite completely and was losing weight rapidly. He was spending a fortune of money on doctor bills and medicines, trying to regain his appetite and his health. Therefore I tell you now, and remember it *always*: you have your health? Then YOU ARE RICH!"

A newly-rich woman was trying to impress her neighbor, the wife of a labor leader. She began to talk about her jewelry. "I clean my diamonds with ammonia," she said, "my rubies with Bordeaux wine, my emeralds with Danzig brandy, and my sapphires with milk."

"I never bother," replied the labor leader's wife. "When my jewels get dirty, I just throw them away."

394

A wise man once said that the wealthy are driven to insanity by their wealth. When asked to explain what he meant by this, this is what he said: "There are some wealthy people who think that accumulating money is man's greatest achievement. They become conceited, consider themselves superior, and develop an obnoxious sense of authority with the right to voice an opinion about everything. Is it not insanity to think that a pile of money can give you divine rights?"

"I am glad to find you as you are," said the old friend. "Your wealth has not changed you."

"Well," replied the candid millionnaire, "it has changed me in one way. I am now eccentric where I used to be impolite, and delightfully witty where I used to be rude."

A preacher borrowed fifty dollars from one of the wealthy men in town with the promise that he would return it the next morning. The loan was made and returned the next morning. On the evening of the same day, he again borrowed fifty dollars to be returned the next morning. This he also returned. For a week, he borrowed daily and returned daily. Finally, the wealthy man could not contain himself and asked, "Reverend, if you need the fifty dollars, why not keep it for a week or two? Why borrow it daily?"

"I really don't need the money at all," replied the preacher. "But you can't realize with what confidence I face my audience when I have fifty dollars in my pocket!"

A farmer one day came to pay his rent to a man whose love of money was widely acclaimed. After settling his account, the farmer said, "I will give you another shilling, if you will allow me to go down to your vault and just have a look at your money." And so the farmer was permitted to see the piles of gold and silver in the miser's safe. As he ascended, he declared, "Now I am as well off as you are."

"How can that be?" asked the miser.

"Why," said the farmer, "you never use any of this money. All you do is look at it. Now I have looked at it too, so I am just as rich as you are."

A man who was considered poor once met a famous millionaire who was working diligently, and becoming richer every year. The poor man made just enough to support a growing family and take them on a little vacation once a year. He said gently to the rich man, "I am richer than you are."

The millionaire looked nettled. "How can that be?" he asked.

The poor man smiled. "Why," he said, "I have as much money as I want, and you haven't."

Wealth was defined in these few lines by William Blake:

> I have mental joys and mental health,
> Mental friends and mental wealth,
> I've a wife that I love and that loves me;
> I've all but riches bodily.

A miser who possessed more wealth than even he himself could keep track of, sought the advice of the sage in his village.

"I am old," lamented the miser. "I have purged my mind and my soul trying to recollect how the world may have benefited from my having lived in it. Alas, there are no such recollections. I have done nothing for anybody. I would be eternally grateful if you could introduce me to an important and worthy poor man to whom I may leave all my money."

The sage's lips twisted into a sardonic smile as he replied, "I fail to see your need to specify that your money must go to a 'worthy and important' person. After all, the fact that this money has fallen into the hands of a man who has spent a worthless life, by your own admission, is sufficient evidence of its baseness."

WILLS

A wealthy man had two sons, the elder badly crippled, but the younger a healthy, capable man. After the father died, it was discovered that he had left the bulk of his estate to his younger son who was to succeed him in business. All who were present at the reading of the will wondered why it had not been the other way around; why the major portion of the estate had not been left to the older son who was crippled, or at least divided equally. The attorney for the deceased explained that he, too, had wondered about this when the will was being drawn up. He reported that the father had explained his decision with the following parable:

396

A blind beggar amassed a great fortune by soliciting alms. He was the father of several children, all in good health but the youngest son, who was blind. Before the beggar left this world, he specified in his will that his entire fortune should belong to his healthy children, and that nothing was to be given to his disabled son. When he was asked why he did so, he answered: "I know what I am doing. My blind son will be taken care of by sympathetic people who will have mercy on him. But who, pray, will take care of my able children?"

WISDOM

A father was giving guidance to his teen-age son who was finding school rather difficult.

"To lack wisdom is no disgrace," he said. "To lack desire for wisdom is a pity. But to desire wisdom and not to know how to find it is a tragedy."

One should speak simply, like the ordinary man, for one must be understood by the average man. But one should *think* as a wise man, for this is a private matter.

The proverb "A wise man is a man of experience" has been interpreted as follows: "A wise man is one who applies his wisdom to his daily activities. A man must act wisely as well as think wisely."

The greatest wisdom is knowing how to play your wisdom down. Think wisely and act wisely, but keep your mouth in check.

A sage once illustrated the verse "Wisdom is too high for a fool" (Proverbs 24:7), with this parable.

An apple was suspended from the ceiling. The foolish man said, "I cannot reach the fruit, it is too high"; but the wise man said, "It may be obtained if I place one box upon another until my arm can reach it." Similarly, the foolish man says, "Only a wise man can study the entire law"; but the wise man claims, "It is not incumbent upon me to acquire the whole."

A pupil once inquired of his teacher, "What is real wisdom?"

The teacher replied, "To judge liberally, to think purely, and to love your neighbor. The wise man is in his smallest actions great: the fool is in his greatest actions small."

A father who had three sons tested their discretion by giving each an apple filled with rotten specks. The first ate his, rotten parts and all; the second threw his apple away because part of it was rotten; the third one picked out the spoiled spots and ate what was good. He was adjudged the wisest.

Mankind may be similarly divided into three types. Some men swallow all that is presented to them; some throw away all truth; the wise choose the good, and refuse the evil.

A stooped old man and a sprightly young man chanced to meet one day. The young man said to the older one, in his usual braggart way: "Why don't you walk straight like me? That is no way to grow old. It is only a habit—at least that's what I am told."

The old man gave him a knowing look and said: "My dear young friend, have you examined your fine wheat field, and noticed the heads that bend? If not, just look them over closely as the harvest time grows nigh. You'll find the heads that are quite empty are standing tall and high, but the heads that are filled, bend low, awaiting the reaper's bright sickle—their time is short, you know."

There was once a man who owned a beautiful garden. One day, he trapped a hummingbird who was eating his finest fruits. The bird promised him three wise teachings as the price of his release. The man agreed.

Safely out of reach, the bird said, "Do not regret the irrevocable. Do not believe the impossible. Do not seek the unattainable," and burst into laughter. "If you had not let me go, you would have found inside of me a pearl the size of a lemon."

Enraged, the man climbed up the tree after the bird. As he came closer, the bird flew higher. With the man in frenzied pursuit, the bird flew to the highest branch of all, and walked to its very tip. The man came scrambling after; the branch snapped, the bird flew off, the man dropped to the ground with a thud.

Bruised, he picked himself up and gazed ruefully at his tormentor. "Wisdom is for the wise," the bird admonished. "I told you not to regret the irrevocable; but no sooner did you let me go, than you came after me again. I told you not to believe the impossible; yet you believed that a bird my size could contain a pearl the size of a lemon. And I told you not to seek the unattainable; yet you climbed a tree to catch a bird. You are a fool!"

Two women in a train were engaged in an argument. At last, one of them called the conductor.

"If this window is open," she declared, "I will catch cold and will probably die."

"If the window is shut," the other announced, "I shall suffocate." The two glared at each other.

The conductor was at a loss, but he welcomed the words of a man who sat near. These were: "First open the window. That will kill one. Next shut it, that will kill the other. Then we can have peace."

Anatole France describes a young eastern king who wished to be wise and good, and rule his people according to the will of Allah. He called together the wisest men of his realm and ordered them to gather all wisdom into books so that he could read and learn for himself how to rule well.

The wise men began their tremendous task, and after thirty years it was finished. A long string of camels, bearing five thousand volumes, came to the palace.

"Here, O King, is all the wisdom in the world."

The king, already middle-aged, was occupied with many duties and plans. He looked at the loaded camels. "I am too busy to read so many books. Take them away and condense them for me."

The work of condensing took fifteen years, and then the wise men proudly produced five hundred volumes.

"Still far too many," said the king, "fifty ought to be enough."

Most of the wise men were dead, but their successors carried on, and in ten years they brought the fifty books to the king. But by this time the king was old and tired.

"You must summarize it all into one book," he said.

It took them five years, and when they brought the precious volume of distilled wisdom to the king, it was too late; he lay on his deathbed.

WISHES

A poor woodsman was granted three wishes by a fairy. Dazed by this gift, the man rushed home. When he arrived, he found that his wife had not yet finished preparing supper and so he said, without thinking, "I wish I had a piece of pudding before me." Immediately, a bowl of pudding appeared on the table and the man explained the matter of the three wishes to his puzzled wife. His wife, furious at his folly in wasting a wish declared, "You are so foolish, I wish the pudding would stick to your nose," and up it flew to the poor man's nose. He tried to pull it off, but to no avail. They had no alternative but to use the final wish to have the pudding removed.

Abraham Lincoln was once consoled by a friend who said, "I hope that the Lord is on your side." To the friend's amazement, Lincoln replied kindly that that was not his hope. "My wish is," he continued, "that I am on the Lord's side."

The man was a poor woodcutter, and with his advancing years his burden grew heavier and heavier.

He was carrying a heavy load of wood on his back one day, trudging wearily along the road, when he suddenly grew weak and dizzy. He let the bundle down and cried bitterly, "O Death, release me from this terrible existence!"

The words were no sooner spoken when the Angel of Death appeared. "You called me?" asked the sinister figure.

Astonished, and frightened beyond imagination, the wood-cutter could only stammer.

"Yes, your excellency—your honor—your majesty—would you mind—er—ah—helping me get this bundle back on my shoulders?"

WOMEN

A middle aged man was standing in the street, obviously engrossed with himself. A friend approached him and asked, "What are you thinking about?"

The man replied, "I'm contemplating a queer phenomenon. You see I believe I'm a strange animal. The king of animals is the lion. The bear is afraid of the lion, the wolf fears the bear,

400

the dog fears the wolf, the cat fears the dog, the reptile fears the mouse, my wife is afraid of the mouse, and I fear my wife. . . . Imagine what a queer animal I am!"

The following card of thanks appeared in a midwestern paper: "I wish to thank the municipal authorities for quarantining my family and me for three weeks recently because one of them had the smallpox. During that time my wife caught up with all her sewing and ironing; we had three homecooked meals a day, as no one came in and she was not permitted to leave; we enjoyed three weeks of good nights' sleep. So for this and other blessings we are very thankful for the quarantine."

He had been pacing up and down the corridor. Finally, the nurse emerged and told him the good news. He had just become the father of twin boys. When he was permitted to enter his wife's room he said, "Honey, won't you ever get over the habit of exaggeration?"

A lady declared that second thoughts were best. As most of the people agreed with her, she explained, "Man was God's first thought; woman was His second."

It has been said that a good woman inspires a man, a brilliant woman interests him, a beautiful woman fascinates him, but a sympathetic woman gets him.

WORDS

Dr. Wilfred Funk, the well-known philologist who gained a wide reputation because of the dictionaries he composed, was once asked to list the 10 most expressive words in the English language. He replied as follows:

The most bitter word is *alone*.
The most reverent is *mother*.
The most tragic is *death*.
The most beautiful is *love*.

The most cruel is *revenge*.
The most peaceful is *tranquil*.
The saddest is *forgotten*.
The warmest is *friendship*.
The coldest is *no*.
The most comforting is *faith*.

~~~~~

An illiterate mililonaire decided to leave his money to a small local college. The son wasn't ready to be cut out of the will. He knew that his father was ignorant and a prude, so he said to the old man one day, "Father, I hope you are aware that at that college—the one you've decided to give all your money—the boys and girls MATRICULATE together."

The father looked startled, and the son continued, "Not only that," he said, "but both boys and girls use the same CURRICULUM."

Now the father's face began to darken, and the son leaned forward to whisper. "But the worst of all, Father, before a girl can graduate she has to show her THESIS to the dean."

"That settles it," roared the father. "That school won't get a penny from me."

~~~~~

"Can you explain the difference between caution and cowardice?" asked the teacher.

"I can," answered George, a rather meticulous person. "Caution is when you are afraid, and cowardice is when the other fellow is afraid."

~~~~~

In *The Mind Alive,* H. and B. Overstreet wrote:

Words are medicine
That can make us whole
And keep us whole—
When they are the right words,
About the right things,
Spoken with the right intention.

~~~~~

WORK

A survey was once conducted of those men and women who had achieved success in their fields. Several hundred letters were mailed to these people. Each letter called for an answer to this question: "What do you consider the first requisite in a young man or woman for a successful career?"

When the answers were tabulated, one thought ran through the greatest majority of them. Concisely expressed, it was "FIND OUT WHAT WORK YOU LIKE TO DO AND THEN DO IT ALL THE TIME."

A woman was watching a potter at his work. One foot, with never-slackening speed, turned the wheel, while the other foot rested patiently on the ground.

The woman said to him sympathetically, "How tired your foot must be!"

Raising his eyes, the man said, "No, ma'am; it's not the foot that works that's tired; it's the foot that's idle."

John W. Carr, the principal of the Friends' Central School, Philadelphia, reared several sons, all of whom were strong in body, well-trained for life, and who, from the very first year of their careers, made good livings.

"How did you do it?" he was asked.

"By teaching them to work," he replied. "We used to have three rules at our house.

"The first was: When school is out in the summer, get something to do, something for which you will be paid if possible;

"Second: Do something, whether you get paid or not;

"And the third, which was called, 'Extreme Unction,' was: If you cannot find anything at all to do, come to father and he will find something for you."

One evening when Thomas Edison came home from work, his wife said to him, "You've worked long enough without a rest. You must go on a vacation."

"But where on earth would I go?" asked Edison.

"Just decide where you would rather be than anywhere else on earth," suggested the wife.

Edison hesitated. "Very well," he said finally, "I'll go tomorrow."

The next morning he was back at work in his laboratory.

"Why is it that the sound of thy flowing waters cannot be heard even a short distance from thy shores?" asked all the other rivers of the Euphrates river.

"It is not necessary that my waters be heard," replied the Euphrates. "My deeds, my fruitful shores, speak for me."

The rivers then asked of the Tigris river, "Why is it that the tumult and splashing of thy waters may be heard for such a great distance?"

"Because," replied the noisy Tigris, "it is necessary that my currents rush with tumultuous rumble and clamor so people may hear and know how important I am."

Likewise did the trees of the forest ask the fruit trees, "Why is it that the rustling of thy leaves may not be heard at the distance?"

"It is not necessary that we attract attention by the rustling of our leaves. Now, we shall ask a question of thee, 'Why do thy leaves rustle constantly?' "

"That," answered the forest trees, "is because we must call the attention of others to our presence."

The Talmud comments on this subject: Man is to be judged by his deeds, not his words. As a tree is known by its fruit, so is man by his works.

~~~~~

When the other fellow takes a long time to do something, he's slow,
But when I take a long time to do something, I'm thorough.
When the other fellow doesn't do it, he's too lazy,
But when I don't do it, I'm too busy.
When the other fellow goes ahead and does something without being told, he's over-stepping his bounds.
But when I go ahead and do something without being told, that's initiative!
When the other fellow states his side of a question strongly, he's bull-headed,
But when I state my side of a question strongly, I'm being firm.
When the other fellow overlooks a few of the rules of etiquette, he's rude,
But when I skip a few of the rules, I'm original.
When the other fellow does something that pleases the boss, he's polishing the apple,
But when I do something that pleases the boss, that's cooperation.

When the other fellow gets ahead, he sure had the lucky breaks.
But when I manage to get ahead, Man!
Hard work did that!

When James B. Conant was president of Harvard University,
he kept among other objects on his desk a little model of a turtle,
under which was the inscription, "Consider the turtle. He makes
progress only when he sticks his neck out."

An almost forgotten legend tells of King David who was
about to embark against an enemy who threatened his country.
He was badly in need of a horse trainer who would put his
cavalry in condition and train his horsemen.

Two famed trainers were summoned and each was asked to
bring six of his best horses.

The first trainer led his six remarkable horses before the king.
One stood on his hind legs for as long as it would take to recite
the Ten Commandments. Another stood on his forelegs and
jumped. A third could dance. A fourth could swim like a fish.
A fifth could carry the load of a camel and the sixth horse could
run as far backwards as forwards.

The king watched the performance with amazement.

Then he summoned the second horse trainer who brought
forth his six stallions, each of which looked pretty much like the
other—clean, trim and well-groomed.

"What can they do?" asked the king.

"Nothing, sir," said the trainer, "that any other good horse
could not do, only mine can do it well and do it consistently."

"You are my man," said the king. "I need horses to carry my
men into battle, not into a circus ring."

WORLD

A man entered a tailor shop and requested that he make a suit
in one week's time. He needed it for an important function. The
tailor told him that he must take at least three weeks to make a
new suit.

"Three weeks?" echoed the man. "What do you mean three
weeks? God created the whole world in seven days and you need
three weeks to make one suit?"

"True enough," answered the tailor. "God created the entire world in seven days and look at the way it looks."

⁓

WORRY

A rabbi used group therapy to help his followers who had no peace of mind. When someone came to him with problems, the rabbi listened attentively and asked him to return on a specified date. On that date, the rabbi arranged to have ten people laden with troubles congregate in his study. When all assembled, he excused himself from their midst, telling them he could not listen for the next hour, and suggested that they share their problems with one another. After the hour was up, the rabbi returned. He found them all gone, except for one man who indicated that he had been delegated to remain. He informed the rabbi that after listening to each other's worries, everyone had decided that his personal burdens were not so difficult to bear.

⁓

"It doesn't pay to be frightened or to worry," I once heard a man of much worldly experience say. "I realized this long ago, and now my only worry is that I am never worried."

⁓

There is a story of a philosophical clock which fell to meditation. It thought about its future as it was placed on the shelf for the first time. It reasoned that it had to tick twice each second, 120 times each minute, 7200 times every hour, and 172,800 every 24 hours. This meant 63,072,000 times every year. And in ten years it would have to tick 630,720,000 times.

The clock became so overwrought at the thought of so much work, that it collapsed from nervous exhaustion. When it was revived by the watchmaker, it perceived in a moment of insight that all it had to do was to tick one tick at a time. So it began to tick again, and continued to tick for a hundred years. It became a most sought-after grandfather clock.

⁓

A physician, who specialized in the treatment of ulcers, stated that he had been doing research in his laboratory and had to abandon the use of dogs. "They just wouldn't worry," he complained, "and worry is the thing that makes ulcers and keeps them active. You can inflict an ulcer upon a dog by artificial methods

406

and he will sit down placidly and cure himself by refusing to be bothered about anything."

～～～

Henry Ward Beecher once was asked how he managed to get through so much work in a day. He replied, "By never doing anything twice. I never anticipate my work and never worry about it. When the time comes to do a thing, I do it, and that's the end of it."

～～～

Toscanini once taught a musician an important lesson. One evening, the bassoon-player came to him in a panic. His instrument was out of order; he couldn't make it reach E-flat. The wise old director looked at him in total silence, thinking hard. Then he laughed, slapped the unhappy worried musician on the shoulder and said, "Never mind. The note E-flat doesn't appear in the music you'll play tonight."

～～～

YOUTH

A description of "modern" youth:

"Our youths love luxury. They have bad manners, contempt for authority; they show disrespect for their elders, and have to chatter in place of exercise. Children are now tyrants, not the servants of their households. They no longer rise when their elders enter the room. They contradict their parents, chatter before company, gobble up their food, and tyrannize their teachers."

If you think this is a description of the twentieth century, you're wrong. This was written by Socrates, the great Greek philosopher, in 400 B.C.E.!

～～～

Rossini, the great Italian musician, said to a friend who had congratulated him on his continued triumphs, "I would give all this glory that the world envies me, all my operas, all that I have done, for some sweet days of YOUTH and LOVE."

～～～

Youth was overjoyed. "The world is mine," she exclaimed. "My future is beautiful. I am strong, powerful, full of energy. Why should I worry about tomorrow when I have today? Tomorrow will also be mine!"

407

Index

409

411